THE HEIDENMAUER;

OR,

THE BENEDICTINES.

A LEGEND OF THE RHINE.

BY J. FENIMORE COOPER.

"From mighty wrongs to petty perfidy,
Have I not seen what human things could do."

BYRON.

COMPLETE IN ONE VOLUME.

NEW EDITION.

NEW YORK:
PUBLISHED BY HURD AND HOUGHTON.
Cambridge: Riverside Press.
1871.

HEIDENMAUER.

INTRODUCTION.

"I shall crave your forbearance a little; may be, I will call upon you anon, for some advantage to yourself."

Measure for Measure.

Contrary to a long-established usage, a summer had been passed within the walls of a large town; but, the moment of liberation arrived, the bird does not quit its cage with greater pleasure, than that with which post-horses were commanded We were four in a light travelling calêche, which strong Norman cattle transported merrily towards their native province. For a time we quitted Paris, the queen of modern cities, with its tumults and its order; its palaces and its lanes; its elegance and its filth; its restless inhabitants and its stationary politicians; its theories and its practices; its riches and its poverty; its gay and its sorrowful; its rentiers and its patriots; its young liberals and its old illiberals; its three estates and its equality; its delicacy of speech and its strength of conduct; its government of the people and its people of no government; its bayonets and its moral force; its science and its ignorance; its amusements and its revolutions; its resistance that goes backward, and its movement that stands still; its milliners, its philosophers, its opera-dancers, its poets, its fiddlers, its bankers, and its cooks. Although so long enthralled within the barriers, it was not easy to quit Paris, entirely without regret—Paris, which every stranger censures and every stranger seeks; which moralists abhor and imitate; which causes the heads of the old to shake, and the hearts of the young to beat;—Paris, the centre of so much that is excellent, and of so much that cannot be named!

That night we laid our heads on rustic pillows, far from the French capital. The succeeding day we snuffed the air of the sea. Passing through Artois and French Flanders, on the fifth morning we entered the new kingdom of Belgium, by the historical and respectable towns of Douaï, and Tournaï, and

Ath. At every step we met the flag which flutters over the pavilion of the Thuileries, and recognized the confident air and swinging gait of French soldiers. They had just been employed in propping the crumbling throne of the house of Saxe. To us they seemed as much at home as when they lounged on the Quai d'Orsay.

There was still abundant evidence visible at Brussels, of the fierce nature of the struggle that had expelled the Dutch. Forty-six shells were sticking in the side of a single building of no great size, while ninety-three grape-shot were buried in one of its pilasters! In our own rooms, too, there were fearful signs of war. The mirrors were in fragments, the walls broken by langrage, the wood-work of the beds was pierced by shot, and the furniture was marked by rude encounters. The trees of the park were mutilated in a thousand places, and one of the little Cupids, that we had left laughing above the principal gate three years before, was now maimed and melancholy, whilst its companion had altogether taken flight on the wings of a cannon-ball. Though dwelling in the very centre of so many hostile vestiges, we happily escaped the sight of human blood; for we understood from the obliging Swiss who presides over the hotel, that his cellars, at all times in repute, were in more than usual request during the siege. From so much proof we were left to infer, that the Belgians had made stout battle for their emancipation, one sign at least that they merited to be free.

Our road lay by Louvain, Thirlemont, Liège, Aix-la-Chapelle, and Juliers, to the Rhine. The former of these towns had been the scene of a contest between the hostile armies, the preceding week. As the Dutch had been accused of unusual excesses in their advance, we looked out for the signs. How many of these marks had been already obliterated, we could not well ascertain; but those which were still visible gave us reason to think that the invaders did not merit all the opprobrium they had received. Each hour, as life advances, am I made to see how capricious and vulgar is the immortality conferred by a newspaper!

It would be injustice to the ancient Bishopric of Liège to pass its beautiful scenery without a comment. The country possesses nearly every requisite for the milder and more rural sort of landscape;—isolated and innumerable farm-houses, herds in the fields, living hedges, a waving surface, and a verdure to rival the emerald. By a happy accident, the road runs for miles on an elevated ridge, enabling the traveller to enjoy these beauties at his ease.

At Aix-la-Chapelle we bathed, visited the relics, saw the scene of so many coronations of emperors of more or less renown, sat in the chair of Charlemagne, and went our way.

The Rhine was an old acquaintance. A few years earlier, I had stood upon the sands, at Katwyck, and watched its periodical flow into the North Sea, by means of sluices made in the short reign of the good King Louis, and, the same summer, I had bestrode it, a brawling brook, on the icy side of St. Gothard. We had come now to look at its beauties in its most beautiful part, and to compare them, so far as native partiality might permit, with the well-established claims of our own Hudson.

Quitting Cologne, its exquisite but incomplete cathedral, with the crane that has been poised on its unfinished towers five hundred years, its recollections of Rubens and his royal patroness, we travelled up the stream so leisurely as to examine all that offered, and yet so fast as to avoid the hazard of satiety. Here we met Prussian soldiers, preparing, by mimic service, for the more serious duties of their calling. Lancers were galloping, in bodies, across the open fields; videttes were posted, the cocked pistol in hand, at every hay-stack; while couriers rode, under the spur, from point to point, as if the great strife, which is so menacingly preparing, and which sooner or later must come, had actually commenced. As Europe is now a camp, these hackneyed sights scarce drew a look aside. We were in quest of the interest which nature, in her happier humors, bestows.

There were ruined castles, by scores; gray fortresses; abbeys, some deserted and others yet tenanted; villages and towns; the seven mountains; cliffs and vineyards. At every step we felt how intimate is the association between the poetry of Nature and that of art; between the hill-side with its falling turret, and the moral feeling that lends them interest.

Here was an island, of no particular excellence, but the walls of a convent of the middle ages crumbled on its surface. There was a naked rock, destitute of grandeur, and wanting in those tints which milder climates bestow, but a baronial hold tottered on its apex. Here Cæsar led his legions to the stream, and there Napoleon threw his corps d'armée on the hostile bank; this monument was to Hoche, and from that terrace the great Adolphus directed his battalions. Time is wanting to mellow the view of our own historical sites; for the sympathy that can be accumulated only by the general consent of mankind, has not yet clothed them with the indefinable colors of distance and convention.

In the mood likely to be created by a flood of such recollections, we pursued our way along the southern margin of this great artery of central Europe. We wondered at the vastness of the Rheinfels, admired the rare jewel of the ruined church at Baccarach, and marvelled at the giddy precipice on which a prince of Prussia even now dwells, in the eagle-like grandeur and security of the olden time. On reaching Mayence, the evening of the second day, we deliberately and, as we hoped, impartially compared what had just been seen, with that which is so well and so affectionately remembered.

I had been familiar with the Hudson from childhood. The great thoroughfare of all who journey from the interior of the state towards the sea, necessity had early made me acquainted with its windings, its promontories, its islands, its cities, and its villages. Even its hidden channels had been professionally examined, and time was when there did not stand an unknown seat on its banks, or a hamlet that had not been visited. Here then was the force of deep impressions to oppose to the influence of objects still visible.

To me i is quite apparent that the Rhine, while it frequently possesses more of any particular species of scenery, within a given number of miles, than the Hudson, has none of so great excellence. It wants the variety, the noble beauty, and the broad grandeur of the American stream. The latter, within the distance universally admitted to contain the finest parts of the Rhine, is both a large and a small river; it has its bays, its narrow passages among the meadows, its frowning gorges, and its reaches resembling Italian lakes; whereas the most that can be said of its European competitor, is that all these wonderful peculiarities are feebly imitated. Ten degrees of a lower latitude supply richer tints, brighter transitions of light and shadow, and more glorious changes of the atmosphere, to embellish the beauties of our western clime. In islands, too, the advantage is with the Hudson, for, while those of the Rhine are the most numerous, those of the former stream are bolder, better placed, and, in every natural feature, of more account.

When the comparison between these celebrated rivers is extended to their artificial accessories, the result becomes more doubtful. The buildings of the older towns and villages of Europe seem grouped especially for effect, as seen in the distant view, though security was in truth the cause, while the spacious, cleanly, and cheerful villages of America must commonly be entered, to be appreciated. In the other hemisphere, the maze of roofs, the church-towers, the irregular faces of wall, and frequently the castle rising to a pinnacle in the rear, give a town the appearance of some vast and antiquated pile devoted to a single object. Perhaps the boroughs of the Rhine have less of this picturesque, or landscape effect, than the villages of France and Italy, for the Germans regard space more than their neighbors, but still are they less commonplace than the smiling and thriving little marts that crowd the borders of the Hudson. To this advantage must be added that which is derived from the countless ruins, and a crowd of recollections. Here, the superiority of the artificial auxiliaries of the Rhine ceases, and those of her rival come into the ascendant. In modern abodes, in villas, and even in seats, those of princes alone excepted, the banks of the Hudson have scarcely an equal in any region. There are finer and nobler edifices on the Brenta, and in other favored spots, certainly, but I know no stream that has so many that please and attract the eye. As applied to moving objects, an important feature in this comparison, the Hudson has perhaps no rival, in any river that can pretend to a picturesque character. In numbers, in variety of rig, in beauty of form, in swiftness and dexterity of handling, and in general grace and movement, this extraordinary passage ranks amongst the first of the world. The yards of tall ships swing among the rocks and forests of the highlands, while sloop, schooner, and bright canopied steam-boat, yacht, periagua, and canoe are seen in countless numbers, decking its waters. There is one more eloquent point of difference that should not be neglected. Drawings and engravings of the Rhine lend their usual advantages, softening, and frequently rendering beautiful, objects of no striking attractions when seen as they exist; while every similar attempt to represent the Hudson, at once strikes the eye as unworthy of its original.

Nature is fruitful of fine effects in every region, and it is a mistake not to enjoy her gifts, as we move through life, on account of some fancied superiority in this, or that, quarter of the world. We left the Rhine, therefore, with regret, for, in its way, a lovelier stream can scarce be found.

At Mayence we crossed to the right bank of the river, and passing by the Duchies of Nassau and Darmstadt, entered that of Baden, at Heidelberg. Here we sat upon the Tun, examined the castle, and strolled in the alleys of the remarkable garden. Thence we proceeded to Manheim, turning our faces, once more, towards the French capital. The illness of one of the party compelled us to remain a few hours in the latter city, which presented little for reflection, unless it were that this, like one or two other towns we had lately seen, served to convince us, that the symmetry and regularity which render large cities magnificent, cause those that are small to appear mean.

It was a bright autumnal day when we returned to the left bank of the Rhine, on the way to Paris. The wishes of the invalid had taken the appearance of strength, and we hoped to penetrate the mountains which bound the Palatinate on its south-western side, and to reach Kaiserslautern, on the great Napoleon road, before the hour of rest. The main object had been accomplished, and, as with all who have effected their purpose, the principal desire was to be at home. A few posts convinced us that repose was still necessary to the invalid. This conviction, unhappily as I then believed, came too late, for we had already crossed the plain of the Palatinate, and were drawing near to the chain of mountains just mentioned which are a branch of the Vosges, and are known in the country as the Haart. We had made no calculations for such an event, and former experience had caused us to distrust the inns of this isolated portion of the kingdom of Bavaria. I was just bitterly regretting our precipitation, when the church-tower of Duerckheim peered above the vineyards; for, on getting nearer to the base of the hills, the land became slightly undulating, and the vine abundant. As we approached, the village or borough promised little, but we had the word of the postilion that the post-house was an inn fit for a king; and as to the wine, he could give no higher eulogium than a flourish of the whip, an eloquent expression of pleasure for a German of his class. We debated the question of proceeding, or of stopping, in a good deal of doubt, to the moment when the carriage drew up before the sign of the Ox. A substantial looking burgher came forth to receive us. There was the pledge of good cheer in the ample development of his person, which was not badly typified by the sign, and the hale hearty character of his hospitality removed all suspicion of the hour of reckoning. If he who travels much is a gainer in knowledge of mankind, he is sure to be a loser in the charities that sweeten life. Constant intercourse with men who are in the habit of seeing strange faces, who only dispose of their services to those that are likely never to need them again, and who, of necessity, are removed from most of the responsibilities and affinities of a more permanent intercourse, exhibits the selfishness of our nature in its least attractive form. Policy may suggest a specious blandishment of air, to conceal the ordinary design on the pocket of the stranger; but it is in the nature of things that the design should exist. The passion of gain, like all other passions, increases with indulgence; and thus do we find those who dwell on beaten roads more rapacious than those in whom the desire is latent, for want of use.

Our host of Duerckheim offered a pledge, in his honest countenance, independent air, and frank manner, of his also being above the usual mercenary schemes of another portion of the craft, who, dwelling in places of little resort, endeavor to take their revenge of fortune, by showing that they look upon every post-carriage as an especial God-send. He had a garden, too, into which he invited us to enter, while the horses were changing, in a way that showed he was simply desirous of being benevolent, and that he cared little whether we staid an hour or a week. In short, his manner was of an artless, kind, natural, and winning character, that strongly reminded us of home, and which at once established an agreeable confidence that is of an invaluable moral effect. Though too experienced blindly to confide in national characteristics, we liked, too, his appearance of German faith, and more than all were we pleased with the German neatness and comfort, of which there were abundance, unalloyed by the swaggering pretension that neutralizes the same qualities among people more artificial. The house was not a beer-drinking, smoking caravanserai, like many hotels in that quarter of the world, but it had detached pavilions in the gardens, in which the wearied traveller might, in sooth, take his rest. With such inducements before our eyes, we determined to remain, and we were not long in instructing the honest burgher to that effect. The decision was received with great civility, and, unlike the immortal Falstaff, I began to see the prospects of taking "mine ease in mine inn" without having a pocket picked.

The carriage was soon housed, and the baggage in the chambers. Notwithstanding the people of the house spoke confidently, but with sufficient modesty, of the state of the larder, it wanted several hours, agreeably to our habits, to the time of dinner, though we had enjoyed frequent opportunities of remarking that in Germany a meal is never unseasonable. Disregarding hints, which appeared more suggested by humanity than the love of gain, our usual hour for eating was named, and, by way of changing the subject, I asked,—

"Did I not see some ruins, on the adjoining mountain, as we entered the village?"

"We call Duerckheim a city, mein Herr," rejoined our host of the Ox; "though none of the largest, the time has been when it was a capital!"

Here the worthy burgher munched his pipe and chuckled, for he was a man that had heard of such places as London, and

Paris, and Pekin, and Naples, and St. Petersburg, or, haply, of the Federal City itself.

"A capital!—it was the abode of one of the smaller Princes, suppose; of what family was your sovereign, pray?"

"You are right, mein Herr. Duerckheim, before the French revolution, was a residence (for so the political capitals are called in Germany), and it belonged to the princes of Leiningen, who had a palace on the other side of the city (the place may be about half as large as Hudson, or Schenectady), which was burnt in the war. After the late wars, the sovereign was *médiatisé*, receiving an indemnity in estates on the other side of the Rhine."

As this term of *médiatisé* has no direct synonyme in English, it may be well to explain its signification. Germany, as well as most of Europe, was formerly divided into a countless number of petty sovereignties, based on the principle of feudal power. As accident, or talent, or alliances, or treachery advanced the interests of the stronger of these princes, their weaker neighbors began to disappear altogether, or to take new and subordinate stations in the social scale. In this manner has France been gradually composed of its original, but comparatively insignificant kingdom, buttressed, as it now is, by Brittany, and Burgundy, and Navarre, and Dauphiny, and Provence, and Normandy, with many other states; and, in like manner has England been formed of the Heptarchy. The confederative system of Germany has continued more or less of this feudal organization to our own times. The formation of the empires of Austria and Prussia has, however, swallowed up many of these principalities, and the changes produced by the policy of Napoleon gave the death-blow, without distinction, to all in the immediate vicinity of the Rhine. Of the latter number were the Princes of Leiningen, whose possessions were originally included in the French republic, then in the empire, and have since passed under the sway of the King of Bavaria, who, as the legitimate heir of the neighboring Duchy of Deux Ponts, had a nucleus of sufficient magnitude in this portion of Germany, to induce the congress of Vienna to add to his dominions; their object being to erect a barrier against the future aggrandizement of France. As the dispossessed sovereigns are permitted to retain their conventional rank, supplying wives and husbands, at need, to the reigning branches of the different princely families, the term *médiatisé* has been aptly enough applied to their situation.

"The young prince was here, no later than last week," continued our host of the Ox; "he lodged in that pavilion, where he passed several days. You know that he is a son of the Duchess of Kent, and half-brother to the young princess who is likely, one day, to be queen of England."

"Has he estates here, or is he still, in any way, connected with your government?"

"All they have given him is in money, or on the other side of the Rhine. He went to see the ruins of the old castle; for he had a natural curiosity to look at a place which his ancestors had built."

"It was the ruins of the castle of Leiningen, then, that I saw on the mountain, as we entered the town?"

"No, mein Herr. You saw the ruins of the Abbey of Limburg; those of Hartenburg, for so the castle was called, lie farther back among the hills."

"What! a ruined abbey, and a ruined castle, too!—Here is sufficient occupation for the rest of the day. An abbey and a castle!"

"And the Heidenmauer, and the Teufelstein."

"How! a Pagan's wall, and a Devil's stone!—You are rich in curiosities!"

The host continued to smoke on philosophically.

"Have you a guide who can take me, by the shortest way to these places?"

"Any child can do that."

"But one who can speak French is desirable—for my German is far from being classical."

The worthy inn-keeper nodded his head.

"Here is one Christian Kinzel," he rejoined, after a moment of thought, "a tailor who has not much custom, and who has lived a little in France; he may serve your turn."

I suggested that a tailor might find it healthful to stretch his knee-joints.

The host of the Ox was amused with the conceit, and he fairly removed the pipe, in order to laugh at his ease. His mirth was hearty, like that of a man without guile.

The affair was soon arranged. A messenger was sent for Christian Kinzel, and taking my little male travelling companion by the hand, I went leisurely ahead, expecting the appearance of the guide. But, as the reader will have much to do with the place about to be described, it may be desirable that he should possess an accurate knowledge of its locality.

Duerckheim lies in that part of Bavaria, which is commonly called the circle of the Rhine. The king, of the country named, may have less than half a million of subjects in this detached part of his territories, which extends in one course from the river to Rhenish Prussia, and in the other from Darmstadt to France. It requires a day of hard posting to traverse this province in any direction, from which it would appear that its surface is about equal to two-thirds of that of Connecticut. A line of mountains, resembling the smaller spurs of the Alleghanies, and which are known by different local names, but which are a branch of the Vosges, passes nearly through the centre of the district, in a north and south course. These mountains cease abruptly on their eastern side, leaving between them and the river, a vast level surface, of that description which is called "flats," or "bottom land" in America. This plain, part of the ancient Palatinate, extends equally on the other side of the Rhine, terminating as abruptly on the eastern as on the western border. In an air line, the distance between Heidelberg and Duerckheim, which lie opposite to each other on the two lateral extremities of the plain, may a little exceed twenty miles, the Rhine running equi-distant from both. There is a plausible theory, which says that the plain of the Palatinate was formerly a lake, receiving the waters of the Rhine, and of course discharging them by some inferior outlet, until time, or a convulsion of the earth, broke through the barrier of the mountains at Bingen, draining off the waters, and leaving the fertile bottom described. Irregular sand-hills were visible, as we approached Duerckheim, which may go to confirm this supposition, for the prevalence of northerly winds might easily have cast more of these light particles on the south-western than on the opposite shore. By adding that the eastern face of the mountains, or that next to the plain, is sufficiently broken and irregular to be beautiful, while it is always distinctly marked and definite, enough has been said to enable us to proceed with intelligence.

It would appear that one of the passes that has communicated, from time immemorial, between the Rhine and the country west of the Vosges, issues on the plain through the gorge near Duerckheim. By following the windings of the valleys, the post-road penetrates, by an easy ascent, to the highest ridge, and following the water-courses that run into the Moselle, descends nearly as gradually into the Duchy of Deux Ponts, on the other side of the chain. The possession of this pass, therefore, in the ages of lawlessness and violence, was, in itself, a title to distinction and power; since all who journeyed by it, lay in person and effects more or less at the mercy of the occupant.

On quitting the town, my little companion and myself immediately entered the gorge. The pass itself was narrow, but a valley soon opened to the width of a mile, out of which issued two or three passages, besides that by which we had entered, though only one of them preserved its character for any distance. The capacity of this valley, or basin, as it must have been when the Palatinate was a lake, is much curtailed by an insulated mountain, whose base, covering a fourth of the area, stands in its very centre, and which doubtless was an island when the valley was a secluded bay. The summit of this mountain or island-hill is level, of an irregularly oval form, and contains some six or eight acres of land. Here stand the ruins of Limburg, the immediate object of our visit.

The ascent was exceedingly rapid, and of several hundred feet; reddish free-stone appeared everywhere through the scanty soil, the sun beat powerfully on the rocks; and I was beginning to weigh the advantages and disadvantages of proceeding, when the tailor approached, with the zeal of new-born courage.

"Voici Christian Kinzel!" exclaimed ———, to whom novelty was always an incentive, and who, in his young life, had eagerly mounted Alp and Apennine, Jura and Calabrian hill tower, monument, and dome, or whatever else served to raise him in the air; "Allons,—grimpons!"

We scrambled up the hill-side, and, winding among terraces on which the vine and vegetables were growing, soon reached the natural platform. There was a noble view from the summit, but it would be premature to describe it here. The whole surface of the hill furnished evidence of the former extent of the Abbey, a wall having encircled the entire place; but the principal edifices had been built, and still remained, near the longitudinal centre, on the very margin of the eastern precipice. Enough was standing to prove the ancient magnificence of the structure. Unlike most of the ruins which border the Rhine, the masonry was of a workmanlike kind, the walls being not only massive, but composed of the sand-stone just mentioned neatly hewn, for immense strata of the material exist in all this region. I traced the chapel, still in tolerable preservation, the refectory, that never-failing solacer of monastic seclusion, several edifices apparently appropriated to the dormitories, and some vestiges of the cloisters. There is also a giddy tower, of an ecclesiastical form, that sufficiently serves to give a character to the ruins. It was closed, to prevent idlers from incurring foolish risks by mounting the crazy steps; but its having formerly been appropriated to the consecrated bells, was not at all doubtful. There is also a noble arch near, with several of its disjointed stones menacing the head of him who ventures beneath.

Turning from the ruin, I cast a look at the surrounding valley. Nothing could have been softer or more lovely than the near view. That sort of necessity, which induces us to cherish any stinted gift, had led the inhabitants to turn every foot of the bottom land to the best account. No Swiss Alp could have been more closely shaved than the meadows at my feet, and a good deal had been made of two or three rivulets that meandered among them. The dam of a rustic mill threw back the water into a miniature lake, and some zealous admirer of Neptune had established a beer-house on its banks, which was dignified with the sign of the "Anchor!" But the principal object in the interior or upland view, was the ruins of a castle, that occupied a natural terrace, or rather the projection of a rock, against the side of one of the nearest mountains. The road passed immediately beneath its walls, a short arrow-flight from the battlements, the position having evidently been chosen as the one best adapted to command the ordinary route of the traveller. I wanted no explanation from the guide to know that this was the castle of Hartenburg. It was still more massive than the remains of the Abbey, built of the same material, and seemingly in different centuries; for while one part was irregular and rude, like most of the structures of the middle ages, there were salient towers filled with embrasures, for the use of artillery. One of their guns, well elevated, might possibly have thrown its shot on the platform of the Abbey-hill, but with little danger even to the ruined walls.

After studying the different objects in this novel and charming scene, for an hour, I demanded of the guide some account of the Pagan's Wall and of the Devil's Stone. Both were on the mountain that lay on the other side of the ambitious little lake, a long musket-shot from the Abbey. It was even possible to see a portion of the former, from our present stand; and the confused account of the tailor only excited a desire to see more. We had not come on this excursion without a fit supply of road-books and maps. One of the former was accidentally in my pocket, though so little had we expected anything extraordinary on this unfrequented road, that as yet it had not been opened. On consulting its pages now, I was agreeably disappointed in finding that Duerckheim and its antiquities had not been thought unworthy of the traveller's especial attention. The Pagan's Wall was there stated to be the spot in which Attila passed the winter before crossing the Rhine, in his celebrated inroad against the capital of the civilized world, though its origin was referred to his enemies themselves. In short, it was believed to be the remains of a Roman camp, one of those advanced works of the empire, by which the Barbarians were held in check, and of which the Hun had casually and prudently availed himself, in his progress south. The Devil's Stone was described as a natural rock, in the vicinity of the encampment, on which the Pagans had offered sacrifices. Of course he liberated limbs of the guide were put in requisition, to con duct us to a spot that contained curiosities so worthy of even his exertions.

As we descended the mountain of Limburg, Christian Kinzei lighted the way, by relating the opinions of the country, concerning the places we had seen and were about to see. It would appear by this legend, that when the pious monks were planning their monastery, a compact was made with the Devi. to quarry the stones necessary for so extensive a work, and to transport them up the steep acclivity. The inducemen: held forth to the evil spirit, for undertaking a work of this nature, was the pretence of erecting a tavern, in which, doubtless, undue quantities of Rhenish wine were to be quaffed, cheating human reason, and leaving the undefended soul more exposed to the usual assaults of temptation. It would seem, by the legends of the Rhine, that the monks often succeeded in outwitting the arch foe in this sort of compact, though perhaps never with more signal success than in the bargain in question. Completely deceived by the artifices of the men of God, the father of sin lent himself to the project with so much zeal, that the Abbey and its appendages were completed in a time incredibly short; a circumstance that his employers took good care to turn to account, after their own fashion, by ascribing it to a miracle of purer emanation. By all accounts the deception was so well managed, that notwithstanding his proverbial cunning, the Devil never knew the true destination of the edifice until the Abbey-bell actually rang for prayers. Then, indeed, his indignation knew no bounds, and he proceeded forthwith to the rock in question, with the fell intent of bringing it into the air above the chapel, and, by its fall, of immolating the monks and their altar together, to his vengeance. But the stone was too firmly rooted to be displaced even by the Devil; and he was finally compelled, by the prayers of the devotees, who were now, after their own fashion of fighting, fairly in the field, to abandon this portion of the country in shame and disgrace. The curious are shown certain marks on the rock, which go to prove the violent efforts of Satan, on this occasion, and among others the prints of his form, left by seating himself on the stone, fatigued by useless exertions. The more ingenious even trace, in a sort of groove, evidence of the position of his tail, during the time the baffled spirit was chewing the cud of chagrin on his hard stool.

We were at the foot of the second mountain when Christian Kinzel ended this explanation.

"And such is your Deurckheim tradition concerning the Devil's Stone?" I remarked, measuring the ascent with the sight.

"Such is what is said in the country, mein Herr," returned the tailor; "but there are people, hereabouts, who do not believe it."

My little travelling companion laughed, and his eyes danced with expectation.

"Allons, grimpons!" he cried again—"Allons voir ce Teufelstein!"

In a suitable time we were in the camp. It lay on an advanced spur of the mountain, a sort of salient bastion made by nature, and was completely protected on every side, but that at which it was joined to the mass, by declivities so steep as to be even descended with some pain. There was the ruin of a circular wall, half a league in extent, the stones lying in a confused pile around the whole exterior, and many vestiges of foundations and intersecting walls within. The whole area was covered with a young growth of dark and melancholy cedars. On the face exposed to the adjoining mountain, there had evidently been the additional protection of a ditch.

The Teufelstein was a thousand feet from the camp. It is a weather-worn rock, that shows its bare head from a high point in the more advanced ranges of the hills. I took a seat on its most elevated pinnacle, and for a moment the pain of the ascent was forgotten.

The plain of the Palatinate, far as eye could reach, lay in the view. Here and there the Rhine and the Neckar glittered like sheets of silver, among the verdure of the fields, and tower of city and of town, of Manheim, Spires, and Worms, of nameless villages, and of German residences, were as plenty in the scene, as tombs upon the Appian Way. A dozen gray ruins clung against the sides of the mountains of Baden and Darmstadt, while the castle of Heidelberg was visible, in its romantic glen, sombre, courtly, and magnificent. The landscape was German, and in its artificial parts slightly Gothic; it wanted the warm glow, the capricious outlines, and seductive beauty of Italy, and the grandeur of the Swiss valleys and glaciers; but it was the perfection of fertility and industry embellished by a crowd of useful objects.

It was easy for one thus placed, to fancy himself surrounded by so many eloquent memorials of the progress of civilization, of the infirmities and constitution, of the growth and ambition of the human mind. The rock recalled the age of furious superstition and debased ignorance—the time when the country lay in forest, over which the hunter ranged at will, contending with the beast for the mastery of his savage domain. Still the noble creature bore the image of God, and occasionally some master mind pierced the shades, catching glimpses of that eternal truth which pervades Nature. Then followed the Roman, with his gods of plausible attributes, his ingenious and specious philosophy, his accumulated and borrowed art, his concerted and overwhelming action, his love of magnificence, so grand in its effects, but so sordid and unjust in its means, and last, the most impressive of all, that beacon-like ambition which wrecked his hopes on the sea of its vastness, with the evidence of the falsity of his system as furnished in his fall. The memorial before me showed the means by which he gained and lost his power. The Barbarian had been taught, in the bitter school of experience, to regain his rights, and in the excitement of the moment, it was not difficult to imagine the Huns pouring into the camp, and calculating their chances of success, by the vestiges they found of the ingenuity and resources of their foes.

The confusion of misty images that succeeded was an apt emblem of the next age. Out of this obscurity, after the long and glorious reign of Charlemagne, arose the baronial castle, with feudal violence and its progeny of wrongs. Then came the abbey, an excrescence of that mild and suffering religion, which had appeared on earth, like a ray of the sun, eclipsing the factitious brilliancy of a scene from which natural light had been excluded for a substitute of a meretricious and deceptive quality. Here arose the long and selfish strife, between antagonist principles, that has not yet ceased. The struggle was between the power of knowledge and that of physical force. The former, neither pure nor perfect, descended to subterfuge and deceit; while the latter vacillated between the dread of unknown causes, and the love of domination. Monk and baron came in collision; this secretly distrusting the faith he professed, and that trembling at the consequences of the blow which his own sword had given; the fruits of too much knowledge in one, and of too little in the other, while both were the prey of those incessant and unwearied enemies of the race, the greedy passions.

A laugh from the child drew my attention to the foot of the rock. He and Christian Kinzel had just settled, to their mutual satisfaction, the precise position that had been occupied by the Devil's tail. A more suitable emblem of his country than that boy, could not have been found on the whole of its wide surface. As secondary to the predominant English or Saxon stock, the blood of France, Sweden, and Holland ran, in nearly equal currents, in his veins. He had not far to seek, to find among his ancestors the peaceful companion of Penn, the Huguenot, the Cavalier, the Presbyterian, the follower of Luther and of Calvin. Chance had even deepened the resemblance; for, a wanderer from infancy, he now blended languages in merry comments on his recent discovery. The train of thought that his appearance suggested was natural. It embraced the long and mysterious concealment of so vast a portion of the earth as America, from the acquaintance of civilized man; its discovery and settlement; the manner in which violence and persecution, civil wars, oppression and injustice, had thrown men of all nations upon its shores; the effects of this collision of customs and opinions, unenthralled by habits and laws of selfish origin; the religious and civil liberty that followed; the novel but irrefutable principle on which its government was based, the silent working of its example in the two hemispheres, one of which had already imitated the institutions that the other was struggling to approach, and all the immense results that were dependent on this inscrutable and grand movement of Providence. I know not indeed but my thoughts might have proached the sublime, had not Christian Kinzel interrupted them, by pointing out the spot where the Devil had kicked the stone, in his anger.

Descending from the perch, we took the path to Deurckheim. As we came down the mountain, the tailor had many philosophical remarks to make, that were chiefly elicited by the forlorn condition of one who had much toil and little food. In his view of things, labor was too cheap, and wine and potatoes were too dear. To what depth he might have pushed reflections bottomed on principles so natural, it is impossible to say, had not the boy started some doubts concerning the reputed length of the Devil's tail. He had visited the Jardin des Plantes at Paris, seen the kangaroos in the Zoological Garden in London, and was familiar with the inhabitants of a variety of caravans encountered at Rome, Naples, Dresden, and other capitals; with the bears of Berne he had actually been on the familiar terms of a friendly visiting acquaintance Having also some vague ideas of the analogies of things, he could not recall any beast so amply provided with such an elongation of the dorsal bone, as was to be inferred from Christian Kinzel's gutter in the Teufelstein. During the discussion of this knotty point, we reached the inn.

The host of the Ox had deceived us in nothing. The viands were excellent, and abundant to prodigality. The bottle of old Deurckheimer might well have passed for Johannisberger, or for that still more delicious liquor, Steinberger, at London or New-York; and the simple and sincere civility with which every thing was served, gave a zest to all.

It would have been selfish to recruit nature, without thought of the tailor, after so many hours of violent exercise in the keen air of the mountains. He too had his cup and his viands, and when both were invigorated by these natural means, we held a conference, to which the worthy post-master was admitted.

The following pages are the offspring of the convocation held in the parlor of the Ox. Should any musty German antiquary discover some immaterial anachronism, a name misplaced in the order of events, or a monk called prematurely from purgatory, he is invited to wreak his just indignation on Christian Kinzel, whose body and soul may St. Benedict of Limburg protect, for evermore, against all critics.

THE HEIDENMAUER.

CHAPTER I.

Stand you both forth now; stroke your chins, and swear by your beards that I am a knave.——*As You Like It.*

THE reader must imagine a narrow and secluded valley, for the opening scene of this tale. The time was that in which the day loses its power, casting a light on objects most exposed, that resembles colors seen through glass slightly stained; a peculiarity of the atmosphere, which, though almost of daily occurrence in summer and autumn, is the source of constant enjoyment to the real lover of nature. The hue meant is not a sickly yellow, but rather a soft and melancholy glory, that lends to the hill-side and copse, to tree and tower, to stream and lawn, those tinges of surpassing loveliness that impart to the close of day its proverbial and soothing charm. The setting sun touched with oblique rays a bit of shaven meadow, that lay in a dell so deep as to owe this parting smile of nature to an accidental formation of the neighboring eminences, a distant mountain crest, that a flock had cropped and fertilized, a rippling current that glided in the bottom, a narrow beaten path, more worn by hoof than wheel, and a vast range of forest, that swelled and receded from the view, covering leagues of a hill-chase, that even tradition had never peopled. The spot was seemingly as retired as if it had been chosen in one of our own solitudes of the wilderness while it was, in fact, near the centre of Europe, and in the sixteenth century. But, notwithstanding the absence of dwellings, and all the other signs of the immediate presence of man, together with the wooded character of the scene, an American eye would not have been slow to detect its distinguishing features, from those which mark the wilds of this country. The trees, though preserved with care, and flourishing, wanted the moss of ages, the high and rocking summit, the variety and natural wildness of the western forest. No mouldering trunk lay where it had fallen, no branch had been twisted by the gale and forgotten, nor did any upturned root betray the indifference of man to the decay of this important part of vegetation. Here and there, a species of broom, such as is seen occasionally on the mast-heads of ships, was erected above some tall member of the woods that stood on an elevated point; land-marks which divided the rights of those who were entitled to cut and clip; the certain evidence that man had long before extended his sway over these sombre hills, and that, retired as they seemed, they were actually subject to all the divisions, and restraints, and vexations, which, in peopled regions, accompany the rights of property.

For an hour preceding the opening of our tale, not a sound of any nature, beyond that of a murmuring brook, had disturbed the quiet of the silent little valley, if a gorge so narrow, and in truth so wild, deserved the name. There was not even a bird fluttering among the trees, nor a hawk soaring above the heights. Once, and for a minute only did a roebuck venture from its cover, and descend to the rivulet to drink. The animal had not altogether the elastic bound, the timid and irresolute movement, nor the wandering eye of our own deer; but it was clearly an inhabitant of a forest; for while it in some degree confided in the protection, it also distrusted the power of man. No sooner was its thirst assuaged, than listening with the keenness of an instinct that no circumstances of accidental condition could destroy, it went up the acclivity again, and sought its cover with troubled steps. At the same instant, a grayhound leaped from among the trees, on the opposite side of the gorge, into the path, and began bounding back and forth, in the well-known manner of that species of dog, when exercising in restlessness, rather than engaged in the hot strife of the chase. A whistle called the hound back from its gambols, and its master entered the path.

A cap of green velvet, bearing a hunting-horn above the shade, a coarse but neat frock of similar color, equally ornamented with the same badge of office, together with the instrument itself suspended from a shoulder, and the arms usual to one of that class, denoted a forester, or an individual charged with the care of the chase, and otherwise intrusted with a jurisdiction in the forest; functions that would be much degraded by the use of the abused and familiar term of gamekeeper.

The forester was young, active, and, notwithstanding the rudeness of his attire, of a winning exterior. Laying his fusee against the root of a tree, he whistled in the dog, and renewing the call, by means of a shrill instrument that was carried for that purpose, he soon succeeded in bringing its fellow to his side. Coupling the grayhounds in a leash, which he attached to his own person, he threw the horn from its noose, and blew a lively and short strain, that rolled up the valley in mellow and melodious notes. When the instrument was removed from his lips, the youth listened till the last of the distant echoes was done, as if expecting some reply. He was not disappointed. Presently an answering blast came down the gorge, ringing among the woods, and causing the hearts of many of its tenants to beat quick and fearfully. The sounds of the unseen instrument were far more shrill and wild than those of the hunting horn, while they wanted not for melancholy sweetness. They appeared both familiar and intelligible to the young forester, who no sooner heard them, than he slung the horn in its usual turn of the cord, resumed the fusee, and stood in an attitude of expectation.

It might have been a minute before another youth appeared in the path, higher in the gorge, and advancing slowly towards the forester. His dress was rustic, and altogether that of a peasant, while in his hand he held a long, straight, narrow tube of cherry wood, firmly wrapped with bark, having a mouth-piece and a small bell at the opposite end, resembling those of a trumpet. As he came forward, his face was not without an expression of ill humor, though it was rather rendered comic than grave, by a large felt hat, the front rim of which fell in an enormous shade above his eyes, rendering the trim cock in the rear, ludicrously pretending. His legs, like those of the forester, were encased in a sort of leathern hose, that left the limbs naked and free below the knee, while the garment above set so loosely and unbuttoned above that important joint, as to offer no restraint to his movements.

"Thou art behind thy time, Gottlob," said the young forester, as the boor approached, "and the good hermit will not give us better welcome for keeping him from prayer. What has become of thy herd?"

"That may the holy man of the Heidenmauer declare, for it is more than I could answer were Lord Emich himself to put the question, and say, in the manner he is wont to use to the Abbot of Limburg—what hath become of thy herd Gottlob?"

"Nay, this is no trifling matter, if thou hast, in sooth, let the cattle stray! Where hadst thou the beasts last in sight?"

"Here in the forest of Hartenburg, Master Berchthold, on the honor of an humble servitor of the Count."

"Thou wilt yet lose this service, Gottlob, by thy carelessness!"

"It would be a thousand pities were thy words to be true, for in that case Lord Emich would lose the honestest cow-herd in Germany, and it would go near to break my heart were the friars of Limburg to get him! But the beasts cannot be far, and I will try the virtue of the horn once more, before I go home to a broken head and a discharge. Dost thou know, Master Berchthold, that the disgrace of which thou speakest never yet befell any of my family, and we have been keepers of cattle longer than the Friedrichs have been electors!"

The forester made an impatient gesture, patted his hounds, and waited for the effects of the new blast, that his companion was by this time preparing to sound. The manner of Gottlob was that of entire confidence in his own knowledge of his calling for notwithstanding his words, his countenance at no time betrayed uneasiness for the fate of his trust. The valley was soon ringing with the wild and plaintive tones of the cherry-wood horn, the hind taking care to give the strains those intonations, which, by a mute convention, had from time immemorial been understood as the signal for collecting a lost herd. His skill and faith were soon rewarded, for cow after cow came leaping out of the forest, as he blew his air, and ere long the necessary number of animals were in the path, the younger beasts frisking along the way, with elevated tails and awkward bounds, while the more staid contributors of the dairy hurried on, with business-like air but grave steps, as better became their years and their characters in the hamlet. In a few minutes they were all collected around the person of the keeper, who having counted his charge, shouldered his horn, and disposed himself to proceed towards the lower extremity of the gorge.

"Thou art lucky to have gotten the beasts together, with so little trouble, Gottlob," resumed the forester, as they followed in the train of the herd.

"Say dexterous, Master Berchthold, and do not fear to make me vain-glorious. In the way of understanding my own merits there is little danger of doing me harm. Thou shouldest never discourage modesty, by an over-scrupulous discretion. It would be a village miracle, were a herd so nurtured in the ways of the church to forget its duty!"

The forester laughed, but he looked aside, like one who would not see that to which he wished to be blind.

"At thy old tricks, friend Gottlob! Thou hast let the beasts roam upon the range of the friars!"

"I have paid Peter's pence, been to the chapel of St. Benedict for prayer, confessed to Father Arnolph himself, and all within the month: what more need a man do, to be in favor with the Brothers?"

"I could wish to know if thou ever entertainest Father Arnolph with the history of thy visits to the pastures of the convent, with Lord Emich's herd, honest Gottlob."

"So! Dost thou fancy, Master Berchthold, that, at a moment when there is every necessity to possess a calm and contemplative spirit, I should strive to put the pious monk in a passion, by relating all the antics of some ill-bred cow, or of a heifer, who is as little to be trusted without a keeper, as your jung-frau before she reaches the years of caution is to be trusted at a fair without her mother, or a sharp-sighted old aunt, at the very least!"

"Well, have a care, Gottlob, for Lord Emich though loving the friars so little, will be apt to order thee into a dungeon, on bread and water for a week, or to make thy back acquainted with the lash, should he come to hear that one of his hinds has taken this liberty with the rights of a neighbor."

"Let Lord Emich then expel the brotherhood from the richest pasturage near the Jaegerthal. Flesh and blood cannot bear to see the beasts of a noble digging into the earth with their teeth, after a few bitter herbs, while the carrion of a convent are rolling the finest and sweetest grasses over their tongues. Look you, Master Berchthold, these friars of Limburg eat the fattest venison, drink the warmest wine, and say the shortest prayers of any monks in Christendom! Potz-Tausend! There are some who accuse them, too, of shriving the prettiest girls! As for bread and water, and a dungeon, I know from experience that neither of the remedies agrees with a melancholy constitution, and I defy the Emperor, or even the Holy Father himself, to work such a miracle, as to make back of mine acquainted with the lash."

"Simply because the introduction hath long since had place."

"That is thy interpretation of the matter, Master Berchthold, and I wish thee joy of a quick wit. But we are getting beyond the limits of the forest, and we will dismiss the question to another conversation. The beasts are full, and will not disappoint the dairy girls, and little matters it whence the nourishment comes—Lord Emich's pastures or a churchly miracle. Thou hast hunted the dogs lightly to-day, Berchthold?"

"I have had them on the mountains for air and movement. They got away on the heels of a roe buck, for a short run, but as all the game in thi chase belongs to our master, I did not see fit to le them go faster than there was need."

"I rejoice to hear thee say it, for I count upon thy company in climbing the mountain when our work is ended; thy legs will only be the fresher for the toil."

"Thou hast my word, and I will not fail thee; in order that no time be lost, we will part here to mee again in the hamlet."

The forester and the cow-herd made signs of leave-taking, and separated. The former quitted the public road, turning short to the right by a private way, which led him across narrow meadows, and the little river that glided among them, towards the foot of the opposite mountain. Gottlob held on his course to a hamlet that was now visible, and which completely filled a narrow pass in the valley at a point where the latter made a turn, nearly at a right angle with its general direction.

The path of the former led him to an habitation very different from the rude dwellings towards which the steps of the cow-herd tended. A massive castle occupied a projecting point of the mountain, overhanging the cluster of houses in the gorge, and frowning upon all that attempted the pass. The structure was a vast but irregular pile. The more modern parts were circular salient towers, that were built upon the uttermost verge of the rock, from whose battlements it would not have been difficult to cast a stone into the road, and which denoted great attention to strength in their masonry, while beauty of form and of workmanship, as they were understood at the period of which we write, were not entirely neglected. These towers, though large, were mere appendages to the main building, which, seen from the position now before the mind of the reader, presented a confused maze of walls, chimneys, and roofs. In some places, the former rose from the greensward which covered the hill-side; while in others, advantage had been taken of the living rock, which was frequently so blended with the pile it supported, both being of the same reddish free-stone, that it was not easy at the first glance to say, what had been done by nature and what by art.

The path of the forester led from the valley up the mountain, by a gradual and lateral ascent to a huge gate, that opened beneath a high arch, communicating with a court within. On this side of the castle there was neither ditch, nor bridge, nor any other of the usual defences, beyond a portcullis, for the position of the hold rendered these precautions in a measure unnecessary. Still great care had been taken to prevent a surprise, and it would have required a sure foot, a steady head, and vigorous limbs, to have effected an entrance into the edifice, by any other passage than its gate.

When Berchthold reached the little terrace that lay before the portal, he loosened his horn, and, standing on the verge of the precipice, blew a hunting strain, apparently in glee. The music echoed among the hills as suited the spot, and more than one crone of the hamlet suspended her toil, in dull admiration, to listen to its wild effect. Replacing the instrument, the youth spoke to his hounds and passed beneath the portcullis, which happened to be raised at the moment.

CHAPTER II.

"What sayest thou to a hare, or the melancholy of moor-ditch?"
King Henry IV.

The light had nearly disappeared from the gorge, n which the hamlet of Hartenburg lay, when Berchthold descended from the castle, by a path different from that by which he had entered it an hour before, and crossing the rivulet by a bridge of stone, he ascended the opposite bank into the street, or rather the road. The young forester having kennelled the hounds, had laid aside his leash and fusee, but he still kept the horn suspended from his shoulder. At his side, too, he carried a couteau-de-chasse, a useful instrument of defence in that age and country, as well as a weapon he was entitled to carry, in virtue of his office under the Count of Lienengen-Hartenburg, the master of the hold he had just quitted, and the feudal lord of most of the adjoining mountains, as well as of sundry villages on the plain of the Palatinate. It would seem that the cow-herd expected his associate, or perhaps we might venture to call him friend, for such in truth did he appear to be, by the easy terms on which they met. Gottlob was in waiting near the cottage of his mother, and when the two joined each other they communicated by a sign, and proceeded with swift steps, leaving the cluster of houses.

Immediately on quitting the hamlet, the valley expanded, and took that character of fertility and cultivation, which has been described to the reader in the Introduction; for all who have perused that opening and necessary preface to our labors, will at once recognize that the two youths introduced to their acquaintance, were now in the mountain basin which contained the Abbey of Limburg. But three centuries, while they have effected little in altering the permanent features of the place, have wrought essential changes in those which were more perishable.

As the young men moved swiftly on, the first rays of the moon touched the tops of the mountains, and ere they had gone a mile, always holding the direction of the pass which communicated with the valley of the Rhine, the towers and roofs of the Abbey itself were illuminated. The conventual buildings were then perfect, resembling, by their number and confusion, the grouping of some village, while a strong and massive wall encircled the entire brow of the isolated hill. The construction resembled one of those warlike ecclesiastical princes of the middle ages, who wore armor beneath the stole; for while the towers and painted windows, the pious memorials and votive monuments, denoted the objects of the establishment, the defences betrayed that as much dependence was placed on human as on other means, for the protection of those who composed the brotherhood.

"There is a moon for a monk as well as for a cow-herd, it would seem," observed Gottlob, speaking however in a voice subdued nearly to a whisper. "There comes the light upon the high tower of the Abbey, and presently it will be glistening on the bald head of every straggler of the convent, who is abroad tasting the last vintage, or otherwise prying into the affairs of some burgher of Deurckheim!"

"Thou hast not much reverence for the pious fathers, honest Gottlob; for it is seldom thou lettest opportunity pass to do them an ill turn, with tongue or hungry beast."

"Look you, Berchthold, we vassals are little more than so much clear water in which our master may see his own countenance, and at need his own humors. Whenever Lord Emich has a sincere hatred for man or horse, dog or cat, town or village, monk or count, I know not why it is so, but I feel my own choler rise, until I am both ready and willing to strike when he striketh, to curse when he curseth, and even to kill when he killeth."

"'Tis a good temper for a servitor, but it is to be hoped, for the sake of Christian credit, that the sympathy does not end here, but that thy affections are as social as thy dislikes."

"More so, as there is faith in man! Count Emich is a huge lover of a venison pasty of a morning, and I feel a yearning for it the day long—Count Emich will dispatch you a bottle of Deurckheim in an hour, whereas two would scarce show my zeal for his honor in the same time; and as for other mortifications of this nature, I am not the man to desert my master for want of zeal."

"I believe thee, Gottlob," said Berchthold laughing, "and even more than thou canst find words to say in thine own favor, on topics like these. But, after all, the Benedictines are churchmen, and sworn to their faith and duty, as well as any bishop in Germany; and I do not see the cause of all the dislike of either lord or vassal."

"Ay, thou art in favor with some of the fraternity, and it is rare that the week passes in which thou art not kneeling before some of their altars; but with me the case is different, for since the penance commanded for that affair of dealing a little freely with one of their herds, I have small digestion for their spiritual food."

"And yet thou hast paid Peter's pence, said thy prayers, and confessed thy sins to Father Arnolph, and all within the month!"

"What wouldst thou have of a sinner? I gave the money on the promise of having it back with usury

I prayed on account of an accursed tooth that torments me, at times, in a manner worse than a damned soul is harrowed; and as to confession, ever since my uncommon candor, concerning the herd, got me into that penance, I confess under favor of a proper discretion. To tell the truth, Master Berchthold, the church is something like a two-year old wife; pleasant enough when allowed her own way, but a devil of a vixen when folded against her will."

The young forester was thoughtful and silent, and as they were now in the vicinity of the hamlet which belonged to the friars of Limburg, his loquacious and prurient companion saw fit to imitate his reserve, from a motive of prudence. The little artificial lake mentioned in the Introduction was in existence, at the time of our tale; but the inn, with the ambitious sign of the anchor, is the fruit of far more modern enterprise. When the young men reached a ravine, that opened into the mountain near the present site of this tavern, they turned aside from the high road, first taking care to observe that no curious eye watched their movements.

Here commenced a long and somewhat painful ascent, by means of a rough path, that was only lighted in spots by the rising moon. The vigorous limbs of the forester and the cow-herd, however, soon carried them to the summit of the most advanced spur of the adjoining mountain, where they arrived upon an open heath-like plain. Although the discourse between them had been maintained during the ascent, it was in more subdued tones even than when beneath the walls of Limburg, the spirits of Gottlob appearing to ooze away the higher he mounted.

"This is a dreary and a courage-killing waste, Berchthold," whispered the cow-herd, as his foot touched the level ground; "and it is even more disheartening to enter on it by the aid of the moon, than in the dark. Hast ever been nearer to the Teufelstein, at this hour?"

"I came upon it once at midnight; for it was there I made acquaintance with him that we are now about to visit—Did I never relate the manner of that meeting?"

"What a habit hast thou of taxing a memory! Perhaps if thou wert to repeat it, I might recall the facts by the time thou wert ended; and to speak truth, thy voice is comfortable on this sprite's common."

The young forester smiled, but without derision, for he saw that his companion, spite of his indifference to all grave subjects, was, as is generally the case, the most affected of the two when put to a serious trial, and perhaps he also remembered the difference that education had made in their powers of thinking. That he did not treat the subject as one of light import himself, was also apparent by the regulated and cautious manner in which he delivered the following account.

"I had been on the chases of Lord Emich since the rising of the sun," commenced Berchthold, "for there was need of more than common vigilance to watch the neighboring boors. The search had led me far into the hills, and the night came, not as it is now seen, but so pitchy dark, that, accustomed as I was from childhood to the forest, it was not possible to tell the direction of even a star, much less that of the Castle. For hours I wandered, hoping at each moment to reach the opening of the valley, when I found myself of a sudden in a field that appeared endless and uninhabited."

"Ay—That was this devil's ball-room!—thou meanest untenanted by man."

"Hast thou ever known the helplessness of being lost in the forest, Gottlob?"

"In my own person, never, Master Berchthold:

but in that of my herd, it is a misfortune that often befalls me, sinner that I am!"

"I know not that sympathy with thy cows can teach thee the humiliation and depression that come over the mind, when we stand on this goodly earth, cut off from all communication with our fellows, in a desert, though surrounded by living men, deprived of the senses of sight and hearing for useful ends, and with all the signs of God before the eyes, and yet with none of the common means of enjoying his bounty, from having lost the clue to his intentions."

"Must the teeth, of necessity, be idle, or the throat dry, Master Forester, because the path is hid?"

"At such a moment the appetites are quieted, in the grand desire to return to our usual communication with the earth. It is like being restored to the helplessness of infancy, with all the wants and habits of manhood besetting the character and wishes."

"If thou callest such a condition a restoration, friend Berchthold, I shall make interest with St. Benedict that I may remain deposed to the end of my days."

"I weigh not the meaning of every word I utter, with the recollection of that helpless moment so fresh. But it was when the desolate feeling was strongest, that I roved out of the chase upon this mountain heath; there appeared something before my sight, that seemed a house, and by a bright light that glittered, as I fancied, at a window, I felt again restored to intercourse with my kind."

"Thou usest thy terms with more discretion now," said the cow-herd, fetching a heavy breath, like one who was glad the difficulty had found a termination. "I hope it was the abode of some substantial tenant of Lord Emich, who was not without the means of comforting a soul in distress."

"Gottlob, the dwelling was no other than the

Teufelstein, and the light was a twinkling star, tha chance had brought in a line with the rock."

"I take it for granted, Master Berchthold, thou didst not knock twice for admission at that door!"

"I am not much governed by the vulgar legends and womanish superstitions of our hills, but——"

"Softly—softly—friend forester; what thou callest by names so irreverent, are the opinions of all who dwell in or about Deurckheim; knight or monk—burgher or count, has equally a respect for our venerable traditions. Tausand Sechs und Zwanziges! what would become of us, if we had not a gory tale, or some alarming and reverend spectacle of this sort, to set up against the penances, and prayers, and masses of the Friars of Limburg!—As much wisdom and philosophy as thou wilt, foster-brother of mine, but leave us our Devil, if it be only to make battle against the Abbot!"

"Notwithstanding thy big words, I well know that none among us has, at heart, a greater dread of this very hill than thyself, Gottlob! I have seen thee sweat cold drops from thy forehead, in crossing the heath after night-fall."

"Art quite sure 'twas not the dew? We have heavy falls of that moisture in these hills, when the earth is parched!"

"Let it then be the dew."

"To oblige thee, Berchthold, I would willingly swear it was a water-spout. But what didst thou make of the rock and the star?"

"I could change the nature of neither. I pretend not to thy indifference to the mysterious power that rules the earth, but thou well knowest that fear never yet kept me from this hill. When a near approach showed me my error, I was about to turn away, not without crossing myself and repeating an Ave, as I am ready to acknowledge; but a glance upward convinced me that the stone was occupied——"

"Occupied?—I have always known that it was possessed, but never before did I think it was occupied!"

"There was one seated on its uppermost projection, as plainly to be seen as the rock itself."

"Whereupon thou madest manifest that good speed which has gained thee the favor of the Count, and thy post of forester."

"I hope the nerve to put the duties of my office in practice, had their weight with Lord Emich," rejoined Berchthold, a little quickly. "I did not run, Gottlob, but I spoke to the being who had chosen a seat so remarkable, and at that late hour."

Spite of his spirits and affected humor, the cow herd unconsciously drew nearer to his companion casting at the same time an oblique glance in the direction of the suspected rock.

"Thou seemest troubled, Gottlob."

"Dost thou think I am without bowels? What, shall a friend of mine be in this strait, and I not troubled! Heaven save thee, Berchthold, were the best cow in my herd off her stomach, I could not be in greater concern. Hadst any answer?"

"I had—and the result has gone to show me," returned the forester, musing as he spoke, like one who was obtaining glimpses of long-concealed truth, "that our fears oftentimes prevent us from seeing things as they are, and are the means of nourishing our mistakes. I got an answer, and certainly, contrary to what most in Deurckheim would have believed, it was given in a human voice."

"That was encouraging, though it were hoarser than the roaring of a bull!"

"It spoke mildly and in reason, Gottlob, as thou wilt readily believe, when I tell thee it was no other than the voice of the Anchorite of the Cedars.

Our acquaintance then and there commenced, since which time, as thou knowest well, it hath not flagged for want of frequent visits to his abode, on my part."

The cow-herd walked on in silence, for more than a minute, and then stopping short, he abruptly addressed his companion:—

"And this then hath been thy secret, Berchthold concerning the manner of commencing on thy new friendship."

"There is no other. I well knew how much thou wert fettered by the opinions of the country, and was afraid of losing thy company in these visits, were I, without caution, to tell all the circumstances of our interview. But now thou hast become known to the anchorite, I do not fear thy desertion."

"Never count upon too many sacrifices from thy friends, Master Berchthold! The mind of man is borne upon by so many fancies, is ruled by so many vagaries, and tormented by so many doubts, when there is question concerning the safety of the body, to say nothing of the soul, that I know no more rash confidence, than to count too securely on the sacrifices of a friend."

"Thou knowest the path, and can return by thyself, to the hamlet, if thou wilt," said the forester peevishly, and not without severity.

"There are situations in which it is as difficult to go back as to go forward," observed Gottlob; "else, Berchthold, I might take thee at thy word, and go back to my careful mother, a good supper, and a bed that stands between a picture of the Virgin, one of St. Benedict, and one of my Lord the Count. But for my concern for thee, I would not go another foot towards the camp."

"Do as thou wilt," said the forester, who appeared, however, to know the apprehension his companion felt of being left alone in that solitary and suspected spot, and who turned his advantage to good account, by quickening his pace in such a manner as would soon have left Gottlob to his own thick-coming fancies, had he not diligently imitated his gait. "Thou canst tell the people of Lord Emich, that thou abandoned me on this hill."

"Nay," returned Gottlob, making a merit of necessity, "if I do that, or say that, may they make a Benedictine of me, and the Abbot of Limburg to boot!"

As the cow-herd, who felt all his master's antipathies against their religious neighbors, expressed this determination in a voice strong as his resolution, confidence was restored between the friends, who continued their progress with swift paces. The place was, sooth to say, one every way likely to quicken any dormant seeds of superstition that education, or tradition, or local opinions had implanted in the human breast.

By this time our adventurers had approached a wood of low cedars, which, apparently encircled in a round wall that was composed of a confused but vast pile of fallen stones, grew upon the advanced spur of the hills. Behind them lay the heath-like plain, while the bald rock which the moon-beams had just lighted, raising its head from out of the earth, resembled some gloomy monument placed in the centre of the waste, to mark and to render obvious, by comparison, the dreary solitude of the naked fields. The back-ground was the dark slopes and ridges of the forest of the Haart mountains. On their right was the glen, or valley, from which they had just ascended; and on their front, looking a little obliquely from the grove, the plain of the Palatinate, which lay in misty obscurity, like a dim sea of cultivation, hundreds of feet beneath their elevated stand.

It was rare, indeed, that any immediate dependant of the Count Emich, and more especially any of those who dwelt in or about his castle, and who were likely to be called into his service at an unexpected moment, ventured so far from the fortress, and in the direction of the hostile Abbey, without providing himself with the means of offence and defence. Berchthold wore, as wont, his hunting-knife, or the short straight sword, which to this day is carried by that description of European dependan called a chasseur, and who is seen, degraded to the menial offices of a footman, standing behind the carriages of ambassadors and princes, reminding the observant spectator of the regular and certain decadency of the usages of feudal times. Neither had Gottlob been neglectful of his personal security, as respects human foes; for on the subject of resisting all such attacks, his manhood was above reproach, as had been proved in more than one of those bloody frays, which in that age were of frequent occurrence between the vassals of the minor German princes. The cow-herd had provided himself with a heavy weapon that his father had often wielded in battle, and which needed all the vigor of the muscular arm of the son, to flourish with a due observance of the required positions and attitudes. Fire-arms were of too much value and of too imperfect use to be resorted to on every light occasion, like that which had now drawn the foster-brothers, for such supported by long habit was the secret of the intimacy between the forester and the cow-herd, from their hamlet to the hill of Deurckheim.

Berchthold loosened his couteau-de-chasse, as he turned by an ancient gate-way, whose position was known merely by an interruption of the ditch that had protected this face of the wall, and an opening in the wall itself, to enter the inclosure, which the reader will at once recognize as the Pagan's Camp of the Introduction. At the same moment Gottlob cast his heavy weapon from his shoulder, and grasped its handle in a more scientific manner. There was certainly no enemy visible to justify these movements, but the increasing solitude of the place, and that impression of danger which besets the faculties, when we find ourselves in situations favorable to deeds of violence, probably induced the double and common caution. The light of the moon, which was not yet full, had not sufficient power to penetrate the thick branches of the cedars; and when the youths were fairly beneath the gloomy foliage, although not left in the ordinary darkness of a clouded night, they were perhaps in that very species of dull and misty illumination, which, by leaving objects uncertain while visible, is the best adapted to undermine the confidence of a distrustful spirit. There was little wind, but the sighs of the night air were plaintively audible, while the adventurers picked their way among the fragments of the place.

It has been elsewhere said, that the Heidenmauer was originally a Roman camp. The warlike and extraordinary people who had erected these advanced works on the remotest frontier of their wide empire, had, of course, neglected none of the means that were necessary, under the circumstances, either for their security or for their comfort. The first had been sufficiently obtained by the nearly isolated position of the hill, protected, as it was, by walls so massive and so high as those must have been, which had consumed the quantity of materials still visible in the large circuit that remained; while the interior furnished abundant proofs that the latter had not been neglected, in its intersecting remains, over which Gottlob more than once stumbled, as he advanced into the shadows of the place. Here and there, a ruined habitation, more or less dilapidated, was still standing, furnishing, like the memo rable remains of Pompeii and Herculaneum, inter esting and infallible evidence of the usages of those who have so long since departed to their eternal rest. It would seem, by the rude repairs which rather injured than embellished these touching, though simple monuments of what the interior of the camp had been in its day of power and pride, that modern adventurers had endeavored to turn them to account by converting the falling huts into habitations appropriated to their own temporary uses. All, however, appeared to have been long before finally abandoned; for as Berchthold and his companion stole cautiously among the crumbling stones, the gaping rents and roofless walls denoted hopeless decay. At length the youths paused, and fastened their looks in a common direction, as if apprized that they were near the goal of their expedition.

In a part of the grove, where the cedars grew more dense and luxuriant than on most of that stony and broken soil, stood a single low building, which, of all there, had the air of being still habitable. Like the others, it either had been originally constructed by the masters of the world, or restored on the foundations of some Roman construction by the followers of Attila, who, it will be remembered, had passed a winter in this camp; and it was now rendered weather-proof by the usual devices of the poor and laborious. There was a single window, a door, and a rude chimney, which the climate and the elevated situation of the place rendered nearly indispensable. The light of a dim torch shone through the former, the only sign that the hut was tenanted; for on the exterior, with the exception of the rough repairs just mentioned, all around it lay in the neglected and eloquent stillness of ruin. The reader will not imagine, in this description, any of that massive grandeur which so insensibly attaches itself to most that is connected with the Roman name; for while, in the nature of things, the most ponderous and the most imposing of the public works of that people are precisely those which are the most likely to have descended to our own times, the traveller often meets with memorials of their power, that are so frail and perishable in their construction, as to owe their preservation, in a great measure, to an accidental combination of circumstances favorable to such a result. Still, the Roman was ordinarily as much greater in little things, if connected with a public object, as he excelled all who have succeeded him, in those which were of more importance. The Ringmauer, or Heidenmauer, is a strong proof of what we say. There is not an arch, nor a tomb, nor a gate, nor a paved road of any description in the vicinity of Deurckheim, to show that the post was more than a temporary military position; and yet the presence of its former occupants is established by more evidence than would probably be found, a century hence were half of the present cities of Christendom to be suddenly abandoned. But these evidences are rude and suited to the objects which had brought them into existence.

The forester and the cow-herd stood long regarding the solitary hut, which had arrested their looks like men hesitating to proceed.

"I had more humor for the company of the honest anchorite, Master Berchthold," said the latter "before thou madest me acquainted with his fondness for taking the night air on the Teufelstein."

"Thou hast not fear, Gottlob? Thou, who bearest so good a name for courage among our youths!"

"I shall be the last to accuse myself of cowardice or of any other discreditable quality, friend forester but prudence is a virtue in a youth, as the Abbot of Limburg himself would swear, were he here——"

"He is not present in his own reverend and respected person," said a voice so nigh the ear of

Gottlob, as to cause him to jump nimbly aside; "but one who may humbly represent some portion of his sanctity, is not wanting to affirm the truth of what thou sayest, son."

The startled young men saw that a monk of the opposite mountain had unexpectedly appeared between them. They were on the lands of the Abbey, or rather on ground in dispute between the burghers of Deurckheim and the convent, but actually in possession of the latter; and they felt the insecurity of their situation as the dependants of the count of Hartenburg. Neither spoke, therefore, for each was striving to invent some plausible pretext for his appearance in a place so unfrequented, and which, in general, was held in so little favor by the neighboring peasantry.

"You are youths of Deurckheim?" asked the monk, endeavoring to observe their features by the imperfect light that penetrated the foliage of the dark cedars. Gottlob, whose besetting infirmity was a too exuberant fluency of tongue, took on himself the task of answering.

"We are youths, reverend father," he said, "as thy quick and sagacious sight hath so well seen. I will not deny my years, and if I would, the devil, who besets all between fifteen and five-and-twenty in the shape of some giddy infirmity, would soon betray the imposture."

"Of Deurckheim, son?"

"As there is question between the Abbey and the town concerning these hills, we might not stand any better in thy favor, holy Benedictine, were we to say yes."

"In that suspicion, thou dost little justice to the Abbey, son: we may defend the rights of the Church, confided in their temporalities as they are to an unworthy and sinful brotherhood, without feeling any uncharitableness against those who believe they have claims better than our own. The love of mammon is feeble in bosoms that are devoted to self-denying and repentant lives. Say then boldly that you are a Deurckheim, and dread not my displeasure."

"Since it is thy good pleasure, benevolent monk, I will say boldly that we are of Deurckheim."

"And you come to consult the holy Anchorite of the Cedars?"

"It is not necessary that I should tell one of thy knowledge of human nature, reverend Benedictine, that the failing of all dwellers in small towns, is an itching to look into the affairs of their neighbors. Himmel! If our worthy burgomasters would spare a little time from the affairs of other people to look into their own, we should all be greatly gainers; they in their property, and we in our comfort!"

The Benedictine laughed, and he motioned for the youths to follow, advancing himself towards the hut.

"Since you have given yourselves this trouble, no doubt with a praiseworthy and pious intention, my sons," he said, "let not respect for my presence change your purpose. We will go into the cell of the holy hermit, in company; and if there should be advantage from his blessing, or discourse, believe me I will not be so unjust as to envy either of you a share."

"The manner in which the friars of Limburg deny themselves advantages, in order to do profit to their fellow-christians, is in the mouths of all, far and near; and this generosity of thine, reverend monk, is quite of a piece with the well-earned reputation of the whole brotherhood."

As Gottlob spoke gravely, and bowed with sufficient reverence, the Benedictine was in a slight degree his dupe; though, as he passed beneath the low portal of the hut, he could not prevent a lurking suspicion of the truth.

CHAPTER III.

"He comes at last in sullen loneliness,
And whence they know not, why they need not guess."
Lara

In those ages in which moral wrongs were chiefly repaired by superstition, and the slaves of the grosser passions believed they were only to be rebuked by signal acts of physical self-denial, the world often witnessed examples of men retiring from its allurements, to caves and huts, for the ostensible purposes of penitence and prayer. That this extraordinary pretension to godliness was frequently the cloak of ambition and deceit is certain, but it would be uncharitable to believe that, in common, it did not proceed from an honest, though it might be an ill-directed, zeal. Hermitages are still far from infrequent in the more southern parts of Europe, though they are of rare occurrence in Germany; but previously to the change of religion which occurred in the sixteenth century, and consequently near the period of this tale, they were perhaps more often met with among the descendants of the northern race, than among the more fervid fancies of the southern stock of that quarter of the world. It is a law of nature that the substances which most easily receive impressions, are the least likely to retain them; and possibly there may be requisite a constancy and severity of character to endure the never-ending and mortifying exactions of the anchorite, that were not so easily found among the volatile and happy children of the sun, as among the sterner offspring of the regions of cold and tempests.

Whatever may be said of the principles of him who thus abandoned worldly ease for the love of

God, it it quite sure, that in practice, there were present and soothing rewards in this manner of life, that were not without strong attractions to morbid minds; especially to those in which the seeds of ambition were dormant rather than extinct. It was rare, indeed, that a recluse established himself in the vicinity of a simple and religious neighborhood, and few were they who sought absolute solitude without reaping a rich harvest of veneration and moral dependence among the untrained minds of his admirers. In this treacherous manner does vanity beset us in our strong-holds of mental security, and he who has abandoned the world, in the hope of leaving behind him those impulses which endangered his hopes, finds the enemy in a new shape, intrenched in the very citadel of his defences. There is little merit, and commonly as little safety, in turning the back on any danger, and he has far less claims to the honors of a hero who outlives the contest in consequence of means so questionable, than he who survives because he has given a mortal blow to his antagonist. The task assigned to man is to move among his fellows doing good, filling his part in the scale of creation, and escaping from none of the high duties which God has allotted to his being; and greatly should he be grateful, that, while his service is arduous, he is not left without the powerful aid of that intelligence which controls the harmony of the universe.

The Anchorite of the Cedars, as the recluse now visited by the monk and his accidental companions was usually termed by the peasants, and by the burghers of Deurckheim, had made his appearance about six months before the opening of our story, in the Ringmauer. Whence he had come, how long he intended to remain, and what had been his previous career, were facts equally unknown to those among whom he so suddenly took up his abode.

None had seen him arrive, nor could any say from what sources he drew the few articles of household furniture which were placed in his hut. They who left the camp untenanted one week, on returning the next, had found it occupied by a man, who had arranged one of the deserted buildings in a manner to shelter him from the storms, and who, by erecting a crucifix at his door, had sufficiently announced the motive of his retirement. It was usual to hail the establishment of a hermit in any particular district, as a propitious event; and many were the hopes excited, and plans of effecting temporal objects concocted, by the intervention of the prayers of the stranger, before his presence had been known a fortnight. All within the influence of the name of the hermit, except Emich of Leinengen-Hartenburg, the burgomasters of Deurckheim, and the monks of Limburg, heard of his arrival with satisfaction. The haughty and warlike baron had imbibed a standing prejudice against all devotees, from an inherited enmity to the adjoining convent, which had contested the sovereignty of the valley with his family for ages; while the magistrates had a latent jealousy of every influence which custom and the laws had not rendered familiar. As to the monks, the secret of their distrust was to be found in that principle of human nature, which causes us to dislike being outdone in any merit of which we make an especial profession, even though superior godliness be its object. Until now the Abbot of Limburg was held to be the judge, in the last resort, of all intercessions between earth and heaven; and as his supremacy had the support of time, he had long enjoyed it in that careless security which lures so many of the prosperous to their downfall.

These antipathies on the part of the honored and powerful might, to say the least, have rendered the life of the anchorite very uncomfortable, if not posi tively insecure, were it not for the neutralizing effect of the antagonist forces which were set in motion Opinion, deepened by superstition, held its shield over the humble hut, and month after month glided away, after the arrival of the stranger, during which he received no other testimonials of the feelings excited by his presence, than those connected with the reverence of the bulk of the population. An accidental communication with Berchthold was ripening into intimacy, and, as will be seen in the course of the narrative, there were others to whom his counsel, or his motives, or his prayers, were not indifferent.

The latter fact was made sufficiently apparent to those who on account of their mutual distrust, now presented themselves with less ceremony than usual, at the threshold of the hut. The light within came from a fagot which was burning on the rude hearth, but it was quite strong enough to show the monk and his companions that the anchorite was not alone. Their footsteps had evidently been heard, and a female had time to arise from her knees, and to arrange her mantle in such a manner as effectually to conceal her countenance. The hurried action was scarcely completed, when the Benedictine darkened the door with his gloomy robes, while Berchthold and his friend stood gazing over his shoulders, with lively curiosity mingled with surprise.

The form and countenance of the anchorite were those of middle age. His eye had lost nothing of its quickness or intelligence, though his movements had the deliberation and care that long experience insensibly interweaves in the habits of those who have not lived in vain. He expressed neither concern nor wonder at the unexpected visits, but regarding his guests earnestly, like one who assured himself of their identity, he mildly motioned for all to enter. There was jealous suspicion in the glance of the Benedictine, as he complied: for until now, he had no reason to believe that the recluse was usurping so intimate and so extensive an influence over the minds of the young, as the presence of the unknown female would give reason to believe.

"I knew that thou wert of holy life and constant prayer, venerable hermit," he said, in a tone that questioned in more than one meaning of the term, "but until this moment, I had not thought thee vested with the Church's power to hearken to the transgressions of the faithful and to forgive sins!"

"The latter is an office, brother, that of right belongs only to God. The head of the Church himself is but an humble instrument of faith, in discharging this solemn trust."

The countenance of the monk did not become more amicable at this reply, nor did he fail to cast a scrutinizing glance at the muffled form of the stranger, in a fruitless endeavor to recognize her person.

"Thou hast not even the tonsure," he continued, while his uneasy eye rolled from that of the recluse to the form of the stranger, who had shrunk, as far as the narrow place would permit, from observation.

"Thou seest, father, I have all the hair that time and infirmities have left me. But is it thought, in thy beneficed and warlike abbey, that the advice of one who has lived long enough to know and to lament his own errors, can injure the less experienced? If unhappily I may have deceived myself, thou art timely present, reverend monk, to repair the wrong."

"Let the maiden come to the confessional of the Abbey Church, if distrust or apprehension weigh upon her mind; doubt it not, she will find great comfort in the experiment."

"As I will testify, from many trials—" abruptly interposed the cow-herd, who advanced intrusively between the two devotees, in a manner to occupy all their attention. "'Go upon the hill, and ease thy soul, Gottlob,' is my good and venerable mother in the practice of saying, whenever my opinion of myself is getting to be too humble, 'and discourse with some of the godly fathers of the Abbey, whose wisdom and unction will not fail to lighten thy heart of even a heavier load. There is Father Ulrich, he is a paragon of virtue and self-denial; and Father Cuno is even more edifying and salutary than he; while Father Siegfried is more balmy to a soul, than the most reverend Abbot, the virtuous and pious Father Bonifacius himself! Whatever thou doest, child, go upon the hill, and enter boldly into the church, like a loaded and oppressed sinner as thou art, and especially seek counsel and prayer from the excellent and beloved father Siegfried.'"

"And thou—who art thou?" demanded the half-doubting monk, "that thus speakest of me, in terms that I so little merit, to my face?"

"I would I were Lord Emich of Hartenburg, or for that matter, the Elector Palatine himself, in order to do justice to those I honor; in which case certain Fathers of Limburg should have especial favor, and that quickly too, after my own flesh and blood! Who am I, father? I wonder that a face so often seen at the confessional should be forgotten. What there is of me to boast of, Father Siegfried, is of thine own forming—but it is no cause of surprise that thou dost not recall me to mind, since the meek and lowly of spirit are sure to forget their own good works!"

"Thou callest thyself Gottlob—but the name belongs to many Christians."

"More bear it, reverend monk, than know now to do it honor. There is Gottlob Frincke, as arrant a knave as any in Deurckheim; and Gottlob Popp might have more respect for his baptismal vow and as to Lord Gottlob of Manheim——"

"We will overlook the transgressions of the remainder of thy namesakes, for the good that thou thyself hast done," interrupted the Benedictine, who, having insensibly yielded to the unction of flattery in the commencement of the interview, began now to be ashamed of the weakness, as the fluent cow-herd poured forth his words in a manner to excite some suspicion of the quality of praise that came from such a source. "Come to me when thou wilt, son, and such counsel as a weak head, but a sincere heart, can render, shall not be withheld."

"How this would lighten the heart of my old mother to hear! 'Gottlob,' would she say——"

"What has become of thy companion, and of the maiden?" hastily demanded the Benedictine.

As the part of the cow-herd was successfully performed, he stood aside, with an air of well-acted simplicity and amazement, leaving the discourse to be pursued between the recluse and the monk.

"Thy guests have suddenly left us," continued the latter, after satisfying himself, by actual observation, that no one remained in the hut but himself, its regular occupant, and the honey-tongued Gottlob; "and, as it would seem, in company!"

"They are gone as they came, voluntarily and without question."

"Thou knowest them, by frequent visits, holy hermit?"

"Father, I question none: were the Elector Friedrich to come into my abode, he would be welcome, and this cow-herd is not less so. To both, at parting, I merely say, 'God speed ye!'"

"Thou keepest the cattle of the burghers, Gottlob?"

"I keep a herd, reverend priest, such as my masters please to trust to my care."

"We have grave cause of complaint against one of thy fellows who serves the Count of Hartenburg, and who is in the daily habit of trespassing on the pastures of the church. Dost know the hind?"

"Potz Tausend! If all the knaves who do these wrongs, when out of sight of their masters, were set in a row before the eyes of the most reverend Abbot of Limburg, he would scarce know whether to begin with prayers or stripes, and they say he is a potent priest at need, with both! I sometimes tremble for my own conduct, though no one can have a better opinion of himself than I, poor and lowly as I stand in your reverend presence; for a hard fortune, and some oversight in the management of my father's affairs, have brought me to the need of living among such associates. Were I not of approved honesty, there might be more beasts on the Abbey lands; and they who now pass their time in fasting in sheer humility, might come to the practice of sheer necessity."

The Benedictine examined the meek countenance of Gottlob with a keen distrustful eye; he next invited the hermit to bestow his blessing, and then motioning for the hind to retire, he entered on the real object of his visit to the hermitage.

We shall merely say, at this point of the narrative, that the moment was extremely critical to all who dwelt in the Palatinate of the Rhine. The Elector had, perhaps imprudently for a prince of his limited resources, taken an active part in the vindictive warfare then raging, and serious reverses threatened to endanger not only his tranquillity but his throne. It was a consequence of the feudal system, which then so generally prevailed in Europe, that internal disorders succeeded any manifest though it might be only a temporary derangement of the power of the potentate that held the right of sovereignty over the infinite number of petty rulers who, at that period, weighed particularly heavy on Germany. To them he was the law, for they were not apt to acknowledge any supremacy that did not come supported by the strong hand. The ascending scale of rulers, including baron, count, landgrave, margrave, duke, elector, and king, up to the nominal head of the state, the emperor himself, with the complicated and varied interests, embracing allegiance within allegiance, and duty upon duty, was likely in itself to lead to dissension, had the Imperial Crown been one of far more defined and positive influence than it was. But, uncertain and indirect in the application of its means, it was rare that any very serious obstacle to tranquillity was removed, without the employment of positive force. No sooner was the Emperor involved in a serious struggle, than the great princes endeavored to recover that balance which had been lost by the long ascendency of a particular family, while the minor princes seldom saw themselves surrounded with external embarrassment, that internal discord did not come to increase the evil. As a vassal was commonly but a rude reflection of his lord's enmities and prejudices, the reader will have inferred from the language of the cow-herd, that affairs were not on the most amicable footing between those near neighbors, the Abbot of Limburg and the Count of Hartenburg. The circumstance of their existing so near each other was, of itself, almost a certain cause of rivalry; to which natural motive of contention may be added the unremitted strife between the influence of superstition and the dread of the sword.

The visit of the monk had reference to certain interests connected with the actual state of things, as they existed between the Abbey and the Castle. As it would be premature, however, to expose his object, we shall be content with saying, that the conference between the priest and the hermit lasted for half an hour, when the former took his leave, craving a blessing from one of a life so pure and self-denying as his host.

At the door of the hut, the monk found Gottlob who had early been gotten rid of, it will be remembered, but who, for reasons of his own, had seen fit to await the termination of the conference.

"Thou here, son!" exclaimed the Benedictine. "I had thought thee at peace, in thy bed, favored with the benediction of a hermit so holy!"

"Good fortune is sure to drive sleep from my eyes, father," returned Gottlob, dropping in by the side of the monk who was walking through the cedars towards the ancient gateway of the camp. 'I am not of your animal kind, that is no sooner filled with a good thing than it lies down to rest; but the happier I become, the more I desire to be up to enjoy it."

"Thy wish is natural, and, although many natural desires are to be resisted, I do not see the danger of our knowing our own happiness."

"Of the danger I will say nothing, father, but of the comfort, there is not a youth in Deurckheim, who can speak with greater certainty than myself."

"Gottlob," said the Benedictine, insensibly edging nearer to his companion, like one willing to communicate confidentially, "since thou namest Deurckheim, canst say aught of the humor of its people, in this matter of contention between our holy Abbot and Lord Emich of Hartenburg?"

"Were I to tell thy reverence the truth that lies deepest in my mind, it would be to say, that the burghers wish to see the affair brought to an end, in such a way as to leave no doubt, hereafter, to which party they most owe obedience and love, since they find it a little hard upon their zeal, to have so large demands of these services made by both parties."

"Thou canst not serve God and Mammon, son so sayeth one who could not deceive."

"And so sayeth reason, too, worshipful monk but to give thee at once my inmost soul, I believe there is not a man in our Deurckheim, who believes himself strong enough in learning to say, in this strife of duties, which is God and which is Mammon!"

"How! do they call in question our sacred mission—our divine embassy—in short, our being what we are?"

"No man is so bold as to say that the monks of Limburg are what they are; that might be irreverent to the Church, and indecent to Father Siegfried; and the most we dare to say is, that they seem to be what they are; and that is no small matter, considering the way things go in this world. 'Seem to be, Gottlob,' said my poor father, 'and thou wilt escape envy and enemies; for in this seemliness there is nothing so alarming to others; it is only when one is really the thing itself, that men begin to find fault. If thou wishest to live peaceably with thy neighbors, push nothing beyond seeming to be, for that much all will bear, since all can seem; whereas being oftentimes sets a whole village in an uproar. It is wonderful the virtue there is in seeming, and the heart-burnings and scandal, ay, and the downright quarrels there are in being just what one seems.' No, the most we say, in Deurckheim, is that the monks of Limburg seem to be men of God."

"And Lord Emich?"

"As to Count Emich, father, we hold it wise to remember he is a great noble. The Elector has not a bolder knight, nor the emperor a truer vassal; we say, therefore, that he seems to be brave and loyal."

"Thou makest great account, son, of these apparent qualities."

"Knowing the frailty of man, father, and the great likelihood of error, when we wish to judge of acts and reasons, that lie deeper than our knowledge, we hold it to be the most prudent. No, let us of Deurckheim alone, as men of caution!"

"For a cow-herd, thou wantest not wit—Canst read?"

"By God's favor, Providence put that little accident in my way when a child, reverend monk, and I picked it up, as I might swallow a sweet morsel."

"'Tis a gift more likely to injure than to serve one of thy calling. The art can do little benefit to thy herd!"

"I will not take upon myself to say, that any of the cattle are much the better for it; though, to deal fairly by thee, reverend Benedictine, there are animals among them that seem to be."

"How! wilt thou attempt to show a fact not only improbable but impossible? Go to, thou hast fallen upon some silly work of a jester. There have been numberless of these commissions of the devil poured forth, since the discovery of that imprudent brother of Mainz. I would gladly hear in what manner a beast can profit by the art of printing?"

"Thy patience, Father Siegfried, and thou shalt know. Now here is a hind that can read, and there is one that cannot. We will suppose them both the servants of Emich of Hartenburg. Well, they go forth of a morning with their herds; this taking the path to the hills of the Count, and that, having read the description of the boundaries between his Lord's land and that of the holy Abbot of Limburg, taking another, because learning will not willingly follow ignorance; whereupon the reader reaches a nearer and better pasture, than he who hath gone about to feed upon ground that has only been trodden upon too often before, by hoof of beast and foot of man."

"Thy learning hath not done much towards

clearing thy head, Gottlob, whatever it may have done for the condition of thy herd!"

"If your worship has any doubts of my being what I say, here is proof of its justice, then—I know nothing that so crams a man and confuses him as learning! He who has but one horn can take it and go his way; whereas he that hath many, may lose his herd while choosing between instruments that are better or worse. He that hath but one sword, will draw it and slay his enemy: but he that hath much armor, may lose his life while putting on his buckler or head-piece."

"I had not thought thee so skilful in answers. And thou thinkest the good people of Deurckheim will stand neuter between the Abbey and the Count?"

"Father, if thou wilt show me by which side they will be the greatest gainers, I think I might venture to say, with some certainty, on which side they will be likely to draw the sword. Our burghers are prudent townsmen, as I have said, and it is not often that they are found fighting against their own interests."

"Thou shouldst know, son, that he who is most favored in this life, may find the balances of justice weighing against him in the next; while he who suffers in the flesh, will be most likely to find its advantage in the spirit."

"Himmel! In that case, reverend Benedictine the most holy Abbot of Limburg himself may fare worse hereafter then even a hind who now lives like a dog!" exclaimed Gottlob, with an air of admiration and simplicity that completely misled his listener. "The one is said to comfort the body in various ways, and to know the difference between a cup of pure Rhenish and a draught of the washy liquors that come from the other side of our mountains; while the other, whether it be of necessity or inclination I will not take upon myself to say drinks only of the spring. 'Tis a million of pities that one never knoweth which to choose, present ease with future pain, or a starving body with a happy soul! Believe me, Father Siegfried, were thy reverence to think more of these trials that befall us ignorant youths, thou wouldst not deal so heavily with the penances, as thine own severe virtue often tempts thee to do."

"What is thus done is done for thy health, future and present. By chastening the spirit in this manner, it is gradually prepared for its final purification, and thou art not a loser in the eyes of thy fellows, by leading a chaste life. Thou wilt have justice at the settlement of the great account."

"Nay, I am no greedy creditor, to dun Providence for my dues. I very well know that what will come cannot be prevented, and therefore I take patience to be a virtue. But I hope these accounts, of which you tell us so often, are kept with sufficient respect for a poor man; for, to deal fairly with thee, father, we have not overmuch favor in settling those of the world."

"Thou hast credit for all thy good deeds with thy fellows, Gottlob."

"I wish it were true! To me it seems that the world is ready enough to charge, while it is as niggardly as a miser in giving credit—I never did an evil act—and as we are all mortal and frail, most holy monk, these accidents will befall even your saint or a Benedictine—that the deed itself and all its consequences were not set down against me, in letters that a short-sighted man might read; while most of my merits—and considering I am but a cow-herd they are of respectable quality—seem to be forgotten. Now your Abbot, or his Highness the Elector, or even Count Emich——"

"The Summer Landgrave!" interrupted the monk, laughing.

"Summer or winter, as thou wilt, Father Siegfried, he is Count of Hartenburg, and a noble of Leiningen. Even he does no deed of charity, or even of simple justice, that all men do not seize upon the occasion to proclaim it, as eagerly as they endeavor to upbraid me for the accidental loss of a beast, or any other little backsliding, that may befall one, who being bold under thy holy instruction, sometimes stumbles against a sin."

"Thou art a casuist, and, at another time, I must look more closely into the temper of thy mind. At present, thou mayst purchase favor of the Church by enlisting a little more closely in her interests. I remember thy cleverness and thy wit, Gottlob, for both have been remarked in thy visits to the convent; but, until this moment, there has not been sufficient reason to use the latter in the manner that we may fairly claim to do, considering our frequent prayers, and the other consolations afforded in thy behalf."

"Do not be too particular Father Siegfried, for thy words reveal grievous penance!"

"Which may be much mitigated in future, if not entirely avoided, by a service that I would now propose to thee, honest Gottlob, and which I will venture to say, from my knowledge of thy reverence for holy things, as is manifest in thy attentions to the pious hermit, and thy love for the Abbey of Limburg, thou wouldst not refuse to undertake."

"So!"

"Nay, I have as good as pledged myself to Father Bonifacius to procure either thee, or one shrewd and faithful as thee, to do a trusty service for the brotherhood."

"The latter might not be easy among the cowherds!"

"Of that I am sure. Thy skill in the management of the beasts may yet gain thee the office of ending the ample herds of the abbey. Thou art already believed fit for the charge."

"Not to deny my own merits, sagacious father, I have already some knowledge of the pastures."

"And of the beasts, too, Gottlob; we keep good note of the characters of all who come to our confessionals. There are worse than thine among them, I do assure thee."

"And yet have I never told thee half that I might say of myself, father!"

"It is not important now. Thou knowest the state of the contest between Count Emich and our Abbey. The service that I ask of thee, son, is this; and by discharging it, with thy wonted readiness, believe me thou wilt gain favor with St. Benedict and his children. We have had reason to know, that there is a strong band of armed men in the castle, ready and anxious to assail our walls, under a vain belief that they contain riches and stores to repay the sacrilege; but we want precise knowledge of their numbers and intentions. Were we to send one of known pursuits on this errand, the Count would find means to mislead him; whereas, we think a hind of thy intelligence might purchase the Church's kindness without suspicion."

"Were Count Emich to get wind of the matter, he would not leave me an ear with which to listen to thy holy admonitions."

"Keep thine own council, and he will not suspect one of thy appearance. Hast no pretext for visiting the castle?"

"Nay, it would be easy to make a thousand. Here, I might say, I wished to ask the cow-herd of Lord Emich for his cunning in curing diseased hoofs, or I might pretend a wish to change my service, or, there is no want of laughing damsels in and about the hold."

"Enough: thou art he, Gottlob, for whom I have sought daily for a fortnight. Go thy way, then, without fail, and seek me, after to-morrow's mass, in the Abbey."

"It may be enough on the side of Heaven, father, but men of our prudence must not forget their mortal state. Am I to risk my ears, do discredit to my simplicity, and neglect my herd, without a motive?"

"Thou wilt serve the Church, son; get favor in the eyes of our reverend Abbot, and thy courage and dexterity will be remembered in future indulgences."

"That I shall serve the Church it is well known to me, reverend Benedictine, and it is a privilege of which a cow-herd hath reason to be proud; but, by serving the Church, I shall make enemies on earth, for two sufficient reasons: first, that the Church is in no great esteem in this valley; and second, because men never love a friend for being any better than themselves. 'No, Gottlob,' used my excellent father to say, 'seem to all around thee conscious of thy unworthiness, after which thou mayst be what thou seemest. On this condition only can virtue live at peace with its fellow-creatures. But if thou wouldst have the respect of mankind,' would he say, 'set a fair price on all thou doest, for the world will not give thee credit for disinterestedness; and if thou workest for naught, it will think thou deservest naught. No,' did he shake his head and add, 'that which cometh easy is little valued, while that which is costly, do men set a price upon.'"

"Thy father was, like thyself, one that looked to his ease. Thou knowest that we inhabitants of cells do not carry silver."

"Nay, righteous Benedictine, if it were a trifle of gold, I am not one to break a bargain for so small a difference."

"Thou shalt have gold, then. On the faith of my holy calling, I will give thee an image of the Emperor in gold, shouldst thou succeed in bringing the tidings we require."

Gottlob stopped short, and kneeling, he reverently asked the monk to bless him. The latter complied, half doubting the discretion of employing such an emissary, between whose cunning and simplicity he was completely at fault. Still, as he risked nothing, except in the nature of the information he was to receive, he saw no sufficient reason for recalling the commission he had just bestowed. He gave the desired benediction, therefore; and our two conspirators descended the mountain in company, discoursing, as they went, of the business on which the cow-herd was about to proceed. When so near the road as to be in danger of observation, they separated, each taking the direction necessary to his object.

CHAPTER IV.

> "And not a matron, sitting at her wheel,
> But could repeat their story—"
>
> ROGERS.

THE female, enveloped in her mantle, had so well profited by the timely interposition of Gottlob Frinck, as to quit the hermit's hut without attracting the notice of the Benedictine. But the vigilance of young Berchthold had not been so easily eluded. He stepped aside as she glided through the door, then stooping merely to catch the eye of the cow-herd, to whom he communicated his intention by a sign, he followed. Had the forester felt any doubts as to the identity of her he pursued, the light and active movement would have convinced him, that age, at least, had no agency in inducing her to conceal her features. The roe-buck of his own forests scarce bounded with more agility than the fugitive fled, on first quitting the abode of the recluse; nor did her speed sensibly lessen, until she had crossed most of the melancholy camp, and reached a spot where the opening of the blue and star-lit void showed that she was at the verge of the wood, and near the margin of the summit of the mountain. Here she paused, and stood leaning against a cedar, like one whose strength was exhausted.

Berchthold had followed swiftly, but without losing that appearance of calmness and of superior physical force which gives dignity to the steps of young manhood, as compared with the timid but more attractive movements of the feebler sex. He seemed conscious of his greater powers, and unwilling to increase a flight that was already swifter than circumstances required, and which he knew to be far more owing to a vague and instinctive alarm, than to any real cause for apprehension. When the speed of the female ceased, his own relaxed, and he approached the spot where she stood panting for breath, like a cautious boy, who slackens his haste in order not to give new alarm to the bird that has just alighted.

"What is there so fearful in my face, Meta, that thou fleest my presence, as I had been the spirit of one of those Pagans that they say once peopled this camp? It is not thy wont to have this dread of a youth thou hast known from childhood, and I will say, in my own defence, known as honest and true!"

"It is not seemly in a maiden of my years—it was foolish, if not disobedient, to be here at this hour," answered the hurried girl:—"I would I had not listened to the desire of hearing more of the holy hermit's wisdom!"

"Thou art not alone, Meta!"

"That were unbecoming, truly, in my father's child!" returned the young damsel, with an expression of pride of condition, as she glanced an eye towards the fallen wall, among whose stones Berchthold saw the well-known form of a female servitor of his companion's family. "Had I carried imprudence to this pass, Master Berchthold, thou wouldst have reason to believe, in sooth, that it was the daughter of some peasant, that by chance had crossed thy footstep."

"There is little danger of that error," answered Berchthold quickly. "I know thee well; thou art Meta, the only child of Heinrich Frey, the Burgomaster of Deurckheim. None know thy quality and hopes better than I, for none have heard them oftener!"

The damsel dropped her head in a movement of natural regret and sudden repentance, and when her blue eye, softened by a ray of the moon, met the gaze of the forester, he saw that better feelings were uppermost.

"I did not wish to recount my father's honors. nor any accidental advantage of my situation, and, least of all, to thee," answered the maiden, with eagerness; "but I felt concern lest thou shouldst imagine I had forgotten the modesty of my sex and condition—or, I had fear that thou mightest—thy manner is much changed of late, Berchthold!"

"It is then without my knowledge or intention. But we will forget the past, and thou wilt tell me, what wonder hath brought thee, to this suspected and dreaded moor, at an hour so unusual?"

Meta smiled, and the expression of her countenance proved, that if she had moments of uncharitable weakness, they were more the offspring of the world's opinions, than of her own frank and generous nature

"I might retort the question on thee, Berchthold,

and plead a woman's curiosity as a reason why I should be quickly answered—Why art thou here, at an hour when most young hunters sleep?"

"I am Lord Emich's forester; but thou, as there has just been question, art a daughter of the Burgomaster of Deurckheim."

"I give thee credit for all the difference. Did my mother know that I was thus about to furnish a reason for my conduct, she would say, 'Keep thy explanations, Meta, for those who have a right to demand them!'"

"And Heinrich Frey?"

"He would be little likely to approve of either visit or explanation."

"Thy father loves me not, Meta?"

"He does not so much disapprove of thee, Master Berchthold, as that thou art only Lord Emich's forester. Wert thou as thine own parent was, a substantial burgher of our town, he might esteem thee much. But thou hast great favor with my dear mother!"

"Heaven bless her, that in her own prosperity she hath not forgotten those who have fallen! I think that, in thy heart as in thy looks, Meta, thou more resemblest thy mother than thy father."

"I would have it so. When I speak to thee of my being the child of Heinrich Frey, it is without thought of any present difference between us, I do affirm to thee, Berchthold, but rather as showing that in not forgetting my station, I am not likely to do it discredit. Nay, I know not that a forester's is a dishonorable office! They who serve the Elector in this manner are noble."

"And they who serve nobles, simple. I am but a menial, Meta, though it be in a way to do little mortification to my pride."

"And what is Count Emich but a vassal of the Elector, who, in turn, is a subject of the Emperor!

Thou shalt not dishonor thyself in this manner Berchthold, and no one say aught to vindicate thee."

"Thanks, dearest Meta. Thou art the child of my mother's oldest and closest friend, and whatever the world may proclaim of the difference that now exists between us, thy excellent heart whispers to the contrary. Thou art not only the fairest, but, in truth, the kindest and gentlest damsel of thy town!"

The daughter, only child, and consequently the heiress of the wealthiest burgher of Deurckheim, did not hear this opinion of Lord Emich's handsome forester without great secret gratification.

"And now thou shalt know the reason of this unusual visit," said Meta, when the silent pleasure excited by the last speech of young Berchthold had a little subsided; "for this have I, in some measure, promised to thee; and it would little justify thy good opinion to forget a pledge. Thou knowest the holy hermit, and the sudden manner of his appearance in the Heidenmauer?"

"None are ignorant of the latter, and thou hast already seen that I visit him in his hut."

"I shall not pretend to give, or to seek, the reason, but sure it is, that he had not been a week in the old Roman abode, when he sought occasion to show me greater notice than to any other maiden of Deurckheim, or than any merit of mine might claim."

"How! is the knave but a pretender to this sanctity, after all!"

"Thou canst not be jealous of a man of his years; and, judging by his worn countenance and hollow eye, years too of mortification and suffering! He truly is of a character to give a youth of thy age, and gentle air, and active frame, and comely appearance, uneasiness! But I see the color in thy cheek, Master Berchthold, and will not offend thee with comparisons that are so much to thy disadvan tage. Be the motive of the holy hermit what it will, on the two occasions when he visited our town and in the visits that we maidens have often made to his cell, he hath shown kind interest in my welfare and future hopes, both as they are connected with this life, and with that to which we all hasten, although it be with steps that are not heard even by our own ears."

"It does not surprise me, that all who see and know thee, Meta, should act thus. And yet I find it very strange!"

"Nay," said the amused girl, "now thou justifiest the exact words of old Ilse, who hath often said to me, 'Take heed, Meta, and put not thy faith too easily in the language of the young townsmen; for, by looking closely into their meaning, thou wilt see that they contradict themselves. Youth is so eager to obtain its end, that it stops not to separate the true from the plausible.' These are her very words, and oft repeated too, which thou hast just verified—I believe the crone fairly sleepeth on that pile of the fallen wall!"

"Disturb her not. One of her years hath great need of rest: nay, it would be thoughtless to rob her of this little pleasure!"

Meta had made a step in advance, seemingly with intent to arouse her attendant, when the hurried words and rapid action of the youth caused her to hesitate. Receding to her former attitude, beneath the shadow of the cedar, she more considerately resumed——

"It would be ungracious, in sooth, to awaken one who hath so lately toiled up this weary hill."

"And she so aged, Meta!"

"And one that did so much for my infancy! I ought to go back to my father's house, but my kind mother will overlook the delay, for she loveth Ilse little less than one of her own blood."

"Thy mother knoweth of this visit to the hermit's hut, then?"

"Dost think, Master Berchthold, that a Burgomaster of Deurckheim's only child would go forth, at this hour, without permission had? There would be great unseemliness in such secret gossiping, and a levity that would better suit thy damsels of Count Emich's village: they say indeed, in our town, that the castle damsels are none too nice in their manner of life."

"They belie us of the mountain strangely, in the towns of the plain! I swear to thee, there is not greater modesty in thy Deurckheim palace, than among our females, whether of the village or of the castle."

"It may be true in the main, and, for the credit of my sex, I hope it is so; but thou wilt scarce find courage, Berchthold, to say aught in favor of her they call Gisela, the warder's child? More vanity have I never seen in female form!"

"They think her fair, in Hartenburg."

"'Tis that opinion which spoileth the creature's manner! Thou art much in her society, Master Berchthold, and I doubt not that use causeth thee to overlook some qualities that are not concealed from strangers. 'Do but regard that flaunting bird from the pass of the Jaegerthal,' said the excellent old Ilse, one morn that we had a festival in our venerable church, to which the country round came forth in their best array; 'one would imagine, from its fluttering, and the movements of its feathers, that it fancied the eye of every young hunter was on its plumage, and that it dreaded the bolt of the archer unexpectedly! And yet have I known animals of this breed, that did not so greatly fear the fowler's hand, if truth were said!'"

"Thou judgest Gisela harshly; for though of some lightness of speech, and haply not without ad miration of her own beauty, the girl is far from being uncompanionable, or, at times, of agreeable discourse."

"Nay, I do but repeat the words of Ilse, Master Berchthold!"

"Thy Ilse is old, and garrulous, and is like to utter foolishness."

"This may be so--but let it be foolish, if thou wilt—the folly of my nurse is my folly. I have gained so much from her discourse, that I fear it is now too late to amend. To deal fairly with thee, she did not utter a syllable concerning thy warder's daughter that I do not believe."

Berchthold was but little practised in the ways of the human heart. Free in the expression of his own sentiments as the air he breathed on his native hills, and entirely without thought of guilt, as respects the feeling which bound him to Meta, he had never descended into the arcana of that passion of which he was so completely the subject, without indeed knowing even the extent of his own bondage. He viewed this little ebullition of jealousy, therefore, as a generous nature regards all injustice, and he entered only the more warmly into the defence of the injured party. One of those sieve-like hearts that have been perforated a hundred times by the shots that Cupid fires, right and left, in a capital, would probably have had recourse to the same expedient, merely to observe to what extent he could trifle with the feelings of a being he professed to love.

Europeans, who are little addicted to looking into the eye of their cis-Atlantic kinsman in search of the mote, say, that the master passion of life is but a sluggish emotion in the American bosom. That those who are chiefly employed in the affairs of this world should be content with the natural course of the affections, as they arise in the honest relations of the domestic circle, is quite as probable, as it is true that they who feed their passions by vanity and variety, are mistaken when they think that casual and fickle sensations compose any of the true ingredients of that purifying and elevated sentiment, which, by investing the admired object with all that is estimable, leads us to endeavor to be worthy of the homage we insensibly pay to virtue. In Berchthold and Meta, the reader is to look for none of that constitutional fervor, which sometimes substitutes impulse for a deeper feeling, or for any of that factitious cultivation of the theory of love, that so often tempts the neophyte to mistake his own hallucinations for the more natural attachment of sympathy and reason. For the former they lived too far north, and for the latter it might possibly be said, that fortune had cast their lot a little too far south. That subtle and nearly indefinable sympathy between the sexes, which we call love, to which all are subject, since its principle is in nature itself, exists perhaps in its purest and least conventional form precisely in the bosoms of those whom Providence has placed in the middle state, between extreme cultivation and ignorance; between the fastidious and sickly perversion of over-indulgence, and the selfishness that is the fruit of constant appeals to exertion; or the very condition of the two young persons that have been placed before the reader in this chapter. Enough has been seen to show that Berchthold, though exercising a menial office, had received opinions superior to his situation; a circumstance that is sufficiently explained by the allusions already made to the decayed fortunes of his parents. His language and manner, therefore, as he generously vindicated Gisela, the daughter of the person charged to watch the approaches of Lord Emich's castle was perhaps superior to what would have been expected in a mere forester.

"I shall not take upon myself the office of pointing out the faults of our castle beauty, if faults she hath," he said; "but this much may I say in her defence, without fear of exceeding truth; her father is grown gray under the livery of Leiningen, and there is not a child in the world that showeth more reverence or affection to him who gave her being, than this same bird of thine, with its flaunting plumes, and the coquetry with the archer's bolt!"

"'Tis said, a dutiful daughter will ever make an excellent and an obedient wife."

"The luckier then will he be who weds old Friedrich's child. I have known her keep the gates, deep into the night, that her father might take his rest, when the nobles have frequented the forest later than common; ay, and to watch weary hours, when most of her years and sex would find excuses for being on their pillows. Now, this have I often seen, going forth, as thou mayst be certain by my office, in Count Emich's company, in most of his hunts. Nay, Gisela is fair, none will deny; and it may be that, among her other qualities, the girl knows it."

"She appeareth not to be the only one of thy Hartenburg pile that is aware of the fact, Master Berchthold!"

"Dost thou mean, Meta, the revelling abbé, from Paris, or the sworn soldier-monk of Rhodes, that now abide in the castle?" asked the young forester, with a simplicity that would have set the heart of a coquette at ease, by its perfect nature and openness. "Now thou touchest on the matter, I will own, though one of my office should be wary of opinions on those his master loves, but I know thy prudence, Meta—Therefore will I say, that I have half suspected these two ill-assorted servants of the church, of thinking more of the poor girl than is seemly."

"Thy poor Gisela hath cause to hang herself

Truly, were wassailers, like these thou namest, to regard me with but a free look, the Burgomaster of Deurckheim should know of their boldness!"

"Meta, they would not dare! Poor Gisela is not the offspring of a stout citizen, but the warder of Hartenburg's child, and there may be some difference in thy natures, too—nay, there is; for thou art not one of those that seek the admiration of each cavalier that passeth, but a maiden that knoweth her worth, and the meed that is her due. That thou hast, in something, wronged our beauty of the hold, I needs must say; but to compare thee with her, either in the excellence of the body or that of the mind, is what could never be done justly. If she is fair, thou art fairer; if she is witty, thou art wise!"

"Nay, do not mistake me, Berchthold, by thinking that I have uttered aught against thy warder's daughter that is harsh and unseemly. I know the girl's cleverness, and moreover I am willing to acknowledge, that one cruelly placed by fortune in a condition of servitude, like her's, may find it no easy matter to be always what one of her sex and years could wish. I dare to say, that Gisela, did fortune and opportunity permit, would do no discredit to her breeding and looks, both of which, sooth to say, are somewhat above her condition."

"And thou saidst, thy mother knew of this visit to the hermit?"

"And said truth. My mother has never made objection to any reverence paid by her daughter to the Church or to its servants."

"That hath she not!—Thou art amongst the most frequent of those who resort to the Abbey in quest of holy offices thyself, Meta!"

"Am I not a Christian! Wouldst have a well-respected maiden forget her duties?"

"I say not that; but there is discourse amongst us hunters, that of late the prior hath much preferred his young nephew, Brother Hugo, to the duty of quieting the consciences of the penitents. It were better that some father, whose tonsure hath a ring of gray, were put into the confessional, in a church so much frequented by the young and fair of Deurckheim."

"Thou wouldst do well to write of this to the Bishop of Worms, or to our holy Abbot, in thine own scholarly hand. Thou hast the clerkly gifts, Master Berchthold, and might persuade!"

"I would that the little I have done in this way had not so failed of its design. Thou hast had frequent proofs of its sincerity, if not of its skill, Meta."

"Well, this is idle, and leads me to forget the hermit: My mother—I know not why—and now thou makest me think of it, I find it different from her common rule; but it is certain that she in nowise discourages these visits to the Heidenmauer. We are very young, Berchthold, and may not yet understand all that enters into older and wiser heads!"

"It is strange that the holy man should seek just us! If he most urges his advice on you among the damsels of the town, he most gives his counsel to me among the youths of the Jaegerthal!"

There was a charm in this idea which held these two young and unpractised minds in sweet thraldom for many fleeting minutes. They conversed of the unexplained sympathy between the man of God and themselves, long and with undiminishing interest in the subject, for it seemed to both that it contained a tie to unite them still closer to each other. Whatever philosophy and experience may pretend on such subjects, it is certain that man is disposed to be superstitious in respect to the secret influences that guide his fortunes, in the dark passage of the world. Whether it be the mystery of the unforeseen future, or the consciousness of how much of even his most prized success is the result of circumstances that he never could or did control, or whether God, with a view to his own harmonious and sublime ends, has implanted this principle in the human breast, in order to teach us dependence on a superior power, it is certain that few reach a state of mind so calculating and reasoning as not to trust some portion of that which is to come, to the chances of Fortune, or to Providence; for so we term the directing power, as the mind clings to or rejects the immediate agency of the Deity, in the conduct of the subordinate concerns of life. In the age of which we write, intelligence had not made sufficient progress to elevate ordinary minds above the arts of necromancy. Men no longer openly consulted the entrails of brutes, in order to learn the will of fate, but they often submitted to a dictation scarcely less beastly, and few indeed were they who were able to separate piety from superstition, or the grand dispensations of Providence from the insignificant interests of selfishness. It is not surprising, therefore, that Berchthold and Meta should cling to the singular interest that the hermit manifested in them respectively, as an omen propitious to their common hopes; common, for though the maiden had not so far relinquished the reserve she still deemed essential to her sex, as to acknowledge all she felt, that subtle instinct which unites the young and innocent left little doubt in the mind of either, of the actual state of the other's inclinations.

Old Ilse had consequently ample time to rest her frame, after the painful toil of the ascent between the town and the camp. When Meta at length approached to arouse her, the garrulous woman broke out in exclamations of surprise at the shortness of the interview with the hermit, for the soundness of her slumbers left her in utter ignorance of the appearance and disappearance of Berchthold.

"It is but a moment, Meta dear," she said, "since we came up the hill, and I fear thou hast not given sufficient heed to the wise words of the holy man. We should not reject a wholesome draught because it proves bitter to the mouth, child, but swallow all to the last drop, when we think there is healing in the cup. Didst deal fairly by the hermit, and tell him honestly of thy evil nature?"

"Thou forgettest, Ilse, the hermit has not even the tonsure, and cannot shrive and pardon."

"Nay, nay—I know not that! A hermit is a man of God; and a man of God is holy; and any Christian may, ay, and should pardon; and as to shriving, give me a self-denying recluse, who passes his time in prayer, mortifying soul and body, before any monk of Limburg, say I! There is more virtue in one blessing from such a man, than in a dozen from a carousing Abbot—I know not but I might say fifty."

"But I had his blessing, nurse."

"Well, that is comforting, and we have not wearied our limbs for naught; but thou shouldst have told him of thy wish to wear the laced boddice, at the last mass, in order that thy equals might envy thy beauty. It would have been wholesome to have acknowledged that sin, at least."

"But he questioned me not of my sins. All his discourse was of my father's house, and of my good mother, and—and of other matters."

"Thou shouldst then have edged the boddice in among the other matters. Have I not always forewarned thee, Meta, of the danger of pride, and of stirring envy in the bosom of a companion? There is naught more uncomfortable than envy, as I know by experience. Oh! I am no longer young; and come to me if thou wouldst wish to know what envy is, or any other dangerous vice, and I warrant thee thou shalt hear it well explained! Ay, thou wert very wrong not to have spoken of the bod dice!"

"Had it been fit to confess, I might have found more serious sins to own, than any that belong to dress."

"I know not that! Dress is a great beguiler of the young heart, and of the handsome face. If thou hast beauty in thy house, break thy mirrors that the young should not know it, is what I have heard a thousand times; and as thou art both young and fair, I will repeat it, though all Deurckheim gainsay my words, thou art in danger if thou knowest it. No, hadst thou told the hermit of that boddice, it might have done much good. What matters it to such a man, whether he hath the tonsure or not? He hath prayers, and fastings, and midnight thought, and great bodily suffering, and these are surely worth as much hair as hath ever fallen from all the monks in the Palatinate. I would thou hadst told him of that boddice, child!"

"Since thou so wishest it, at our next meeting it shall be said, dear Ilse; so set thy heart at peace."

"This will give thy dear mother great pleasure; else, why should she consent that a daughter of her's should visit a heathenish camp, at so late an hour? I warrant thee that she thought of the boddice!"

"Do cease speaking of the garment, nurse; my thoughts are bent on something else."

"Well, if indeed thou thinkest of something else, it may be amiss to say more at present, though, Heaven it knows! thou hast great occasion to recall that vain-glorious mass to thy mind. How suddenly thy communion with the hermit ended tonight, Meta!"

"We have not been long on the mountain, truly Ilse. But we must hasten back, lest my mother should be uneasy."

"And why should she be so? Am I not with thee? Is age nothing, and experience, and prudence, and an old head, ay, and, for that matter, an old body too, and a good memory, and such eyes as no other in Deurckheim of my years hath—I say of my years, for thou hast better; and thy dear mother's are little worse than thine—but of my years, few have their equal. At thy age, girl, I was not the old Ilse, but the lively Ilse, and the active, and, God forgive me if there be vain-glory in the words! but truth should always be spoken—the handsome Ilse, and this too without aid from any such boddice as that of thine."

"Wilt never forget the boddice! here, lean on me, nurse, or thy foot may fail thee in the steep descent."

Here they began to descend, and as they were now at a point of the path where much caution was necessary, the conversation in a great measure ceased.

He who visits Deurckheim now, will find sufficient remaining evidence to show that the town formerly extended more towards the base of the mountain than its present site would prove. There are the ruins of walls and towers among the vineyards that ornament the foot of the hill, and tradition speaks of fortifications that have long since disappeared, rendered useless by those improvements in warfare that have robbed so many other strong places of their importance. Then, every group of houses on an eminence was more or less a place of defence; but the use of gunpowder and artillery centuries ago rendered all these targets useless, and he who would now seek a citadel, is most sure to find it buried in some plain or morass. The world has reached another crisis in improvement for the introduction of steam is likely to alter all its systems of offence and defence both by land

and sea; but be the future as it may, the skill of the engineer had not so far ripened at the period of our tale, as to prevent Meta and her attendant from entering within walls of ancient construction, clumsily adapted to meet the exigencies of the imperfect state of the existing art. As the hour was early, they had no difficulty in reaching the Burgomaster's door without attracting remark.

CHAPTER V

"What news?"
"None, my lord; but that the world is grown honest."
"Then is doomsday near!"
Hamlet.

Within the whole of these widely extended states, there is scarcely a single vestige of the manner of life led by those who first settled in the wilderness. Little else is found to arrest the eye of the antiquary in the shape of a ruin, except the walls of some fortress or the mounds of an intrenchment of the war of independence. We have, it is true, some faint remains of times still more remote; and there are even a few circumvallations, or other inventions of defence, that are believed to have once been occupied by the red man; but in no part of the country did there ever exist an edifice, of either a public or a private nature, that bore any material resemblance to a feudal castle. In order, therefore, that the reader shall have as clear a picture as our feeble powers can draw, of the hold occupied by the sturdy baron who is destined to act a conspicuous part in the remainder of this legend, it has become necessary to enter at some length into a description of the surrounding localities, and of the building itself. We say of the reader, for we profess to write only for the amusement—fortunate shall we be if instruction may be added—of our own countrymen: should others be pleased to read these crude pages, we shall be flattered and of course grateful; but with this distinct avowal of our object in holding the pen, we trust they will read with the necessary amount of indulgence.

And here we shall take occasion to hold one moment's communion with that portion of the reading public of all nations, that, as respects a writer, composes what is termed the world. Let it not be said of us, because we make frequent reference to opinions and circumstances as they exist in our native land, that we are profoundly ignorant of the existence of all others. We make these references, crime though it be in hostile eyes, because they best answer our end in writing at all, because they allude to a state of society most familiar to our own minds, and because we believe that great use has hitherto been made of the same things, to foster ignorance and prejudice. Should we unheedingly betray the foible of national vanity—that foul and peculiar blot of American character! we solicit forgiveness; urging, in our own justification, the aptitude of a young country for falling insensibly into the vein of imitation, and praying the critical observer to overlook any blunders in this way, if perchance we should not manifest that felicity of execution which is the fruit only of great practice. Hitherto we believe that our modesty cannot justly be impeached. As yet we have left the cardinal virtues to mankind in the gross, never, to our knowledge, having written of "American courage;" or "American honesty," nor yet of "American beauty," nor haply of "American manliness," nor even of "American strength of arm," as qualities abstracted and not common to our fellow-creatures:

but have been content, in the unsophisticated language of this western clime, to call virtue, virtue—and vice, vice. In this we well know how much we have fallen short of numberless but nameless classical writers of our own time, though we do not think we are greatly losers by the forbearance, because we have sufficient proof that when we wish to make our pages unpleasant to the foreigner, we can effect that object by much less imposing allusions to national merits; since we have good reason to believe, there exists a certain querulous class of readers who consider even the most delicate and reserved commendations of this western world, as so much praise unreasonably and dishonestly abstracted from themselves. As for that knot in our own fair country, who aim at success by flattering the stranger, and who hope to shine in their own little orbits by means of borrowed light, we commit them to the correction of a reproof which is certain to come, and, in their cases, to come embittered by the consciousness of its being merited by a servility as degrading as it is unnatural. As they dive deeper into the secrets of the human heart, they will learn there is a healthful feeling that cannot be repulsed with impunity, and that as none are so respected as they who fearlessly and frankly maintain their rights, so none are so contemned as those who ignobly desert them.

During the time that Berchthold was holding converse with Meta, on the mountain of the Heidenmauer, Emich of Leiningen was at rest in his castle of Hartenburg. It has already been said, that the hold was of massive masonry, the principal material being the reddish sand-stone, that is so abundantly found in nearly the whole region of the ancient Palatinate. The building had grown with time, and that which had originally been a tower had swelled into a formidable and extensive fortress. In the ages which succeeded the empire of Charlemagne, he who could rear one of these strong places, and maintain it in opposition to his neighbors, became noble, and in some measure a sovereign. He established his will as law for the contiguous territory, and they who could not enjoy their own lands, without submitting to his pleasure, were content to purchase protection by admitting their vassalage. No sooner was one of these local lords firmly established in his hold, by receiving service and homage from the husbandmen, than he began to quarrel with his nearest neighbor of his own condition. The victor necessarily grew more powerful by his conquests, until, from being the master of one castle and one village, he became in process of time the master of many. In this manner did minor barons swell into power and sovereignty, even mighty potentates tracing their genealogical and political trees into roots of this wild growth. There still stands on an abrupt and narrow ledge of land, in the confederation of Switzerland and in the Canton of Argovie, a tottering ruin, that, in past ages, was occupied by a knight, who from his aerie overlooked the adjoining village, and commanded the services of its handful of boors. This ruined castle was called Hapsbourg, and is celebrated as the cradle of that powerful family which has long sat upon the throne of the Cæsars, and which now rules so much of Germany and Upper Italy. The King of Prussia traces his line to the House of Hohenzollern, the offspring of another castle; and numberless are the instances in which he who thus laid the corner-stone of a strong place, in ages when security was only to be had by good walls, also laid the foundation of a long line of prosperous and puissant princes.

Neither the position of the castle of Hartenburg, however, nor the period in which it was founded, was likely to lead to results great as these just named. As has been said, it commanded a pass important for local purposes, but not of so much moment as to give him who held the hold any material rights beyond its immediate influence. Still, as the family of Leiningen was numerous, and had other branches and other possessions in more favored portions of Germany, Count Emich was far from being a mere mountain chief. The feudal system had become methodized long before his birth, and the laws of the Empire secured to him many villages and towns on the plain, as the successor of those who had obtained them in more remote ages. He had recently claimed even a higher dignity, and wider territories, as the heir of a deceased kinsman; but in this attempt to increase his power, and to elevate his rank, he had been thwarted by a decision of his peers. It was to this abortive assumption of dignity, that he owed the soubriquet of the Summer Landgrave; for such was the rank he had claimed, and the period for which he had been permitted to bear it.

With this knowledge of the power of their family, the reader will not be surprised to hear that the castle of the Counts of Hartenburg, or, to be more accurate, of the Counts of Hartenburg-Leiningen, was on a commensurate scale. Perched on the advanced spur of the mountain, just where the valley was most confined, and at a point where the little river made a short bend, the pass beneath lay quite at the mercy of the archer on its battlements. In the fore-ground, all that part of the edifice which came into the view was military, and, in some slight degree, fitted to the imperfect use that was then made of artillery; while in the rear arose that maze of courts, chapels, towers, gates, portcullises, state-rooms, offices, and family apartments, that marked the usages and tastes of the day. The hamlet which lay in the dell, immediately beneath the walls of the salient towers, or bastions, for they partook of both characters, was insignificant, and of little account in estimating the wealth and resources of the feudal lord. These came principally from Deurckheim, and the fertile plains beyond, though the forest was not without its value, in a country in which the ax had so long been used.

We have said that Emich of Leiningen was taking his rest in the hold of Hartenburg. Let the reader imagine a massive building, in the centre of the confused pile we have mentioned, rudely fashioned to meet the wants of the domestic economy of that age, and he will get a nearer view of the interior. The walls were wainscoted, and had much uncouth and massive carving; the halls were large and gloomy, loaded with armor, and at this moment pregnant with armed men; the saloons of the medium size which suited a baronial state, and all the appliances of that mingled taste in which comfort and luxury, as now understood, were unknown, but which was not without a portion of the effect that is produced by an exhibition of heavy magnificence. With few but signal exceptions, Germany, even at this hour, is not a country remarkable for the elegancies of domestic life. Its very palaces are of simple decoration, its luxuries of a homebred and inartificial kind, and its taste is rarely superior, and indeed not always equal, to our own. There is still a shade of the Gothic in the habits and opinions of this constant people, who seem to cultivate the subtle refinements of the mind, in preference to the more obvious and material enjoyments which address themselves to the senses.

Quaint and complicated ornaments, wrought by the patient industry of a race proverbial for this description of ingenuity; swords, daggers, morions, cuirasses, and all sorts of defensive armor then in use; such needle-work, as it befitted a noble dame to produce; pictures that possessed most of the faults and few of the beauties of the Flemish school; furniture that bore some such relation to the garniture of the palaces of electors and kings, as the decorations of a village drawing-room in our own time, bear to those of the large towns; a profuse display of plate, on which the arms of Leiningen were embossed and graven in every variety of style, with genealogical trees and heraldic blazonry in colors, were the principal features.

Throughout the whole pile, there was little appearance, however, of the presence of females, or even of the means of their accommodation. Few of that sex were seen in the corridors, or offices, or courts; though men crowded the place in unusual numbers. The latter were chiefly grim and whiskered warriors, who loitered in the halls, or in the more public parts of the castle, like idlers waiting for the expected movement of exertion. None among them were armed at all points, though this carelessly wore his morion, that had buckled on a breast-plate, and another leaned listlessly on his arquebuse or handled his pike. Here a group exercised, in levity, with their several weapons of offence; there a jester amused a crowd of sluggish listeners, with his ribaldry and humor; and numberless were those who quaffed of the Rhenish of their lord. Although this continent had then been discovered, the goodly portion which has since fallen to our heritage was still in the hands of its native proprietors; and the plant, so long known as the weed of Virginia, but which has since become a staple of so many other countries in this hemisphere, was not in its present general use amongst the Germans: else would it have been our duty to finish this hasty sketch, by enveloping it all in mist. Notwithstanding the general air of indifference and negligence, which reigned within the walls of Hartenburg without the gates, in the turrets, and on the advanced towers, there was the appearance of more than the customary watchfulness. Had one been there to note the circumstance, he would have seen, in addition to the sentries who always guarded the approaches of the castle, several swift-footed spies on the look-out, in the hamlet, on the rocks of the mountain-side, and along the winding paths; and as all eyes were turned towards the valley in the direction of Limburg, it was evident that the event they awaited was expected to arrive from that quarter.

While such was the condition of his hold and of so strong a body of his vassals, Count Emich himself had retired from observation, to one of the quaint, half-rude, half-magnificent saloons of the place. The room was lighted by twenty tapers, and other well-known signs indicated the near approach of guests. He paced the large apartment with a heavy and armed heel; while care, or at least severe thought, contracted the muscles around a hard and iron brow, which bore evident marks of familiar acquaintance with the casque. Perhaps this is the only country of Christendom, even now, in which the profession of the law is a pursuit still more honorable and esteemed than that of arms—the best proof of a high and enviable civilization—but at the age of our narrative, the gentleman that was not of the Church, the calling which nearly monopolized all the learning of the times, was of necessity a soldier. Emich of Leiningen carried arms therefore as much in course, as the educated man of this century reads his Horace or Virgil; and as nature had given him a vigorous frame, a hardy constitution, and a mind whose indifference to personal suffering amounted at times to ruthlessness, he was more successful in his trade of violence, than many a pale and zealous student proves in the cultivation of letters.

The musing Count scarce raised his looks from the oaken floor he trod, as menial after menial appeared, moving with light step in the presence of one so dreaded and yet so singularly loved. At length a female, busy in some of the little offices of her sex, glided before his half-unconscious sight. The youth, the bloom, the playful air, the neat coif, the tight boddice, and the ample folds of the falling garments, at length seemed to fill his eye with the form of his companion.

"Is it thou, Gisela?" he said, speaking mildly, as one addresses a favored dependant. "How fareth it with the honest Karl?

"I thank my lord the Count, his aged and wounded servant hath less of pain than is commonly his lot. The limb he has lost in the service of the House of Leiningen——"

"No matter for the leg, girl—thou art too apt to dwell upon that mischance of thy parent."

"Were my lord the Count to leave a limb on the field, it might be missed when he was hurried!"

"Thinkest thou, child, that my tongue would never address the Emperor without naming the defect? Go to, Gisela; thou art a calculating hussy, and rarely permittest occasion to pass without allusion to this growing treasure of thy family. Are my people actively on the watch, with or without their limbs?"

"They are as their natures and humors tend. Blessed Saint Ursula knows where the officers of the country have picked up so ungainly a band, as these that now inhabit Hartenburg! One drinketh, from the time his eyes open in the morn until they shut at even; another sweareth worse than the northern warriors that do these ravages in the Palatinate; this a foul dealer in ribaldry: that a glutton who never moveth lip but to swallow; and none, nay, not a swaggerer of them all, hath civil word for a maiden, though she be known as one esteemed in their master's household."

"They are my vassals, girl, and stouter men at need are not mustered in Germany."

"Stout in speech, and insolent of look, my Lord Count, but most odious company to all, of modest demeanor and of good intentions, in the hold."

"Thou hast been humored by thy mistress, girl, until thou sometimes forgettest discretion. Go and look my guests are informed that the hour of the banquet is at hand;—I await the pleasure of their presence."

Gisela, whose natural pertness had been somewhat heightened by an indulgent mistress, and in whom consciousness of more beauty than ordinarily falls to the share of females of her condition had produced freedom of language that sometimes amounted to temerity, betrayed her discontent in a manner very common to her sex, when it is undisciplined, or little restrained by a wholesome education. She pouted, taking care however that Emich's eye was again turned to the floor, tossed her head and quitted the room. Left to himself, the Count relapsed into his reverie. In this manner did several minutes pass unheeded.

"Dreaming, as usual, noble Emich, of escalades and excommunication!" cried a gay voice at his elbow, the speaker having entered the saloon unseen —"of revengeful priests, of vassalage, of shaven abbots, the confessional and penance dire, thy rights redressed, the frowning conclave, the Abbey cellar, thy morion, revenge, and, to sum up all, in a word that covers every deadly sin, that fallen angel the Devil!"

Emich forced a grim smile at this unceremonious and comprehensive salutation, accepting the offered hand of him who uttered it, however, with the frank freedom of a boon companion.

"Thou art right welcome, Albrecht," he replied, "for the moment is near when my ghostly guests should arrive; and to deal fairly by thee, I never feel myself quite equal to a single combat of wits with the pious knaves; but thy support will be enough, though the whole Abbey community were of the party."

"Ay, we are akin, we sons of Saint John and these bastards of Saint Benedict. Though more martial than your monks of the hill, we of the island are sworn to quite as many virtues. Let me see," he added, counting on his fingers with an air of bold licentiousness; "firstly are we vowed to celibacy and your Benedictine is no less so—then are we self-dedicated to chastity, as is your Limburg monk; next we respect our oaths, as does your Father Bonifacius; then both are servants of the holy cross;" by a singular influence the speaker and the Count made the sacred symbol on their bosoms, as the former uttered the word, "and, doubt it not, I shall be the equal of the reverend brotherhood. They say sin can match sin, and saint should surely be saint's equal! But, Emich, thou art graver than becometh a hot carousal, like this we meditate!"

"And thou gay as if about to gallant the dames of Rhodes to one of thy island festivals!"

The Knight of Saint John regarded his attire with complacency, strutting by the side of his host, as the latter resumed his walk, with the air of a bird of admired plumage. Nor was the remark of the Count of Hartenburg misapplied, since his kinsman and guest had, in reality, expended more labor on his toilette than was customary in the absence of females, and in that rude hold. Unlike the stern and masculine Emich, who rarely divested himself of all his warlike gear, the sworn defender of the Cross appeared entirely in a peaceful guise, if the long rapier that dangled at his side, and which to a much later period formed an indispensable accompaniment of one of gentle condition, could be excepted from the implements of war. His doublet, fully decorated with embroidery, fringes, and loops, and dotted with buttons, was of a pale orange stuff, that was puffed and distended about his person, in the liberal amplitude of the prevailing fashion. The nether garment, which scarce appeared, however, essential as it might be, was of the same material, and cut with a similar expenditure of cloth. The hose were pink, and, rolling far above the knee, gave the effect of a rich coloring to the whole picture. He wore shoes whose upper-leather rose high against the small of the leg, buckles that covered the instep, and about the throat and wrists there was a lavish display of lace. The well-known Maltese cross dangled by a red ribbon, at a button-hole of the doublet; not above the heart, as is the custom at present among the chevaliers of the other hemisphere, but, by a vagary of taste, so low as to demonstrate, if indeed there is any allusion intended by the accidental position of these jewels, that the honorable badge was assumed in direct reference to that material portion of the human frame which is believed to be the repository of good cheer; an interpretation that, in the case of Albrecht of Viederbach, the knight in question, was perhaps much nearer to the truth than he would have been willing to own. After poising himself, first on the point of one shoe, and then on the other, smoothing his ruffles, shoving the rapier more aside, and otherwise adjusting his attire to his mind, the professed soldier of Saint John of Jerusalem pursued the discourse.

"I am decent, kinsman," he replied; "fit to be a guest at thy hospitable board, if thou wilt, in the absence of its fair mistress, but beyond that unworthy to be named. As for the dames of our unhappy and violated Rhodes, dear cousin, thou knowest little of their humors, if thou fanciest that this rude guise would have any charm in their refined eyes. Our knights were used to bring into the island the taste and improvements of every distant land; and small though it be, there are few portions of the earth, in which the human arts, for so I call the decoration of the human body, flourished more than in our circumscribed, valiant, and much regretted Rhodes. Thus was it, at least, until the fell Ottoman triumphed!"

"'Fore God, I had thought thee sworn to all sorts of modesty, in speech, life, and other abstinences!"

"And art thou not sworn, most mutinous Emich, to obey thy liege lords, the Emperor and the Elector—nay, for certain of thy lands and privileges, art thou not bound to knight's service and obedience to the holy Abbot of Limburg?"

"God's curse on him and on all the others of that grasping brotherhood!"

"Ay, that is but the natural consequence of thy oath, as this doublet is of mine. If the rigid performance of a vow is as agreeable to the body, as we are taught it may be healthful to the soul, Count of Leiningen, where would be the merit of observance? I never don these graceful garments, but a wholesome remembrance of watchful nights passed on the ramparts, of painful sieges and watery trenches, or of sickly cruises against the Mussulmans, do not present themselves in the shape of past penances. In this manner do we sweeten sin, by our bodily pains, and by the memory of hours of virtuous hardships!"

"By the three sainted Kings of Koeln, and the eleven thousand virgins of that honored city, Master Albrecht! but thou wert much favored in thy narrow island, if it were permitted to thee to s n in this fashion, with the certainty of tempering punishment with so light service! These griping monks of Limburg make much of their favors, and he who would go with a safe skin, must needs look to an indulgence had and well paid for, in advance. I know not the number of goodly casks of the purest Rhenish that little sallies of humor may have cost me, first and last, in this manner of princely expenditure; but certain am I, that did occasion offer, the united tributes would leave little empty space in Prince Friedrich's vaunted tun, in his ample cellars of Heidelberg!"

"I have often heard of that royal receptacle of generous liquor, and have meditated a pilgrimage in honor of its capacity. Does the Elector receive noble travellers with a hospitality suited to his rank and means?"

"That doth he, and right willingly, though this war presses sorely, and giveth him other employment. Thy wayfaring will not be weary, for thou mayst see the towers of Heidelberg from off these hills, and a worthy steed might be pricked from this court of mine into that of Duke Friedrich in a couple of hours of hard riding."

"When the merits of thy cellar are exhausted, noble Emich, it will be in season to put the Tun to the proof," replied the Knight of Rhodes, "as our esteemed friend here, the Abbé, will maintain, in the face of all the reformers with which our Germany is infested."

In introducing another character, we claim the reader's patience for a moment of digression. Whatever may be said of the merits and legality of the Reformation, effected chiefly by the courage of Luther (and we are neither sectarian nor unbeliever, to deny the sacred origin of the church from which he dissented,) it is very generally admitted, that the long and undisputed sway of the prevailing authority of that age, had led to abuses, which called loudly for some change in its administration. Thousands of those who had devoted their lives to the administrations of the altar, were quite as worthy of the sacred office as it falls to man's lot to become; but thousands had assumed the tonsure, the cowl, or the other symbols of ecclesiastical duty, merely to enjoy the immunities and facilities the character conferred. A long and nearly undisputed monopoly of letters, the influence obtained by the unnatural union between secular and religious power, and the dependent condition of the public mind, the legitimate consequence of both, induced all who aspired to moral pre-eminence, to take this, the most certain, because the most beaten, of the paths that led to this species of ascendency. It is not alone to the religion of Christendom, as it existed in the time of Luther, that we are to look for an example of the baneful consequence of spiritual and temporal authority, as blended in human institutions. Christian or Mahommedan, Catholic or Protestant, the evil comes in every case from the besetting infirmity which tempts the strong to oppress the weak, and the powerful to abuse their trusts. Against this failing there seems to be no security but an active and certain responsibility. So long as the severe morality required of its ministers, by the Christian faith, is uncorrupted by any gross admixture of worldly advantage, there is reason to believe that the altar, at least, will escape serious defilement; but no sooner are these fatal enemies admitted to the sanctuary, than a thousand spirits, prompted by cupidity, rush rashly into the temple, willing to bear with the outward exactions of the faith, in order to seek its present and visible rewards.

However pure may be a social system, or a religion, in the commencement of its power, the possession of an undisputed ascendency lures all alike into excesses fatal to consistency, to justice, and to truth. This is a consequence of the independent exercise of human volition, that seems nearly inseparable from human frailty. We gradually come to substitute inclination and interest for right, until the moral foundations of the mind are sapped by indulgence, and what was once regarded with the aversion that wrong excites in the innocent, gets to be not only familiar, but justifiable by expediency and use. There is no more certain symptom of the decay of the principles requisite to maintain even our imperfect standard of virtue, than when the plea of necessity is urged in vindication of any departure from its mandate, since it is calling in the aid of ingenuity to assist the passions, a coalition that rarely fails to lay prostrate the feeble defences of a tottering morality

It is no wonder, then, that the world, at a period when religious abuses drove even churchmen reluctantly to seek relief in insubordination, should exhibit bold instances of the flagrant excesses we have named. Military ambition, venality, love of ease. and even love of dissipation, equally sought the mantle of religion as cloaks to their several objects and if the reckless cavalier was willing to flesh his sword on the body of the infidel, in order that he might live in men's estimation as a hero of the cross, so did the trifler, the debauchee, and even the wit of the capital, consent to obtain circulation by receiving an impression which gave currency to all coin, whether of purer or of baser metal, since it bore the outward stamp of the Church of God.

"Reformers, or rather revilers, for that is the term they most merit," returned the Abbé, alluded to in the last speech of Albrecht of Veiderbach, "I consign without remorse to the devil. As for this pledge of our brave Knight of Saint John, noble Count Emich, so far as I am concerned, it shall be redeemed: for I am certain the cellars of Heidelberg can resist a heavier inroad than any that is likely to invade them by such means. But I am late from my chamber, and I had hoped, ere this, to have seen our brethren of Limburg! I hope no unnecessary misunderstanding is likely to deprive us of the satisfaction of their presence, Lord Count?"

"Little fear of that, so far as it may depend on any disappointment in a feast. If ever the devil tempted these monks of the hill, it has been in the shape of gluttony. Were I to judge by the experience of forty years passed in their neighborhood, I should think they deem abstinence an eighth deadly sin."

"Your Benedictine is privileged to consider hospitality a virtue, and the Abbot has fair license for the indulgence of some little cheer. We will not judge them harshly, therefore, but form our opinions of their merits by their deeds. Thou hast many servitors without, to do them honor to-night, Lord Emich."

The Count of Leiningen frowned, and, ere he answered, his eye exchanged a glance with that of his kinsman, which the Abbé might have interpreted into a hidden meaning, had it attracted his observation.

"My people gather loyally about their lord, for they have heard of this succor sent by the Elector to uphold the lazy Benedictines," was the reply "Four hundred mercenaries lie within the Abbey walls this night, Master Latouche, and it should not cause surprise that the vassals of Emich of Hartenburg are ready with hand and sword to do service in his defence. God's mercy! The cunning priests may pretend alarm, but if any here hath cause to be afraid, truly it is the rightful and wronged lord of the Jaegerthal!"

"Thy situation, Cousin of Hartenburg," observed the wearer of the cross of Saint John, "is, in sooth one of masterly diplomacy. Here dost thou stand at sword's point with the Abbot of Limburg, ready at need to exchange deadly thrusts, and to put this long-disputed supremacy on the issue of battle, while thou callest on the keeper of thy cellar to bring forth the choicest of its contents, in order to do hospitality and honor to thy mortal foe! This beateth, in all niceties, Monsieur Latouche, the situation of an abbé of thy quality, who is scarce churchman enough to merit salvation, nor yet deep enough in sin to be incontinently damned in the general mass of evil-doers."

"It is to be hoped that we shall share the common lot of mortals, which is to receive more grace than they merit," returned the Abbé, a title that in fact scarce denoted one seriously devoted to the Church. "But I trust this present meeting between the hostile powers may prove amicable; for, not to conceal the truth, unlike our friend the Knight here, I am of none of the belligerent orders."

"Hark!" exclaimed the host, lifting a finger to command attention: "Heard ye aught?"

"There is much of the music of thy growlers in the courts, cousin, and some oaths in a German that needs be translated to be understood; but that blessed signal the supper-bell is still mute."

"Go to!—'Tis the Abbot of Limburg and his brethren, Fathers Siegfried and Cuno. Let us to the portal, to do them usual honor."

As this was welcome news to both the Knight and the Abbé, they manifested a suitable desire to be foremost in paying the required attention to a personage, as important in that region as the rich and powerful chief of the neighboring religious establishment.

CHAPTER VI.

"Why not?—The deeper sinner, better saint."
BYRON.

A WILD and plaintive note had been sounded on a horn far in the valley towards the hill of Limburg. This melodious music was of common occurrence, for of all that dwell in Europe, they who inhabit the banks of the Rhine, the Elbe, the Oder, and the Danube, with their tributaries, are the most addicted to the cultivation of sweet sounds. We hear much of the harshness of the Teutonic dialects, and of the softness of those of Latin origin; but, Venice and the regions of the Alps excepted, nature has amply requited for the inequality that exists between the languages, by the difference in the organs of speech. He who journeys in those distant lands must, as a rule, expect to hear German warbled and Italian in a grand crash, though exceptions are certainly to be found in both cases. But music is far more common on the vast plains of Saxony than on the Campagna Felice, and it is no uncommon occurrence to be treated by a fair-haired postilion of the former country, as he slowly mounts a hill, with airs on the horn that would meet with favor in the orchestra of a capital. It was one of these melancholy and peculiar strains which now gave the signal to the spies of Count Emich, that his clerical guests had quitted the convent.

"Heard ye aught, brothers?" demanded Father Bonifacius of the companions who rode at his side, nearly at the same moment that the Lord of Leiningen put the same question in his hold; "that horn spoke in a meaning strain!"

"We may be defeated in our wish to reach the castle suddenly," returned the monk, already known to the reader as Father Siegfried; "but though we fail in looking into Count Emich's secret with our own eyes, I have engaged one to do that office for us, and in a manner, I trust, that shall put us on the scent of his designs. Courage, most holy Abbot, the cause of God is not likely to fail for want of succor. When were the meek and righteous ever deserted?"

The Abbot of Limburg ejaculated, in a manner to express little faith in any miraculous interposition in behalf of his cure, and he drew about him the mantle that served in some degree to conceal his person, spurring the beast he rode only the quicker, from a feverish desire, if possible, to outstrip the sounds, which he intuitively felt were intended to announce his approach. The prelate was not deceived, for no sooner did the wild notes reach the castle, than the signal, which had caught the attention of its owner, was communicated to those within the walls.

At the expected summons there was a general movement among the idlers of the courts. Subordinate officers passed among the men, hurrying those away to their secret lodging places who were intractable from excess of liquor, and commanding the more obedient to follow. In a very few minutes, and long before the monks, who however pricked their beasts to the utmost, had time to get near the hamlet even, all in the hold was reduced to a state of tranquil repose; the castle resembling the abode of any other powerful baron, in moments of profound security. Emich had seen to this disposition of his people in person, taking strict caution that no straggler should appear, to betray the preparations that existed within his walls. When this wise precaution was observed, he proceeded, with his two companions, to take a station near the door of the building more especially appropriated to the accommodation of himself and his friends, in order to await the arrival of the monks.

The moon had ascended high enough to illuminate the mountain-side, and to convert the brown towers and ramparts of Hartenburg into picturesque forms, relieved by gloomy shadows. The signals appeared to have thrown all who dwelt in the hamlet, as well as they who inhabited the frowning hold which overhung that secluded spot, into mute attention For a few minutes the quiet was so deep and general, that the murmuring of the rivulet which meandered through the meadows was audible. Then came the swift clattering of hoofs.

"Our churchmen are in haste to taste thy Rhenish, noble Emich," said Albrecht of Viderbach, who rarely thought; "or is it a party of their sumpter mules that I hear in the valley?"

"Were the Abbot about to journey to some other convent of his order, or were he ready to visit his spiritual master of Spires, there is no doubt that many such cattle would be in his train; for of all lovers of fat cheer, Wilhelm of Venloo, who has been styled Bonifacius in his baptism of office, is he that most worships the fruits of the earth. I would he and all his brotherhood were spiritually planted in the garden of Eden! They should be well watered with my tears!"

"The wish hath a saintly odor, but may not be accomplished without mortal aid—unless thou hast favor with the Prince Elector of Koeln, who might haply do thee that service, in the way of miracle."

"Thou triflest, knight, in a matter of great gravity," answered Emich roughly, for, notwithstanding his inherited and deadly dislike of the particular portion of the church which interfered with his own power, the Count of Hartenburg had all the dependence on superior knowledge that is the unavoidable offspring of a limited education. "The Prince Elec tor hath served many noble families in the way thou namest, and he might do honor to houses less deserving of his grace, than that of Leiningen. But here cometh the Abbot and his boon associates God's curse await them for their pride and avarice!'

The clattering of hoofs had been gradually increasing, and was now heard even on the pavement of the outer court; for in order to do honor to his guests, the count had especially ordered there should be no delay or impediment from gate, portcullis, or bridge.

"Welcome, and reverence for thy churchly office, right holy Abbot!" cried Emich, from whose lips had just parted the malediction, advancing officiously to aid the prelate in dismounting—"Thou art welcome, brothers both; worthy companions of thy respected and honored chief."

The churchmen alighted, assisted by the menials of Hartenburg, with much show of honor on the part of the Count himself, and on that of his friends. When fairly on their feet, they courteously returned the greetings.

"Peace be with thee, son, and with this cavalier and servitor of the Church!" said Father Bonifacius, signing with the rapid manner in which a Catholic priest scatters his benedictions. "St. Benedict and the Virgin take ye all in their holy keeping! I trust, noble Emich, we have not given thee cause of vexation, by some little delay?"

"Thou never comest amiss, father, be it at morn, or be it at even; I esteem Hartenburg more than honored, when thy reverend head passeth beneath its portals."

"We had every desire to embrace thee, son, but certain offices of religion, that may not be neglected, kept us from the pleasure. But let us within; for I fear the evening air may do injury to those tha are uncloaked."

At this considerate suggestion, Emich, with much show of respect to his guests, ushered them into the apartment he had himself so lately quitted. Here recommenced the show of those wily courtesies which, in that semi-barbarous and treacherous age, often led men to a heartless and sometimes to a blasphemous trifling with the most sacred obligations, to effect their purposes, and which, in our times, has degenerated to a deception, that is more measured perhaps, but which is scarcely less sophisticated and vicious. Much was said of mutual satisfaction at this opportunity of commingling spirits, and the blunt professions of the sturdy but politic baron, were more than met by the pretending sanctity and official charity of the priest.

The Abbot of Limburg and his companions had come to the intended feast with vestments that partially concealed their characters; but when the outer cloaks and the other garments were removed, they remained in the usual attire of their order, the prelate being distinguished from his inferiors by those symbols of clerical rank, which it was usual for one of his authority to display, when not engaged in the ministrations of the altar.

When the guests were at their ease, the conversation took a less personal direction, for though rude and unnurtured as his own war-horse, as regards most that is called cultivation in our bookish days, Emich of Hartenburg wanted for none of the courtesies that became his rank, more especially as civilities of this nature were held to be worthy of a feudal lord, and in that particular region.

" 'Tis said, reverend Abbot," continued the host pushing the discourse to a point that might favor his own secret views, that our common master, the Prince Elector, is sorely urged by his enemies, and that there are even fears a stranger may usurp the rule in the noble Castle of Heidelberg. Hast thou heard aught of his late distresses, or of the necessities that bear upon his house?"

"Masses have been said for his benefit in all our chapels, and there are hourly prayers that he may prevail against his enemies. In virtue of a concession made to the abbey, by our common father at Rome, we offer liberal indulgences, too, to all that take up arms in this behalf."

"Thou art much united in love with Duke Friedrich, holy prelate!" muttered Emich.

"We owe him such respect as all should willingly pay to the strong temporal arm that shields them; our serious fealty is due alone to heaven. But how comes it that so stout a baron, one so much esteemed in warlike exercises, and so well known in dangerous enterprises, rests in his doublet, at a time when his sovereign's throne is tottering? We had heard that thou wert summoning thy people, Herr Count, and thought it had been in the Elector's interest."

"Friedrich hath not of late given me cause to love him. If I have called my vassals about me, 'tis because the times teach every noble to be wary of his rights. I have consorted so much of late with my cousin of Viederbach, this self-denying Knight of Rhodes, that martial thoughts will obtrude even on the brain of one, peaceful and homebred as thy poor neighbor and penitent."

The Abbot bowed and smiled, like one who gave full credit to the speaker's words, while a by-play arose between the wandering and houseless knight, the abbé, and the brothers of Limburg. In this manner did a few minutes wear away, when a flourish of trumpets announced that the expected banquet awaited its guests. Menials lighted the party to the hall in which the board was spread, and much ceremonious form was observed in assigning to each of the individuals the place suited to his rank and character. Count Emich, who in common was of a nature too blunt and severe to waste his efforts in superfluous breeding, now showed himself earnest to please, for he had a heart an object that he knew was in danger of being baffled by the more practised artifices of the monks. During the preliminary movements of the feast, which had all the gross and all the profuse hospitality which distinguished such entertainments, he neglected no customary observance. The robust and sensual Abbot was frequently plied with both cup and dish, while the inferior monks received the same agreeable attentions from Albrecht of Viederbach, and Monsieur Latouche, who, notwithstanding it suited his convenience to pass through life under the guise of a churchman, was none the worse at board or revel. As the viands and the generous liquors began to operate on the physical functions of the brothers, however, they insensibly dropped their masks, and each discovered more of those natural qualities, which usually lay concealed from casual observation.

It was a rule of the Benedictines to practise hospitality. The convent door was never closed against the wayfarer, and he who applied for shelter and food was certain of obtaining both, administered more or less in a manner suited to the applicant's ordinary habits. The practice of a virtue so costly was a sufficient pretence for accumulating riches, and he who travels at this day in Europe will find ample proofs that the means of carrying into effect this law of the order were abundantly supplied. Abbeys of this particular class of monks are still of frequent occurrence in the forest cantons of Switzerland, Germany, and in most of the other Catholic states. But the gradual and healthful transfer of political power from clerical to laical hands, has long since shorn them of their temporal lustre. Many of these abbots were formerly princes of the empire, and several of the communities exercised sovereign sway over territories that have since taken to themselves the character of independent states.

While the spiritual charge and the mortifications believed to characterize a brotherhood of Benedictines, were more especially left to a subordinate monk termed the prior, the abbot, or head of the establishment, was expected to preside not only over the temporalities, but at the board. This frequent communication with the vulgar interests of life, and the constant indulgence in its grosser gratifications, were but ill adapted to the encouragement of the monastic virtues. We have already remarked that the intimate connexion between the interests of life and those of the church is destructive of apostolical character. This blending of God with Mammon, this device of converting the revealed ordinances of the Master of the Universe into a species of buttress to uphold temporal sway, though habit has so long rendered it familiar to the inhabitants of the other hemisphere, and even to a large portion of those who dwell in this, is, in our American eyes, only a little removed from blasphemy; but the triumphs of the press, and the changes made by the steady advances of public opinion, have long since done away with a multitude of still more equivocal usages, that were as familiar to those who existed three centuries ago, as our own customs to us at this hour. When prelates were seen in armor, leading their battalions to slaughter, it is not to be supposed that the other dignitaries of this privileged class, would be more tender of appearances than was exacted by the opinions of the age.

Wilhelm of Venloo, known since his elevation as Bonifacius of Limburg, was not possessed of all that temporal authority, however, which tempted so many of his peers to sin. Still he was the head of a rich, powerful, and respected brotherhood, that had many allodial rights in lands beyond the abbey walls, and which was not without its claims to the fealty of sundry dependants. Of vigorous mind and body, this dignified churchman commanded much influence by means of a species of character that often crosses us in life, a sturdy independence of thought and action that imposed on the credulous and timid, and which sometimes caused the bold and intelligent to hesitate. His reputation was far greater for learning than for piety, and his besetting sin was well known to be a disposition to encounter the shock between the powers of mind and matter, as both were liable to be affected by deep potations and gross feeding—a sort of degeneracy to which all are peculiarly liable, who place an unnatural check on the ordinary and healthful propensities of nature—just as one sense is known to grow in acuteness as it is deprived of a fellow. The abbot loosened his robe, and threw his cowl still farther from his neck, while Emich pledged him in Rhenish, cup after cup; and by the time the meats were removed, and the powers of digestion, or we might better say of retention, would endure no more, his heavy cheeks became flushed, his bright, deeply-seated, and searching gray eyes flashed with a species of ferocious delight, and his lip frequently quivered, as the clay gave eloquent evidence of its enjoyment. Still his voice, though it had lost its rebuked and schooled tones, was firm, deep, and authoritative, and ever and anon he threw into his discourse some severe and pointed sarcasm, bitingly scornful. His subordinates, too, gave similar proofs of the gradual lessening of their caution, though in degrees far less imposing, we had almost said less grand, than that which rendered the sensual excitement of their superior so remarkable. Albrecht and the abbé also betrayed, each in his own manner the influence of the banquet, and all became garru lous, disputative, and noisy.

Not so with Emich of Hartenburg. He had eaten in a manner to do justice to his vast frame and bodily wants, and he drank fairly; but, until this moment, the nicest observer would have been puzzled to detect any decrease of his powers. The blue of his large leaden eyes became brighter, it is true, but their expression was yet in command, and their language courteous.

"Thou dost but little compliment to my poor fare, most holy Abbot," cried the host, as he witnessed a lingering look of the prelate, whose eye followed the delicious fragments of a wild boar from the hall —"If the knaves have stinted thee in the choice of morsels, by St. Benedict! but the mountains of my chase can still furnish other animals of the kind—How now——"

"I pray thee, mercy, noble Emich! Thy forester hath done thee fair justice with his spear; more savory beast never smoked at table."

"It fell by the hand of young Berchthold, the burgher of Deurckheim's orphan. 'Tis a bold youth in the forest, and I doubt not, his will one day be a ready hand in battle. Thou knowest him I mean, father, for he is often at thy abbey confessionals."

"He is better known to the prior than to one so busied with worldly cares as I. Is the youth at hand? I would fain render him thanks."

"Hear ye that, varlet! Bid my head forester appear. The reverend and noble Abbot of Limburg owes him grace."

"Didst thou say the youth was of Deurckheim?"

"Of that goodly town, reverend priest; and, though reduced by evil chances to be the ranger of my woods, a lad of mettle in the chase, and of no bad discourse in moments of ease."

"Thou claimest hard service, Cousin of Hartenburg, of these peaceful townsmen! Were they left freely to choose between the ancient duty of our convent, and this stirring life thou leadest the artisans, we should have more penitents within our walls."

The feality of Deurckheim was a long mooted point between the corporation of Limburg and the house of Leiningen, and the allusion of the monk was not thrown away upon his host. Emich's brow clouded, and for a moment it threatened a storm; but, recovering his self-command, he answered in a tone of hilarity, though with sufficient coolness:—

"Thy words remind me of present affairs, reverend Bonifacius, and I thank thee that thou hast put a sudden check on festivities which were getting warm without an object." The Count arose, and filled to the brim a cup of horn, elaborately ornamented with gold, drawing the attention of all at table to himself by the action. "Nobles and reverend servants of God," he continued, "I drink to the health and happiness of the honored Wilhelm of Venloo, the holy Abbot of Limburg, and my loving neighbor. May his brotherhood never know a worse guide, and may the lives and contentment of all that now belong to it, be as lasting as the abbey walls."

Emich concluded the potent cup at a single draught. In order to do honor to the mitred monk, there had been placed by the side of Bonifacius, a vessel of agate richly decorated with jewelry, an heir-loom of the house of Leiningen. While his host was speaking, the looks of the latter watched every expression of his countenance, through gray, overhanging, shaggy brows, that shaded the upper part of his face like a screen of shrubbery planted to shut out prying eyes from a close; and he paused when the health was given. Then, rising in his turn, he quaffed a compliment in return.

"I drink of this pure and wholesome liquor," he said, "to the noble Emich of Leiningen, to all of his ancient and illustrious house, to his and their present hopes, and to their final deliverance. May this goodly hold, and the happiness of its lord, endure as long as those walls of Limburg of which the Count has spoken, and which, were his loving wishes consulted, would doubtless stand for ever."

"By the life of the emperor, learned Bonifacius!" exclaimed Emich, striking his fist on the table with force, "you as much exceed one of my narrow wit in wishes, as in godliness and other excellencies! But I pretend not to set limits to my desires in your behalf, and throw the fault of my imperfect speech on a youth that had more to do with the sword than with the breviary. And now let us to serious concerns. It may not be known to you, Cousin of Viederbach, or to this obliging churchman who honors Hartenburg with his presence, that there has been subject of amicable dispute between the brotherhood of Limburg and my unworthy house, touching the matter of certain wines, that are believed by the one party to be its dues, and by the other to be a mere pious grace accorded to the church——"

"Nay, noble Emich," interrupted the Abbot, "we have never held the point to be disputable in any manner. The lands in question are held of us in soccage; and, in lieu of bodily service, we have long since commuted for the produce of vines that might be named."

"I cry you mercy; if there be dues at all, they come of naught else than knight's service. None of my name or lineage ever paid less to mortal!"

"Let it be thus," Bonifacius answered more

mildly. "The question is of the amount of liquor, and not of the tenure whence it comes."

"Thou sayest right, wise Abbot, and I cry mercy of these listeners. State thou the matter, reverend Bonifacius, that our friends may know the humor on which we are madly bent."

The Count of Hartenburg succeeded in swallowing his rising ire, and made a gesture of courtesy towards the Abbot, as he concluded. Father Bonifacius rose again, and notwithstanding the physical ravages that excess was making within, it was still with the air of calmness and discipline that became his calling.

"As our upright and esteemed friend has just related," he said, "there is truly a point, of a light but unseemly nature to exist between so dear neighbors, open between him and us servants of God. The Counts of Leiningen have long considered it a pleasure to do favor to the Church, and in this just and commendable spirit, it is now some fifty years that, at the termination of each vintage, without regard to seasons or harvest, without stooping to change their habits at every change of weather, they have paid to our brotherhood——"

"Presented, priest!"

"Presented,—if such is thy will, noble Emich,—fifty casks of this gentle liquor that now warms our hearts towards each other, with brotherly and praiseworthy affection. Now, it has been settled between us, to avoid all future motive of controversy, and either the better to garnish our cellars, or to relieve the house of Hartenburg altogether of future imposition, that it shall be decided this night, whether the tribute henceforth shall consist of one hundred casks, or of nothing."

"By're Lady! A most important issue, and one likely to impoverish or to enrich!" exclaimed the Knight of Rhodes.

"As such we deem it," continued the monk, "and in that view, parchments of release, with all due appliances and seals, have been prepared by a clerkly scholar of Heidelberg. This indenture, duly executed," he added, drawing from his bosom the instruments in question, "yieldeth to Emich all the Abbey's rights to the vines in dispute, and this wanteth but his sign of arms and noble name, to double their present duty."

"Hold!" cried the Chevalier of the Cross, whose faculties began already to give way, though it was only in the commencement of the debauch: "Here is matter might puzzle the Grand Turk, who sits in judgment in the very seat of Solomon! If thou renderest thy claims, and my cousin Emich yieldeth double tribute-money, both parties will be the worse, and neither possessed of the liquor!"

"In a merry mood, it hath been proposed that there shall be the trial of love and not of battle, between us, for the vines. The question is of liquor, and it is agreed,—St. Benedict befriend me, if there be sin in the folly! to try on whose constitution the disputed liquor is the most apt to work good or evil. Let the Count of Hartenburg give to his parchment the virtue that hath already been given to this of ours, and we shall leave both in some place of observation;—then, when he alone is able to rise and seize on both, let him give the victor's cry; but should he fail of that power, and there be a servant of the Church ready, and able to grasp the instruments, why let him go, and think no more of land that he hath right merrily lost."

"By St. John of Jerusalem, but this is a most unequal contest—three monks against one poor baron, in a trial of heads!"

"Nay, we think more of our honor, than to permit this wrong. The Count of Hartenburg hath full right to call in equal succor, and I have taken thee gallant cavalier of Rhodes, and this learned Abbé, to be his chosen backers!"

"Let it be so!" cried the two in question,—"We ask no better service than to drain Count Emich's cellars to his honor and profit!"

But the lord of the hold had taken the matter, as indeed it was fully understood between the principals, to be a question on which depended a serious amount of revenue, for all futurity. The wager had arisen, in one of those wild contests for physical and gross supremacy, which characterize ages and countries of imperfect civilization; for next to deeds in arms and other manful exercises, like those of the chase and saddle, it was deemed honorable to be able to undergo the trials of the festive board with impunity. Nor should it occasion surprise to find churchmen engaged in these encounters; for, independently of our writing of an age when they appeared in the field, there is sufficient evidence that our own times are not entirely purified from so coarse abuses of the gown. But Bonifacius of Limburg, though a man of extensive learning and strong intellectual qualities, had a weakness on this particular point, for which we may be driven to seek an explanation in his peculiar animal construction. He was of a powerful frame and sluggish temperament, both of which required strong excitement to be wrought up to the highest point of physical enjoyment; and neither the examples around him, nor his own particular opinions, taught him to avoid a species of indulgence that he found so agreeable to his constitution. With these serious views of a contest, to which neither party would probably have consented, had not each great confidence in himself as a well-tried champion, both Emich and the Abbot required that the instruments should be openly read. The discharge of this duty was assigned to Monsieur Latouche, who forthwith proceeded to wade through a torrent of unintelligible terms, that were generated in the obscurity of feudal times for the benefit of the strong, and which are continued to our own period through pride of professional knowledge, a little quickened by a view to professional gain. On the subject of the true consideration of the respective releases, the instruments themselves were silent, though nothing material was wanting to give them validity, especially when supported by a good sword; or the power of the Church, to which the parties looked respectively in the event of flaws.

Count Emich listened warily as his guest the Abbé read clause after clause of the deed. Occasionally his eye wandered to the firm countenance of the Abbot, betraying habitual distrust of his hereditary and powerful enemy, but it was quickly riveted again on the heated features of the reader.

"This is well," he said, when both papers had been examined: "These vines are to remain for ever with me and mine, without claim from any grasping churchman, so long as grass shall grow or water run, or henceforth they pay double tribute, a tax that will leave little for the cellar of their rightful lord."

"Such are our terms, noble Emich. But to confirm the latter condition, thy seal and name are wanting to the instrument."

"Were the latter to be written by a good sword, none could do the office better than this poor arm, reverend Abbot; but thou knowest well, that my youth was too much given to warlike and other manly exercises befitting my rank, to allow much time for acquiring clerkly skill. By the holy Virgins of Koeln! It were, in sooth, a shame to confess, that one of my class in these stirring times had leisure for such lady games! Bring hither an eagle's feather—hand of mine never yet touched aught from meaner wing—that I may do justice to the monks."

The necessary implements being produced, the Count of Hartenburg proceeded to execute the instrument on his part. The wax was speedily attached and duly impressed with the bearings of Leiningen, for the noble wore a signet-ring of massive size, ready at all times to give this token of his will. But when it became necessary to subscribe the name, a signal was made to a domestic, who disappeared in quest of the Count's man of charge. This individual manifested some reluctance to perform the customary office, but, as there was just then a clamorous dialogue among the party at table, he seized the moment to examine into the nature of the document, and the consideration that was to decide the ownership of the vineyard. Grinning in satisfaction, at a species of payment in which he held it to be impossible Lord Emich could fail to acquit himself honorably, the dependant took the hand of his master, and, accustomed to the duty, he so guided it as to leave a very legible and creditable signature. When this had been done, and the papers were properly witnessed, the Count of Hartenburg glanced suspiciously from the deed in his hand to the indomitable face of the Abbot, as if he still half repented of the act. "Look you, Bonifacius," he said, shaking a finger,—"Should there be flaw, or doubt of any intention in this our covenant, sword of mine shall cut it!"

"First earn the right, Count of Leiningen. The deeds are of equal virtue, and he who would lay claim to their benefits must win the wager. We are but poor brothers of St. Benedict, and little worthy to be named with warlike barons and devoted followers of St. John, but we have an humble trust in our patron."

"By St. Benedict, it shall pass for a miracle, if

thou prevailest!" shouted Emich, yielding the deed in a burst of delight. "Away with these cups of agate and horn, and bring forth vessels of glass, that all may see we deal fairly by each other, in this right manly encounter. Look to your wits, monks.—By the word of a cavalier, your Latin will do little service in this dispute."

"Our trust is in our patron," answered Father Siegfried, who had already done so much honor to the banquet, as to give reason to believe, that, in his case, the fraternity leaned upon a fragile staff. "He never yet deserted his children, when fairly enlisted in a good cause."

"You are cunning in reasons, fathers," put in the knight—"and I doubt not that sufficient excuses would be forthcoming, were you pushed to justify service to the devil."

"We suffer for the church," was the Abbot's answer, after taking a bumper in obedience to a signal from his host. "We hold it to be commendable to struggle with the flesh, that our altars may flourish."

As soon as executed, the two deeds had been placed on a high and curiously wrought vessel of silver, that contained cordials, and which occupied the centre of the board, and more fitting cups having been brought, the combatants were compelled to swallow draught after draught, at signals from Emich, who, like a true knight, saw that each man showed loyalty. But, as the conflict was between men of great experience in this species of contention, and as it endured hours, we deem it unworthy of the theme to limit its description to a single chapter. Before closing the page, however, we shall digress for a moment, in order to express our opinions concerning the great human properties involved in this sublime strife.

It has been the singular fortune of America to be the source of numberless ingenious theories, that taking their rise in the other hemisphere, have been let loose upon the world to answer ends that we shall not stop to investigate. The dignified and beneficed prelate maintains there is no worship of God within our land, probably because there are no dignified and beneficed prelates; a sufficiently logical conclusion for all who believe in the efficacy of that self-denying class of Christians; while the neophyte, in some lately invented religion, denounces us all in a body, as so many miserable bigots, devoted to Christ! In this manner is a pains-taking and plain-dealing nation of near fourteen millions of souls kept, as it were, in abeyance in the opinions of the rest of mankind, one deeming them as much beyond, as another fancies them to be short of, truth. In the fearful catalogue of our deadly sins, is included a propensity to indulge in excesses similar to that it is now our office to record. As we are confessedly democrats, dram-drinking in particular has been pronounced to be a "democratic vice."

It has been our fortune to have lived in familiarity with a greater variety of men, either considered in reference to their characters or their conditions, than ordinarily falls to the lot of any one person. We have visited many lands, not in the capacity of a courier, but staidly and soberly, as becomes a grave occupation, setting up our household gods, and abiding long enough to see with our eyes and to hear with our ears; and we feel emboldened to presume on these facts, in order to express a different opinion, amid the flood of assertions that has been made by those who certainly have no better claim to be heard. And, firstly, we shall here say that, as in the course of justice, an intelligent, upright, single-minded, and discriminating witness is, perhaps, the rarest of all desirable instruments in effecting its sacred ends, so do we acknowledge a traveller, entitled to full credit, to be the mortal of all others the least likely to be found.

The art of travelling, we apprehend, is far more practised than understood. To us it has proved a laborious, harassing, puzzling, and oftentimes a painful pursuit. To divest oneself of impressions made in youth; to investigate facts without referring their merits to a standard bottomed on a foundation no better than habit; to analyze, and justly to compare the influence of institutions, climate, natural causes, and practice; to separate what is merely exception from that which forms the rule; or even to obtain and carry away accurate notions of physical things, and, most of all, to possess the gift of imparting these results comprehensively and with graphical truth, requires a combination of time, occasion, previous knowledge, and natural ability, that rarely falls to the lot of a single individual. One assumes the task prepared by acquaintance with established opinions, which are commonly no more than prejudices, the result of either policy, or of the very difficulties just enumerated; and he goes on his way, not only ready but anxious to receive the proofs of what he expects, limiting his pleasure to the sort of delight, that dependent minds feel in following the course pointed out by those that are superior. As the admitted peculiarities of every people are sufficiently apparent, he converts self-evident facts into collateral testimony, and faithfully believes and imagines all that is concealed on the strength of that which is obvious. For such a traveller time wears away men and things in vain; he accords his belief to the last standard opinion of his sect, with a devotion to convention that might purchase salvation in a better cause. To him Vesuvius is just as high, produces the same effect in the view, and has exactly the same outline as before the crater fell; and he watches the workmen disinterring a house at its base, and goes away rejoicing at having witnessed the resurrection of a Roman dwelling after eighteen hundred years of interment, simply because it is the vulgar account that Pompeii was lost for that period. If he should happen to be a scholar, what is his delight in following a cicerone (a title assumed by some wily *servitore di Piazza*) to the little garden that overlooks the Roman Forum, and in fancying that he stands upon the Tarpeian Rock! His faith in moral qualities, his graduation of national virtue, and his views of manners, are equally the captives of the last popular rumor. A Frenchman may roll incontinently in the *gras de Paris*, filled with an alcohol inflammable as gunpowder, and in his eyes it shall pass for pure animal light-heartedness, since it is out of all rule for a Frenchman to be intoxicated, while the veriest tyro knows that the nation dances to a man! The gallant general, the worshipful alderman, the right honorable adviser of the king, may stammer around a subject for half an hour, in St. Stephen's, in a manner to confound all conclusion, and generalize so completely as to baffle particularity, and your hearer shall go away convinced of the excellence of the great school of modern eloquence, because the orator has been brought up at the "feet of Gamaliel." When one thoroughly imbued with this pliant faculty, gets into a foreign land, with what a diminished reverence for his own does he journey! As few men are endowed with sufficient penetration to pierce the mists of received opinion, fewer still are they that are so strong in right as to be able to stem its tide. He who precedes his age is much less likely to be heard, than he who lingers in its rear; and when the unwieldy body of the mass reaches the eminence on which he has long stood the object of free comment, it may be assumed as certain, that they who were his bitterest deriders when his doctrine was new, will be foremost in claiming the honors of the advance. In short, to instruct the world, it is necessary to watch the current, and to act on the public mind like the unseen rudder, by slight and imperceptible variations, avoiding, as a seaman would express it, any very rank sheer, lest the vessel should refuse to mind her helm and go down with the stream.

We have been led into these reflections, by frequent opportunities of witnessing the facility with which opinions are adopted concerning ourselves, because they have come from the pens of those who have long contributed to amuse and instruct us, but which are perfectly valueless, both from the unavoidable ignorance of those who utter them, and from the hostile motives that gave them birth. To that class which would wish to put in a claim to *bon ton*, by undervaluing their countrymen, we have nothing to say, since they are much beyond improvement, and are quite unable to understand all the high and glorious consequences dependent on the great principles of which this republic is the guardian. Their fate was long since settled by a permanent and wise provision of human feeling; but, presuming on the opportunities mentioned, and long habits of earnest observation in the two hemispheres, we shall conçlude this digression by merely adding, that it is the misfortune of man to abuse the gifts of God, let him live in what country or under what institutions he may. Excess of the description in question is the failing of every people, nearly in proportion to their means; nor are there any certain preventives against a vice so destructive, but absolute want, or a high cultivation of the reasoning faculties.

He who has accurately ascertained how far the people of this republic are behind or before the inhabitants of other lands, in mental improvement and moral qualities, will not be far from the truth in assigning to them a correspondent place in the scale of sobriety. It is true that many foreigners will be ready enough to deny this position, but we have had abundant opportunities of observing, that all those who visit our shores do not come sufficiently prepared, by observation at home, to make just comparisons, and what we have here said has not been ventured without years of close and honest investigation. We shall gladly hail the day when it can be said, that not an American exists, so lost to himself as to trifle with the noblest gift of the Creator; but we cannot see the expediency of attaining an end, desirable even as this, by the concession of premises that are false.

CHAPTER VII.

"What a thrice-double ass
Was I, to take this drunkard for a god!
Caliban.

Physical qualities are always prized in proportion o the value that is attached to those that are purely intellectual. So long as power and honor depend on the possession of brute force, strength and agility are endowments of the last importance, on the same principle that they render the tumbler of more account in his troop; and he who has ever had occasion to mingle much with the brave, and subject to a qualification that will readily be understood, we might add, the noble savages of this contirient, will have remarked, that, while the orators are in general a class who have cultivated their art for want of qualifications to excel in that which is deemed still more honorable, the first requisite in the warrior is stature and muscle. There exists a curious document to prove how much even their successors a people in no degree deficient in acuteness, have been subject to a similar influence. We allude to a register that was made of the thews and sinews among the chiefs of the army of Washington, during the moment of inaction that preceded the recognition of Independence. By this report it would seem, that the animal entered somewhat into the ideas of our fathers, when they made their original selection of leaders, a circumstance that we attribute to the veneration that man is secretly disposed to show to physical perfection, until a better training and experience have taught him there is still a superior power. Our first impressions are almost always received through the senses, and the connexion between martial prowess and animal force seems so natural, that we ought not to be surprised that a people so peaceful and unpractised, in their simplicity, betrayed a little of this deference to appearances. Happily, if they sometimes put matter into stations which would have been better filled by mind, the honesty and zeal that were so general in the patriotic ranks carried the country through in triumph.

It was a consequence of the high favor enjoyed by all manly or physical qualities in the sixteenth century, that men were even prized for their excesses. Thus he who could longest resist the influence of liquor was deemed, in a more limited sense, as much a hero as he who swung the heaviest mace, or pointed the surest cannon in battle. The debauch in which the Abbot of Limburg and his neighbor Emich of Leiningen, were now engaged, was one of no unusual nature; for, in a country in which prelates appeared in so many other doubtful characters, it should not excite surprise that some of the class were willing to engage in a strife that and little danger, while it was so highly in favor with the noble and the great.

The reader will have seen that great progress had been made towards the issue of the celebrated encounter it is our duty to relate, even before its precise object had been formally introduced among the contending parties. But while the monks came to the struggle apprized of its motive, and prepared at all points to maintain the reputation of their ancient and hospitable brotherhood, the Count of Leiningen, with a sullen reliance on his own powers, that was somewhat increased by his contempt for priestcraft, had neglected to bestow the same care on his auxiliaries. It is scarcely necessary to add that both the Abbé and the knight of Rhodes had become heated to garrulousness, before they perfectly understood the nature of the service that was expected at their hands, or, we ought rather to say, of their heads. With this explanation we shall resume the narrative, taking up its thread some two hours later than the moment when it was last dropped.

At this particular juncture of the strife, Fathers Siegfried and Cuno had become thoroughly warmed with their endeavors, and habitual and profound respect for the Abbot was gradually giving way before the quickening currents of their blood. The eyes of the former glistened with a species of forensic ferocity, for he was ardently engaged on a controversial point with Albrecht of Viederbach, all of whose faculties appeared to be rapidly exhaling with his potations. The other Benedictine and the Abbé from time to time mingled in the dispute, in the character of seconds, while the two most interested in the issue sat, warily collecting their powers, and sternly regarding each other, like men who knew they were not engaged in idle sport.

"This is well, with thy tales of L'Isle Adam, and

the Ottoman power," continued Father Siegfried pursuing the discourse from a point, beyond which we consider it unnecessary to record all that passed —"This will do to repeat to the dames of our German courts, for the journey between these Rhenish plains and yonder island of Rhodes is far, and few are inclined to make it, in order to convict thy chiefs of neglect, or their sworn followers of forgetfulness of their vows."

"By the quality of my order! reverend Benedictine, thou pushest words to unseemliness! Is it not enough, that the chosen and the gentlest of Europe should devote soul and body to services that would better become thy lazy order—that all that is noble and brave should abandon the green fields and pleasant rivers of their native lands, to endure hot suns and sultry winds from Africa, in order to keep the unbeliever in his limits, but they must be taunted with gibes like these? Go, count the graves and number the living, if thou wouldst learn the manner in which our illustrious master held out against Solyman, or wouldst know the services of his knights!"

"It would sound ill in thy ears, were I to bid thee enter purgatory, to inquire into the fruits of our masses and prayers, and yet one and the other are equally easy to perform. Thou knowest well, that Rhodes is no longer a Christian island, and that none bearing the cross dare be seen on its shores. Go to, Count Albrecht, thy order is fallen into disuse, and it is better where it is, hid beneath the snowy mountains of the country of Nice, than it might be in the front ranks of Christendom. There is not a crone in Germany that does not bewail the backsliding of an order so esteemed of old, or a maiden that does not speak lightly of its deeds!"

"Heavenly patience! hearest thou this, Monsieur Latouche? and from the mouth of a chanting Benedictine, who passeth his days between safe walls of stone, here in the heart of the Palatinate, and his nights on a warm pallet, beyond sound even of the rushing winds, unless, in sooth, he be not bent on offices of midnight charity among the believing wives of the faithful!"

"Boy! dost presume to scandalize the Church, and dare its anger?" demanded Bonifacius, in a voice of thunder.

"Reverend Abbot," answered Albrecht, crossing himself, for habit and policy equally held him subject to the predominant authority of the age, "the little I say is more directed to the man than to his cloth."

"Let him give utterance to all he fancies," interrupted the wily Siegfried. "Is not a knight of Rhodes immaculate, and shall we refuse him right of speech?"

"It is held at the court of the chivalrous Valois," observed the Abbé, who perceived it was necessary to interfere, in order to preserve the peace, "that the defence of Rhodes was of exceeding valor, and few survived it, who did not meet with high honors from Christian hands. We have seen numberless of the brave knights among us, in the most esteemed houses of Paris, and at the merry castle of Fontainebleau, and believe me, none were more sought, or better honored. The scars of even Marignano and of Pavia are less prized than those given by the hands of the infidel."

"Thou dost well, my learned and self-denying brother," answered Siegfried, with a sneer, "to remind us of the fight of Pavia, and of thy great master's present abode! Are these tidings of late from the Castiles, or is it not permitted to thy prince to dispatch couriers to his own capital?"

"Nay, reverend monk, thou pressest with unkind allusions, and forgettest that, like thee, we are both servitors of the Church."

"We count thee not—one nor the other. Martyred St. Peter! what would become of thy keys, were they intrusted to the keeping of such hands!—Go, doff thy vanities—lay aside that attire of velvet, if thou wouldst be known as of the flock."

"Master Latouche," exclaimed Emich, who was boiling with indignation, but who preserved his self-command in order to circulate the cups, and to see that each man did true service in the prescribed contest, "tell him of his brother of Wittenberg, and of these late doings in the hive. Stick that thorn into his side, and thou shalt see him shrink like a jaded and galled steed, under a pointed spur! Who art thou, and why dost thou disturb my pleasures?"

This sudden interruption of himself was addressed by the baron to a youth, in neat but modest attire, who had just entered the banqueting-room, and who, passing by the menial that filled the glasses at the beck of his master's hand, now stood, with a firm but respectful mien, at the elbow of the speaker.

"'Tis Berchthold, my lord's forester. They bid me come to do your pleasure, noble Count."

"Thou art seasonably arrived to keep the peace between a sworn knight of Rhodes and a garrulous monk of Limburg.' This reverend Abbot would do thee favor, boy."

Berchthold bowed respectfully, and turned towards the prelate.

"Thou art the orphan of our ancient liegeman, he who bore thy name, and was well esteemed among the townsmen of Deurckheim?"

"I am the son of him your reverence means, but that he was liegeman of any of Limburg, I deny."

"Bravely answered, boy!" shouted Emich, striking his fist on the table so hard as to threaten destruction to all it held: "Ay, and as becomes thy master's follower! Hast enough, Father Bonifacius, or wilt dip deeper into the youth's catechism?"

"The young man has been tutored to respect his present ease," returned the Abbot, affecting indifference equally to the exultation of the Count and to the disrespect of his forester. "When he next comes to our confessionals, there will be occasion to give him other schooling."

"God's truth! that hour may never happen. We are half disposed to live on in our sins, and to take soldier's fortune, in these stirring times; which is ever the chance of sudden death, without the church's passport. We are fast getting of this mind—are we not, brave Berchthold?"

The youth bowed respectfully, but without answering, for he saw by the inflamed countenances and swimming eyes of all at table, that the moment was one in which explanations would be useless. Had it been possible to doubt the cause of the scene he witnessed, the manner in which glass after glass was swallowed, at the will of the cup-bearer, would have explained its nature. But, far advanced as Father Bonifacius had now become in inebriety, in common with the other guests, he retained enough of his faculties, to see that the words of Emich contained an allusion of a dangerously heretical character.

"Thou art resolved to despise our counsel and our warnings!" he exclaimed, glancing fiercely at one and the other. 'Twere better to say at once, that thy wish is to see the walls of Limburg Abbey lying on the side of Limburg hill."

"Nay, reverend and honored priest, thou pushest a few hasty words beyond their meaning. What is it to a Count of the noble house of Leiningen, that a few monks find shelter for their heads, and ease for their souls, beneath a consecrated roof within cannon-shot of his own towers. If thy walls do not tumble until hand of mine helps to unsettle them, they may stand till the fallen Angel that set them up, shall aid in their overthrow. Truly, Father Bonifacius, for a godly community, this tale of thy sanctuary's origin makes it of none of the best parentage!"

"Hear ye that!" sputtered Albrecht of Viederbach, who, though his tongue had continued to sound a sort of irregular accompaniment to his cousin's speeches, was no longer able to articulate clearly—"Here ye that! imp of St. Benedict! The devil set ye up, and the devil will be your downfall. L'Isle Adam is a saint to thy holiest; and his—good—sword——"

At this word, the knight of Rhodes succumbed, losing his balance in an animated effort to gesticulate, and fairly falling under the table. A sarcastic smile crossed the Abbot's face, at this overthrow of one of his adversaries, while Emich scowled in disdain at the ignoble exhibition made by his kinsman; who, finding it impossible to rise, resigned himself to sleep on the spot where he had fallen.

"Swallow thy Rhenish, monk, and count not on the slight advantage thou hast got in the overthrow of that prating fool," said the host, whose tones grew less and less amicable, as the plot thickened—"But to a more fitting subject; Berchthold is worthy of his lord, and is a youth that thinks of things as things appear. We may quit thy confessionals for divers reasons, as thou knowest. Here is the Monk of Erfurth! Ha! what think you of his new teaching, and of the manner in which he advises the faithful to come to the altar? You have had him at Rome, and at Worms, and among ye in many councils, and yet the honest man stands fast in all reasonable opinions. Thou hast heard of Luther, is it not so, young Berchthold?"

"'Tis certain, my Lord Count, that few in the aergerthal escape the tidings of his name."

"Then are they in danger of a most damnable

heresy!" interrupted Bonifacius, in a voice of thunder. "Why tell me of this driveller of Erfurth, Lord Emich, if thou art not in secret praying that his rebellious wishes may prosper at the Church's cost! But we mark thee, irreverent Count, and hard and griping penance may yet purge thee of these prurient fancies—" Here the Abbot, inflamed as he was with wine and resentment, paused; for the silent monk, Father Cuno, fell from his seat like a soldier shot in battle; the simple inferior having entered into the trial of heads, more with a relish for the liquor than with any thought of victory, and having, in consequence, done so much honor to the potations, as to become an easy sacrifice to the common enemy. The Abbot looked at his prostrate follower with grim indifference, showing by his hard, scowling, and angry eye, that he deemed the loss of little moment to the main result. "What matters the impotency of a fool!" he muttered, turning away to his principal and only dangerous opponent, with a full return of all his angry feelings:—"That the devils are suffered to gain a momentary and specious triumph, we are well aware, Baron of Hartenburg——"

"By my father's bones, proud priest, but thou strangely forgettest thyself! Am I not a prince of Leiningen, that one of the cowl should please to call me less?"

"I should have said the Summer Landgrave!" answered Bonifacius sneeringly, for long-smothered hatred was beginning to break through the feeble barriers that their reeling faculties still preserved. "I crave pardon of your highness; but a short reign leaves brief recollections. Even thy subjects, illustrious Emich, may be forgiven, that they know not their sovereign's title. The coronet that is worn from June to September scarce gets the fit of the head!"

"It was worn longer, Abbot, than ever head of thine will wear a saintly crown. But I forget my ancient house, and the forbearance due to a guest, in honest anger at an artful and malignant monk!"

Bonifacius bowed with seeming composure, and while each appeared to recover his moderation, in a misty recollection of the true affair in Land, the dialogue between the Abbé and Father Siegfried, which had been drowned by the stentorian lungs of the principal disputants, broke out in the momentary pause.

"Thou sayest true, reverend father," said the former, "but were our fair and sprightly dames of France to perform these pilgrimages to distant shrines, of which thou speakest, rude treatment in the wayfaring, evil company, and, haply, designing confessors, might tarnish the present lustre of their graces, and leave them less ornaments to our brilliant and gallant court, than they at present prove. No, I espouse no such dangerous opinions, but endeavor, by gentle persuasion and courtly arguments, to lead their precious souls nearer to the heaven they so well merit, and which it were scarce impious to say, they will so rarely become."

"This may be well for the towering fancies of thy French imaginations, but our slower German minds must be dealt with differently. By the mass! I would give little for the success of the confessor, that should deal only in persuasive and gentle discourse! Here, we throw out manifold hints of damnation, in plainer speech."

"I condemn no usage on speculation, Benedictine; but truly this directness of condemnation would be thought indecorous in our more refined presences. As yet, thou wilt acknowledge, we are less tainted with heresies than thy northern courts."

Here the deep voice of Emich, who had recovered a little self-command, again drowned the by-play of the subordinates.

"We are not children, most reverend Bonifacius," he resumed, "to irritate ourselves with names. That I have been denied the honors and rights of my birth and line, for one come of no direct descent, is admitted; but let it be forgotten. Thou art welcome to my board, and there is no dignitary of the church, or of thy brotherhood, that I esteem more than thee and thine, within a hard ride of these towers. Let us be friends, holy Abbot, and drink to our loving graces."

"Count Emich, I pledge thee, and pray for thee, as thou meritest. If there have been misunderstandings between our convent and thy house, they have come of the misguiding of the devil. We are a peaceful community, and one given more to prayer and a just hospitality, than to any grasping desire to enrich our coffers."

"On these points we will not dwell, father, for it is not easy for baron and abbot, layman and priest, to see at all times with the same eyes. I would that this question of authority in Deurckheim were fairly disposed of, that there might always be good neighborhood in the valley. Our hills shut in no wide plain, like yon of the river, that we must needs turn the little level land we have into a battle-ground. By the mass, most holy Abbot, but thou wouldst do well to dismiss the Elector's troops, and trust this matter between us, to gentle and friendly argument."

"If it were the last prayer I uttered, before passing into the fruition of a self-denying and holy life, princely Emich, thy wish should not want support! Have we not often professed a willingness to refer the question to the Holy Father, or any other high church authority, that can fittingly take cognizance of so knotty a point. Less than this arbitration would scarce become our apostolic mission."

"God's truth! mein Herr Wilhelm, but ye are too grasping for those who mortify the flesh! Is it meet, I ask ye, that a goodly number of valiant and pains-taking burghers should be led by shaven crowns, in the day of strife, in fair and foul, evil and good, like so many worthless women, who, having lived in the idleness and vanities of gossip and backbiting, are fain to hope that their sex's sins may be hid beneath a monk's frock? Give me up, therefore, this question of Deurckheim, and certain other rights that might be fairly written out, and the saints in Paradise shall not live in more harmony than we of the Jaegerthal."

"Truly, Lord Emich, the means of fitting us for the heavenly state thou namest have not been forgotten, since thou hast made a purgatory of the valley these many years——"

"By the mass, priest, thou again pushest thy remarks beyond discreet speech! In what manner have I done aught to bring this scandal on the neighborhood, beyond a mere forethought to mine own interest. Hast thou not opened thy abbey-gates to receive armed and irreligious men?—are not thy ears hourly wounded by rude oaths, and thy eyes affronted by sights that should be thought unseemly in a sanctuary?—Nay, that thou mayest not suppose I am ignorant of thy hidden intentions, do not the armed bands of Duke Friedrich lie at watch, this very moment, within thy cloisters?"

"We have a just caution of our rights and of the church's honor," answered Bonifacius, who scarce endeavored to conceal the contemptuous smile the question excited.

"Believe me, Abbot of Limburg, so far from being the enemy of our holy religion, I am its sworn friend; else should I long since have joined the pros elytes of this brother Luther, and have done thee harm openly."

"'Twere better than to pray at our altars by day, and to plot their fall at night."

"I swear by the life of the Emperor that thou urgest me too far, haughty priest!"

The clamor created by the Abbé and Father Siegfried here caused the two principal speakers to direct their attention, for the moment, to the secondary combatants. From a courtly dispute, the argument had got to be so confused and warm, between the latter, that each raised his voice in a vain endeavor to drown that of his adversary. It was but an instant, before the whirling senses of M. Latouche, who had only maintained his present place in the debauch by fraud, gave way to so rude an assault, and he staggered to a settee, where, gesticulating wildly, he soon sunk at his length, unable to lift his head. Father Siegfried witnessed the retreat of his mercurial foe with a grin of exultation; then he raised a ferocious shout, which, coming from lungs that had so lately chanted to the honor of God, caused the young Berchthold to shudder with horror. But the glazed eyes of the monk, and his failing countenance, betrayed an inability to endure more. After staring wildly about him, with the unmeaning idiotcy of a drunkard, he settled himself in his chair, and closed his eyes in the heavy sleep that nature unwillingly furnishes to those who abuse her gifts.

The Abbot and the Count witnessed the manner in which their respective seconds were thus put *hors de combat*, in sullen silence. Their growing warmth, and the feelings excited by the mention of their several grievances, had insensibly drawn their attention from the progress of the contest, but each now regained a certain glimpse of its nature and of its results; the recollection served to recall the temper of both, for they were too well practised in these scenes, not to understand the value of presence of mind in maintaining the command of their faculties.

"Our brother Siegfried hath yielded to the frailties of nature, noble Emich," resumed Boniface. smiling as placidly on his remaining companion, as flushed features and a heated eye would permit. "The flesh of priest can endure no more than that of layman, else would he have seen thy flasks drained of their last drop, for better intention never filled grateful heart, in doing honor to the gifts of Providence."

"Ay, thou passest thy debauches to the account of this subtilty, while we of the sword, Master Abbot, sin to-night, and ask forgiveness to-morrow, without other pretence than our pleasures. But the hood of a monk is a mask, and he who wears it thinks he hath a right to the benefit of the disguise. I would I knew, to a boddice, the number of burghers' wives thou hast shrived since Corpus Domini!"

"Jest not with the secrets of the confessional, Count Emich; the subject is too sacred for profane tongues. There has been bitter penance for greater than thou!"

"Nay, mistake me not, holy Abbot," returned the baron, hurriedly crossing himself; "but your bold talkers say there is discontent in Deurckheim on this point, and I deem it friendly to communicate the accusations of the enemy. This is a moment in which our German monks are in danger for, in sooth, thy brother of Erfurth is no driveller in his cry against Rome."

The eye of Father Boniface flashed fire, for none are so quick to meet, or so violent to resent attacks, on what they consider their rights, as those who have long been permitted to enjoy monopolies however frail or unjust may be the tenure of their possession.

"In thy heart, rude Emich, thou clingest to this heresy!" he said: "Beware, in what manner thou castest the weight of thy example and name into the scale, against the commands of God and the authority of the church! As for this Luther, a backsliding wretch, that unquiet ambition and love for a professed but misguided nun, having urged to rebellion, the devils are rejoicing in his iniquity, and imps of darkness stand ready to riot in his final and irretrievable fall."

"By the mass! father, to a plain soldier it seemeth better to wive the sister honestly, than to give all this scandal in Deurckheim, and otherwise to do violence to the peace of families on the fair plains of the Palatinate. If brother Luther hath done no more, than thou sayest here, he hath fairly cheated Satan, which is what thy community did of old when it got the evil spirit to aid in raising thy chapel, and then, with no great regard to a debtor's obligations, sent him away penniless."

"Were the truth known, Emich, I fear it would be found that thou hast faith in this silly legend!"

"If thou hast not outwitted the devil, priest, it hath been that his prudence hath kept him from bargaining with those he knows to be his betters in cunning. By the rood! 'twas a bold spirit that would grapple, wit to wit, with the monks of Limburg!"

Disdain kept the Abbot from answering, for he was too superior to vulgar tradition to feel even resentment at an imputation of this kind. His host perceived that he was losing ground, and he began to see, by the manner in which his senses were slowly receding, that he was in imminent danger of forfeiting the important stake that now depended wholly on his powers of endurance. The Abbot had a well-earned reputation of having the strongest head of all the churchmen of the Palatinate, and Count Emich, who was nowise wanting in physical excellence of this sort, began to feel that species of failing which is commonly the forerunner, as it is often the cause, of defeat. He swallowed bumper after bumper, with a reckless desire to overwhelm his antagonist, without thought of the inroads that he was producing on his own faculties. Bonifacius, who saw and felt his superiority, willingly indulged his antagonist in this feverish desire to drive the struggle to a premature issue, and several glasses were taken in a sort of sullen defiance, without a syllable issuing from the lips of either. In this strait, the Count turned his swimming eyes towards his attendants, in a vague hope that they who served him so faithfully on ordinary occasions, might aid him in the present desperate emergency.

Young Berchthold Hintermayer stood near his lord, in respectful attendance on his pleasure, for habit prevented him from withdrawing without an order. Enough had fallen from the parties in this singular contest to let him into the secret of its object. He appeared to understand the appeal, and advancing to do the office of cup-bearer, a duty that in truth required some such interference, for he who should have discharged it had been too diligently imitating those at the board, to be able any longer to acquit himself with propriety of his functions.

"If my Lord Abbot would but relieve the passing time," said Berchthold, as he poured out the wine, "by descanting more at large on this heresy, he might be the instrument of saving a doubting soul; I freely confess, that for one, I find much reason to distrust the faith of my fathers."

This was attacking the Abbot on his weakest, not to say his only vulnerable, point.

"Thou shalt smart for this, bold boy!" he cried, striking the table with a clenched fist. "Thou harborest heresies, unfledged and paltry reasoner on apostolic missions! 'Tis well—'tis well—the impudent avowal is noted!"

Emich made a sign of gratitude, for in his rage the priest took a heavy draught, unconscious of what he was about.

"Nay, my Lord, the most reverend Abbot will pardon imprudent speech in one little gifted in knowledge of this sort. Were it to strike a wild-boar, or to stop a roe-buck, or haply to do harm to my master's enemies, this hand might prove of some account; but is it matter of fair surprise that we of simple wit should be confounded, when the most learned of Germany are at a loss what to believe? I have heard it said, that Master Luther made noble answers in all the councils and wise bodies, in which he hath of late appeared."

"He spoke with the tongue of Lucifer!" roared the Abbot, fairly frothing with the violence of ungovernable rage. "Whence cometh this new and late-discovered religion! Of what stock and root is it? Why hath it been so long hid, and where is its early history? Doth it mount to Peter and Paul, or is it the invention of modern arrogance and rank conceit?"

"Nay, father, the same might be asked of Rome itself, before Rome knew an apostle. The tree is not less a tree after it hath been trimmed of its decayed branches, though it may be more comely."

Father Bonifacius was both acute and learned, and, under ordinary circumstances, even the monk of Wittenberg might have found him a stubborn and subtle casuist; but in his actual condition, the most sophistical remark, if it had but the aspect of reason, was likely to inflame him. Thus assailed, therefore he exhibited an awful picture of the ferocity of human passions when brutalized by indulgence. His eyes seemed starting from his head, his lips quivered, and his tongue refused its functions. He was now

.n the predicament, in which the Count had so lat y stood; and, though he foresaw the consequen s with the desperation of an inebriated man, he sou ;ht the renewal of his forces in the very agent which had undermined them. Count Emich himself was past intelligible utterance, but eloquence not being his strongest arm, he still maintained sufficient command of his physical powers to continue the conflict. He flourished his hand in defiance, and muttered words that seemed to breathe hatred and scorn. In this manner did a noble of an illustrious and princely house, and a mitred prelate of the church, stand at bay, with little other consciousness of the existence of the nobler faculties of their being, than that connected with the common mercenary object which had induced this trial of endurance.

"The church's malediction on ye all!" Boniface at length succeeded in uttering:—then falling back in his elbowed and well-cushioned chair, he yielded his faculties to the sinister influence of the liquor he had swallowed.

When Emich of Leiningen witnessed the overthrow of his last antagonist, a gleam of intelligence and triumph shot from beneath his shaggy brows. By a desperate effort he raised himself, and stretching forth an arm, he gained possession of the deed by which the community of Limburg formally released its claims upon the products of the disputed vineyards. Arising, with the air of one accustomed to command even in his cups, he signed for his forester to approach, and aided by his young and nervous arm, he tottered from the room, leaving the banqueting-hall, like a deserted field, a revolting picture of human infirmity in its degradation and neglect.

As the Count fell heavily upon his couch, clad as had been at table, he shook the parchment ards his young attendant, till the folds rattled

Then closing his eyes, his deep and troubled breathing soon announced, that the victor of this debauch lay like the vanquished, unconscious, feverish, and unmanned.

Thus terminated the well-known debauch of Hartenburg, a feat of physical endurance on the part of the stout baron who prevailed, that gained him little less renown among the boon companions of the Palatinate, than he would have reaped from a victory in the field ; and which, strange as it may now appear, derogated but little from any of the qualities of the vanquished.

CHAPTER VIII.

> And from the latticed gallery came a chant
> Of psalms, most saint-like, most angelical,
> Verse after verse sung out most holily."
>
> ROGERS.

THE succeeding day was the Sabbath. The morning of the weekly festival was always announced to the peasants of the Jaegerthal with the usual summons to devotion. The matin bell had been heard on the abbey walls, even before the light penetrated to the bottom of the deep vale; and all the pious had bent, in common, wherever the sounds happened to reach their ears, in praise and thanksgiving. But as the hours wore on, a more elevated display of Roman worship was prepared in the high mass, a ceremony addressed equally to the feelings and the senses.

The sun was fairly above the hills, and the season bland to seduction. The domestic cattle, relieved from their weekly toil, basked against the hill-side, ruminating in contentment, and filled with the quiet pleasures of their instinct. Children gambolled before the cottage doors; the husbandman loitered, in the habiliments that had borne the fashions of the Haard through many generations, regarding the silent growth of his crops, and the housewife hurried from place to place, in the excitement of simple domestic enjoyment. The month was the most grateful of the twelve, and well filled with hopes. The grass had reached its height, and was throwing out its exuberance, the corn was filling fast, and the vine began to give forth its clusters.

In the midst of this scene of rural tranquillity, the deep-toned bells of the abbey called the flock to its usual fold. Long practice had made the brotherhood of Limburg expert in all the duties that were necessary to the earthly administration of their functions. Even the peals of the bells were regulated and skilful. Note mournfully succeeded note, and there was not a silent dell, for miles, into which the solemn call did not penetrate. Bells were heard too from Deurckheim, and even from the wide plain beyond; but none rose fuller upon the air, or came so sweet and melancholy to the ear, as those which hung in the abbey towers.

Obedient to the summons, there was a gathering of all in the valley towards the gate of Limburg. A crowd appeared also in the direction of the gorge. for devotion, superstition, or curiosity, never failed to attract a multitude on these occasions, to witness mass in that celebrated conventual chapel. Among the latter came equally the sceptical and the believing, the young and the old, the fair and her who deemed it prudent to shade a matronly countenance with the veil, the idle, the half-converted follower of Luther, and the lover of music. It was customary for one of the brothers to preach, when mass was ended; and Limburg had many monks that were skilled in the subtleties of the times, and some even who had names for eloquence.

With a management and coquetry that enter into most human devices that are intended to act on our feelings, especially in matters that it is not thought safe to confide too much to naked reason, the peals of the bells were continued long, with a view to effect As group after group arrived, the court of the abbey slowly filled, until there appeared a congregation sufficiently numerous to gratify the self-love of even a clerical star of our own times. There was much grave salutation among the different dignitaries that were here assembled, for of all those who doff the cap in courtesy, perhaps the German is the most punctilious and respectful. As the neighboring city was fully represented in this assembly of the religious and curious, there was also a profitable display of the duties that are due to station. A herald might have obtained many useful hints, had he been there to note the different degrees of simple homage that were paid, from the Burgomaster to the Bailiff. Among the variety of idle and ill-digested remarks that are lavisned on the American people and their institutions, it is a received pleasantry to joke on their attachment to official dignities. But he who has not only seen, but observed both his own countrymen and strangers, will have had numberless occasions to remark that this, like most similar strictures, is liable to the imputation of vapidity, and of being proof of a narrow observation. The functionary that is literally a servant of the people, whatever may be his dispositions, can never triumph over his masters; and, though it be an honest and commendable ambition to wish to be so distinguished, we need only examine the institutions to see that in this, as in most other similar circumstances, there is no strict analogy between ourselves and European nations. The remark has probably been made, because a respect for official authority has been found among us, when there was the expectation, and possibly the wish, to find anarchy.

At the high mass of Limburg there was more ceremony observed in ushering the meanest village dignitary to his place in the church, than would be observed in conducting the head of this great republic to the high station he occupies; and care was had, by an agent of the convent, to see that no one should approach the altar of the Lord of the Universe, without his receiving the deference he might claim in virtue of his temporal rank! Here, where all appear in the temple as they must appear in their graves. equals in dependence on divine support as they are equals in frailty, it will not be easy to understand the hardihood of sophistry which thus teaches humility and penitence with the tongue, and invites to pride and presumption in the practice; and which, when driven to a reason for its conduct, defends itself against the accusation of inconsistency, by recriminating the charge of envy!

There had been a suitable display of ceremony when several functionaries of Deurckheim appeared but the strongest manifestation of respect was reserved for a burgher, who did not enter the gates, until the people were assembled in the body of the church. This personage, a man whose hair was just beginning to be gray, and whose solid, vigorous frame denoted full health and an easy life, came in the saddle; for at the period of which we write, there was a bridle path to the portal of Limburg. He was accompanied by a female, seemingly his spouse, who rode an ambling nag, bearing on the crupper a crone that clung to her well-formed waist, with easy, domestic familiarity, but like one unused to her seat. A fair-haired, rosy girl sat the pillion of the father, and a serving-man, in a species of official livery, closed the cavalcade.

Sundry of the more substantial citizens of Deurckheim hastened to the reception of this little party, for it was Heinrich Frey, with Meta, her mother, and Ilse, that came unexpectedly to the mass of Limburg. The affluent and flourishing citizen was ushered to the part of the church or chapel, where especial chairs were reserved for such casual visits of the neighboring functionaries, or for any noble that devotion, or accident, might lead to worship at the abbey's altars.

Heinrich Frey was a stout, hale, obstinate, sturdy burgher, in whom prosperity had a little cooled benevolence, but who, had he escaped the allurements of office and the recollection of his own success, might have passed through life, as one that was wanting in neither modesty nor humanity. He was, in short, on a diminished scale, one of those examples of desertion from the ranks of mankind to the corps d'élite of the lucky, that we constantly witness among the worldly and fortunate. While a youth, he had been sufficiently considerate for the burthens and difficulties of the unhappy; but a marriage with a small heiress, and subsequent successes, had gradually brought him to a view of things, that was more in unison with his own particular interests, than it was either philosophical or christian-like. He was a firm believer in that dictum which says none but the wealthy have sufficient interest in society to be intrusted with it control, though his own instinct might have detected the sophistry, since he was daily vacillating between opposing principles, just as they happened to affect his own particular concerns. Heinrich Frey gave freely to the mendicant, and to the industrious; but when it came to be a question of any serious melioration of the lot of either, he shook his head, in a manner to imply a mysterious political economy, and uttered shrewd remarks on the bases of society, and of things as they were established. In short, he lived in an age when Germany, and indeed all Christendom, was much agitated by a question that was likely to unsettle not only the religion of the day, but divers other vested interests; and he might have been termed the chief of the conservative party, in his own particular circle. These qualities, united to his known wealth; a reputation for high probity, which was founded on the belief that he was fully able to repair any pecuniary wrong he might happen to commit; a sturdy maintenance of his own opinions, that passed with the multitude for the consistency of rectitude; and a perfect fearlessness in deciding against all those who had not the means of disputing his decrees, had procured for him the honor of being the first Burgomaster of Deurckheim.

Were the countenance a certain index of the qualities of the mind, a physiognomist might have been at a loss to discover the motives which had induced Ulricka Hailtzinger, not only the fairest but the wealthiest maiden of the town, to unite herself in marriage with the man we have just delineated. A mild, melancholy, blue eye, that retained its lustre in despite of forty years, a better outline of features than is common to the region in which she dwelt, and a symmetry of arm and bust that, on the other hand, are rather peculiar to the natives of Germany, still furnished sufficient evidence of the beauty for which she must have been distinguished in early life. In addition to these obvious and more vulgar attractions, the matronly partner of Heinrich had an expression of feminine delicacy and intelligence, of elevated views, and even of mysterious aspirations, which rendered her a woman that a nice observer of nature might have loved to study—and have studied to love.

In personal appearance, Meta was a copy of her mother, engrafted on the more ruddy health and less abstracted habits of the father. Her character will be sufficiently developed as we proceed in the tale. We commit Ilse to the reader's imagination, which will readily conceive the sort of attendant that has been introduced.

The Herr Heinrich did not take possession of his customary post before the high altar, without causing the stir and excitement among the simple peasants of the Jaegerthal, and the truant Deurckheimers who were present, that became his condition in life. But even city importance cannot predominate for ever in the house of God, and the bustle gradually subsiding, expectation began to take precedency of civic rank.

The Abbey of Limburg stood high among the religious communities of the Rhine, for its internal decorations, its wealth, and its hospitality. The chapel was justly deemed a rare specimen of monastic taste, nor was it wanting in most of those ornaments and decorations, that render the superior buildings, devoted to the service of the Church of Rome, so imposing to the senses, and so pleasing to the admirers of solemn effect. The building was vast, and, as prevailed throughout that region and in the century of which we write, sombre. It had numerous altars, rich in marbles and pictures, each celebrated in the Palatinate for the kind mediation of the particular saint to whom it was dedicated, and each loaded with the votive offerings of the suppliant, or of the grateful. The walls and the nave were painted *al fresco*, not indeed with the pencil of Raphael, or Buonorotti, but creditably, and in a manner to heighten the beauty of the place. The choir was carved in high relief, after a fashion much esteemed, and that was admirably executed in the middle states of Europe, no less than in Italy, and whole flocks of cherubs were seen poising on the wing around the organ, the altar, and the tombs

The latter were numerous, and indicated, by their magnificence, that the bodies of those who had enjoyed the world's advantages, slept within the hallowed precincts.

At length a door, communicating with the cloisters, opened, and the monks appeared, walking in procession. At their head came the Abbot, wearing his mitre, and adorned with the gorgeous robes of his ecclesiastical office. Two priests, decorated for the duties of the altar, followed, and then succeeded the professed and the assistants, in pairs. The whole procession swept through the aisles, in stately silence; and, after making the tour of most of the church, paying homage and offering prayers at several of the most honored altars, it passed into the choir. Father Bonifacius was seated on his episcopal throne, and the rest of the brotherhood occupied the glossy stalls reserved for such occasions. During the march of the monks, the organ breathed a low accompaniment, and, as they became stationary, its last strain died in the vaulted roof. At this moment the clattering of horses' hoofs was audible without, causing the startled and uneasy priests to suspend the mass. The rattling of steel came next, and then the heavy tread of armed heels was heard on the pavement of the church itself.

Emich of Hartenburg came up the principal aisle, with the steady front of one confident of his power, and claiming deference. He was accompanied by his guests, the Knight of Rhodes and Monsieur Latouche, while young Berchthold Hintermayer kept at his elbow, like one accustomed to be in close attendance. A small train of unarmed dependants brought up the rear. There was a seat of honor, in the choir itself, and near the master altar, to which it was usual to admit princes and nobles of high consideration. Passing through the crowd, that had collected at the railing of the choir, the Count inclined towards one of the lateral aisles, and was soon face to face with the Abbot. The latter arose, and slightly recognized the presence of his guest, while the whole brotherhood imitated his example, though with greater respect; for, as we have said, it was usual to pay this homage to worldly rank, even in the temple. Emich seated himself, with a scowl on his visage, while his two noble associates found seats of honor near. Berchthold stood at hand.

An inexperienced eye could have detected no outward signs of his recent defeat, in the exterior of Wilhelm of Venloo. His muscles had already regained their tone, and his entire countenance its usual expression of severe authority, a quality for which it was more remarkable than for any lines of mortification or of thought. He glanced at the victor, and then, by a secret sign, communicated with a lay brother. At this moment the mass commenced.

Of all the nations of Christendom, this, compared with its numbers, is the least connected with the Church of Rome. The peculiar religious origin of the people, their habits of examination and mental independence, and their prejudices (for the Protestant is no more free from this failing than the Catholic,) are likely to keep them long separated from any policy, whether of church or state, that exacts faith without investigation, or obedience without the right to remonstrate. An opinion is sedulously disseminated in the other hemisphere, that busy agents are rapidly working changes in this respect, and a powerful party is anxiously anticipating great ecclesiastical and political results from the return of the American nation to the opinions of their ancestors of the middle ages. Were the fact so, it would give us little concern, for we do not believe sal vation to be the peculiar province of sects; but, had we any apprehensions of the consequences of such a conversion, they would not be excited by the accidental accumulations of emigrants in towns, or on the public works in which the country is so actively engaged. We believe that where one native Protestant becomes a Catholic in America, ten emigrant Catholics drop quietly into the ranks of the prevailing sects; and, without at all agitating the point of which is the gainer or the loser by the change, we shall proceed to describe the manner of the mass, as a ceremony, that ninety-nine in a hundred of our readers have never had, nor probably ever will have, an opportunity of witnessing.

There is no appeal to the feelings of man, which has given rise to opinions so decidedly at variance as those which are entertained of the Roman ritual. To one description of Christians, these ceremonies appear to be vain mummeries, invented to delude, and practised for unjustifiable ends; while, to another, they contain all that is sublime and imposing in human worship. As is usual in most cases of extreme opinions, the truth would seem to lie between the two. The most zealous Catholic errs when he would maintain the infallibility of all who minister at the altar, or when he overlooks the slovenly and irreverent manner in which the most holy offices are so frequently performed; and, surely, the Protestant who quits the temple, in which justice has been done to the formula of this church, without perceiving that there is deep and sublime devotion in its rites, has steeled his feelings against the admission of every sentiment in favor of a sect that he is willing to proscribe. We belong to neither class, and shall, therefore, endeavor to represent things as they have been seen, not disguising or affecting a single emotion because our fathers happened to take refuge in this western world, to set up altars of a different shade of faith.

The interior of the Abbey-church of Limburg, as has just been stated, was renowned in Germany for its magnificence. Its vaulted roof was supported by many massive pillars, and ornamented with scriptural stories, by the best pencils of that region. The grand altar was of marble, richly embellished with agate, containing as usual a labored representation of the blessed Mary and her deified child. A railing of exquisite workmanship and richly gilded, excluded profane feet from this sanctified spot, which, in addition to its fixtures, was now glittering with vessels of gold and precious stones, being decorated for the approaching mass. The officiating priests wore vestments stiffened with golden embroidery, while the inferior attendants were as usual clad in white, and bound with scarfs of purple.

Upon this scene of gorgeous and elaborate splendor, in which the noble architecture united with the minute preparations of the service, to lead the spirit to lofty contemplations, the chant of the monks, and the tones of the organ, broke in a deep and startling appeal to the soul. Lives dedicated to the practices of their community, had drilled the brotherhood into perfection, and scarce a note issued among the vaults that was not attuned to the desired effect. Trombones, serpents, and viols, lent their aid to increase the solemn melody of powerful masculine voices, which were so blended with the wind instrument as to comprise but one deep, grand, and grave sound of praise. Count Emich turned on his seat, clenching the handle of his sword, as if the clamor of the trumpet were in his ears: then his unquiet glance met that of the Abbot, and his chin fell upon a hand. As the service proceeded, the zeal of the brotherhood seemed to increase, and, as it was afterwards remarked, on no occasion had the mass of Limburg, at all times known for its power in music, been so remarkable for its strong and stirring influence. Voice rolled above voice, in a manner that must be heard to be understood, and there were moments when the tones of the instruments, full and united as they were, appeared drowned in the blending of a hundred human aspirations. From the deepest of one of these solemn peals there arose a strain, at whose first tone all other music was hushed. It was a single human voice, of that admixture of the male and female tones which seems nearest allied to the supernatural, being in truth, a contr'alto of great compass, roundness, and sweetness. Count Emich started, for, when these heavenly strains broke upon his ear, they seemed to float in the vault above the choir; nor could he, as the singer was concealed, assure himself of the delusion, while the solo lasted. He dropped his sword, and gazed about him, for the first time that morning, with an expression of human charity. The lips of young Berchthold parted in admiration, and as he just then met the blue eye of Meta, there was an exchange of gentle feeling in that quiet and secret glance. In the mean time, the chant proceeded. The single unearthly voice that had so stirred the spirits of the listeners ceased, and a full chorus of the choir concluded the hymn.

The Count of Leiningen drew a breath so heavy that it was audible to Bonifacius. The latter suffered his countenance to unbend, and, as in the case of the youthful pair, the spirit of concord appeared to soothe the tempers of these fierce rivals. But here commenced the ritual of the mass. The rapid utterance of the officiating priest, gesticulations which lost their significance by being blended and indistinct, and prayers in a tongue that defeated their object, by involving instead of rendering the medium of thought noble and clear, united to weaken the effect produced by the music. Worship lost its character of inspiration, by assuming that of business, neither attracting the imagination, influencing the feelings, nor yet sufficiently convincing the reason. Abandoning all these persuasive means, too much was left to the convictions of a naked and settled belief.

Emich of Hartenburg gradually resumed his repulsive mien, and the effect of all that he had so lately felt was lost in cold indifference to words that he did not comprehend. Even young Berchthold sought the eye of Meta less anxiously, and both the Knight of Rhodes and Monsieur Latouche gazed listlessly towards the throng grouped before the railing of the choir. In this manner did the service commence and terminate. There was another hymn, and a second exhibition of the power of music, though with an effect less marked than that which had been produced when the listeners were taken by surprise.

Against a column, near the centre of the church, was erected a pulpit. A monk rose from his stall, at the close of the worship, and, passing through the crowd, ascended its stairs like one about to preach. It was Father Johan, a brother known for the devotedness of his faith and the severity of his opinions. The low receding forehead, the quiet but glassy eye, and the fixedness of the inferior members of the face, might readily have persuaded a physiognomist that he beheld a heavy enthusiast. The language and opinions of the preacher did not deny the expectations excited by his exterior. He painted, in strong and ominous language, the dangers of the sinner, narrowed the fold of the saved within metaphysical and questionable limits, and made frequent appeals to the fears and to the less noble passions of his audience. While the greater number in the church kept aloof, listening indifferently, or gazing at the monuments and other rich decorations of the place, a knot of kindred spirits clustered around the pillar that supported the preacher's desk, deeply sympathizing in all his pictures of pain and desolation.

The sharp, angry, and denunciatory address of Father Johan was soon ended; and, as he re-entered the choir, the Abbot arose and retired to the cloisters, followed by most of the brotherhood. But neither the Count of Hartenburg, nor any of his train, seemed disposed to quit the church so soon. An air of expectation appeared, also, to detain most of those in the body of the building. A monk, towards whom many longing eyes had been cast, yielded to the general and touching appeal, and quitting his stall, one of high honor, he took the place just vacated by Father Johan.

This movement was no sooner made, than the name of Father Arnolph, the Prior, or the immediate spiritual governor of the community, was buzzed among the people. Emich arose, and, accompanied by his friends, took a station near the pulpit, while the dense mass of uplifted and interested faces, that filled the middle aisle, proclaimed the interest of the congregation. There was that in the countenance and air of Father Arnolph to justify this plain demonstration of sympathy. His eye was mild and benevolent, his forehead full, placid, and even, and the whole character of his face was that of winning philanthropy. To the influence of this general and benevolent expression, must be added evident signs of discipline, much thought, and meek hope.

The spiritual part of such a man was not likely to belie the exterior. His doctrine, like that of the divine being he served, was charitable and full of love. Though he spoke of the terrors of judgment, it was with grief rather than with menace: and it was when dwelling on the persuasive and attractive character of faith, that he was most earnest and eloquent. Again Emich found his secret intentions shaken, and his frown relaxed to gleamings of sympathy and interest. The eye of the preacher met that of the stern baron, and, without making an alarming change of manner, he continued, as it were, by a natural course of thought—"Such is the church in its purity, my hearers, let the errors, the passions, or the designs of man pervert it in what manner they may. The faith I preach is of God, and it partakes of the godlike qualities of his divine essence. He who would impute the sins of its mistaken performance to aught but his erring creatures, casts odium on that which is instituted for his own good; and he who would do violence to its altars, lifts a hand against a work of omnipotence!"

With these words in his ears, Emich of Hartenburg turned away, and passed musingly up the church.

CHAPTER IX.

"Japhet, I cannot answer thee."
BYRON.

THE Abbey of Limburg owed its existence and its rich endowments chiefly to the favor of an emperor of Germany. In honor of this great patron, an especial altar, and a gorgeous and elaborate tomb, had been erected. Similar honors had been also paid to the Counts of Leiningen, and to certain other noble families of the vicinity. These several altars were in black marble, relieved by ornaments of white, and the tombs were decorated with such heraldic devices as marked the particular races of the different individuals. They stood apart from those already described in the principal church, in a sort of crypt, or semi-subterranean chapel, beneath the choir. Thither Count Emich held his way, when he quitted the column against which he had leaned, while listening to the sermon of Father Arnolph.

The light of the upper church had that soft and melancholy tint, which is so peculiar and so ornamental to a Gothic edifice. It entered through high, narrow windows of painted glass, coloring all within with a hue that it was not difficult for the imagination to conceive had some secret connexion with the holy character of the place. The depth and the secluded position of the chapel rendered this light still more gloomy and touching in the crypt. When the Count reached the pavement, he felt its influence deeply, for few descended into that solemn and hallowed vault without becoming sensible to the religious awe that reigned around. Emich crossed himself, and, as he passed before the altar reared by his race, he bent a knee to the mild and lovely female countenance that was there to represent the Mother of Christ. He thought himself alone, and he uttered a prayer; for, though Emich of Leiningen was a man that rarely communed seriously with God, when exposed to worldly and deriding eyes, he had in his heart deep reverence for his power. As he arose, a movement at his elbow attracted a look aside.

"Ha!—Thou here, Herr Prior!" he exclaimed suppressing as much of his surprise as self-command enabled him to do with success; "Thou art swift in thy passage from the stall to the pulpit, and swifter from the pulpit to the chapel!"

'We that are vowed to lives of monkish devotion, need to be often at all. Thou wert kneeling, Emich, before the altar of thy race?"

"By St. Benedict, thy patron! but thou hast, in good sooth, found me in some such act, holy father. A weakness came over me, on entering into this gloomy place, and I would fain do reverence to the spirits of those who have gone before me."

"Callest thou the desire to pray a weakness? At what shrine could one of thy name worship more fittingly than at this, which has been reared and enriched by the devout of his own kindred; or in what better mood canst thou look into thyself, and call upon divine aid, than in that thou hast mentioned?"

"Herr Prior, thou overlookest the occasion of my visit, which is to hear the Abbey mass, and not to confess and be shrived."

"It is long since thou hast had the benefit of these sacred offices, Emich!"

"Thou hast done well in thy way, father, at the desk; and I question not that the burghers of Deurckheim and their gossips will do thee credit in their private discourses. Thy fame as a preacher is not of mean degree even now, and this effort of to-day would well-nigh gain thee a bishopric, were the women of our valley in the way of moving Rome. How fareth it with the most holy Abbot this morning, and with those two pillars of the community, the Fathers Siegfried and Cuno?"

"Thou sawest them in their places at the most holy mass."

"'Fore heaven! but they are worthy companions! Believe me, father, more honest boon associates do not dwell in our merry Palatinate, nor men that I love in a better fashion, according to their merits! Did'st hear, reverend Prior, of their visit to Hartenburg, and of their deeds in the flesh?"

"The humor of thy mind is quickly changed

Herr Count, and pity 'tis 'twere thus. I came not here to listen to tales of excesses in thy hold, nor of any forgetfulness of those, who having sworn to better things, have betrayed that they are merely men.

"Ay, and stout men, if any such dwell in the empire! I prize my good name as another, or I would tell thee the number of vessels that my keeper of the cellar sweareth are no better than so many men-at-arms fallen in a rally or an onset."

"This love of wine is the curse of our region and of the times. I would that none of the treacherous liquor should again enter the gates of Limburg!"

"God's justice! reverend Prior, thou wilt in sooth find some decrease of quantity in future," returned Emich, laughing, "for the disputed vineyards have at last found a single, and, though it might better come from thee, as one that hath often looked into my interior, as it were, by confession, a worthy master. I pledge thee the honor of a noble, that not a flask of that which thou so contemnest shall ever again do violence to thy taste."

The Count cast a triumphant glance at the monk, in the expectation, and possibly in the hope, that, notwithstanding his professions of moderation, some lurking signs of regret might betray themselves at this announcement of the convent's loss. But Father Arnolph was what he seemed, a man devoted to the holy office he had assumed, and one but little influenced by worldly interests.

"I understand thee, Emich," he said mildly, but unmoved. "This scandal was not wanting at such a moment, to bring obloquy upon a reverend and holy church, against which its enemies have been permitted to make rude warfare, for reasons that are concealed in the inscrutable mysteries of him who founded it."

"Thou speakest in reason, monk, for, to say truth,

yon fellow of Saxony, and his followers, who are any thing but few or weak, begin to move many in this quarter to doubts and disobedience. Thou must most stoutly hate this brother Luther in thy heart, father !"

For the first time that day, the countenance of the Prior lost its even expression of benevolence. But the change was so imperceptible to a vulgar eye, as to escape the scrutiny of the Count; and the feeling, a lingering remnant of humanity, was quickly mastered by one so accustomed to hold the passions in subjection.

"The name of the schismatic hath troubled me !" returned the Prior, smiling mournfully at the consciousness of his own weakness; "I hope it has not been with a feeling of personal dislike. He stands on a frightful precipice, and from my soul do I pray, that not only he, but all the deluded that follow in his dangerous track, may see their peril in time to retire unharmed !"

"Father, thou speakest like one that wishest good to the Saxon rather than harm !"

"I think I may say, the words do not belie the thoughts."

"Nay, thou forgettest the damnable heresies he practiseth, and overlooketh his motive ! Surely one that can thus sell soul and body for love of a wanton nun, hath little claim to thy charity !"

There was a slight glow on the temples of Father Arnolph.

"They have attributed to him this craven passion," he answered, "and they have tried to prove, that a mean wish to partake of the pleasures of the world, lies at the bottom of his rebellion; but I believe it not, and I say it not."

"God's truth ! thou art worthy of thy holy office, Herr Prior, and I honor thy moderation. Were there more like thee among us, we should have a better neighborhood, and less meddling with the concerns of others. With thee, I see myself no such necessity of his openly wiving the nun, for it is very possible to enjoy the gifts of life even under a cowl, should it be our fortune to wear it."

The monk made no answer, for he perceived he had to do with one unequal to understanding his own character.

"Of this we will say no more," he rejoined, after a brief and painful pause; "let us look rather to thine own welfare. It is said, Count Emich, that thou meditatest evil to this holy shrine; that ambition, and the longings of cupidity, have tempted thee to plot our abbey's fall, in order that none may stand between thine own baronial power and the throne of the Elector!"

"Thou art less unwilling to form unkind opinions of thy nearest neighbor, than of that mortal enemy of the Church, Luther, it would appear, Herr Prior. What hast thou seen in me, that can embolden one of thy charity to hazard this accusation?"

"I do but hazard what all in our convent think and dread. Hast thou reflected well, Emich, of this sacrilegious enterprise, and of what may be its fruits? Dost thou recall the objects for which these holy altars were reared, or the hand that laid the corner-stone of the edifice thou wouldst so profanely overthrow?"

"Look you, good Father Arnolph, there are two manners of viewing the erection of thy convent, and more especially of this identical church in which we stand. One of our traditions sayeth that the arch-knave himself had his trowel in thy masonry."

"Thou art of too high lineage, of blood too noble, and of intelligence too ripe, to credit the tale."

"These are points in which I pretend not to dip too deeply. I am no scholar of Prague or Wittenberg, that thou shouldst put these questions so closely to me. It were well that the brotherhood had bethought itself of this imputation in season, that the question might have been settled, for or against, as justice needed, when the learned and great among our fathers were met at Constance, in grave and general council."

Father Arnolph regarded his companion in serious concern. He too well knew the deplorable ignorance, and the consequent superstition, in which even the great of his time were involved, to manifest surprise; but he also knew the power the other wielded sufficiently to foresee the evils of such a union between force and ignorance. Still it was not his present object to combat opinions that were only to be removed by time and study, if indeed they can ever be eradicated, when fairly rooted in the human mind. He pursued his immediate design, therefore, avoiding a discussion, which, at that moment, might prove worse than useless.

"That the finger of evil mingles more or less with all things that come of human agency, may be true," he continued, taking care that the expression of his eye should neither awaken the pride, nor arouse the obstinacy of the noble—"but when altars have been reared, and when the worship of the Most High God hath continued for ages, we have reason to hope that his holy spirit presideth in majesty and love around the shrines. Such hath been the case with Limburg, Count Emich: and doubt it not, we who stand here, holding this discourse, stand also in the immediate presence of that dread Being who created heaven and earth, who guideth our lives, and who will judge us in death!"

"God help us, Herr Prior! Thou hast already done thy office in the desk this day, and I see no occasion that thou shouldst doubly perform a function, that was so well acquitted at first. I like not the manner of being ushered, as it were unannounced, into so dread a presence as this thou hast just proclaimed. Were it but the Elector Friedrich. Emich of Leiningen could not presume to this familiarity, without some consultation as to its fitness."

"In the eyes of the Being we mean, Electors and Emperors are equally indifferent. He loveth the meek, and the merciful, and the just, while he scourgeth them that deny his authority. But thou hast named thy feudal prince, and I will question thee in a manner suited to thy habits. Thou art, in truth, Emich of Leiningen, a noble of name in the Palatinate, and one known to be of long-established authority in these regions. Still art thou second, or even third, in worldly command, in this thy very country. The Elector and the Emperor both hold thee in check, and either is strong enough to destroy thee at pleasure, in thy vaunted hold of Hartenburg."

"To the last I yield the means, if thou wilt, worthy Prior"—interrupted the Count—"but for the first, he must needs dispose of his own pressing enemies, before he achieves this victory!"

Father Arnolph understood the other's meaning, for it was no secret that Friedrich was, just then, so pressed as to sit on a tottering throne; a circumstance that was known to have encouraged the long meditated designs of the Count of Hartenburg to get rid of a community, that thwarted his views, and diminished his local authority.

"Forgetting the Elector, we will turn only to the Emperor, then," rejoined the Prior. "Thou believest him to be in his palace, and remote from thy country, and certainly he hath here no visible force to restrain thy rebellious hand. We will imagine that a family he protected—nay, that he loved—stood in the way of some of thy greedy projects, and that the tempter had persuaded thee it would be well to remove it, or to destroy with the strong hand. Art thou weak enough, Count Emich, to listen to such advice, when thou knowest that the arm of Charles is long enough to reach from his distant Madrid to the most remote corner of Germany, and that his vengeance would be as sure as it would be fearful?"

"It would be a bold warfare, Herr Prior, that of Emich of Leiningen against Charles Quintus! Left to mine own humor, holy monk, I would rather choose another enemy."

"And yet thou wouldst war with one mightier than he! Thou raisest thy impotent arm, and thy audacious will, against thy God! Thou wouldst despise his promises, profane his altars, nay, thou wouldst fain throw down the tabernacle that he hath reared! Dost thou think that omnipotence will be a nerveless witness of this sin; or that an eternal and benign wisdom will forget to punish?"

"By St. Paul! thou puttest the matter altogether in thine own interest, Father Arnolph, for there is yet no proof that this Abbey of Limburg hath any such origin, or, if it had, that it hath not fallen into disfavor, by the excesses of its own professed. 'Twere well to send for the right reverend Abbot, and those pillars of sanctity the Fathers Cuno and Siegfried, to bear witness in thy behalf. God's wisdom! I reason better with those worthies, in such a matter, than with thee!"

Emich laughed, the sound echoing in that vaulted chapel to the ears of the monk, like the scoffing of a demon. Still, the natural equity of Father Arnolph told him that there was too much to justify the taunt of the noble, for he had long and bitterly mourned the depravity of many of the brotherhood.

"I am not here to sit in judgment on those who err, but to defend the shrines at which I worship, and to warn thee from a fatal sin. If thy hand is ever lifted against these walls, it is raised against that which God hath blessed, and which God will avenge. But thou art of human feeling, Emich of Hartenburg; and though, doubting of the sacred character of that which thou wouldst fain destroy, thou canst not deceive thyself concerning these tombs—In this holy chapel have prayers been often raised, and masses said, for the souls of thine own line!"

The Count of Leiningen looked steadily at the speaker. Father Arnolph had placed himself, without design, near the opening which communicated between that sombre chapel and the superior church. Rays of bright light shot through the eastern window, and fell upon the pavement at his feet, throwing around his form the mild and solemn lustre which comes from the stained glass of the Gothic ages. The services of the morning had also spread throughout the entire building, that soothing atmosphere which is usually the attendant of Roman worship. The incense had penetrated to the crypt, and unconsciously the warlike noble had felt its influence quieting his nerves and lulling the passions. All who have entered the principal Basilica of modern Rome, have been subject to a combination of moral and physical causes that produce the result we mean, and which, though more striking in that vast and glorious pile, resembling a world with attributes and an atmosphere of its own, is also felt in every Catholic temple of consequence in a lessened degree.

"Here lie my fathers, Arnolph," answered the Count, huskily; "and here, as thou sayest, have masses been said for their souls!"

"And thou contemnest their graves—thou wouldst violate even their bones!"

"'Twere not an act for a Christian!"

"Look hither, Count. This is the monument of

the good Emich, thy ancestor. He honored his God, and did not scruple to worship at our altars."

"Thou knowest, holy Prior, that I have often bared my soul at thy knees."

"Thou hast confessed, and hast been shrived; that thou didst not lay up future griefs——"

"Say rather damnation"—interrupted one behind, whose voice, issuing suddenly from that sepulchral chapel, seemed to come from the tombs themselves —"Thou triflest, reverend Prior, with our holy mission, to deal thus tenderly with so sore a sinner."

The Count of Leiningen had started, and even quailed, at the first words of interruption; but looking around, he beheld the receding front, the sunken eye, and the bending person of Father Johan."

"Monks, I leave you," said Emich, firmly. "It is good for ye to pray, and to frequent these gloomy altars; but I, who am a soldier, cannot waste further time in your vaults. Herr Prior, farewell. Thou hast a guardian that will protect the good."

Before the Prior could recover his voice, for he too had been taken by surprise, the Count stalked, with a heavy footstep, up the marble stairs, and the tread of his armed heel was soon heard on the flags above.

CHAPTER X.

"The way is but short; away—"
Armado.

While all must be conscious of the fearful infirmities that beset human nature, there are none so base as not to know that their being contains the seeds of that godlike principle which still likens them to their divine Creator. Virtue commands the respect of man, in whatever accidental stage of civilization, or of mental improvement, he may happen to exist; and he who practises its precepts is certain of the respect, though he may not always secure the protection of his contemporaries.

As the Count of Leiningen walked down the rich and vast aisle of the Abbey-church, his thoughts vacillated between the impressions produced by the Prior, and his latent, but still predominant, intentions. He might have been likened to one who listened to the councils of a good and of an evil genius; that exhorting to forbearance and mercy, and this tempting to violence by the usual array of flattery and hopes. While he brooded over the exactions of the community, which were founded on a legal superiority that was alike hurtful to his power and galling to his pride, its manner of thwarting his views, and its constant opposition to his supremacy in the valley, motives of enmity that were justly heightened by the dissolute and audacious deportment of too many of its members, the effect of all was secretly opposed by the image of Father Arnolph, surrounded by the mild and noble characteristics of Christian virtue. Emich could not, though he fain would, chase from his imagination the impression of meekness, charity, and of self-denial, that a long acquaintance with the monk had made, and which the recent interview had served both to freshen and to render more deep. But a spectacle was prepared to meet his eyes in the court of the convent, that did as much towards weakening this happy influence of the Prior, by setting the pride of the noble in opposition to his better feelings, as could have been wished by the bitterest enemy of Limburg.

It has been said that the outer wall of the Abbey encircled the entire brow of the hill, or mountain, on which the convent stood. Though the buildings were spacious and numerous, the size of the little plain on the summit left ample space for exercise and air. Besides the cloisters, which were vast, though possessing the character of monkish seclusion, there were gardens in the rear of the Abbot's abode, and a court of considerable extent, immediately in front of the church. Athwart this court, in which sundry groups of the late congregation yet lingered, was drawn up, in military order, a band of soldiers, wearing the colors, and acknowledging the authority, of the Elector Friedrich. The secret signal given by Father Bonifacius, when the Count entered the choir, had prepared this unwelcome sight for his neighbor.

While the men-at-arms leaned on their arquebuses, in grave attention to discipline, the Knight of Rhodes and the Abbé were occupied in paying their court to the fair wife of the Burgomaster of Deurckheim, and to her scarce fairer daughter. Young Berchthold stood aloof; watching the interview with feelings allied equally to envy and jealousy.

"A fair morning and a comfortable mass to you, high-born Emich!" cried the husband and father heartily, but lifting his cap, as the noble approached the spot where the burgher stood, waiting for this meeting ere he put foot into the stirrup; "I had thought the sight of your fathers' altar was like to cheat me of this honor, and to send me away without a word from your friendly and much-prized grace."

"Between thee and me, Heinrich, this slight could not happen," answered the Count, grasping the hand of the Burgomaster, which he squeezed with the cordiality and vigor of a soldier. "How fareth it with all in Deurckheim, that town of my affection, not to say of my right?"

"As you could wish, noble Count, and well-disposed to the house of Leiningen. In all that pertaineth to love of your name and race, we lack nothing."

"This is well, honest Heinrich; it may yet be better—But thou wilt do me grace this summer morning?"

"Nay, it is for your grace to command in this particular, and for one like me to obey."

"Herr Heinrich, hast looked well at these knaves of Friedrich? Ha! are they not melancholy and ill-disposed at being cooped with Benedictines, when there are stirring times in the Palatinate, and when their master hath as much as he can do to hold his court in Heidelberg! Seest thou aught of this?"

Emich had dropped his voice, and the burgher was not a man to express more in answer, than the circumstances actually required. He looked eloquently, however, and the exchange of glances between him and the Count betrayed the nature of the understanding that connected the castle and the city.

"You spoke of commanding my duty, mein Herr Graf, and it is fitting I should know in what manner to do you pleasure."

"Nay, 'tis no pain-giving penance I ask. Turn thy horse's head towards Hartenburg, and share of my poor fare, with a loving welcome, for an hour or so."

"I would it were within compass, my Lord Count," returned Heinrich, casting a doubting look towards Meta and his wife—"but these Sunday masses are matters in which the women love to deal; and from the first sound of the matin bell, till we shut the gates at even, I scarce call myself master of a thought."

"By the Virgin! 'Twould seem ill indeed, did not Hartenburg contain a roof to shelter all of thy name and love."

"There are noble gentlemen already on your hospitality, and I would not fain——"

"Name them not. This in the gay doublet, that weareth the white cross, is but a houseless Knight of Rhodes, one that wandereth like the dove from the ark, uncertain where to place his foot; and he of black vestments, an idle Abbé from among the French, who doth little else but prate with the women. Leave thy female gender in their hands, for they are much accustomed to these gallantries."

"Zum Henker! most nobly born eccellenz, I never doubted their handiness in all idlenesses; but my wife hath little humor for vain attentions of this nature, and not to conceal from my lord any of our humors, I will confess it is as little to my pleasure to witness so much ceremony with a woman. Were the well-born Ermengarde, your noble consort, in the castle, my female charge might be glad to pay their court to her, but in her absence I doubt that they will cause more encumbrance than they will afford satisfaction."

"Name it not, honest Heinrich, but leave the matter to me. As for these idlers, I will find them occupation, when fairly out of the saddle; so will I not excuse the youngest of thy name."

The warm, frank manner of the noble prevailed,

though the arrangement was not altogether agreeable to the Burgomaster; but in that age hospitality was always of so direct a character as seldom to admit denial without sufficient excuse. Emich now paid his court to the females. Smoothing his moustache and beard, he saluted the cheeks of Ulricke, with affectionate freedom, and then, presuming on his years and rank, he pressed a kiss on the ruby lips of Meta. The girl blushed and laughed, and in her confusion curtesied, as if in acknowledgment of the grace from one of so high quality. Heinrich himself, though he so little liked the coquetry of the strangers, witnessed these liberties not only without alarm but with evident contentment.

"Many thanks, noble Emich, for this honor to my women," he cried, lifting his bonnet again. "Meta is not used to these compliments, and she scarce knoweth rightly how to acknowledge the grace, for to say truth, it is not often that her cheek feeleth the tickling of a beard. I am no saluter of her sex, and there are none in Deurckheim that may so presume."

"St. Denis defend me!" exclaimed the Abbé; "in what shameful negligence have we fallen!" saluting the mild Ulricke on the instant, and repeating the same ceremony with the daughter, so suddenly, as to leave none present time to recover from their surprise. "Sir Knight of Rhodes, we appear in this affair as but of indifferent breeding!"

"Hold, cousin of Viederbach," said Emich, laughing, while he placed a hand before his kinsman—'We forget, all this time, that we are in the court of Limburg, and that salutations which savor so much of earth may scandalize the holy Benedictines. We will to horse, and keep our gallantries for a better season."

The forward, impatient movement of young Berchthold was self-checked, and, swallowing his discontent, he turned aside to conceal his vexation.

In the mean time, the whole party prepared to mount. Although repulsed in his effort to obtain a salute from the fair girl, who had so passively received these liberties from his kinsman and the Abbé, the Knight of Rhodes busied himself in assisting the damsel upon the crupper of her father's saddle. A similar office was performed for Ulricke by the Count of Leiningen himself, and then the noble threw his own booted and heavy leg across the large and strong-jointed war-horse that was pawing the pavement of the court. The others imitated his example, even to the mounted servitors, who were numerous; when, doing stately reverence to the large crucifix that stood before them, the whole cavalcade ambled from the court.

There were many curious spectators around the outer gate, among whom were sundry of the more humble dependants of Hartenburg, purposely collected there, by an order of their lord, in the event of any sudden violence arising from his visit to the Abbey, together with a crowd of mendicants.

"Alms, great Emich! Alms, worthy and wealthy Burgomaster! God's blessing on ye both, and holy St. Benedict heed ye in his prayers! We are a-hungred and a-cold, and we crave alms at your honorable hands!"

"Give the rogues a silver pence," said the Count to the purse-bearer, who rode in his train—"They have a starving look, in sooth. These godly Benedictines have, of late, been so busied between their garrison and their masses, that they have forgotten to feed their poor. Come nearer, friend; art of the Jaegerthal?"

"No, noble Count. I come from a pilgrimage to a distant shrine, but want and suffering have befallen me by the way."

"Hast pressed the monks for charity? or dost

thou find them toc much engaged in godliness to remember human suffering?"

"Great Count, they give freely; but where there are many mouths to feed, there needs be much gold. I say naught against the holy community of Limburg, which is godly in charity, as in grace."

"Give the knave a kreutzer;" growled Heinrich Frey; "hast thou aught to show in the way of authority for undertaking this pilgrimage, and for assailing the Elector's subjects and servitors in a public horse-path?"

"Naught but this, illustrious Burgomaster,"—Heinrich wore his chain of office—"naught but the commands of my confessor, and this pass of our own chief men."

"Callest this naught? Thou speakest of a legal instrument of high quality, an' it were but a copy of silly rhymes! Hold! thou must not be led into temptation by too much want. Meta, wench, hast a kreutzer?"

"Here is a silver pence, that may better suit the pilgrim's necessities, father."

"God keep thee, child! Dost expect to escape want thyself, with such prodigality? But stay—there are many of them, and the piece justly distributed might do good. Come nearer, friends. Here is a silver zwanziger, which you will divide honestly into twenty parts, of which two are for the stranger, for to him are we most indebted by the commands of God, and one for each inhabitant of the valley, not forgetting the poor woman that, in your haste, and by reason of her years, you have prevented from drawing near. For this boon, I ask prayers of you in behalf of the Elector, the city of Deurckheim, and the family of Frey."

So saying, the Burgomaster pushed ahead, and was soon at the foot of the mountain of Limburg. The train of footmen, who had lingered to witness the largess of the magistrate, and who had considered the indifference of Emich as what was no more than natural in one, placed by Providence in a situation so far removed from vulgar wants, was about to follow, when a lay-brother of the convent touched one of the party on the arm, signing for him to re-enter the court.

"Thou art needed further, friend," whispered the lay-brother. "Amuse thyself with these men-at-arms till they retire; then seek the cloisters."

A nod sufficed to tell the lay-brother that he was understood, and he immediately disappeared. The follower of Count Emich did as commanded, loitering in the court until the object of the Abbot was accomplished, that of exhibiting the protection of the Elector to his dangerous neighbor, and the arquebusiers marched to their quarters. The road was no sooner clear, than the peasant who had been detained proceeded to do as he had been ordered.

In each conventual edifice of the other hemisphere, there is an inner court surrounded by low and contemplative arcades, called the cloisters. The term, which is given to the seclusion of monastic life in general, and to the objects of the institution itself, in an architectural sense, is limited to the secluded and sombre piazzas just mentioned. When this part of the building is decorated, as often happens, with the elaborate ornaments of the Gothic style, it is not easy to conceive a situation more happily imagined for the purposes of reflection, self-examination, and religious calm. To us the cloisters have ever appeared pregnant with the poetry of monkish existence, and, Protestant as we are, we never yet entered one without feeling the influence of that holy and omnipotent power that is thought to be propitiated by conventual seclusion. In Italy, the land of vivid thought and of glorious realities, the pencils of the greatest masters have been put in requisition to give the cloisters a mild attraction, blended with lessons of instruction, that are in strict consonance with their uses. Here are found some of the finest remains of Raphael, of Domenichino, and of Andrea del Sarto; and the traveller now enters vaulted galleries, that the monk so long paced in religious hope or learned abstraction, to visit the most prized relics of art.

The dependant of Count Emich had no difficulty in finding his way to the place in question, for, as usual, there was a direct communication between the cloisters of Limburg and the church. By entering the latter, and taking a lateral door, which was known to lead to the sacristy, he found himself beneath the arcades, in the midst of the touching seclusion described. Against the walls were tablets with Latin inscriptions, in honor of different brothers who had been distinguished by piety and knowledge; and here and there was visible, in ivory or stone, that constant monitor of Catholic worship, the crucifix.

The stranger paused, for a single monk paced the arcades, and his mien was not inviting for one who doubted of his reception. At least so thought the dependant of Emich, who might easily have mistaken the chastened expression of Father Arnolph's features, clouded as they now were with care, for severity.

"What wouldst thou?" demanded the Prior, when a turn brought him face to face with the intruder.

"Reverend monk, thy much-prized blessing."

"Kneel, and receive it, son. Thou art doubly blest; in seeking consolation from the Church, and in avoiding the fatal heresies of the times."

The Prior repeated the benediction, made the usual sign of grace, and motioned for the other to rise.

"Wouldst thou aught else?" he asked, observing

that the peasant did not retire, as was usual for those who received this favour.

"Naught—unless yonder brother hath occasion for me."

The face of Siegfried was thrust through a door which led to the cells. The countenance of the Prior changed like that of one who had lost all confidence in the intentions of his companion, and he pursued his way along the arcade. The other glided past, and disappeared by the door which he had been covertly invited to enter.

It has already been said that the Benedictine is an order of hospitality. A principal building of the hill was especially devoted to the comforts of the Abbot, and to those of the travellers it was always his duty, and in the case of Father Bonifacius scarcely less often his pleasure, to entertain. Here were seen some signs of the great wealth of the monastery, though it was wealth chastened by forms, and restricted by opinion; still there was little of self-denial, or indeed of any of that self-mortification which is commonly thought to be the inseparable attendant of the cell. The rooms were wainscoted with dark oak; emblems of religious faith, in costly materials, abounded; nor was there any want of velvet and other stuffs, all however of sober colours, though of intrinsic value. Father Siegfried ushered the peasant into one of the most comfortable of these rooms. It was the cabinet of the Abbot, who, having thrown aside the robes of office in which he had so lately appeared in the choir, and, ungirt and divested of all the churchly pomp in which he had just shown himself to the people, was now taking his ease, with the indolence of a student, and with some of the negligence of a debauchee.

"Here is the youth I have named to you, holy Abbot," said Father Siegfried, motioning his companion to advance.

Bonifacius laid down a parchment-covered and illuminated volume, one but lately issued from the press, rubbing his eyes like a man suddenly roused from a dreamy abstraction.

"Truly, brother Siegfried, these knaves of Leipzig have done wonders with their art! Not a word can I find astray, or a thought concealed. God knows to what pass of information this excess of knowledge, so long sacred to the learned, may yet lead us! The office of a librarian will no longer be of rare advantages, or scarcely of repute."

"Have we not proofs of the evil, in the growing infidelity, and in the manifest insubordination of the times?"

"It were better for all their souls, and their present repose, that fewer did the thinking in this troublesome world—Thou art named Johan, son?"

"Gottlob, most reverend Abbot, by your leave, and with the Church's favor."

"'Tis a pious appellation, and I trust thou dost not forget to obey the duty of which it should hourly remind thee."

"In that particular I can say that I praise God, father, for all the benefits I receive, and were they double what they are, I fee that within me which says I could go on rendering thanks for ever, for gracious gifts."

The answer of Gottlob caused the Abbot to turn his head. After studying the demure expression of the young man's face intently, he continued—

"This is well; thou art a huntsman in Count Emich's household?"

"His cow-herd, holy Abbot, and a huntsman in the bargain; for a more scampering, self-losing trouble-giving family is not to be found in the Pa'atinate, than this of mine!"

"I remember it was a cow-herd; thou dealt a ittle lightly with my brother Siegfried here, in pretending thou wert of Deurckheim, and not of the castle."

"To speak fairly to your reverence, there was some business between us; for be it known to you, holy Abbot, a cow-herd is made to suffer for all the frolics of his beasts, and so I preferred to do penance simply for my own backslidings, without white-washing the consciences of all Lord Emich's cattle in the bargain."

The Abbot turned again, and this time his look was still longer and more scrutinizing than before.

"Hast thou heard of Luther?"

"Does your reverence mean the drunken cobbler of Deurckheim."

"I mean the monk of Wittenberg, knave: though, by St. Benedict! thou hast not unaptly named the rebel; for truly doth he cobble that would fain mend the offices or discipline of Holy Church! I ask if thou hast sullied thy understanding and weakened thy faith, by lending ear to this damnable heresy, that is abroad in our Germany?"

"St. Benedict and the blessed Maria keep your reverence in mind, according to your deserts! What hath a poor cow-herd to do with questions that trouble the souls of the learned, and cause even the peaceably disposed to become quarrelsome and warlike?"

"Thou hast received a schooling above thy fortune—Art of the Jaegerthal?"

"Born and nurtured, holy Abbot. We are of long standing in the valley, and few families are better known for skill in rearing beeves, or for dealing cunningly with a herd, than that of which I come, humble and poor as I may seem to your reverence."

"I doubt but there is as much seeming as reality in this indifferent opinion of thyself. But thou hast had an explanation with brother Siegfried, and we count on thy services. Thou knowest the power of the Church, son, and cannot be ignorant of its disposition to deal mercifully with those that do it homage, nor of its displeasure when justly angered. We are disposed to deal in increased kindness with those who do not stray from the fold, at this moment when the Devils are abroad scattering the ignoran and helpless."

"Notwithstanding all you have said, most reverend Abbot, concerning the trifle I have gleaned in the way of education, I am too little taught to understand aught but plain speech. In the matter of a bargain it might be well to name the conditions clearly, lest a poor, but well-meaning, youth should happen to be damned, simply because he hath little knowledge of Latin, or cannot clearly understand what hath not been clearly said."

"I have no other meaning than that thy pious conduct will be remembered at the altar and the confessional; and that indulgences, and other lenities, will not be forgotten when there is question of thee."

"This is excellent, holy Abbot, for those that may profit by it—but, Saint Benedict help us! of what account would it all be, were Lord Emich to threaten his people with the dungeon and stripes, should any dare to frequent the altars of Limburg, or otherwise to have dealings with the reverend brotherhood?"

"Dost think our prayers, or our authority, cannot penetrate the walls of Hartenburg?"

"Of that, most powerful Bonifacius, I say nothing, since I never have yet profited in the way you mean. The dungeon of Hartenburg and I are not strangers to each other; and, were I to speak my most intimate thoughts, it would be to say, that Saint Benedict himself would find it no easy matter to open its doors, or to soften its pavements, so long as the Count was in an angry humour. Potz Tau send, holy Abbot! it is well to speak of miracles and of indulgences; but let him who imagines that either is about to make that damp and soul-chilling hole warm and pleasant, pass a night within its walls in November! He may enter with as much faith in the Abbey prayers as he will; but if he do not come forth with great dread of Lord Emich's displeasure, why he is not flesh and blood, but a burning kiln in the form of mortality!"

Father Bonifacius saw that it was useless endeavoring to influence the mind of the cow-herd in the vulgar manner, and he had recourse to surer means. Motioning his companion to hand him a little casket, externally decorated with many of the visible signs of the Christian faith, he took out of it a purse, that wanted for neither size nor weight. The eyes of Gottlob glistened—had not the monks been much occupied in examining the gold, they might have suspected that the pleasure he betrayed was a little affected—and he manifested a strong disposition to know the contents of a bag that had so many outward signs of value.

"This will make peace and create faith between us," said the Abbot, handing a golden mark to Gottlob. "Here is that which the dullest comprehension can understand; and whose merits, I doubt not, will be sufficiently clear to one of thy ready wit."

"Your reverence does not overvalue my means," answered the cow-herd, who pocketed the piece without further ceremony. "Were our good Mother of the Church to take this method of securing friends, she might laugh at all the Luthers between the Lake of Constance and the ocean, him of Wittenberg among the number: but, by some strange oversight, she has of late done more towards taking away the people's gold, than towards bestowing! I am rejoiced to find that the mistake is at last discovered; and chiefly am I glad, that one, poor and unworthy as I, has been among the first that she is pleased to make an instrument of her new intentions!"

The Abbot appeared at a loss to understand the character of his agent; but, being a worldly and selfish man himself, he counted rather loosely on the influence of a mediator whose potency is tacitly admitted by all of mercenary propensities. He resumed his seat, therefore, like one who saw little necessity for farther concealment, and went directly to the true object of the interview.

"Thou hast something to communicate from the Castle of Hartenburg, good Gottlob?"

"If it be your reverence's pleasure to listen."

"Proceed—Canst tell aught of the force Emich hath gathered in the hold?"

"Mein Herr Abbot, it is no easy matter to count varlets that go staggering about, from the moment the sun touches your Abbey towers, to that in which he sets behind the Teufelstein."

"Hast thou not means of separating them in divisions, and of making the enumerations of each apart?"

"Holy Abbot, that experiment hath failed. I divided them into the drunk and the sober; but, for the life of me, I could never get them all to be long enough of the same mind, to hunt up those that were in garrets and cellars; for while this slept off his debauch, that swallowed cup after cup, in a manner to recruit the drunkards as fast as they lost. It were far easier to know the Emperor's policy, than to count Lord Emich's followers!"

"Still they are many."

"They are and they are not, as one happens to view soldiership. In the way of draining a butt, Duke Friedrich would find them a powerful corps even in an attack against his Heidelburg tun; and yet I doubt whether he would think them of much account in the pressing warfare he wageth."

"Go to—thou art too indirect in thy answers for the duty thou hast undertaken. Return the gold if thou refusest the service."

"I pray thee, reverend Abbot, to remember the risks I have already run in this desperate undertaking, and to consider that the trifle you have so munificently bestowed, is already more than earned by the danger of my ears, to say nothing of great loss of reputation, and some pricking of conscience."

"This clown hath tampered with thee, Father Siegfried," said the Abbot, in a tone of reproach to the attending monk: "he even dares to make light of our presence and office!"

"We have the means of recalling him to his respect, as well as to a remembrance of his engagements."

"Thou sayest true: let the remedies be applied—but hold!"

During this brief colloquy between the Benedictines, Father Siegfried had touched a cord, and a lay-brother, of vigorous frame, showed himself. At a signal from the monk, he laid a hand on an arm of the unresisting Gottlob, and was about to lead him from the room, when the last words of the Abbot, and another signal from Father Siegfried, caused him to pause.

Bonifacius leaned a cheek on his hand, and mused long on the policy of the step he was about to take. The relations between the Abbey and the Castle, to adopt diplomatic language, were precisely in that awkward state in which it was almost as hazardous to recede as to advance. To imprison a vassal of the Count of Hartenburg, might bring matters to an immediate issue; and yet, to permit him to quit the convent, was to deprive the brotherhood of the means of extracting the information it was so important to obtain, and to procure which had been the principal inducement of attending the debauch already described, at a moment when there was so little real amity between the revellers. The precaution of Emich had frustrated this well-laid scheme, and the result of the experiment had been too cost'y to admit of repetition. There was also hazard in permitting Gottlob to return to Hartenburg, for the expectations and hostile spirit of the Abbey had been so unadvisedly exposed to the hind, as to render it certain he would relate what had occurred. It was desirable, too, to maintain an appearance of confidence, although so little was felt; for the monk well knew, that next to friendship, its apparent existence was of account in preventing the usual expedients of open hostility. Agents were at Heidelburg, pressing the Elector on a point of the last concern to the welfare of the brotherhood; and it was particularly material that Emich should not be driven to any overt act before the result of this mission was known. In short, these too little powers were in a condition similar to that in which some greater communities have been known to exist, instinctively alive to the opposing character of their respective interests, and yet tampering with the denouement, because neither was yet prepared to proclaim all it wished, meditated, and hoped to be able to attain, In the mean time, there was an ostensible courtesy between the belligerent parties, occasionally obscured by bursts of natural feeling, which, in politics, the world calls bonhommie, but which would, perhaps, be better termed by the frank designation of artifice.

The Abbot was so much accustomed to this sort of politic reflection, that all these considerations passed before his mind in less time than we have consumed in enumerating them. Still the pause was salutary; for, when he resumed the discourse, he spoke like one whose decision was supported by thought.

"Thou wilt tarry with us a little, Gottlob, for the good of thy soul," he said, making a sign that was understood by his inferiors.

"A thousand thanks, humane and godly Abbot. Next to the present good of my body, I look with most concern to the future condition of my poor soul; and there is great comfort and consolation in your gracious words. It is but the soul of a poor man; but, being my all, in the way of souls, it must needs be taken care of."

"The discipline we meditate will be healthful Brothers, lead the penitent to his cell."

The singular indifference with which Gottlob heard his doom, might have given the Abbot motive for reflection, had he not been so much occupied by other thoughts. As it was, the hind accompanied the lay brother without resistance, and indeed with the manner of one who appeared to think he was a gainer by this especial notice from the community of Limburg. So natural and easy was the air of Gottlob, as they took the direction of a gloomy corridor, that Father Siegfried began to believe he had employed an agent whose mind, shrewd and peculiar as it seemed at times, was in truth subject to moments of more than usual imbecility and dullness. He placed the cow-herd in a cell, pointed to a crucifix, its only article of furniture, and, without deeming it necessary even to secure the door retired.

CHAPTER XI.

——— "The Lady Valeria is come
To visit you."

Coriolanus.

A SHORT ride brought the cavalcade of Count Emich to the gates of Hartenburg. When all had alighted, and the guests, with the more regular inmates of the castle, were ushered into the hall, the lord of the hold again saluted Ulrike and her daughter. This freedom was the privilege of his rank, and of his character as host; and for its exercise, he once more received the grateful acknowledgments of Heinrich Frey. The females were then committed to the care of Gisela, the warder's daughter, who, in the absence of its more noble mistress, happened to be the presiding person of her sex in the place.

"Thou art thrice welcome, upright and loyal Heinrich!" exclaimed the Count, heartily, while he led the Burgomaster by the hand, into one of the rooms of honor—"None know thy worth, and thy constancy to thy friends, better than the master of this poor castle; and none love thee better."

"Thanks, well-born Emich, and such duty as one of poor birth and breeding can and should pay to a noble so honoured and prized. I am little used to courtesies, beyond those which we burghers give and take in the streets, and may not do myself full justice in the expression of reverence and respect, but I pray you, Herr Count, to take the desire for the performance."

"Wert thou the Emperor's most favored chamberlain, thy speech could not do thee more credit. Though Deurckheim be not Madrid, it is a well respected and courtly city, and none need envy the Roman, or the Parisian, that dwelleth there. Here is my kinsman of Viederbach, a knight that Providence hath cast a little loosely upon the world since the downfall of his Mediterranean island of Rhodes, and who hath travelled far and near, and he swears, daily, thy town hath no parallel, for its dimensions."

"Considered as a mountain city of no great magnitude, meine Herren, we do not blush at the aspect of our ancient walls."

"Thou needest not, and thou must have noted that I spoke in reference to its size. Monsieur Latouche is a gentleman that cometh from the capital of King Francis itself; and no later than this morning, he remarked on the neatness, and wealth, and other matters of consideration, that make themselves apparent, even to the stranger, in thy well-governed and prosperous borough."

The Burgomaster acknowledged the compliment, by a profound inclination and a gratified eye, for no flattery is so palpable as not to meet a welcome with those who labor for public distinction; and Emich well knew, that the police and order of his city were weak spots in Heinrich Frey's humility.

"Lord Emich scarce does me justice," returned the pliant Abbé, "since I found many other causes of admiration. The deference that is paid to rank in thy populace, and the manner in which the convenience of the honourable is respected, are particularly worthy of commendation."

"The churchman is right, Lord Emich—for, of all the towns in Germany, I do not think it easy to find another in which the poor and base are so well taught to refrain from thrusting their importunities and disadvantages on the gentle, as in our Deurckheim. I think my lord the Count must have observed the strict severity and cautious justice of our rules in this particular?"

"None know them better, nor does any heed them more. I cannot recall the moment, cousin Albrecht when any unpleasant intrusion on my privileges hath ever occurred within its gates. But I keep you from refreshing yourselves, worthy friends. Give us leave a little ;—we will seek you again, at your own convenience."

The Knight and the Abbé took this intimation of the desire of the Count to be alone with the Burgomaster in good part, and withdrew without unnecessary delay. When alone, Emich again took Heinrich Frey by the hand, and led him away into a part of the castle where none presumed to intrude without an especial errand. Here he entered one of those narrow rooms, which were devoted to secret uses, and which was well termed a closet, being in effect but little larger and scarcely better lighted, than the straitened apartments to which we give the same appellation in these later times.

When fairly protected from observation, and removed beyond the danger of eaves-droppers and spies, the Count threw aside his cloak, unbuckled his sword-belt, and assumed the manner of one at his ease. The Burgomaster took a seat on a stool, in deference to his companion's rank; while the latter, without seeming sensible of the act, seated himself at his side, in the only chair that the closet contained. Whoever has had much intercourse with Asiatics, or with Mussulmans of the southern shore of the Mediterranean, must have frequently observed the silent, significant, manner with which they regard each other, when disposed to court or to yield confidence; the eye gradually kindling, and the muscles of the mouth relaxing, until the feeling is fully betrayed in a smile. This is one of the means employed by men who dwell under despotic and dangerous governments, and where the social habits are much tinctured with violence and treachery, of assuring one another of secret faith and ready support. There is a sort of similar freemasonry in all conditions of life, in which frank and just institutions do not spread their mantle equally over the powerful and the weak, superseding, by the majesty of the law, the necessity of these furtive appeals to the pledges and sympathies of confidants. Such, in some degree, was the nature of the communication with which Emich of Hartenburg now commenced his private intercourse with Heinrich Frey. The Count first laid his square, bony, hand on the knee of the Burgomaster, which he squeezed until the iron fingers were nearly buried in the fleshy protuberance. Each turned his head toward his companion, looking askance, as if they mutually understood the meaning of what was conveyed by this silent coquetry. Still, notwithstanding the apparent community of thought and confidence, the countenance and air of each was distinguished by the personal character and the social station of the individual. The eye of the Baron was both more decided, and more openly meaning, than that of the Burgomaster; while the smile of the latter appeared rather like a faint reflection of the inviting expression of the former, than the effect of any inward impulse.

"Hast heard of last night's success?" abruptly demanded the Count.

"Nothing of the sort hath gladdened me, Herr Count; my heart yearns to know all, if it touches your high interests."

"The mass-singing rogues are stripped of their wine-tribute! Of that much are they fairly and legally disburthened! Thou knowest of our long-intended trial of heads; I had intended to have prayed thee to be a second at the banquet, but the presence of these idlers put some restraint on my hospitality. Thou wouldest have proved a stanch second in such an onset, Heinrich!"

"I thank my lord the Count, and shall deem the grace as good as accomplished in the wish. I am not worse than another at board, and may boast of some endurance in the way of liquor, but the seriousness of the times admonishes us, of civic authority, to be prudent. There is a wish in the people to be admitted to certain unreasonable and grave privileges, such as the right of vending their wares in the market-place at unseasonable hours, when the convenience of the burgomasters would be much vexed by the concession; and other similar innovations, against which we must make a firm stand, lest they come, in time, to invade our general authority and cause an unnatural convulsion. Were we to give way to pretensions so extravagant, Herr Count, the town would come to general confusion; and the orderly and respectable city of Deurckheim would justly merit to be compared to the huts of those countries of which they speak in the distant land of America, that hath so much, of late, given cause to writings and conversation. We need, therefore, look to the example set; for we have busy enemies, who make the most of the smallest indulgences. At another time, I would gladly have drained Heidelburg to your gracious honor."

"Thou wouldest not have been in danger of observation here; and, by the three holy Kings of Koeln, I should know how to tutor any prying knave that might chance to thrust a curious eye within these walls! But thy discretion is worthy of thy prudence, Heinrich; for, with thee, I deem the time serious for all lovers of established order, and of the peace of mankind. What would the knaves, that they thus trouble thy authority? Are they not fed and clad? and do they not now possess privileges out of number? The greedy rogues, if left to their humors, would fain envy their betters each delicate morsel they carry to their mouths, or each drop of generous rhenish that moistens their lips!"

"I fear, well-born Emich, that this spirit of cov

etousness is in their vile natures! I have rarely consented to any little yielding to their entreaties, such as a wish to swell out the time of their merry-makings, or a desire like this of the market-place, that the taste of the indulgence hath not given a relish for fuller fare. No; he that would govern quietly, and at his own ease, must govern thoroughly, else shall we all become illiterate savages, fitter for the forests of these Indies, than for our present rational and charitable civilization."

"Braver words were never uttered in thy council-hall, and well do I know the head that conceived them! Had there been occasion to have summoned thee hither for the banquet, the excuse should have satisfied, though the vineyards were the forfeiture. But what didst think, friend Heinrich, of the priests to-day, and of their warlike company!"

"'Tis plain Duke Friedrich still upholds them, and to deal frankly with my lord the Count, the men-at-arms have the air of fellows that are not likely to yield the hill without fair contention."

"Thinkest thou thus, Burgomaster? 'Twere a thousand pities that men of tried mettle should do each other harm, for the benefits and pleasure of a community of shaven Benedictines! What is there to urge in favor of pretensions so audacious as these they prefer, and which are so offensive, both to me, as a noble of the empire, and to all of any note or possessions in Deurckheim?"

"They lay great stress, Herr Count, on the virtue of ancient usages, and on the sacred origin of their mission."

"As much respect as thou wilt for rights that are sealed by time, for such is the stamp that gives value to my own fair claims; and many of thy city privileges come chiefly of use. But the matter between us is of abuse; and I hold it to be unworthy of those who can right themselves, to submit to wrong Do the monks still press the town for dues?"

"With offensive importunity. If matters be not quickly stayed, we shall come to open and indecen dissension."

"I would give a winter's enjoyment of my chases, were Friedrich more sorely pressed!" exclaimed the Count, laying his hand again on the Burgomaster's knee, whose countenance he studied with a significance that was not lost on his companion. "I speak merely in the manner of his being driven to know his true and fast friends from those who are false."

Heinrich Frey remained silent.

"The Elector is a mild and loving prince, but one sorely ridden by Rome! I fear we shall never have a tranquil neighborhood, notwithstanding our long forbearance, until the Church is persuaded to limit its authority to its duties."

The eyelids of the Burgomaster lowered, as it might be in reflection.

"And chiefly, Heinrich, am I troubled lest my good and loving Deurckheimers lose this occasion to do themselves right," continued the Count, squeezing the knee he still grasped, until even the compact citizen flinched with the force of the pressure. "What say they in the council-hall touching this matter?"

There was no longer any plausible apology for the silence of the Burgomaster, who did not answer, however, without working the heavy muscles of his face, as if delivered of his opinions with pain.

"Men speak their minds among us, noble-born Count, much as Duke Friedrich prospers, or fails, in his warfare. When we hear good tidings from the other side of the river, the brotherhood fares but badly in our discourses; but when the Elector's warriors triumph, we hold it prudent to remember they have friends."

"God's truth! Herr Heinrich, it is full time that you come to certain conclusions, else shall we be saddled to the end of our days by these hard-riding priests! Art thou not wearied with all their greedy exactions, that thou waitest patiently for more?"

"In that particular, a little sufficeth for our humors. There is not a city between Constance and Leyden, that is more quickly satisfied with paying than our Deurckheim: but we are husbands and fathers, Herr Count, and men that bear a heavy burthen of authority; and we must be wary, lest in throwing aside one portion of the load, space be found on our shoulders to place another that is heavier. When I would speak of your strong love to the town, there are distrustful tongues, that question me sorely of its fruits, and of your own honorable intentions in our behalf."

"To all of which thou couldest not be wanting of replies! Have I not often entertained thee with my loving wishes in behalf of the citizens?"

"If wishes in our behalf could serve our interests, the townsmen might, in their proper right, put in a claim to high favor. In the way of longing for our own success, Antwerp itself is not our better."

"Nay, thou takest my meaning unkindly: what Emich of Hartenburg wishes for his friends, he finds means to perform. But we will not trouble digestion, as we are about to feed, with these tiresome details—"

"I pray you, Herr Count, not to doubt my means; —little troubles me, when——"

"Thou shalt yield to my humor. What! is not the Count of Leiningen master in his own castle. Not a word more will I hear till thou hast tasted of my poor hospitality. Did my knaves serve thee, as I commanded yesterday, with the fat buck that fell by my own hand, Heinrich?"

"A thousand thanks, mein Herr—they did, and right cheerfully. I gave the rogues a silver penny for their largess; and the dust of the Jaegerthal w washed away in heavy draughts of our wine of the plain."

"I would have it so; between friends, there should be no niggardly reserve, in the way of courtesies," said Emich, rising. "Dost not bethink thee, Burgo master, of looking among the youths of Deurck heim for a son to stay thy age? Meta hath reache the years when maidens gladly become wives."

"The wench is not ignorant of her time of life, and the search of a suitable husband hath not failed to give me fatherly concern. I do not presume to compare our conditions and early lives in aught that is disrespectful, mein Herr Graf; but, touching all that is common to great and little, the youth of this day seem not as they were in the time of our young manhood."

"Priest-ridden, Burgomaster;—too much of Rome in our laws and habits. God's my life! when I first mounted steed, in the court below, I could have leaped the convent towers, did a Benedictine dare gainsay the feat!"

"That would have been a miracle little short o the raising of their convent walls," answered Heinrich, laughing at his companion's flight, and rising in deference to the attitude the noble had been pleased to take. "These Benedictines have been careless of their advantages, else might they still have kept the circumstance of that miracle as much beyond dispute, as it was in our young days, Lord Count."

"And what say they in Deurckheim, now, touching the affair?"

"Nay, men treat it, at present, as they treat other disputable subjects. Since this outcry of Brother Luther, there have appeared many who call in question not only that, but divers others of the Abbey's feats."

The Count unconsciously crossed himself, seeming to ponder gloomily on the subject, within his own mind. Then glancing towards his companion, he perceived that he was standing.

"I cry thy mercy, worthy Burgomaster; but my inattention hath given thee this pain. My leg hath been so much of late suspended in the stirrup, that it hath need of straightening; but it should not, in justice, cause thee this inconvenience. I pray thee, Herr Frey, be seated."

"That would ill become my station in your presence, noble and well-born Emich; nor would it do fit credit to my reverence and affection."

"Nay, I will hear none of this. Thy seat, Master Heinrich, and that without delay, lest I seem to overlook thy merits."

"I pray mein Herr Graf not to do himself this wrong; nay, if it be your honorable will—I blush at mine own daring—if I consent, I call my lord to witness 'tis only in profound respect for his will!"

During this struggle of courtesy, the Count succeeded, by means of gentle violence, in forcing the Burgomaster to resume his seat. Heinrich had yielded with a species of maiden coyness; but when he found that, instead of occupying his own humble stool, he had unwittingly been forced into the arm-chair of the noble, he rebounded from the cushion, as if the leather contained enough of the electric fluid to bid defiance to the nonconductor qualities of the ample woollen garment in which his nether person was cased.

"Gott bewahre!" exclaimed the Burgomaster, in harsh, energetic German: "The empire would cry out against this scandal, were it known! I owe it to my reputation to deny myself an honor so little deserved."

"And I to my authority to enforce my will, and to proclaim thy deserts."

Here the amiable force on the part of the Count, and the courteous coquetry of Heinrich Frey, were resumed, until the latter, fearful of offending by longer resistance, was obliged to submit, protesting however, to the last, against the apparent presumption on his own part, and against the great injustice which the lord of the hold was doing to hi own rights, by thus insisting.

A distinguished foreign orator once pronounced the titles of honor, and the social distinctions that are conferred by the European governments, to be the "cheap defence of nations." This opinion strikes us to be merely one of the thousand bold fallacies that have been broached to uphold existing interests, without reference to their true effects, or to their inherent justice. This "cheap defence," like the immortal Falstaff, who was not only witty himself, but the cause of wit in others, is the origin of a hundred sufficiently costly habits, that leave him who bears the burthen but little reason to exult in its discovery. We recommend to all one-eyed economists, who still retain any faith in this well-known opinion of the English orator, to read that letter in the Spectator, in which a city youth relates the manner he is driven to vindicate his own reserve to his fair country cousins, who would fain reproach him with an ungraceful disrespect of his holiday privileges, by reminding them of the calculations of the individual who refused to indulge in cheese-cakes, because they brought with them so many other unnecessary expenditures.

But whether honors of the description just alluded to, do or do not form any portion of the economy of a nation, there is little question but flattery, like this which Emich has just bestowed on the Burgomaster, is one of the subtle and most powerful agents of the great in effecting their secret purposes. Few are they—alas, how few!—that possess a vision sufficiently clear, and an ambition so truly noble, as to look beyond the narrow and vulgar barriers of human selfishness, and to regard truth as it came from God, without respect for persons and things, except as they are the instruments of his will. It is certain that Heinrich Frey had little pretension to be one of this scrutinizing and elevated class; for when he found himself fairly seated in the chair of the Count of Hartenburg, with the noble himself standing, his sensations were like those which are felt by the philosopher of the other hemisphere, who is authorized to put a ribbon at his button-hole;—or the tradesman of this, who is elected to the common-council of his native city, after being run on both tickets. Still he greatly regretted there was no one to envy his preferment; for, after the first soothing effect on his own self-love, that unquiet spirit which haunts us to the last, disfiguring the fairest pictures, and casting its alloy into every scheme of happiness, suggested that his triumph would be imperfect without a witness. Just as this rebellious feeling became troublesome, there appeared at the door of the closet, the very being of all others that the Burgomaster would have chosen to see him in the enjoyment of this high honor. A gentle tap announced the presence of the intruder, and when the authoritative voice of Emich had given the permission, the mild Ulrike appeared on the threshold.

Surprise was strongly painted on the features of the Burgomaster's wife. The husband had crossed his legs, and was indulging in his ease, with a sort of noble indifference to the unusual situation in which he was placed, when this extraordinary sight greeted the eyes of his amazed consort. So absolute and so tenacious were the rules of Germany on all things that concerned the respect due to rank, that even one as little troubled by ambition as the meek

Ulrike, had great difficulty in believing her senses when she beheld Heinrich Frey thus suddenly elevated to a seat of honor in the presence of a Coun of Leiningen.

"Nay, enter without fear, my good Ulrike," said Emich, graciously; "thy worthy husband and I do but indulge in mutual friendship, while my varlets prepare an unworthy banquet. Do not think to break our discourse."

"I only hesitate, noble Emich, at seeing Heinrich Frey preferred to that seat, while the Lord of Hartenburg stands, like one of humble birth, at his side!"

"Touch not the matter, meine Frau," said the husband condescendingly. "Thou art a loving consort, and art well enough amid thy sex, and in questions that belong to thy breeding; but in an affair, like this, between mein Herr Graf and me, thou mayest only mar what thou canst not mend."

"By the life of the princely Karl! master Heinrich, you do insufficient justice to Ulrike's discernment! Were mine own Ermengarde among us, thou shouldst see that we prize thy loving wife little less than we esteem thee. But it were better that we inquire of Ulrike the occasion of her visit, before we attempt to school her on matters of deportment."

Though so rough and unnurtured on many of the points that are now deemed essential even to an indifferent civilization, Emich had a quick interest for the perception of character, and possessed as much of the refinement that marks a superior condition in life, as the state of the age and the situation of his own country permitted. There can be no greater mistake than to imagine that mere nominal rank is any pledge for a correspondent degree of refinement, since every thing is relative in this world, and where the base of the pillar is rude and little polished, it would be a violation of all architectural keeping, to expect a capital of a different style. Thus it is that we, without any social orders but those of convention, are struck with so many glaring discrepancies among people whose patricians, having studied all that is factitious and plausible in breeding, are still deficient in the grand essentials of reason and humanity, simply because the roots of the society, of which they are only the more luxuriant branches, are planted in the soil of ignorance and debasement. The Count of Hartenburg had possessed ample opportunities of witnessing how much the intellectual qualities of the Burgomaster's wife were superior to those of her husband; and he had sufficient discrimination and experience to be quite aware of the importance of conciliating such an ally in advancing his own particular views. It was in this spirit, therefore, that he ventured on so blunt a reproof of Heinrich's superciliousness, and volunteered the compliment to the spouse; probably hazarding the latter, from an intimate conviction that most husbands are content to hear eulogies on those who are so completely in their power as their own wives.

"Since it is your honorable pleasure, Herr Count, for God's sake let the woman come in," answered Heinrich, still, however, without changing an attitude so soothing to his self-esteem. "If she should see me seated in a presence in which it would much better become me to kneel, why it may help to show that God hath given her a companion that is not altogether without the world's esteem, little as he may merit it. Enter freely, therefore, good Ulrike, since it is my lord's pleasure; but presume not on his condescension to me, which is rather a mark of great love for our town, than any matter connected with domestic life."

"In all that the high-born Count hath done honor to any of us, whether as of Deurckheim, or as his unworthy neighbors, I desire respectfully to be grateful," returned the wife, who, by this time, had recovered from her surprise, and who now advanced farther into the narrow room, with the modest self-possession which ordinarily distinguished her manner:—"If I do not come amiss, I crave to be heard of both, in a matter that toucheth nearly a mother's heart; and a matter, as it is of Heinrich Frey's child I would fain speak, that I trust may not be indifferent to my lord the Count."

"Were it of mine own little Kunigunde, the subject should not be more welcome!" said the noble. "Speak freely then, gentle Ulrike, and with the same simplicity thou wouldest use were it only to thy husband's ear."

"Thou hearest, woman! mein Herr Graf enters, as it were, into all our tribulations and happiness, an' he were no other than a brother. So mince not the matter, but deal frankly with us; though I admonish thee not to push thy words to all the familiarity of household discourse."

"As it is of a subject so near, I pray leave to close the door, before more is uttered."

The words of Ulrike were cut short by a hasty gesture of approbation from her husband, and by the Count himself, who, with more of the consideration and manner of a gentleman, performed the desired office with his own hands, thus admitting the wife, as it were, into the very cabinet of their secret councils.

CHAPTER XII.

> "You would be another Penelope: yet they
> Say, all the yarn she spun, in Ulysses' absence, did
> But fill Ithaca full of moths."
>
> *Coriolanus.*

When Ulrike found herself fairly closeted with the Count and her husband, and was quietly seated on the stool which the former, spite of the latter's protestations to the contrary, had insisted on her taking, she cast her mild eyes about her, with that expressive and touching appeal that a woman is apt to make, when she feels called on to act as the adviser, if not the guardian, of him whom nature intended and the law presumes, is both able and willing to discharge those offices for her. Notwithstanding Heinrich's obstinacy and masculine swaggering, many occasions had arrived, in the course of their matrimonial life, to produce a latent conviction in both, that the order of things was a little inverted, as respects judgment and moral authority, by inclining one to lean, though with but an indifferent grace, where he should have supported; and tempting the other, at times, to overstep her sex's duties, though it was always done with an intuitive perception of her sex's seemliness and means.

"For this condescension I thank my Lord Emich, and thee, Heinrich," commenced the thoughtful matron; "for it is not, at all times, advisable for the wife to intrude unbidden even to her husband's presence."

A significant ejaculation, which might almost merit a coarser term, was the manner in which the Burgomaster expressed his assent, during the brief pause that succeeded this excuse of Ulrike. The more courteous host bowed with sufficient respect, though, even by his manner, it was evident he was getting impatient to know the real motive of the interruption.

"We are too well pleased to receive thee, to remember the usages and rights of manhood," answered the latter, with a kindness of manner that was insensibly extorted by the winning and feminine qualities of her he addressed, and which, in some degree, softened the pretensions of his language—"Proceed with thy matter, for none can be more ready to listen."

"Thou hearest, good Ulrike! the Herr Count is willing to remember thou art a Burgomaster's consort; and, as he is pleased to say, we are truly impatient to be let into the cause of thy sudden visit."

The thoughtful Ulrike received this encouragement like one accustomed to be treated, in some measure, as a being inferior in capacity and force to her husband, but not without a shade like that which is produced by unmerited humiliation. Smiling—and few, even in early and attractive youth, had so sweet an expression, when her countenance thus gleamed, whether it were in pleasure, or in melancholy—smiling, as it might be, partly in female gentleness, and partly in sadness, she commenced the purport of her visit, coming, however, to her true object with great reserve and with the caution of a woman accustomed to influence, rather than to control.

"For the great kindness and condescension of the Herr Emich, in behalf of Heinrich Frey, and of all that are his, no one is more grateful than I," she said; "if I may now seem to trouble him with the concerns of a family on which he has already so freely lavished favors"——

"And friendship, good Ulrike."

"And friendship, since you permit me, noble Count, to use the word—but, if I now seem to trespass beyond breeding, by troubling your mind with a concern that is so remote from your own interests, I trust you will remember a mother's tenderness, and think of the highborn Ermengarde, whose anxiety for her own offspring may furnish some excuse for that I feel for mine."

"Hath aught befell the blooming Meta?"

"God's my life!" exclaimed the troubled Heinrich, abandoning his much-prized seat, in the suddenness of paternal alarm. "Hath the wench suffered from the over-rich eels of the Rhine? or is she massed to death by these accursed monks?"

"Our child is well in the body, and, the blessed Maria be praised! she is pure and innocent in mind," returned Ulrike. "I have little cause for aught but gratitude in either of these behalfs;—but, she is of an age when girlish fancies become unsettled, and the flexible female spirit seeks impressions from others than those whom nature hath made its guardians."

"This is some of thy usual incomprehensibilities, good woman, and language that is not easily understood by any but thyself. The noble Graf hath no leisure to hunt up new ideas to maintain a discourse in subtleties. Had the girl indeed tasted too freely of the rare dish which the honest Burgomaster of Mannheim so kindly sent me, as I at first feared, no doubt the means to cure might be found in Hartenburg; but thou askest too much, wife of mine, when thou wouldest have any but thine own husband enter into all the cunning niceties that sometimes beset thy imagination."

"Nay, Master Heinrich, here may be more urgent matter than thou thinkest: thy dame is not a woman whose opinions are to be neglected. Wilt proceed with thy recital, good Ulrike?"

"Our child is at that period of life," continued the mother, too much accustomed to the manner of her husband to permit it to divert her thoughts from their main intention—"when the young of every sort begin to think of the future. It is a principle that God hath implanted, Herr Emich, and therefore it is for good; and we, who have watched over the infancy of our offspring with so much anxiety, have trained their youth with so much care, and have so often trembled for their noon-time, must, sooner or later, consent to loosen the sweet ties that bind us to our second selves, in order that the great ends of the creation shall be accomplished."

"Umph!" ejaculated Heinrich.

"Nay, gentle Ulrike," said the Count, "maternal love hath drawn this picture in stronger colors than may be necessary. When the time for matrimony comes, God's my life! daughter of thine and honest Heinrich Frey, need not wear maiden's coif a day longer than is necessary to do suitable reverence to the church. Here have I youths, out of number, that look to the house of Leiningen for grace, any one of whom would be glad to wive with the damsel I should name. There is young Friedrich Zantzinger, the orphan of my last deputy in the villages of the plain; he is a lad that would gladly do harder service to gain my love."

"When old Friedrich left the boy fatherless, he left him without a penny," drily rejoined the Burgo master.

"That is a fault which might be mended; but I have others that can be named. What thinkest thou of the eldest son of my Heidelburg attorney, worthy Conrad Walther?"

"Curse the knave! I hate him from my heart."

"Thou art warm, Master Heinrich, against one that I both trust and favor."

"I cry your mercy, Herr Graf; but a sudden rising of the bile, at the mention of the fellow's name, got the better of respect," answered the Burgomaster, with more moderation, who, as he saw by the owering look of Emich's brow, the necessity of explanation, continued, with rather more openness than he might have thought necessary under circumstances of less urgency: "Perhaps the high-born Count was never possessed of the matter of our late controversy?"

"Nay, I pretend not to judge my friends,—"

"Let but my lord condescend to hear me, and I leave him arbiter between us. It is well known to you, Herr Emich, that collections were made, and charity asked, in behalf of the peasants who suffered, the past year, from the sudden rising of the Rhine. Among others, the good Christians of our town were importuned for succor; and, for none will deny that it was a sad visitation of Providence, we gave freely as became our several means. To prevent improper uses of the money, in all cases of liberal donations, the sealed bond of the donor, at a near day, was asked in preference to the silver; and mine was granted for the fair sum of twelve crowns, as a poor donation suited to my hopes and station. It so fell out, Herr Graf, that those charged with the distribution had occasion for their money before the instruments were up; and they sent agents among us, in order to enter into such negotiations as the cases might need. Gold was scarce at the moment; and because, in regaining my bond, I had a heedful regard to mine own interests, the misdealing Conrad would fain transport me, like a thief, before the authorities of Heidelburg, to undergo the penalties of a usurer. Son of his shall never call me father, with your gracious leave, nobly-born Count of Leiningen!"

"This truly offereth some impediment to the affair; but, failing of young Conrad, I have others that may be accounted worthy of this advantage. So put thy maternal heart at ease, good Ulrike, and trust to my active friendship to dispose of the girl."

"The Burgomaster's consort had been a patien listener during the short but characteristic digression of her husband. Trained in the opinions of the times, she did not possibly endure all that a mother and a wife, of equal native sensibility, might now suffer at so evident a debasement of her sex; but as the laws of nature are permanent, neither did she escape a pang of wounded feeling as she heard the different expedients that were so hastily devised for the future disposal of one who formed her chief happiness in life. There was less of that hectic color, which commonly gave a lustre to eyes that were by nature rather melancholy than bright, and her voice was fuller of emotion than before, as she continued.

"For all this heed of me and mine, I again thank the Herr Count; but there is a power that is stronger with the young than the counsel of the experienced, or even than the wishes of their friends," she said. "My intent, in intruding myself unbidden into this secret conference, was to say that Meta had listened to the voice of her sympathies more than to the usages of her class, and chosen for herself."

The Count and Heinrich Frey stared at the speaker in mute surprise, for neither fully comprehended her meaning; while Ulrike herself, one of her objects being accomplished, in having made this long-dreaded declaration in the presence of a person able to repress the anger of her husband, sate silent, inwardly trembling for the consequences.

"Wilt thou explain the meaning of thy worthy consort, Herr Heinrich?" abruptly asked the Count.

"Zum Henker! you ask me to perform an office, Lord Count, that might better fit a Benedictine, or a clerk. When Ulrike, who is an excellent and obedient companion in the main, once gets upon the stilts of fancy, I never pretend to be able to raise an idea to the level of her shoe-buckle. Go to! thou hast well spoken, wife of mine; and it will now be better to seek our child, lest yonder cavalier of Rhodes be oiling her ears with the unction of flattery."

"Nay, by my house's honors! but I will know more of this matter, thy fair and virtuous consort consenting, Master Heinrich. Wilt explain thyself freely, dame?"

Whether it be from the instinct of weakness and delicacy, or only the fruit of precepts constantly inculcated, a virtuous woman rarely admits the existence of the sentiment of love, either in herself or in any that is dear to her, without a feeling of shame, and possibly not without an intuitive knowledge that she is conceding some of the vantage-ground of her sex's privileges.

This feeling was apparent in Ulrike, by the slow but complete suffusion of her cheek, and by the manner in which her looks avoided those of Emich, spite of the self-possession and calm of her years.

"I would merely say, Herr Emich," she replied, "that Meta, like all who are young and innocent, hath fancied an image of perfection, and that she hath found an original for her picture in a youth of the Jaegerthal. While of this mind, she cannot, in honesty or in maidenly respect, become the bride of any other than him she loves."

"The affair grows clearer," returned the Count, smiling like one who took no very deep interest in the matter; "and it is as well explained as heart could wish—at least, heart of the youth in question. What thinkest thou of this, Herr Burgomaster?"

The comprehension of Heinrich Frey could not altogether misconceive so plain an explanation, and, since the moment when his wife had ceased speaking, he sat regarding her mild but troubled countenance, with parted lips and open eyes, like a man that first learns some unlooked-for intelligence of great moment.

"Herr Teufel!" exclaimed Heinrich, taking up the last words of the Baron, unconscious of the disrespect of what he did—"Art talking of our own natural-born child?"

"Of none other. In whom else have I this motherly affection?—or for what other can I feel this deep concern?"

"Dost mean that Meta—my daughter, Meta Frey—hath inclination for son of woman, except it may be the natural love and reverence she beareth her own father?—that the girl hath truant and free fancies?"

"I say nothing to give this opinion of Meta—my daughter, Meta," returned Ulrike, with womanly dignity. "Our child has done no more than listened to the secret whisperings of nature; and, in yielding her affections to a youth whom she hath often seen, and long known, she hath merely paid an homage to merit, that the most virtuous are the most apt to yield."

"Go to, Ulrike! Thou art well enough among thy household, and a woman for whom I have esteem; but these visions with which thou art so often troubled, give thee an air, at times, of being of less discernment than thou mayest fairly claim to be. Excuse the dame, Herr Count; for, though her own husband, and a little weak on the subject of her infirmities perhaps, there is not a more thrifty manager, a more faithful spouse, or a kinder mother in the Palatinate."

"Nay, thou little need say this to me! None know the worth of Ulrike better; and, I may add, few respect her so much. It were well to hear further of this matter, Heinrich; for, to treat thee in candor, there may lay more beneath this opening of the excellent wife, than is at first apparent

Our Meta hath seen the qualities of some worthy youth sooner than they have struck the eye of her quick-sighted father, thou wouldst say. Is it not so, dame?"

"I would say that the heart of my child is so closely bound in that of another, as to leave little hope of happiness, should her matrimonial duties teach her to forget him."

"Thou thinkest then, good dame, that the young fancies of a female, when once indulged, are not to be removed by the offices of wife and mother?—that a caprice of the imagination is stronger than a vow made at the altar?"

Though the eyes of both the Count and the Burgomaster were riveted on the fine and speaking countenance of Ulrike, the volume of eloquent nature, that was thus opened to their observation, proved little better than a blank. Strong and dramatic exhibitions of feeling require but little interpretation for the dullest faculties; but few indeed are they who are capable of comprehending the secret workings of a spirit chastened and restrained as that of a virtuous, but unhappily paired woman. There is, perhaps, no one aspect of human nature more common-place, or more easily understood, than that which is hourly offered by a worldly-minded and capricious fair. She runs her little career, seemingly as erratic as a comet, though, in truth her course is always to be calculated on the infallible principles of vanity and selfishness; but no secret is more hermetically sealed against impertinent and vulgar curiosity, than the elevated sentiments which sustain the suffering and silent female who is truly instinct with the high qualities of her sex.

We are no railer at the domination of man; for we are persuaded that he who would wish to transform the being that was created to be his solacer and companion—his guide in moral darkness, and his sharer in sorrow as in joy—into a worldly competitor, changing love and confidence to rivalry and contention, is but miserably instructed in that sublime ordinance of nature, which has thus separated the highest order of its creation into two great classes, so replete with mutual consolation and happiness.

Had the wife of the Burgomaster arisen, and, in chosen terms, made an appeal to the sympathies of her companions, in which language should unite with manner to produce an effect, she might have been understood, as the every-day reader understands all such pictures of female character; but where she sat, silent, suffering, and meek, she was completely concealed from any means of comprehension possessed by either. Her eye did not kindle, for long and patient subordination had taught her to submit to the misconstructions of her husband; nor scarcely did the faint color of her cheek deepen, since the load at her heart counteracted the natural impulses of pride and resentment.

"I think, Lord Count, that when an innocent and youthful female heart yields to a power that nature perhaps has made irresistible," she said, "it, at least, merits to be treated tenderly. Meta hath few fancies of the kind you mention; and the attachment she feels, though doubtless deepened by those colors which the least experienced in the truths of life are the most apt to paint, is but the natural consequence of much association, and of great deserving on the part of the young man."

"This is getting to be plain, Herr Emich," said Heinrich Frey, pithily, "and must needs be looked to. Wilt condescend to name the youth thou meanest Ulrike?"

"Berchthold Hintermayer."

"Berchthold Teufelstein!" exclaimed the Burgomaster, laughing, though there was something like a secret consciousness of danger in the very manner in which he gave loose to his merriment. "A penniless boy is truly a fit husband for child of mine!"

The quiet, blue eye of Ulrike was fastened on her husband; but she averted it with sensitive haste, lest it might betray that she was thinking of the time when her own father had consented to her marriage with one nearly as poor, merely because the penetration of the parent had discovered those qualities of prudence and gainful industry in his townsman, which after-experience so fully developed.

"He is not rich, Heinrich," was her answer; "but he is worthy: and why need a chill be thrown on the heart of Meta, for the desire of that which she already hath in sufficient plenty?"

"Hear you this, Herr Emich? My wife is lifting the curtain of privacy before your respected eyes, with a freedom for which I could fain cry mercy."

"Berchthold is a youth I love," gravely observed the Count.

"In that case, I shall say nothing disrespectful of the lad, who is a worthy forester, and in all things suited to his service in the family of Hartenburg; still, he is but a forester, and a very penniless one. I had not thought to dispose of the girl so soon, for a little maidenly leisure does none of the sex injury, Lord Count; but as she hath her head set upon this Berchthold, it may be well to wrap it in a matron's coif, by way of filling it with ideas more suited to her hopes."

"The remedy may prove fatal, Heinrich!" mildly observed Ulrike, raising her tearful eye to the obstinate features of the Burgomaster

"Nay, I ought to know the constitution of the family; what has so well succeeded with the mother, cannot harm the child."

The wife did not reply. But Emich of Hartenburg had been deeply interested by her gentle and winning manner, for he had watched her counte nance closely, and understood the womanly effort by which the appearance of calm was preserved. Turning to the Burgomaster, he laid a hand on his shoulder, with a friendly smile, and said—

"Herr Heinrich, thou hast a fair and gentle consort; but, I think, too, thou hast scarce less faith in me than in thy wife. Give us leave; I would fain reason this matter with Ulrike, without the aid of thy influence."

"A thousand thanks for the honor to me and mine, high-born Count! As to faith, I would leave the dame a year on Limburg-hill, without other thought than for her convenience; for none know the worth of Ulrike better, though she is so difficult to comprehend when her fancy is moulting. Now kiss me, dame, and prithee do no dishonor to the Count's counsel."

Thus saying, Heinrich Frey placed a hearty kiss on the soft cheek that the obedient Ulrike freely offered, and left his wife alone with the noble, without other thought than of the high distinction that was conferred on his name. The manner in which he prized the notice of the Baron was sufficiently manifested by the readiness with which he communicated the circumstance that Emich and his consort were closeted, on an affair touching the interests of the family of Frey, to all who would listen to his tale.

CHAPTER XIII.

Ah me! for aught that ever I could read,
Could ever hear by tales or history,
The course of true love never did run smooth!"
Shakspeare.

When the door was closed on the husband, the Count turned to the wife, and continued the discourse.

"I love young Berchthold Hintermayer, good Ulrike," he said, "and would gladly be of aid in this affair, which, I see plainly, thou hast much at heart."

"The mother would be unnatural that had not anxiety for the happiness of her child. In youth, Lord Count, we gaze before us, filling the dim ascent with scenes drawn after our wishes, and peopling the world with the beings that we deem most necessary to our hopes; but when we have reached the eminence, whence the commencement and the end of life can both be plainly seen, do we first find truth. I am as little disposed as another to venture rashly on a union that has no better security for its fruits than a blind and feverish passion, that will be certain to consume itself by its own fierceness; but, on the other hand, none who have known life as I, can be disposed to consider lightly those resemblances of taste and opinions, those gentle touches of character and disposition, that are most likely to conduce to wedded love."

"Thou art esteemed lucky in thine own consorting, dame?"

"God hath much blessed me in many mercies—the question is of Meta, my Lord Count."

Ulrike, spite of herself, had changed color; but, aided by the manner of matronly reserve she immediately assumed, the little emotion passed with

Emich as no more than a display of feminine reserve, that was intended to repress a curiosity he had no title to indulge.

"The question is of Meta, in sooth," he answered; "and, by Saint Benedict! the youth shall not want for friendly and free support. But favor should have favor's reward. If I give into thy humor in this concern of thy daughter's marriage, good Ulrike in return, I expect of thee a service on which I scarce lay less stress."

The matron raised her eyes to the countenance of her companion, in surprise. One who had not so uniformly preserved her own self-respect, might have doubted of what she heard; but the look of the Burgomaster's wife merely conveyed a meaning of curiosity and innocence.

"You will deserve far more than I can bestow, Herr Count, should you do aught to secure the happiness of Meta."

"Fair wife," continued Emich, seating himself, and taking her hand, with the freedom which his superior rank and the usages of the country allowed, "thou knowest the manner in which these Benedictines have so long vexed our valley; and, being so deeply in the confidence of the honest Heinrich, thou must have suspected that, wearied of their insolence and exactions, we have seriously bethought us of the means by which to reduce them to the modesty that becometh their godly professions, and which might better justify their pretensions?"

Emich paused, and sat intently regarding the face of his quiet listener. He had unwittingly touched upon the very subject that had been the chief inducement with the Burgomaster's wife for intruding upon the privacy of the conspirators. She had long suspected their intentions; and, though she felt deep care for the future lot of Meta, and had gladly availed herself of a favorable occasion to break the ice on a subject that, sooner or later, must be disclosed, her real object was to warn Heinrich against the probable consequences of the plot. In this disposition, then, she heard the Count with secret pleasure, and prepared herself to reply, in the manner she had long meditated.

"All that you say, Herr Count," she answered, "has more than once crossed my mind; and deeply have I grieved that those I so love and honor should thus meditate injury to the altars of God—plan desperate devices to interrupt his praise."

"How! dost thou call the whinings of these knaves praise of aught but their own hypocrisy?" interrupted Emich. "Are they not the instigators of most of our sins, by their example?—the parents of all the contention that troubles the neighborhood?—Consider, good Ulrike, that heaven is not a close into which souls are to be driven blindfolded; but that we, who are of the flock, have at least the right, as we have the means, of judging whether the shepherds are fit for their office, or not."

"And should they prove unequal to, or unworthy of their duties, where do we find authority to do them harm?"

"God's my life! good wife; are our swords nothing? Are a noble name, an ancient and high descent, a long-standing claim to command, and a stout heart, nothing?"

"Arrayed against the Almighty, they count as the leaves of your own forest, when fluttering in a gale;—less than the flakes of snow that drive, in winter, against the battlements of your strong castle. Limburg is reared in honor of God; and he that raises a hand against the sacred walls, will be apt to repent the rashness in woe. If there are unworthy ministers at its altars, there are also those that are worthy; and, were it not so, the mission is too high to be sullied by any frailty of those who abuse their trusts."

The Count was disturbed; for Ulrike spoke earnestly, and in a voice of sweet persuasion. He leaned his chin upon a hand, as a man that pondered well on the hazards of his enterprise.

"What thinkest thou, Ulrike, of this brother of Wittenberg " he at length asked. "Could we but fairly make him out honest and wise, ecclesiastical authority for lowering the pride of Limburg might be had!"

"I am one of those who think Brother Luther honest; I am also one of those who think him mistaken: but even he is far from urging to deeds of violence."

"By Saint Benedict! woman, thou hast had converse with Father Arnolph, touching this question. Echo does not answer sound more faithfully than thou repeatest the sentiments of the Prior."

"It is not strange that they who love God should feel and speak alike in a matter affecting his honor. I have said naught to Father Arnolph, nor to any other of the Abbey, of your designs; for it is not easy for Ulrike Frey to forget she is both wife and mother. But I have prayed often, that the hearts of those who contemplate this dangerous sacrilege may be softened; and that, for their own safety, they may yet see the evil of their plot. Believe me, Count, the Dread Being who is worshipped in Limburg, will not forget to avenge himself of those who despise his power!"

"Thou art certain, Ulrike, that thy opinions have weight with me, for since childhood have I known and respected thy wisdom. Nay, had there not been want of those claims which birth can alone give, thou wouldst now be sitting in this castle its mistress, and not a guest. The self-denial which was practised, in order to do my father pleasure cost me much pain for many years; nor did I rightly regain my freedom, until the birth of my eldest born turned my hopes towards posterity."

It is seldom woman hears the acknowledgment of her influence with the stronger sex, without secret satisfaction. As there had been nothing in the attachment to which the Count alluded, to alarm her principles or to offend her delicacy, Ulrike listened to this reference to the feelings and incidents of their younger days, with a smile that produced an effect on her gentle features, which resembled the melancholy light which illuminated the chapel of the religious community in question; or which was mild, placid, and, if we may be permitted an expression so vague, tinged with hues of the past.

"We are no longer young, Emich," she answered, withdrawing her hand, under a keen impulse of its propriety—"and that which thou speakest belongs to a former age. But if thou dost, in sooth, entertain this opinion of my discretion, I have never said aught of thee but in thy honor. There were other reasons than the late Count's will, why I could not listen to thy suit, as thou wert then informed; for we are none of us the controllers of those sentiments which so much depend on taste or accident."

"By the sainted eleven thousand of Koeln! Heinrich Frey was scarce a youth to do this disadvantage to the heir of my line and name!"

"Heinrich Frey received my troth, as the nobl Ermengarde received thine, Herr von Hartenburg," answered Ulrike, with the composure of one whose feelings had never been interested in the refusal to which she alluded, and with the dignity of a woman sensitively alive to her husband's character. "By Heaven's favor, we are both happier than if wedded either above or beneath our hopes. But if thou couldst deny thyself this boon—for such, in thy young fancies, didst thou believe my hand—to oblige thy father of earth, wilt thou still defy him of Heaven, to gratify a longing less excusable?"

"Go to, Ulrike; thou pressest me out of reason, I know not fairly that I even meditate the enterprise thou meanest."

"Or, in other language, thou art not yet decided to commit the sacrilege. Before thy hand strikes the irretrievable blow, Herr Count, hear one that, in thy youth, thou professed to love, and who yet remembers thy preference, with grateful kindness."

"Thou art more indulgent as a matron than as a maid! This is the first word of pity for all the sorrow thou causedst my youth, that hath ever escaped thee!"

"Pity is a term it would ill become Ulrike Haitzinger to use to Emich von Leiningen. I said gratitude, Herr Count; for the woman that pretendeth not to feel this sentiment towards the honorable youth that has preferred her to all others of her sex, payeth an indifferent compliment to her own heart. I never disavowed that thy suit gave me both gratification and sorrow—gratification, that one of thy hopes could find sufficient in me to justify thy choice; sorrow, that thou wert necessarily disappointed."

"And had our births been nearer an equality, gentle Ulrike, hadst thou, like me, come of noble parentage, or I, like thee, been of more humble origin, couldst thou, in sooth, have found, in thy heart, the excuse for a different answer?"

"We are here to discuss other matters, Herr von Hartenburg, than these recollections of childish feelings."

"God's my life! Callest thou the pain of disappointed affection a childish sorrow? Thou wert ever tranquil in temper, and too much disposed to indifference on the subject of any warmth of heart beyond the cold duties of family regard."

"This may be my fault, if you will, Count Emich, but I esteem it an advantage to feel strongest where duty most directs the affections."

"I remember thy final answer, made through thy friend young Berchthold's mother—I owe the lad no grace for the boon, were justice done—but thou answered, that the daughter of a Burgomaster was unfit to be the partner of a Baron; and thou prayedst me to render all duty to the Count my father, that his blessing might lighten the disappointment. Now, were the truth known, that reply cost thee no more than a simple refusal to one of thy maidens of some trifling grace!"

"Were the truth known, Emich, it would tell a different tale. Thou wert then young, and, though violent and hot-headed, not without many manly virtues; and thou greatly overratest the power of a thoughtful girl, if thou supposest she would gladly give pain, where she has received naught but esteem."

"And had I been thy neighbor's child—or wert thou the daughter of some equal of the Empire?—"

"In that case, Lord Count, the answer would have been the same," said the other, firmly, though her countenance evidently lost its tranquil brightness in a transient cloud: "The heart of Ulrike Haitzinger spoke in that reply, as well as her prudence."

"God's truth! thou art of cutting simplicity!" cried the Count, rising abruptly, and losing the expression of gentleness that the recollection of his better days and youthful feelings had given his features, in their usual hardened character. "Thou forgettest, Frau Frey, that I am a poor Count of Leiningen!"

"If I have failed in meet respect," returned the mild Ulrike, "I am now reminded of the fault, and will sin no more"

"Nay, I would say naught unkind or ungentle—but thou bruised my spirit, with a sore answer. We were conversing of the accursed monks, too, and blood gets hot at the mention of their names. Thou thinkest, then, my excellent neighbor, that, as Christians, we are bound to submit to all the exactions of these reverend knaves, and that to presume to right ourselves, is flying in the face of Heaven's authority?"

"You put the case in your own humor, Count. I have said naught of abject forbearance, or of unnecessary submission. If the Limburg monks are forgetful of their vows, the question is of their own safety:—as for us, we have to look that we do nothing wrongful of itself, or nothing that may be accounted disrespectful to Him we worship"——

"Prithee, good Ulrike," interrupted Emich, resuming his seat, in the familiar manner he had used at the commencement of the dialogue, "let us converse, in freedom, of this inclination of thy child. I love young Berchthold, and would fain do him service were the means offering; but I greatly fear we shall have difficulty in bringing Heinrich to a complying state of mind."

"The apprehension of his refusal hath caused me much uneasiness, Herr von Hartenburg," returned the tender mother; "for the Burgomaster is not one of those who change their opinions readily. The over-zealous persuasion of friends increases his faith in himself, at times, instead of softening those resolutions which the wisest of us are apt to form hastily and without thought."

"This quality of thy excellent consort hath not escaped me. But Heinrich Frey was wived so happily himself, and with so little claim to riches on his own part, that he should not, in reason, bear too heavily on a youth that might have known better days, but for a hard fortune befalling his parents.

He that hath been poor, should have respect for poverty in others."

"I fear that such is not the working of human nature," answered the thoughtful wife, nearly unconscious of what she uttered. "Our experience in life would prove that they who have risen show the least tolerance for those who tarry in the rear; and, as none prize the gifts of rank and consequence so much as they to whom they are novelties, we ought not to expect the successful man too soon to forget the longings he felt when in adversity, nor him to whom honors are new, to look too closely into their vanity."

"Nay, Heinrich is not so young in consideration, or so new to fortune, as to be classed with these."

"Heinrich!" exclaimed the matron, across whose chaste brow there stole a crimson suffusion, that resembled the flush of even upon the snowy peaks of the Alps—"There is not question, here, of Heinrich Frey!"

The Count smiled till the mustachios curled upon his brown cheeks.

"Thou art right," he answered courteously; "it is in Berchthold and Meta that we are most interested. I think I see the means of accomplishing all we wish in their behalf, and means that offer so readily as to wear the air of being a gift of Providence."

"They are only the more welcome for their character"

"Thou knowest, Ulrike, that I am greatly burthened with charges that lay heavily on all of my rank. Ermengarde hath most of the qualities of her station, and a love of splendor that is costly; besides, this outfit of my young heir, who travels with the Emperor, hath much drained me of means, of late; else would I offer, of pure love for thee and thine that which would make the connexion acceptable to

Heinrich. In this strait, borne down, as we all are by the war, and saddled with the cost of keeping on foot so many men in Hartenburg, I see no other present means than that I have just mentioned."

"Or have not mentioned; for, in the desire to prove your inability to serve the youth, nothing hath yet been said of this favorable chance offered by Providence."

"I cry thy mercy! Thou hast rightly judged me, Ulrike, for I feel it a reproach to be able to do nothing for one I so esteem."

"Put no undue meaning on my words," interrupted the matron, smiling like one who wished to reassure her companion. "It has never entered my thoughts that the Counts of Leiningen are bound to portion all who serve them, according to their several hopes. It would lighten the heaviest purse in the Palatinate, Herr Emich, to furnish an equal marriage-gift to that which may be the share of Meta Frey."

"None know this better than I. Heinrich and I have often discoursed of the affair, and I could fain wish there existed no inequality of rank—but this is idle, and we will talk only of Berchthold and his hopes. Thou are aware, Ulrike, that there are heavy issues between me and the brotherhood concerning certain dues, not only in the valley, but on the plain, and that the contest fairly settled in my favor will much increase my revenues. Now were this unhappy dissension decided as I could wish, it would not only be in my power, but it would become my wish, to bestow such grace on all my principal followers, and on none so much as on Berchthold, as might leave a favorable opinion of my bounty. We want but this affair rightly settled to possess the means of winning Heinrich to our desires."

"Could this be honestly done, my blessing on him that shall effect it!"

"I rejoice to hear thee say this, good Ulrike

Thou, of all others, mayest be most useful in the matter. Heinrich and I have well nigh decided on the fitness of disturbing the monks in their riotous abominations"——

"The words are strong, when applied to professed Benedictines!"

"By the holy Magi! they are more than merited. Here, has not the day twice turned since I had Bonifacius himself weltering in wine beneath the roof of Hartenburg, an' he had been a roisterer of a suburb! Bonifacius, Limburg's Abbot, have I seen in this unfit condition, Frau Ulrike, within mine own good castle walls!"

"And in thine own good castle company, Herr Emich?"

"Dost thou make no difference between Baron and Monk? Am I a sworn professor of godliness, a shaven crown, or one that looketh to be accounted better than his fellows? That I am noble is the chance of fortune, and as such I receive and profit by the advantage, though, I trust, always in fitting reason; but no man can say that Emich of Leiningen pretends aught to the especial virtues of a monkish character. We that are modest may claim to indulge our failings, but justice should heavily visit him that sins under a cloak of sanctity."

"I know not that thy exception may avail thee in the end. But thou wouldest say something to Berchthold Hintermayer's advantage?—"

"That would I, and right heartily. Could Heinrich be brought to a firm mind, that I might count on the support of the townsmen, these reprobates in cowls should be quickly disposed of; and, as of necessity, my dues would be much augmented, by clothing Berchthold with a deputy's authority over the recovered fields and villages, he should so gain in men's respect, as to soften the reluctance of the hardest-hearted Burgomaster in all Germany."

"And in what manner dost thou look to me, in effecting this object?"

"One of thy understanding need scarce put the question. Thou hast been long a wife, Ulrike, and art skilled in the persuasions of thy sex. I know not thy practice with Heinrich; but when Ermengarde would have her way, spite of her husband's inclinations, she has various manners of coming to her wishes. To-day she is smiling, to-morrow silent; now she fondles, and then she frowns; and, most of all, is she ready in seizing the moments of idle confidence to press on my unprepared reason the arguments of kisses and coquetry."

"It were idle to say I do not understand you, Herr von Hartenburg. I wish not to raise the curtain of your domestic confidence, nor do I feel disposed that any should presume to lift mine. Heinrich and I pursue our several ways, as each deems right, though, I trust, always with the harmony of wedded interests, and I am little practised in the influence you mention. But, dear as Meta is to the heart of her mother—and surely no shoot from the parent stem ever gave fonder hopes, or justified more tender regard"—Ulrike folded her hands, and turned her meek blue eyes to heaven—"much as I esteem young Berchthold, who is the child of my youth's nearest friend; and gladly as I would see their young hearts for ever bound up in the same ties of family concord and matrimonial love, the common parents of lisping laughing babes that should cluster at my knee, giving the evening of life some compensation for the chill of its noon-tide—rather than aid thee in this unhallowed design; rather than do aught, even in rebellious thought, against the altars of my God; rather than set my selfishness in array against his dread power, or fancy wish of mine can prove excuse for sacrilege—I could follow the girl to her grave, with a fearless eye, and place my own head by her side, without regret for that calm decline which, when the weary probation of life is ended, Heaven grants to the deserving."

The Count of Leiningen recoiled at the energy with which his companion spoke; for none are so commanding as the mild when aroused to resistance, or so authoritative as the good when required to exhibit the beauty of their principles. He was disappointed; but, though a sort of instinct warned him that he had no further hopes of gaining the assistance of Ulrike, and, almost without knowing it himself, the respect which he had always entertained for his companion was increased. Taking the hand she extended to him, in amity, the moment her excitement had a little abated, he was about to reply, when a footstep in the adjoining room, and a timid tap at the door, interrupted him.

"Thou canst enter," said the Baron, believing that one of the castle maidens was without, and glad for the relief.

"A million of thanks for the honor," returned Ilse, curtsying to the floor as she availed herself of the privilege. "This is the first time so great a favor ever befell me in Hartenburg, though, when a girl, as it might be a ruddy maiden like our Meta, I once was admitted to a closet in Heidelburg. There was I, and the late Burgomaster, Ulrike's father, and the good wife, her mother, on a junketing, in our young days, to see the curiosities of the Elector's Palace, and we had visited the tun"——

"Thou art sent to seek me?" interrupted the mistress. "Hath Meta need of her mother?"

"That may be always said of a certainty, for girls of that age are like the young of the nest, Herr Count, who are ever in danger of breaking their necks, if they take a hasty flight, without the example of the old to give them prudence as well as courage. Twenty times each day—I know not an' it be not fifty—do I say to our Meta, 'Do as thou wilt, child, an' thou dost nothing amiss.' I hold it to be wrongful to curb young humors so long as they are innocent; and therefore do I say, that kindness is a better rod than anger; and, in this reproving and chastening manner, Herr von Hartenburg, have I reared both Meta and her mother. Well, here you both are, in friendly communion, an' you were children of the same cradle!—and Heinrich Frey is yon, without, tasting the rhenish with the two churchmen that infect the castle"——

"Thou wouldst surely say frequent, good-nurse."

"What matters a word, child! Infect or frequent are much the same, when one speaketh of the gentle and gay! I remember ye both young and handsome, and a pair that the whole town of Duerckheim said ought never to be parted; for if one was noble, the other was good; if one was strong and valiant, the other was fair and virtuous; but the ways of the world led ye on different paths, and Heaven forbid that I should say aught against ways that so many travel!"

"And thou hast left Meta with those that infect the castle, to come and say this?"

"Naught like it. It is true I let the girl listen to a few of their idle words, for without experience a maiden may not know when to repulse an improper freedom; but for any levity to escape my eye, were as impossible as for my Lord Count to fail in duty to the Limburg altars. No, I complain not of the stranger nobles; for while he of Rhodes did many gentle offices in behalf of Meta, the reverend Abbé held me in discourse touching this heresy of Luther, and, I warrant you, ecclesiastic as he is, he went not away the worse for my opinion of the schismatic! We had goodly discourse on the dangers and tribu ations of the times, and might have had much earning between us, but for young Berchthold, who fancied himself beating the forest, by the manner in which he threshed among the old armor of the hall, disturbing all present with the idle pretence of seeking a cross-bow for the Count's pleasure in the morning; as if the Herr Count would have hunted with less satisfaction because there were wise words uttered in his halls! The Hintermayers are a race I love, but this youth seemeth to be wanting of respect for years."

"And what hast done with my child?"

"Thou knowest it was thy desire she should say a few greetings to the fallen Lottchen; and when I thought the wandering cavalier had had his say, I beckoned the child away, in order that she might go to the hamlet on that errand. She will be none the worse for the discourse with that free cavalier, for naught so quickens virtue of the pure stamp as a little contamination with vice—it is like the base metal they put in gold, to make the precious ore hard and able to undergo many hands."

"Thou hast not suffered Meta to go unattended?"

"Didst ever know me fail in duty? Thy motherly heart is quick to take alarm, like the bird fluttering at each leaf that rustles. Not I, in sooth: I sent the vain Gisela to keep her company, and whispered our Meta well, as they departed, not to fail to draw instruction from her companion's light discourse, which, I will warrant, turns on naught else but the gallantries of these strangers. Oh! leave old Ilse to profit by any thing edifying that may turn up, in the way of accident! I that never yet lost a good moral for want of pushing an opportunity! and here stands Ulrike as proof of what I have done. I owe you excuses, Herr Emich, for sending away your forester; but the boy vexed me with his clatter among the shields and arquebuses, and, in order to give him a wholesome lesson in silence, I sent him to see Meta safe to his mother's door, under the pretence of its being necessary to have a manly arm present, to beat off the barking curs of the hamlet."

"Does Heinrich know this?"

"In sooth, he is so beset with thy honor in being closeted with my Lord the Count, that he does little besides talk of it, and take his cup. When the child was thus cared for, by the one who first held her in arms, and one, too, whose experience is little short of threescore and fourteen, I saw not the necessity of calling him from his pleasures."

Ulrike smiled, and turning to the Count, who had been so much lost in thought as to give little heed to the words of the nurse, she offered him her hand, and they left the closet in company

CHAPTER XIV.

"Ah, now soft blushes tinge her cheeks,
And mantle on her neck of snow."
Rogers.

THE cottage of Lottchen, the mother of Berchtnold, was distinguished from the other habitations of the hamlet, only by its greater neatness, and by that air of superior comfort which depends chiefly on taste and habit, and of which poverty itself can scarcely deprive those who have been educated in the usages and opinions of a higher caste. It stood a little apart from the general cluster of humble roofs: and, in addition to its other marks of superiority, it possessed the advantage of a small inclosure, by which it was partially removed from the publicity and noise that rob most of the villages and hamlets of Europe of a rural character.

We have had frequent occasions to allude to the difficulty of conveying accurate ideas of positive things, or even of moral and political truths, while using the terms which use has appropriated to the two hemispheres, but which are liable to so much qualification in their respective meanings. What is comfort in one country would be thought great discomfort in another, and even the two higher degrees of comparison must always be understood subject to a right knowledge of their positive qualities. Thus most beautiful conveys nothing clear, unless we can agree on what is beautiful; while neatness and elegance, and even size, taken in their popular significations, become purely terms of local convention. Were we to say that the cottage of Lottchen Hintermayer resembled, in the least, one of those white and spotless dwellings, with its Venetian blinds and pillared piazzas, its grassy court in front, and its garden teeming with golden fruit in the rear its acacias and willows shading the low roof, and its shrubbery exhaling the odors that a generous sun can extract, we should give such a picture to the reader as Europe nowhere presents—nowhere, because in those regions in which nature has been bountiful, man has been held in mental duress; and in those in which man is sufficiently advanced and free to require the indulgences we have named, nature denies the boons so necessary to their existence. Here, and here only, do those whom fortune has not smiled upon, possess the union of comfort, space, retirement, and luxury, which depend on the causes named, for it is only here that are found the habits necessary to their production, in conjunction with the required climate and a cheapness of material and land, to place the whole within the reach of those who are not affluent. We wish, therefore, to be understood as speaking, at all times, under the consciousness of this difference in the value of terms, for, without such an understanding, there will be little intelligence between us and our countrymen.

We have made this explanation, lest the reader might fancy some affinity between the hamlet of Hartenburg and one in the older settlements of the Union. The remoteness of the period might indeed give some reason to suspect such a resemblance, but were the tale one of our own times, it would be scarcely probable. The Germans, like all the more northern nations, are neat, in proportion to their several degrees of civilization; and the great frequency of the little capitals which dot its surface, and which have all been, more or less, beautified by their respective princes, has caused it to possess a greater number of spacious and cleanly towns, in proportion to its population, than are to be met with in most of the other countries of the European continent; but, as elsewhere in that quarter of the world, the poor are poor indeed.

The little cluster of houses that were grouped beneath the salient bastions of Hartenburg, had the general character of poverty and humility which still belongs to nearly all such hamlets. The buildings were constructed of timber and mud, with thatched roofs, and openings to which, in that age, glass was a stranger. In speaking of the comfort of the dwelling of Lottchen, we wish to say little more than that it was superior to its fellows in these particulars, and that it had the additional merit of faultless neatness. The furniture, however, gave much stronger evidence of the former condition of its tenant. Enough of this description of property had been saved from the wreck of her husband's fortunes, to leave before the eyes of its mistress these traces of happier days—one of those melancholy consolations in adversity which are common among those whose fall has been broken by some light circumstances of mitigation, and which, as monitors to delicacy and tenderness, make touching appeals to the recollections of the spectator. But Berchthold's mother had still better claims to the respect of those who came beneath her humble lintel. As we have already said, she had been the bosom friend of Ulrike in early youth, and, by education and character, she was still every way worthy of holding so near a trust with the wife of the Burgomaster. The allowance of her son was small in money, but the Count permitted his forester to use the game freely; and, as German frugality left her mistress of the wardrobes of several generations, the respectable matron had never known absolute want, and was at all times able to make such a personal appearance as better suited her former than her present means. In addition to these advantages, Ulrike never visited the Jaegerthal without thought of her friend's necessities; and full often, at times and seasons when this sacred duty could not be performed in person, was Ilse dispatched to the hamlet as the substitute of her considerate and affection ate mistress.

The cavalcade from the Abbey had, of necessity, passed the door of Lottchen, and she was fully aware of the intended visit. When, therefore, Meta, blooming and happy, entered the cottage, attended by the warder's daughter, and accompanied by Berchthold, though secretly rejoicing in what she saw, the pleased and watchful matron neither expressed nor felt surprise.

"Thy mother?" were the first words which passed the lips of the widowed Lottchen, after she had kissed the glowing and warm cheek of the girl.

"Is closeted with the Herr Emich, my father says; else would she be sure to be here. She has sent me to say this."

"And thy father?" added Lottchen, with emphasis, glancing an uneasy eye from Meta to her son.

"He drinks of rhenish with the castle wassailers. Truly, my mother Lottchen, thou must find the hamlet unquiet with these graceless spirits in the hold. Our Limburg monks are scarcely so thirsty; and for idle discourse, I know not their equal in Duerckheim, town of vanities and folly though it be, as good Ilse is apt to say."

Lottchen smiled, for she saw by the playful eye of her young visitor, that nothing unpleasant had occurred; and giving Gisela welcome, she led the way within.

"Does Heinrich know of this visit?" asked the

widow, when her young guests were seated, and with a painful interest in the answer.

"I tell thee, Lottchen, that my father quaffs with the strangers. Here is Berchthold, thy son—the restless, impatient Berchthold—he can tell thee mother, into what goodly company the Burgomaster of Duerckheim hath fallen!"

As Meta said this, she laughed, though, in very sooth, she scarce knew why. The more experienced Lottchen saw little else in the mirth of her young visitor than one of those buoyant impulses of youth which lead equally to gaiety and sorrow, without sufficient cause; but she watched the countenance of her own child with solicitude, to note how far he sympathized with the merriment of Meta. Berchthold, by speaking, was the interpreter of his own thoughts.

"Since thou appealest to me," he said, "my answer is, that Heinrich Frey consorts at present with two as hopeless idlers as ever darkened door in Hartenburg. Truly, Brother Luther needs bestir himself for the Church, when such as these go forth in its garments!"

"Say what thou wilt, Master Berchthold," cried Gisela, "of the prating half-shaven Abbé, but respect him of Rhodes, as a soldier in evil fortune, and one that is both gentle and gallant."

"As gallant as thou wilt," cried Meta, with warmth. "Thy humor for mild discourse must be formed by the rude company of the bold, if thou stylest these gentle!"

Lottchen had examined each face earnestly, and her countenance brightened with the frankness and fervor of the last speaker. She was about to say something in guarded commendation of her judgment, when a light step was heard before the outer door, and Ulrike herself entered. Notwithstanding the early departure of the young people from the castle, and the trifling distance between its walls and the hamlet, so much leisure had been wasted in idle laughter by the way, or in culling flowers on the hill-side, that she had sufficient time to exhaust all that old Ilse had to recount concerning the manner in which she had disposed of her charge, and to follow them to the cottage, ere the discourse had gone farther. The meeting between the friends was, as wont, warm and happy. When the usual inquiries were exhausted, and a few unmeaning observations had been made by the girls, the younger part of the company were gotten rid of, under pretence of conducting Meta to witness the manner in which Berchthold had arranged the nests for some doves, which had been a present from herself to his mother. The two parents saw the departure of their children, always accompanied by Gisela, with satisfaction; for each had need of a secret conference with the other, and both knew how apt youth and inclination were to prolong their absence, by means of those thousand little delays which form the unconscious and innocent coquetry of love.

When left to themselves, Ulrike and Lottchen sat, for some time, with hands interlocked, regarding one another earnestly.

"Thou hast borne the trying season of the spring time well, good Lottchen," said the former, with affection. "I have no longer any fear that thy health might suffer in this damp abode."

"And thou lookest youthful and fair as when we strolled, like thy Meta there, laughing and thoughtless girls, on the heath of the Heidenmauer. Of all I have known, Ulrike, thou art the least changed by time, either in form or heart."

The gentle pressure, before they released each other's hands, was a silent pledge of their mutual esteem.

"Thou findest Meta blooming and happy?"

"As she meriteth to be—and Berchthold—I think him fast growing into the comeliness and form of his sire?"

"He is all I could wish—one qualification excepted, my friend; and that, thou well knowest, I do not wish him for any other reason than to satisfy Heinrich's scruples."

"For my child, that qualification is hopeless Berchthold has too much generous indifference to gold, ever to accumulate, were the means his. But what hope is there for an humble forester, who travels his range of chase, follows his lord to ceremonies, or attends him in battle?"

"The Herr Emich values thy son, and I do think would fain do him favor. Were the Count earnestly to reason with Heinrich, all hope would not yet be lost."

Lottchen dropped her eyes to the work on which her needle was employed, for necessity had rendered her systematically industrious. The pause was long and thoughtful. But while Ulrike pondered on the chances of overcoming her husband's love of money and his worldly views, a very different picture had presented itself to the mind of her friend. The eye-lids of the latter trembled, and a hot tear fell upon the linen in her lap.

"I have thought much of late, Ulrike," she said, "of the justice of burthening thy happiness and golden fortunes with the load of our adversity. Berchthold is young and brave, and there seems as little necessity as there is right, in weighing thee and Meta down to our own level. I have anxiously wished for the means of counselling with some friend less interested than thou, on the fitness of what we do; but it is difficult to speak of so delicate a subject without wronging thy daughter."

"If thou wouldest have the most disinterested and

wisest of all advisers, Lottchen, take counsel of thine own heart."

"That tells me to be just to thee and Meta."

"Dost thou know aught of Berchthold's manners or mind, that may have escaped the observation of an anxious mother, who desires to match her own child with none but the deserving?"

Lottchen smiled through her tears, and gazed at the mild features of Ulrike with reverence.

"If thou wouldest hear evil of the youth, do not come to her who hath no other hope, for the tidings. The orphan is the sole riches of his widowed mother, and thou mayest not get the truth from one that regards her treasure wth so much covetousness."

"And dost thou fancy, Lottchen, that thy son in poverty is dearer to thee than is Meta to her mother, though Providence may have left us wealth and consideration? Misfortune hath indeed changed thee, and thou art no longer the Lottchen of my young days!"

"I will say no more, Ulrike," answered the widow, in a low voice, speaking like one rebuked; "I leave all to heaven and thee! Thou art certain that were Berchthold Count of Leiningen, his and my desire would be to see Meta his bride."

A nearly imperceptible smile played upon the sweet mouth of Ulrike, for she bethought her of the recent discourse with Emich; but there was neither suspicion nor discontent in the passing thought. She was too wise to put human nature to very severe tests, and much too meek to believe all who fell short of perfection unworthy of her esteem.

"We will think of things as they are," she answered, "and not dwell on impossible chances. Wert thou Ulrike and I Lottchen, none can believe more fervently than I, that these opinions would undergo no change. Of Meta thou art sure, my friend; but truth bids me say, that I fear Heinrich will never yield. His mind is much occupied with what the world deems its equality of interests; and it will be hard, indeed, to bring him to balance virtues against gold."

"And is he so wrong? Of what excellence is Berchthold possessed, that does not find at least its equal in Meta?"

"Happiness cannot be bartered for, as we would look into the value of houses and lands. He is wrong; and I could weep—oh, how bitterly I have wept!—that Heinrich Frey should be thus bent on casting the happiness of that artless and unpractised child, on the rude chances of so narrow calculations. But we will still hope," added Ulrike, drying her tears, "and turn our thoughts to the more cheerful side."

"Thou saidst something of the power of my boy with the Count, and of his wish to do us service?"

"I know no other means to move Heinrich's mind. Though kind and yielding to me, in all matters that he believes touch my state, he believes that no woman is a fit judge of the world's interests; and, I fear I should add, that, from too much familiarity with my poor means, he places his wife lowest among her sex in this particular: there is no hope, therefore, that any words of mine can change him. But the Lord Emich has great hold on his judgment, for, Lottchen, they who prize the world's smiles, ever yield reverence to those that chance to possess them largely."

The widow dropped her eyes, for rarely, in their numerous and friendly conferences, did her friend allude to the weaknesses of her husband.

"And the Herr Emich?" she asked, desirous to change the discourse.

"The Count is much disposed to aid us, as I have said; for I have laid bare to him our wishes this morning, and have much entreated him to do this kind act."

"It is not wont for thee to be the solicitor with the Herr von Hartenburg, Ulrike!" rejoined Lottchen, raising her eyes again to the countenance of her friend, across whose cheek there passed a flush so faint as to resemble the reflection of some bright color of her attire, while a still less obvious smile dimpled the skin. The looks that were exchanged told of recollections that were both joyous and melancholy, being, as it were, hasty but comprehensive glances into the pregnant volume of the past.

"It was the first request," resumed Ulrike; "nor can I say the boon was absolutely refused, though its gift was coupled with a condition impossible to grant."

"If it were too much for thy friendship, it must have been hard indeed!"

Lottchen spoke under the influence of one of those sudden and keen impulses of disappointment, which sometimes make the strong in principle momentarily forget their justice; and Ulrike perfectly understood the meaning of her words. The difference in their fortunes, the hopelessness of the future with the fallen Lottchen, and all the bitterness of unmerited contumely and poverty, the severe judgments which a thoughtless world inflicts on the unlucky, passed quickly through the mind of the latter, amid a tumult of regrets and recollections.

"Of this thou shalt judge for thyself, Lottchen," she answered calmly; "and when thou hast heard me, I require thy unconcealed reply, conjuring thee, by that long and constant friendship across which no cloud has ever yet passed, to lay bare thy soul, shading no thought, nor desiring to color even the most latent of thy wishes!"

"Thou hast only to speak."

"Hast thou never suspected, that all this warlike

preparation in the hold, in the presence of the men-at-arms in Limburg, tends to no good?"

"Both speak of war; but the Elector is sore pressed, and it is now long since our Germany was at perfect peace."

"Nay, thy surmises must have gone beyond these general causes."

The look of surprise assured Ulrike she was mistaken.

"And Berchthold? Has he said naught of his Lord's intentions?" continued the latter.

"He talks of battles and sieges, like most of his years, and he often essays the armor of his grandfather, which lumbers yon closet; for thou knowest, though not of knightly rank, we have had soldiers in our race."

"Is he not angered against Limburg?"

"He is, and yet is he not. There is a little flame of resentment, I regret to say, in all of the Jaegerthal against the monks, which is much fanned in my son by his foster-brother, Gottlob, the cow-herd."

"This flame hath descended to the hind from his Lord. All that Gottlob says, Emich hath more than hinted."

"Nay, there was revelling in the hold, between Bonifacius and the Count, no later than the night past!"

"Too much blindness to that which passeth before thy eyes, dear Lottchen, is a virtuous feeling of thy nature. The Count of Hartenburg plots the downfall of the Abbey-altars, and he has this day sworn to me, that if I will win Heinrich to his wishes, no influence or authority of his shall be wanting to make Berchthold and Meta happy."

Lottchen heard this announcement with the silent amazement with which the unsuspecting and meek first hearken to the bold designs of the ambitious and daring.

"This would be sacrilege!" she exclaimed with emphasis.

"'Twould be to disgrace the altars of God, that our desires might prevail."

There was a pause. Lottchen rose from her chair, with so little effort, that, to the imagination of her excited friend, it seemed her stature grew by supernatural means. Then raising her arms, the widowed mother poured out her feelings in words.

"Ulrike, thou knowest my heart," she said: "thou who art the sister of my love, if not of my blood—thou, from whom no childish thought was hid, no maiden feeling concealed—thou, to whom my mind was but a mirror of thine own, reflecting every wish, all impulses, each desire—and well dost thou know how dear to me is Berchthold! Thou canst say, that when Heaven took his father, the yearnings of a mother alone tempted me to live; that for him, I have borne adversity with contentment, smiling when he smiled, and rejoicing when the buoyancy of youth made him rejoice; that as for him I have lived, so that for him would I die. Thou canst say, Ulrike, that my own youthful and virgin affections were not yielded with greater delight and confidence than I have witnessed this growing tenderness for Meta; and yet do I here declare, in the presence of God and his works, that before a rebel wish of mine shall aid Count Emich in this act, there is no earthly sorrow I will not welcome, no humility that I will dread!"

The pious Lottchen sank into her seat, pale, trembling, and exhausted with an effort so unusual. The widowed mother of Berchthold had never possessed the rare personal attractions of her friend, and those which were left by time, had suffered cruel marks from sorrow and depression. Still, where she now sat, her face beaming with the inspiration of the reverence she felt for the Deity, and her soul charged to bursting, Ulrike thought she had never seen one more fair. Her own eyes brightened with delight, for at that moment of spiritual elevation, neither thought of any worldly interests; and her strongest wish was that the Count of Hartenburg could be a witness of this triumph of principle over selfishness. Her own refusal, though so similar in manner and words, the natural result of their great unity of character, seemed destitute of all merit; for what was the simple denial of one of her means, compared to this lofty readiness to encounter a contumely that was already so bitterly understood.

"I expected no less," answered Ulrike, when emotion permitted speech: "from thee, Lottchen, less would have been unworthy, and more could scarcely come! We will now speak of other things, and trust to the power of the dread Being whose majesty is menaced. Hast thou yet visited the Heidenmauer?"

Notwithstanding the excited state of her own feelings, which were, however, gradually subsiding to their usual calm, Lottchen took heed of the change of manner in her friend as she uttered the last words, and the slight tremor of the voice with which her question was put.

"The kindness of the anchorite to Berchthold, and his great reputation for sanctity, drew me thither I found him of mild discourse, and a recluse of great wisdom."

"Didst note him well, Lottchen?"

"As the penitent regards him who offers consolation."

"I would thou hadst been more particular!"

The widow glanced towards her friend in surprise, but immediately turned her eyes, that were still filled with tears, to her work. There was a moment of musing and painful pause, for each felt the want of their usual and entire confidence

"Dost thou distrust him, Ulrike?"

"Not as a penitent, or one willing to atone."

"Thou disapprovest of the deference he receives from the country round?"

"Of that thou mayest judge, Lottchen, when I tell thee that I suffer Meta to seek counsel from him."

Lottchen showed greater surprise, and the silence was longer than before, and still more embarrassing

"It is long since thou hast named to me, good Lottchen, one that was so much and so warmly in our discourse when we were girls!"

The amazement of the listener was sudden and marked. She dropped her work, and clasped her hands together with force.

"Dost thou believe this?" burst from her lips.

Ulrike bowed her head, apparently to examine the linen, though really unconscious of the act, while the hand she extended trembled violently.

"I have sometimes thought it," she answered, scarce speaking above a whisper.

A merry laugh, one of those joyous impulses which spring from the gaiety of youth, was heard at the door, and Meta entered, followed by Berchthold and the warder's daughter. At this interruption the friends arose, and withdrew to an inner room.

CHAPTER XV.

I pray thee, loving wife, and gentle daughter,
Give even way unto my rough affairs."
King Henry IV.

About an hour after the moment when Ulrike and Lottchen disappeared, as described in the close of the last chapter, the cavalcade of Heinrich Frey was seen moving along the Jaergerthal, beneath the hill of Limburg, on its way towards the town. Four light-armed followers of Emich accompanied the party on foot, under the pretence of doing honor to the Burgomaster, but in truth to protect him against insult from any stragglers belonging to the men-at-arms who lay in the Abbey—a precaution that was not altogether without utility, as the reader will remember that the path ran within call of the ecclesiastical edifices.

As the beasts ambled past the imposing towers and wide roofs, that were visible even to those who journeyed in that deep glen, Heinrich's countenance, which had been more than usually thoughtful ever since he passed beneath the gate of Hartenburg, grew graver; and Meta, who rode as usual at his crupper, heard him draw one of those heavy respirations which were so many infallible signs that the mental part of her worthy parent was undergoing extraordinary exercises.

Nor did this shade appear only on the face of the Burgomaster. A deep and thoughtful gloom clouded the fine features of his wife, while the countenance of the blooming daughter betrayed that sort of sombre rest which is apt to succeed high excitement; a moment in which the mind appears employed in examining the past, as if disposed to dissect the merits and demerits of its recent enjoyments. Of them all, the male attendants alone excepted, old

Ilse returned as she had gone, self-satisfied, unmoved, and talkative.

"Count Emich hath displeased thee, father," Meta said quickly, when a respiration, which in one less physical would have been termed a sigh, gave her reason to think the Burgomaster's bosom was struggling with some bitter vexation; "else wouldest thou be more cheerful, and better disposed to give me thy parental counsel, as is thy habit, when we go together on the pillion."

"The occasion shall not fail, girl; and these Abbey-walls offer in good time to prick my fatherly memory. But thou art in error, if thou thinkest that the souls of the Herr Emich and mine are not bound together like those of David and Jonathan. I know not the man I more love, or, the Emperor and the Elector apart, as is my duty, the noble I so much respect."

"It is well it is so, for I greatly value these airy rides among the hills, and most of all do I prize a visit to the cottage of Lottchen!"

Heinrich ejaculated audibly. Then, riding a short distance in silence, he continued the dialogue.

"Meta," he said, "thou art now getting to be of a womanish age, and it is time to fortify thy young mind in a manner that it may meet the cunning and malice of the world. Life is of great precariousness, especially to the valiant and enterprising, and we live in perilous times. He that is in his prime to-day, honored and of credit, may be cut down to-morrow, or even to-night, to bring the allusion more closely to ourselves; and thine own parent is as mortal as any reptile that creeps, or even as the most worthless roisterer of the Electorate, that wasteth his substance, the saving of some gainful parent perhaps, in riotousness!"

"This is true, father," rejoined the girl, who, though accustomed to the homely morality of the good citizen, never before had heard the Burgomaster deal with so little deference to himself, and who spoke in a lowered tone, as if the reflection of his sudden humility produced a withering influence on her own self-esteem. "We are no better than the poorest of Deurckheim, and scarcely as good as poor Lottchen and Berchthold."

A stronger ejaculation betrayed Heinrich's displeasure.

"Let these honest people alone," he answered, "since each must be saved or be damned on his own account, let Lottchen and her son take such fare as Providence shall send; we have just now serious matters of great family concernment to occupy us. I would reason with thee gravely, child, and therefore I have need of thy closest attention. It being conceded that I am mortal—an admission thou mayest be certain, Meta, I should not loosely make or without necessity—it follows, as a consequence, that, sooner or later, I must be taken from thee, when thou wilt be left an orphan. Now this great calamity may befall us both much sooner than thou fanciest; for, I repeat it, we live in perilous times, when hot-headedness and valor may any day bring a man to a premature end."

The round arm of Meta clung more forcibly to the body of the Burgomaster, who took the gentle pressure as so much proof of his child's concern in his suppositious end.

"Why tell me of this, fatner?" she exclaimed, "when thou knowest it only makes both unhappy! Though young, it may be my fate to die first."

"That is possible, but little probable," returned Heinrich, with a melancholy air. "Giving nature a fair chance, it will be my turn to precede even thy mother, since I have ten good years the start of her; and as for thee, I greatly dread it will be, one day, thy misfortune to be left an orphan. God knows what will be the end of all these contentions that now beset us, and therefore I hold it wise to be prepared. Whenever the evil day of parting may come, Meta, thou wilt be left with a sore companion for one of tender years and little experience."

"Father!"

"I mean money, child, which is a blessing, or a curse, as it proveth. Were I taken suddenly away, many idle and dissolute gallants would beset thee, swearing by their mustachios and beards, that thou wert dearer to them than the air they breathe, when in truth their sole desire would be to look into the leavings of the departed Burgomaster. There is great difficulty in marrying one of thy neutral condition happily, for, while want of birth closeth the door of the castle and the palace against thy entrance, ample means give thee right to look beyond the mere burgher. I would fain have one of good hopes for a son-in-law, and yet no spendthrift."

"That may not be so easy of accomplishment, good father," returned Meta, laughing, for few girls of her years listen to conjectures or plans concerning their future establishment, without a nervous irritability that easily takes the appearance of merriment—"to me the world seems divided into those who get and those who spend."

"Or into the wise and foolish. There are three great ingredients that commonly enter into all marriages of girls in thy condition, and without which there is little hope of happiness, or even of every-day respect. The first is the means of livelihood, the second is the consent and blessing of the parents, and the third is equality of condition."

"I had thought thee about to say something of tastes and inclinations, father!"

"Idle conceit, child, that any whim may change. Look at yonder peasant, who is trimming the Abbey vines—dost think him less happy with his cup of sour iquor, than if he quaffed of the best rhenish in Bonifacius's cellar? And yet, had the hind his choice doubt it not he would be ready to swear none but the liquor of Hockheim should wet lip of his! The fellow might make himself miserable, by mere dint of fancy, were he once to set his mind on other fare; but, taking life soberly and industriously, who so content as he? Oh! I have often envied these knaves their happiness, when vexation and losses have weighed upon my spirits!"

"And wouldest thou change conditions with these vine-trimmers, father?"

"What art thinking of, wench? Is there not such a thing as order and propriety on earth?—And this brings me to my purpose. There has been question to-day concerning some silliness, not to say presumption, on the part of young Berchthold Hintermayer, in wishing to couple his poverty with thy means"

The head of Meta fell abashed, and the arm, which clasped the body of her father, trembled perceptibly.

"I doubt that Berchthold has not thought of this," she answered, in a voice but little above her breath. though her respiration was very audible.

"All the better for him, since such a desire would be just as unreasonable as it would be, on thy part, to wish to wed with Count Emich's heir."

"Nay, that silly thought never crossed me!" exclaimed Meta, frankly.

"All the better for thee, girl, since the Herr von Hartenburg has had the boy betrothed these many years. Well, as we now understand each other so well, leave me to my thoughts, for weighty matters press on my mind."

So saying, Heinrich composed himself to reflection, fully content with the parental lesson he had just imparted to his daughter. But, in the few and vague remarks that had fallen from the Burgomaster, Meta found sufficient food for uncomfortable conjecture for the rest of the ride.

During the short dialogue between Heinrich and Meta, there had also been a discourse between Ulrike and the crone that rode on her pillion. The propensity of old Ilse to talk, and the well-tried indulgence of her mistress, induced the former to break silence the moment they were clear of the hamlet, and were so far advanced beyond the rest of the party, as to render it safe to speak freely.

"Well," exclaimed the nurse, "this hath been, truly, a day! First had we matins in Deurckheim; and then, the stirring words of Father Johan, with the Abbey mass; and lastly, this high demeanor of the Count Emich! I do not think, good wife, that thou hast ever before seen the Burgomaster so preferred!"

"He is ever in the graces of the Herr von Hartenburg, as thou mayest know, Ilse," returned Heinrich's partner, speaking like one that thought of other things. "I would that they were less friendly at this moment."

"Nay, therein thou dost little justice to thy husband. It is honorable to be honored by the world's honored, and thou shouldest wish the Burgomaster favor with all such, though it were even with the Emperor. But thou wert ever particular, even as a child; and I should not deal too harshly with a propensity that, coming as it were of nature, is not without reason. Ah! Heaven is ever tender with the good! Now, what a happy life is thine, Ulrike; here canst thou go forth before all that were once thy equals, a Burgomaster's companion,—and not a varlet between Deurckheim-gate, or indeed thine own gate, and the hold of Hartenburg, shall stand covered as thy steed shuffles past. This is it to be fortunate! Then have we worthy Heinrich for a master, and such another for keeping all in due respect, is not to be seen in our town; and Meta, who, beyond dispute, is both the fairest and the wisest of her years among all the maidens, and thyself scarcely less blooming than of old, with such health and contentment as might even disarm widowhood of its sorrows. Ah! what a life hath been thine!"

Ulrike seemed to arouse herself from a trance, as the nurse thus chanted praises in honor of her good fortune, and the sigh she drew, unconscious of its meaning, was long and tremulous.

"I complain not of my fate, good Ilse."

"If thou didst, I would cause tne beast to halt, that I might quickly descend, for nothing good could come of a journey so blasphemous! No, gratitude before all other virtues, except humility; for humility leadeth to favors, and favor is the lawful parent of gratitude itself. I would thou couldest have been at my last shriving, Ulrike, and thou shouldest have heard questions of nice meaning closely reasoned! It happened that Father Johan was in the confessional, and when he had got the little I had to say of myself in the way of acknowledgment, (for, though a great sinner like all human, it is little I can do against Heaven at threescore and ten,) we came to words concerning doctrine. The Monk maintained that the best of us might fall away, so as to merit condemnation; while I would have sworn, had it been seemly to swear in such a place, that the late Prior, than whom none better ever dwelt in Limburg, always gave comfortable assurance of mercy being safe, when fairly earned. I wonder not that these heresies should be abroad, when the professed throw this discouragement in the way of the old and weak!"

"Thou art too apt, good Ilse, to dwell on subtleties, when a meeker faith might better become thy condition."

"And what is this condition, pritnee, that thou namest it as a disqualifier? Am I not aged—and can any say better what is sin, or what not? Didst thou know what sin was thyself, child, till I taught thee? Am I not mortal, and therefore frail—am I not a woman, and therefore inquiring—and am I not aged, and therefore experienced? No, come to me, an' thou wouldest get an insight into real sin—sin that hath much need of grace!"

"Well, let it be thus. But, Ilse, I would recall thy mind to days long past, and take counsel of thy experience in a matter that toucheth me nearly."

"That must be some question of Meta; naught else could touch a mother nearly."

"Thou hast reason in part: 'tis of Meta, and of us all, in sooth, that I would speak. Thou hast now been to the Heidenmauer more than once with our girl, in quest of the holy Anchorite?"

"Have I not! Thou mayest well say more than once, since I have twice made that weary journey; and few of my years would have come off so lightly from the fatigue."

"And what is said in the country round of the holy man—of his origin and history, I mean?"

"Much is said; and much that is good and edifying is said. It is thought that one blessing of his is as good as two from the Abbey; for of him no harm is known, whereas there is much reputed of Limburg that had better not be true. For myself, Ulrike—and I am one that does not treat these matters lightly—I should go away with more surety of favor with a single touch of the Hermit's hand, than if honored with blows from all of Limburg But, from the account I except Father Arnolph, who if he be not an Anchorite, well deserves, from his virtues, to be one. Oh! that is a man, were justice done him, who ought never to taste other liquor than water of the spring, or other food than bread hard as a rock?"

"And hast thou seen him of the Heidenmauer?"

"It hath been sufficient for me to be in sight of his hut. I am none of those that cannot have a good thing in possession, without using it up. I have never laid eyes on the holy man, for that is a virtue I keep in store against some of the sore evils that beset all in age. Let any of the autumn plagues come upon me, and thou shalt see in what manner I will visit him!"

"Ilse, thou mayest yet remember the days of my infancy, and hast some knowledge of most of the events of Deurckheim for these many, many years?"

"I know not what thou callest infancy, but if it mean the first cry thy feeble voice ever made, or the first glance of thy twinkling eyes, I remember both an' it were yesterday's vespers."

"And thou hast not forgotten the youths and maidens that then sported at our merry-makings, and were gay in their time, as these we see to-day?"

"Call you these gay? These are hired mourners compared to those of my youth. You that have been born in the last fifty years know little of mirth and gaiety. If thou wouldest learn"——

"Of this we can speak at another season. But since thy memory remains so clear, thou canst not have forgotten the young Herr von Ritterstein; he that was well received of old within my father's doors?"

Ulrike spoke in a low voice, but the easy movement of the beast they rode suffered every word to reach the ear of her companion.

"Do I remember Odo von Ritterstein?" exclaimed the crone. "Am I a heathen, to forget him or his crime?"

"Poor Odo! Bitterly hath he repented that transgression in banishment, as I have heard. We may hope that his offence is forgiven!"

"Of whom—of Heaven? Never, as thou livest, Ulrike, can such a crime be pardoned. It will be twenty years this night since he did that deed, as all in the Jaegerthal well know; for there have beer masses and exorcisms without number said in th Abbey-chapel on his account. What dost take Heaven to be, that it can forget an offence like that!"

"It was a dreadful sin!" answered Ulrike, shuddering, for though she betrayed a desire to exonerate the supposed penitent, horror at his offence was evidently uppermost in her mind.

"It was blasphemy to God, and an outrage tc man. Let him look to it, I say, for his soul is in cruel jeopardy!"

A heavy sigh was the answer of the Burgomaster's wife.

"I knew young Odo von Ritterstein well," continued the crone, "and, though not ill gifted as to outward appearance, and of most seductive discourse to all who would listen to a honied tongue, I can boast of having read his inmost nature at our very first acquaintance."

"Thou understood a fearful mystery!" half whispered Ulrike.

"It was no mystery to one of my years and experience. What is a comely face, and a noble birth, and a jaunting air, and a bold eye, to your woman that hath had her opportunities, and who hath lived long? Nay, nay—young Odo's soul was read by me, as your mass-saying priest readeth his missal; that is, with half a glance."

"It is surprising that one of thy station should have so quickly and so well understood him, that most have found inexplicable. Thou knowest he was long in favor with my parents?"

"Ay, and with thee, Ulrike; and this proves the

great difference of judgments. But not a single day, nay not even an hour, was I mistaken in his character. What was his name to me? They say he had crusaders among his ancestors, and that nobles of his lineage bore the sign of the cross, under a hot sun and in a far land, in honor of God; but none of this would I hear. I saw the man with mine own eyes, and with mine own judgment did I judge."

"Thou sawest one, Ilse, of no displeasing mien."

"So thought the young and light-minded. I deny not his appearance; 'twas according to Heaven's pleasure—nor do I say aught against his readiness in exercises, or any other esteemed and knightly qualities, for I am not one to backbite a fallen enemy. But he had a way! Now, when he came first to visit thy father, here did he enter the presence of the honest Burgomaster an' he had been the Elector, instead of a mere Baron; and though there I stood, waiting to do him reverence as became his rank and my breeding, nay, doing him reverence, and that oft repeated, not a look of grace, nor a thank, nor a smile of condescension did I get, for my pains. His eyes could not stoop to the old nurse, but were fastened on the face of the young beauty, besides many other levities.—Oh! I quickly accounted him for what he was!"

"He was of contradictory qualities."

"Worse than that—a hundred-fold worse. I can count you up his graces in brief speech—First was he a roisterer, that never missed occasion to enter into all debaucheries with the very monks he dishonored,——"

"Nay, that I did never hear!"

"Is it reasonable to suppose otherwise, after what we know of a certainty? Give me but one bold vice in a man, and I will quickly show you all its companions."

"And is this true? Ought we not rather to think that most yield in their weakest points, while they may continue to resist in their strongest?—That there are faults, which, inviting the world's condemnation, produce indifference to the world's opinion, may be true; but I hope few are so evil as not to retain some portion of their good qualities."

"Hadst thou ever seen a siege, good wife, thou wouldest not say this. Here is your enemy, without the ditch, shouting, and screaming, and doing his worst to alarm the garrison.—I say now but what I have thrice seen here, in our very Deurckheim—but so long as the breach is not made, or the ladders placed, each goes his way in the streets, quietly and unharmed. But let the enemy once enter, though it be but by a window, or down a chimney, open fly the gates, and in pour the columns, horsemen and footmen, till not a house escapes rifling, nor a sanctuary violation. Now this blasphemy of Herr Odo was much as if a curtain of wall had fallen at once, letting in whole battalions and squadrons of vices in company."

"That the act was fearful, is as certain as that it was heavily punished; but still may it have been the fault of momentary folly, or of provoked resentment."

"It was blasphemy, and as such it is punished; why then say more in its defence? Here cometh Meta within call, and it were well she should not hear her mother justify sin. Remember thou art a mother, and bear thy charge with prudence."

As the horse ridden by the Burgomaster and his daughter drew near, Ulrike ceased speaking, with the patient forbearance that distinguished her intercourse with the old woman. And during the rest of the ride, little more passed among the equestrians. On reaching his own abode, however, Heinrich hastened to hold a secret council with the chief men of the place.

The remainder of the day passed as was wont in the towns of that age. The archers practised with their bows, without the walls; the more trained arquebusiers were exercised with their unwieldy but comparatively dangerous weapons; the youthful of the two sexes danced, while the wine-houses were thronged with artisans, who quaffed, after the toil of the week, the cheap and healthful liquor of the Palatinate, in a heavy animal enjoyment. Here and there a monk of the neighboring Abbey appeared in the streets, though it was with an air less authoritative and assured, than before the open promulgation of the opinions of Luther had brought into question so many of the practices of the prevailing Church.

CHAPTER XVI.

"Thus I renounce the world and worldly things."

ROGERS.

It will be remembered, that the time of this tale was in the winning month of June. When the sun had fallen beneath those vast and fertile plains of the west, among which the Rhine winds its way, a swift and turbid though noble current, that, like some bold mountaineer, has made a descent from the passes of Switzerland, to gather tribute from every valley on his passage, there remained in the air the bland and seductive warmth of the season.—Still the evening was not a calm moonlight night, like those which grace a more alluring climate; but there reigned in its quiet, a character of sombre repose that constantly reminded all of the hour. It seemed a moment more adapted to rest than to indulgence. The simple habits of Deurckheim caused its burghers to shut their doors early, and, as usual, the gates of the town were closed when the bells sounded the stroke of eight. The peasants of the Jaegerthal had not even waited so long, before they sought their beds.

It was, however, near ten, when a private door in the dwelling of Heinrich Frey opened, and a party of three individuals issued into the street. All were so closely muffled as effectually to conceal their persons. The leader, a man, paused to see that the way was clear, and then, beckoning to his companions, who were of the other sex, to follow, he pursued his way within the shadows thrown from the houses. It was not long ere they all reached the gate of the town, which opened to the hill of the Heidenmauer.

There was a stronger watch afoot that night, than was usual in Deurckheim, though the city, and especially at a moment when armies ravaged the Palatinate, was never left without a proper guard. A few armed men paced the street, at the point where it terminated with the defences, and a sentinel was visible on the superior wall.

"Who cometh?" demanded an arquebusier.

The muffled man approached, and spoke to the leader of the guard in a low voice. It would seem, that he spoke him fair; for no sooner did he utter the little he had to say, than a bustle among the citizens announced an eager desire to do his pleasure. The keys were produced, and a way made for the exit of the party. But the man went no farther. Having procured the egress of his companions, he returned into the town, stopping, however, to hold discourse with those on watch, before he disappeared.

When without the gate, the females began to ascend. The way was difficult, for it lay among terraces and vineyards, by means of winding narrow foot paths, and, as it appeared, the limbs of those who were now obliged to thread them, felt all the difficulties of the steep acclivity. At length, though not without often stopping to breathe and rest, they reached the fallen pile of the ancient wall of the camp. Here both seated themselves, to recover their strength, in profound silence. They had mounted by means of a path that conducted them towards that extremity of the mountain which overlooked the valley of our tale.

The sky was covered with fleecy clouds, that dimmed the light of the moon so as to render objects beneath uncertain and dull; though occasionally the mild orb seemed to sail into a little field of blue, shedding all its light below. But these momentary illuminations were too fitful to permit the eye to become accustomed to the change, and ere any saw distinctly, the driving vapor would again intercept the rays. To this melancholy character of the hour, must be added the plaintive sound of a night-breeze, which audibly rustled the cedars.

A heavy respiration from the one of the two who, by her air and attire, was evidently the superior, was taken by the other as a permission to speak.

"Well, thrice in my life have I mounted this hill, at night!" she said: "and few of my years could do the deed, by the light of the sun——"

"Hist, Ilse! Hearest thou naught uncommon?"

"Naught but mine own voice, which, for so mute a person, is, in sooth, of little wont,—"

"Truly, there is other sound! Come hither to the ruin; I fear we are abroad at a perilous moment!"

As both arose, there was but a minute before their persons were concealed in such a manner as to render it little probable that any but a very curious eye would remark their presence. It was evident that many footsteps were approaching, and nearly in their direction. Ilse trembled, but her companion, more self-possessed, and better supported by her reason, was as much or even more excited by curiosity than by fear. The ruined hut, in which they stood, was within the cover of the cedars, where a dull light alone penetrated. By means of this light, however, a band of men was seen moving across the camp. They came in pairs, and their march was swift and nearly noiseless. The glittering of a morion, as it passed beneath some opening in the trees, and the reclining arquebuses, no less than their order, showed them to be warriors.

The line was long, extending to some hundreds of men. They came, in this swift and silent manner, from the direction of the Jaegerthal, and passed away, among the melancholy cedars, in that of the plain of the Rhine.

When the last of this long and ghost-like band had disappeared, Ilse appeared to revive.

"In very sooth," she said, "they seem to be men! Do they, too, come to visit the Holy Hermit?"

"Believe it not. They have gone down by the rear of Deurckheim, and will soon be beyond our wishes, or our fears."

"Lady! Of what origin are they—and on what errand do they come?"

This exclamation of old Ilse sufficiently betrayed the nature of her own doubts, though the firmness of her companion's manner proved that, now the armed men were gone, she no longer felt distrust.

"This may, or may not, be a happy omen," she answered, musingly. "There was a goodly number, and warriors, too, of fair appearance!"

"Thrice have I visited this camp at night, and never before has it been my fate to view its tenants! Thinkest thou they were Romans—or are they the followers of the Hun?"

"They were living men—but let us not forget our errand."

Without permitting further discourse, the superior of the two then took the way towards the hut of the Hermit. At first her footstep was timid and unassured; for, strengthened as she was by reflection and knowledge, the sudden and sprite-like passage of such a line of warriors across the deserted camp, was indeed likely to affect the confidence of one even more bold.

"Rest thy old limbs on this bit of fallen wall, good nurse," said the muffled female, "while I go within. Thou wilt await me here."

"Go, of Heaven's mercy! and speak the holy Anchorite fair. Take what thou canst of comfort and peace for thine own soul, and if there should be a blessing, or a relic more than thou needest, remember her who fondled thy infancy, and who, I may say, and say it I do with pride, made thee the woman of virtue and merit thou art."

"God be with thee—and with me!" murmured the female, as she moved slowly away.

The visitor of the Anchorite hesitated at the door of his hut. Encouraged by sounds within, and certain that the holy man was still afoot, by the strong light that shone through the fissures of the wall, she at length summoned resolution to knock.

"Enter, of God's will!" returned a voice from within.

The door opened, and the female stood confronted to the person of the Anchorite. The cloak and hood both fell from the female's head, as by an involuntary weakness of her hands—and each stood gazing long, wistfully, and perhaps in doubt, at the other. The female, more prepared for the interview, was the first to speak.

"Odo!" she said, with melancholy emphasis.

"Ulrike!"

Eye then studied eye, in that eager and painful gaze, with which the memory traces the changes that time and the passions produce in the human face. In that of Ulrike, however, there was little to be noted but the development of more mature womanhood, with such a shadowing of thought as deeper reflection and diminished hopes are apt to bring; but, had she not been apprized of the person of him she sought, and had her memory not retained so vivid an impression of the past, it is probable that the wife of Heinrich Frey might not have recognized the features of the gayest and handsomest cavalier of the Palatinate, in the sunken but still glowing eye, the grizzled beard, and the worn though bold lineaments of the Anchorite.

"Thou Odo, and a penitent!" Ulrike added.

"One of a stricken soul. Thou seest me, sworn to mortifications and sorrow."

"If repentance come at all, let it be welcome. Thou leanest on a rock, and thy soul will be upheld."

The Recluse made a vague gesture, which his companion believed to be the usual sign of the cross. She meekly imitated the symbol, and, bowing her head, repeated an *ave*. In all great changes in religions and politics, the spirit of party attaches importance to immaterial things, which, by practice and convention, come to be considered as the evidences of opinion. Thus it is, when revolutions are sudden and violent, that so many mistake their symbols for their substance, and men cast their lives on the hazards of battle, in order to support an empty name, a particular disposition of colors in an ensign, or some idle significations of terms that were never well explained, long after the real merits of the controversy have been lost by the cupidity and falsehood of those intrusted with the public welfare; and thus it is, that here, where all change has been gradual and certain, that the neglect of these trifles has subjected the country to the imputation of inconsistency, because, in attending so much to the substance of their work, it has overlooked so many of those outward signs, which, by being the instruments of excitement in other regions, obtain a value that has no influence among ourselves. The Reformation made early and rude inroads upon the formula of the Romish church. The cross ceased to be a sign in favor with the Protestant; and, after three centuries, it is just beginning to be admitted that this sacred symbol is a more fitting ornament of one of "those silent fingers pointing to the skies," which so touchingly adorn our churches, than the representation of a barn-yard fowl! Had Ulrike been more critical in this sort of distinctions, or had her mind been less occupied with her own sad reflections, she might have thought the movement of the Hermit's hand, when he made the sign alluded to, had such a manner of indecision and doubt, as equally denotes one new in practices of this nature, or one about to abandon any long-established ritual. As it was, however, she noted nothing extraordinary, but silently took the seat to which the Anchorite pointed, while he placed himself on another.

The earnest, wistful, and half mournful look of each was renewed. They sat apart, with the torch throwing its light fully upon both.

"Grief hath borne heavily upon thee, Odo," said Ulrike. "Thou art much changed!"

"And innocence and happiness have dealt tenderly by thee! Thou hast well merited this favor, Ulrike."

"Art thou long of this manner of life—or touch I on a subject that may not be treated?"

"I know not that I may refuse to give the world the profit of my lesson—much less can I pretend to mystery with thee."

"I would gladly give thee consolation. Thou knowest there is great comfort in sympathy."

"Thy pity is next to the love of angels—but why speak of this? Thou art in the hut of a Hermit condemned, of his own conscience, to privation and penitence. Go to thy happy home, and leave me to the solemn duty which I have allotted to be done this night."

As he spoke, the Anchorite folded his head in a mantle of coarse cloth, for he was evidently clad to go abroad, and he groaned.

"Nay, Odo, I quit thee not, in this humor of thy mind. The sight of me hath added to thy grief, and it were uncharitable—more, it were unkind, to leave thee thus."

"What wouldest thou, Ulrike?"

"Disburthen thy soul; this life of seclusion hath heaped a load too heavy on thy thoughts. Where hast thou passed the years of thy prime, Odo—what hath brought thee to this condition of bitterness?"

"Hast thou still so much of womanly mercy, as to feel an interest in the fate of an outcast?"

The paleness of Ulrike's cheek was succeeded by a mild glow. It was no sign of tumultuous feeling, but a gentle proof that a heart like hers never lost the affinities it had once fondly and warmly cherished.

"Can I forget the past?" she answered. "Wert thou not the friend of my youth—nay, wert thou not my betrothed?"

"And dost thou acknowledge those long-cherished ties? Oh Ulrike! with what maddened folly did I throw away a jewel beyond price! But listen and thou shalt know in what manner God hath avenged himself and thee."

The Burgomaster's wife, though secretly much agitated, sat patiently awaiting, while the Hermit seemed preparing his mind for the revelation he was about to make.

"Thou hast no need to hear aught of my youth

he at length commenced. "Thou well knowest that, an orphan from childhood, of no mean estate, and of noble birth, I entered on life exposed to all the hazards that beset the young and thoughtless. I had most of the generous impulses of one devoid of care, and a heart that was not needlessly shut against sympathy with the injured, and, I think, I may say one that was not closed against compassion——"

"Thou dost not justice to thyself, Odo! Say that thy hand was open, and thy heart filled with gentleness."

The Anchorite, humbled as he was by penitence and self-devotion, did not hear this opinion, uttered by lips so gentle and so true, without a change of features. His eye lighted, and for a moment it gazed towards his companion with some of its former bright youthful expression. But the change escaped Ulrike, who was occupied with the generous impulse that caused her, thus involuntarily, to vindicate the Hermit to himself.

"It might have been so," the latter resumed, coldly, after a moment of thought; "but in youth, unless watched and wisely directed, our best qualities may become instruments of our fall. I was of violent passions above all; miserable traces in that unerring index, the countenance, prove how violent!"

Ulrike had no answer to this remark; for she had felt how easy it is for the strong of character to attach the mild, and how common it is for the human heart to set value on qualities that serve to throw its own into relief.

"When I knew thee, Ulrike, the influence of thy gentleness, the interest thou gavest me reason to believe thou felt in my happiness, and the reverence which the young of our sex so readily pay to innocence, and beauty, and faith, in thine, served to tame the lion of my reckless temper, and to bring me, for a time, in subjection to thy gentleness."

His companion looked grateful for his praise, but she remained silent.

"The tie between the young and guiltless is one of nature's holiest mysteries! I loved thee, Ulrike, purely, and in perfect faith! The reverence I bear, here in my solitude and penance, to these signs of sacred character, is not deeper, less tinctured with human passion, or more fervent, than the respect I felt for thy virgin innocence!"

Ulrike trembled, but it was like the leaf quivering at the passage of a breath of air.

"For this I gave thee credit, Odo," she whispered, evidently afraid to trust her voice.

"Thou didst me justice. When thy parents consented to our union, I looked forward to the marriage with blessed hope; for young though I was, I so well understood myself, as to foresee that some spirit, persuasive, good, and yet firm as thine, was necessary to tame me. Woman winds herself about the heart of man by her tenderness, nay, by her very dependence, in a manner to effect that which his pride would refuse to a power more evident.

"And couldst thou feel all this?"

"Ulrike, I felt more, was convinced of more, and dreaded more, than I ever dared avow. But all feelings of pride are now past. What further shall I say? Thou knowest the manner in which bold spirits began to assail the mysteries and dogmas of the venerable Church that has so long governed Christendom, and that some were so hardy as to anticipate the reasonings and changes of more prudent heads, by rash acts. 'Tis ever thus with young and heated reformers of abuses. Seeing naught but the wrong, they forget the means by which it has been produced, and overlook the sufficient causes which may mitigate, if they do not justify the evil."

"And this unhappily was thy temper?"

"I deny it not. Young, and without knowledge of the various causes that temper every theory when reduced to practice, I looked eagerly to tne end alone."

Though Ulrike longed to extort some apology from the penitent for his own failings, she continued silent. After minutes of thought, the discourse at length proceeded.

"There were some among thy friends, Odo, who believed the outrage less than the convent reported?"

"They trusted too much to their wishes," said the Anchorite, in a subdued tone. "It is most true, that, heated with wine, and maddened with anger, I did violence, in presence of my armed followers, to those sacred elements which Catholics so reverence. In a moment of inebriated frenzy, I believed the hoarse applause of drunken parasites, and the confusion of a priest, of more account than the just anger of God! I impiously trampled on the host, and sorely hath God since trampled on my spirit!"

"Poor Odo!—That wicked act changed the course of both our lives! and dost thou now adore that Being to whom this great indignity was offered—Hast thy mind returned to the faith of thy youth?"

"Tis not necessary, in order to feel the burthen of my guilt!" exclaimed the Anchorite, whose eye began to lose the human expression which had been kindled by communion with this gentle being, in gleamings of a remorse that had been so long fed by habits of morbid devotion. "Is not the Lord of the universe my God? The insult was to him; whether there be error in this or that form of devotion, I was in his temple, at the foot of his altar, in the presence of his spirit—There did I mock his rule, and defy his power; and this for a silly triumph over a terrified monk!"

"Heart-stricken Odo! Where soughtest thou refuge, after the frantic act?"

The Anchorite looked intently at his companion, as if a flood of distressing and touching images were pressing painfully upon his memory. "My first thought was of thee," he said; "the rash blow of my sword was no sooner given, than it seemed suddenly to open an abyss between us. I knew thy gentle piety, and could not, even in that moment of frenzy, deceive myself as to thy decision. When in a place of safety, I wrote the letter which thou answered, and which answer was so firm and admirable a mixture of holy horror and womanly feeling. When thou renounced me, I became a vagrant on earth, and from that hour to the moment of my return hither, have I been a wanderer. Much influence and heavy fines saved my estates, which the life of a pilgrim and a soldier has greatly augmented, but never till this summer have I felt the courage necessary to revisit the scenes of my youth.'

"And whither strayed thou, Odo?"

"I have sought relief in every device of man:—the gaiety and dissipation of capitals—hermitages (for this is but the fourth of which I am the tenant)—arms—and rude hazards by sea. Of late have I much occupied myself in the defence of Rhodes, that unhappy and fallen bulwark of Christendom. But wherever I have dwelt, or in whatever occupation I have sought relief, the recollection of my crime, and of its punishment, pursues me. Ulrike, I am a man of woe!"

"Nay, dear Odo, there is mercy for offenders more heavy than thou. Thou wilt return to thy long-deserted castle, and be at peace."

"And thou, Ulrike! hath my crime caused thee sorrow? Thou, at least, art happy?"

The question caused the wife of Heinrich Frey uneasiness. Her sentiments towards Odo von Ritterstein had partaken of passion, and were still clothed with hues of the imagination; while her attachment to the Burgomaster ran in the smoother channel of duty and habit:—Still time, a high sense of her sex's obligations, and the common bond of Meta, kept her feelings in the subdued state which most fitted her present condition. Had her will been consulted, she would not have touched on this portion of the subject at all; but since it was introduced, she felt the absolute necessity of meeting it with composure.

"I am happy in an honest husband and an affectionate child," she said; "set thy heart at rest on this account—we were not fitted for each other, Odo; thy birth, alone, offered obstacles we might not properly have overcome."

The Anchorite bowed his head, appearing to respect her reserve. The silence that succeeded was not free from embarrassment. It was relieved by the tones of a bell that came from the hill of Limburg. The Anchorite arose, and all other feeling was evidently lost in a sudden return of that diseased repentance which had so long haunted him, and which, in truth, had more than once gone nigh to unsettle his reason.

"That signal, Ulrike, is for me."

"And dost thou go forth to Limburg at this hour?"

"An humble penitent. I have made my peace with the Benedictines by means of gold, and I go to struggle for my peace with God. This is the anniversary of my crime, and there will be midnight masses for its expiation."

The wife of Heinrich Frey heard of his intention without surprise, though she regretted the sudden interruption of their interview.

"Odo, thy blessing!" said Ulrike, kneeling.

"Thou, ask this mockery of me!" cried the Hermit, wildly.—"Go, Ulrike!—leave me with my sins."

The Anchorite appeared irresolute for a moment, and then he rushed madly from the hut, leaving the wife of Heinrich Frey still kneeling in its centre.

CHAPTER XVII.

Mona, thy Druid rites awake the dead!
ROGERS.

ULRIKE was in the habit of making frequent and earnest appeals to God, and she now prayed fervently, where she knelt. Her attention was recalled to earth, by a violent shaking of the shoulder.

"Ulrike, child!—Frau Frey!" exclaimed the assiduous Ilse.—"Art glued to the ground by necromancy? Why art thou here, and whither hath the holy man sped?"

"Sawest thou Odo von Ritterstein?"

"Whom! Art mad, Frau? I saw none but the blessed Anchorite, who passed me an' he were an angel taking wing for heaven; and though I knelt and beseeched but a look of grace, his soul was too much occupied with its mission to note a sinner Had I been evil as some that might be named, this slight might give some alarm; but being that I am, I set it down rather to the account of merit than to that of any need. Nay, I saw naught but the Hermit."

"Then didst thou see the unhappy Herr von Ritterstein!"

Ilse stood aghast.

"Have we harbored a wolf in sheep's clothing." she cried, when the power of speech returned. "Hath the Palatinate knelt, and wept, and prayed at the feet of a sinner, like ourselves—nay, even worse than ourselves, after all! Hath what hath passed for true coin been naught but base metal—our unction, hypocrisy—our hopes, wicked delusions—our holy pride, vanity?"

"Thou sawest Odo von Ritterstein, Ilse," returned Ulrike, rising, "but thou sawest a devout man."

Then giving her arm to the nurse, for of the two the attendant most required assistance, she took the way from the hut. While walking among the fallen walls of the deserted camp, Ulrike endeavored to bring her companion to consider the character and former sins of the Anchorite with more lenity. The task was not easy, for Ilse had been accustomed to think the truant Odo altogether abandoned of God, and opinions that have been pertinaciously maintained for twenty years, are not gotten rid of in a moment. Still there is a process by which the human mind can be made to do more than justice, when prejudice is finally eradicated. It is by this species of reaction, that we see the same individuals now reprobated as monsters, and now admired as heroes; the common sentiment as rarely doing strict justice in excessive applause as in excessive condemnation.

We do not mean to say, however, that the sentiment of Ilse towards the Anchorite underwent this violent revulsion from detestation to reverence; for the utmost that Ulrike could obtain in his favor, was an admission that he was a sinner in whose behalf all devout Christians might without any manifest impropriety occasionally say an *ave.* This small concession of Ilse sufficiently favored the wishes of her mistress, which were to follow the Hermit to the Abbey church, to kneel at its altars, and to mingle her prayers with those of the penitent, on this the anniversary of his crime, for pardon and peace. We pretend not to show by what cord of human infirmity the wife of Heinrich Frey was led into the indulgence of a sympathy so delicate, with one to whom her hand had formerly been plighted; for we are not acting here in the capacity of censors of female propriety, but as those who endeavor to expose the workings of the heart, be they for good or be they for evil. It is sufficient for our object, that the result of the whole picture shall be a lesson favorable to virtue and truth.

So soon as Ulrike found she could lead her companion in the way she wished, without incurring the risk of listening to stale morals dealt out with a profuse garrulity, she took the path directly towards the convent. As the reader has most probably perused our Introduction, there is no necessity of saying more than that Ulrike and her attendant proceeded by the route we ourselves took in going from one mountain to the other. But the progress of Ilse was far slower than that described as our own, in ascending to the Heidenmauer under the guidance of Christian Kinzel. The descent itself was long and slow, for one of her infirmities and years, and the ascent far more tedious and painful. During the latter, even Ulrike was glad to halt often, to recover breath, though they went up by the horse-path over which they had ridden in the morning.

The character of the night had not changed. The moon appeared to wade among fleecy clouds as before, and the light was misty but sufficient to render the path distinct. At this hour, the pile of the convent loomed against the sky, with its dark Gothic walls and towers, resembling a work of giants, in which those who had reared the structure were reposing from their labors. Accustomed as she was to worship at its altars, Ulrike did not now approach the gate without a sentiment of admiration She raised her eyes to the closed portal, to the long ranges of dark and sweeping walls, and every where she met evidences of midnight tranquillity. There was a faint glow upon the side of the narrow giddy tower, that contained the bells, and which flanked the gate; and she knew that it came from a lamp that burnt before the image of the Virgin in the court. This gave no sign that even the porter was awake. She stepped. however, to the wicket, and rang the night-bell. The grating of the bolts quickly announced the presence of one within.

"Who cometh to Limburg at this hour?" demanded the porter, holding the wicket chained, as if distrusting treachery.

"A penitent to pray."

The tones of the voice assured the keeper of the gate, who had means also of examining the stranger with the eye, and he so far opened the wicket as to permit the form of Ulrike to be distinctly seen.

"It is not usual to admit thy sex within these holy walls, after the morning mass hath been said, and the confessionals are empty."

"There are occasions on which the rule may be broken, and the solemn ceremony of to-night is one."

"I know not that.—Our reverend Abbot is severe in the observance of all decencies,—"

"Nay, I am one closely allied to him in whose behalf this service is given," said Ulrike, hastily.—"Repel me not, for the love of God!"

"Art thou of his kin and blood?"

"Not of that tie," she answered, in the checked manner of one who felt her own precipitation, "but bound to his hopes by the near interests of affection and sympathy."

She paused, for at that instant the form of the Anchorite filled the space beside the porter. He had been kneeling before the image of a crucifix hard by, and had been called from his prayers by the soft appeal that betrayed Ulrike's interest in him, very tone of which went to his heart.

"She is mine," he said, authoritatively;—"she nd her attendant are both mine.—Let them enter!"

Ulrike hesitated—she scarce knew why,—and Ilse, wearied with her efforts, and impatient to be at rest, was obliged to impel her forward. The Hermit, as if suddenly recalled to the duty on which he had come to the convent, turned and glided awav

The porter, who had received his instructions relative to him for whom the mass was to be said, offered no further obstacle, but permitted Ilse to conduct her mistress within. No sooner were the females in the court, than he closed and barred the wicket.

Ulrike hesitated no longer, though she trembled in every limb. Dragging the loitering Ilse after her with difficulty, she took the way directly towards the door of the chapel. With the exception of the porter at the wicket, and the lamp before the Virgin, all seemed as dim and still within as it had been without the Abbey-walls. Not even a sentinel of Duke Friedrich's men-at-arms was visible; but this occasioned no surprise, as these troops were known to keep as much aloof from the more religious part of the tenants of Limburg, as was possible. The spacious buildings, in the rear of the Abbot's dwelling, might well have lodged double their number, and in these it was probable they were now housed. As for the monks, the lateness of the hour, and the nature of the approaching service, fully accounted for their absence.

The door of the Abbey-church was always open. This usage is nearly common to every Catholic place of worship in towns of any size, and it contains an affecting appeal, to the passenger, to remember the Being in whose honor the temple has been raised. The custom is, in general, turned to account equally by the pious and the inquisitive, the amateur of the arts, and the worshipper of God; and it is to be regretted that the former, more especially when they belong to a different persuasion or sect, should not oftener remember, that their taste becomes bad, when it is indulged at the expense of that reverence which should mark all the conduct of man in the immediate presence of his Creator. On the present occasion, however, there were none present tc treat either the altar or its worship with levity. When Ulrike and Ilse entered the chapel, the candles of the great altar were lighted, and the lamps of the choir threw a gloomy illumination on its sombre architecture. The fretted and painted vault above, the carved oak of the stalls, the images of the altar, and the grave and kneeling warriors in stone, that decorated the tombs, stood out prominent in the relief of their own deep shadows.

If it be desirable to quicken devotion by physical auxiliaries, surely all that was necessary to reduce the mind to deep and contemplative awe existed here. The officials of the altar swept past the gorgeous and consecrated structure, in their robes of duty; grave, expectant monks were in their stalls, and Boniface himself sat on his throne, mitred and clad in vestments of embroidery. It is possible that an inquisitive and hostile eye might have detected in some weary countenance or heavy eyelid, longings for the pillow, and little sympathy in the offices; but there were others who entered on their duties with zeal and conviction. Among the last was Father Arnolph, whose pale features and thoughtful eye were seen in his stall, where he sat regarding the preparations with the tranquil patience of one accustomed to seek his happiness in the duties of his vow. To him might be put in contrast the unquiet organs and severe, rather than mortified, lineaments of Father Johan, who glanced hurriedly from the altar, and its rich decorations, to the spot where the Anchorite knelt, as if to calculate to what degree of humiliation and bitterness it were possible to reduce the bruised spirit of the penitent.

Odo of Ritterstein, for there no longer remains a reason for refusing to the Anchorite his proper appellation, had placed himself near the railing at the foot of the choir, on his knees, where he continued with his eyes fixed on the golden vessel that contained the consecrated host he had once outraged—the offence which he had now come, as much as in him lay, to expiate. The light fell but faintly on his form, but it served to render every furrow that grief and passion had drawn athwart his features more evident. Ulrike studied his countenance, seen as it was in circumstances of so little flattery; and, trembling, she knelt by the side of Ilse, on the other side of the little gate that served to communicate between the body of the church and the choir. Just as she had assumed this posture, Gottlob stole from among the pillars, and knelt in the distance, on the flags of the great aisle. He had come to the mass as a ceremony refused to none.

So strong was the light around the altar, and so obscure the aisles below, that it was with difficulty Bonifacius could assure himself of the presence of him in whose behalf this office was had. But when, by contracting his heavy front, so as to form a sort of screen of his shaggy brows, he was enabled to distinguish the form of Odo, he seemed satisfied, and motioned for the worship to proceed.

There is little need to repeat the details of a ceremony it has been our office already to relate in these pages; but as the music and other services had place in the quiet and calm of midnight, they were doubly touching and solemn. There was the same power of the single voice as in the morning, or rather on the preceding day, for the turn of the night was now passed, and the same startling effect was produced, even on those who were accustomed to its thrilling and superhuman melody. As the mass proceeded, the groans of the Anchorite became so audible, that, at times, these throes of sorrow threatened to interrupt the ceremonies. The heart of Ulrike responded to each sigh that escaped the bosom of Odo, and, ere the first prayers were ended her face was bathed in tears.

The examination of the different countenances of the brotherhood, during this scene, would have been a study worthy of a deep inquirer into the varieties of human character, or of those who love to trace the various forms in which the same causes work on different tempers. Each groan of the Anchorite lighted the glowing features of Father Johan with a species of holy delight, as if he triumphed in the power of the offices; and, at each minute, his head was bent inquiringly in the direction of the railing, while his ear listened eagerly for the smallest sound that might favor his desires. On the other hand, the workings of the Prior's features were those of sorrow and sympathy. Every sigh that reached him awakened a feeling of pity—blended with pious joy, it is true—but a pity that was deep, distinct, and human. Bonifacius listened like one in authority, coldly, and with little concern in what passed, beyond that which was attached to a proper observance of the ritual; and, from time to time, he bent his head on his hand, while he evidently pondered on things that had little connexion with what was passing before his eyes. Others of the fraternity manifested more or less of devotion, according to their several characters; and a few found means to obtain portions of sleep, as the rites admitted of the indulgence.

In this manner did the community of Limburg pass the first hours of the day, or rather of the morning, that succeeded the sabbath of this tale. It may have been, afterwards, source of consolation to those among them that were most zealous in the observance of their vows, that they were thus passed; for events were near that had a lasting influence not only on their own destinies, but on those of the very region in which they dwelt.

The strains of the last hymn were rising into the vault above the choir, when, amid the calm that exquisite voice never failed to produce, there came a low rushing sound, which might have been taken for the murmuring of wind, or for the suppressed hum of a hundred voices. When it was first heard, stealing among the ribbed arches of the chapel, the cow-herd arose from his knees, and disappeared in the gloomy depths of the church. The monks turned their heads, as by a general impulse, to listen, but the common action was as quickly succeeded by grave attention to the rites. Bonifacius, indeed, seemed uneasy, though it was like a man who scarce knew why. His gray eyes roamed over the body of darkness that reigned among the distant columns of the church, and then they settled, with vacancy, on the gorgeous vessels of the altar. The hymn continued, and its soothing power appeared to quiet every mind, when the sound of tumult at the great gate of the outer wall became too audible and distinct to admit of doubt. The whole brotherhood arose as a man, and the voice of the singer was mute. Ulrike clasped her hands in agony, while even Odo of Ritterstein forgot his grief, in the rude nature of the interruption.

CHAPTER XVIII.

"Thy reason, dear venom, give thy reason!"
Twelfth Night.

It is scarcely necessary to explain, that the man who had accompanied Ulrike and Ilse to the gate of Deurckheim, was Heinrich Frey. No sooner had his wife disappeared, and his short conference with the men on watch was ended, than the Burgomaster hurried towards that quarter of the town which lay nearest to the entrance of the Jaegerthal. Here he found collected a band of a hundred burghers, chosen from among their townsmen, for resolution and physical force. They were all equipped, according to the fashion of the times, with such weapons of offence as suited their several habits and experience. We might also add, that, as each good man, on going forth on the present occasion, had seen fit to consult his bosom's partner, there was more than the usual display of headpieces, and breastplates, and bucklers.

When with his followers, and assured of their exactitude and numbers, the Burgomaster, who was a man nowise deficient in courage, ordered the postern to be opened, and issued first himself into the field. The townsmen succeeded in their allotted order, observing the most profound silence. Instead of taking the direct road to the gorge, Heinrich crossed the rivulet, by a private bridge, pursuing a footpath that led him up the ascent of the most advanced of the mountains, on that side of the valley. The reader will understand, that this movement placed the party on the hill which lay directly opposite to that of the Heidenmauer. At the period of the tale, cedars grew on the two mountains alike, and the townsmen, of course, had the advantage of being concealed from observation. A half-hour was necessary to effect this lodgment, with sufficient caution and secrecy; but once made, the whole band seemed to consider itself beyond the danger of discovery. The men then continued the march with less attention to order and silence, and even their leaders began to indulge in discourse. Their conversation was, however, guarded, like that of those who felt they were engaged in an enterprise of hazard.

" 'Tis said, neighbor Dietrich," commenced the Burgomaster, speaking to a sturdy smith, who acted on this occasion as lieutenant to the commander-in-chief, an honor that was mainly due to the power of his arm, and who, emboldened by his temporary rank, had advanced nearly to Heinrich's side, " 'Tis said, neighbor Dietrich, that these Benedictines are like bees, who never go forth but in the season of plenty, and rarely return without rich contribution to their hive. Thou art a reflecting and solid townsman; one that is little moved by the light opinions of the idle, and a burgher that knoweth his own rights, which is as much as to say, his own interests, and one that well understandeth the necessity of preserving all of our venerable usages and laws, at least in such matters as touch the permanency of the welfare of those that may lay claim to have a welfare. I speak not now of the varlets who belong, as it were, neither to heaven nor earth, being condemned of both to the misery of houseless and irresponsible knaves; but of men of substance, that, like thee and thy craft, pay scot and lot, keep bed and board, and are otherwise to be marked for their usefulness and natural rights;—and this brings me to my point, which is neither more nor less than to say, that God hath created all men equal, and therefore it is our right, no less than our duty, to see that Deurckheim is not wronged, especially in that par' of her interests that belong, in particularity, to her substantial inhabitants. Do I say that which is reasonable, or do I deceive both myself and thee, friend smith?"

Heinrich had a reputation for eloquence and logic, especially among his own partisans, and his appeal was now made to one who was little likely to refuse him any honor. Dietrich was one of those anima philosophers who seem specially qualified by nature to sustain a parliamentary leader, possessing a good organ, with but an indifferent intellect to derange its action. His mind had precisely the description of vacuum which is so necessary to produce a good political or moral echo, more particularly when the proposition is false; for the smallest addition to his capacity might have had such an effect on his replies, as a sounding-board is known to possess in defeating the repetitions of the voice.

"By Saint Benedict, Master Heinrich," he answered, "for it is permitted to invoke the saint though we so little honor his monks, it were well for Duke Friedrich had he less wine in his Heidelburg tuns, and more of your wisdom in his councils! What you have just proclaimed, is no other than what I have myself thought these many years, though never able to hammer down an idea into speech so polished and cutting as this of your worship! Let them that deny what I say, take up their weapons, and I will repose on my sledge as on an argument not to be answered. We must, in sooth, see Deurckheim righted, and more is the need, since there is this equality between all men, as hath just been so well said."

"Nay, this matter of equality is one much spoken of, but as little understood. Look you, good Dietrich; give me thy ear for a few minutes, and thou shalt get an insight into its justice. Here are we of the small towns born with all properties and wants of those in your large capitals—are we not men to need our privileges—or are we not human, that air is unnecessary for breath—I think thou wilt not gainsay either of these truths."

"He that would do it, is little better than an ass!"

"This being established, therefore, naught remains but to show the conclusion. We, having the same rights as the largest towns in the Empire, should be permitted to enjoy them; else is language little better than mockery, and a municipal privilege of no more value than a serf's oath."

"This is so clear, I marvel any should deny it! And what say they of the villages, Master Burgomaster? Will they, think you, sustain us in this holy cause?"

"Nay, I touch not on the villages, good smith, since they have neither burgomasters nor burghers; and where there is so little to sustain a cause, of what matter is resistance. I speak chiefly of ourselves, and of towns having means, which is a case so clear, that it were manifest weakness to confound it with any other. He that hath right of his side were a fool to enter into league with any of doubtful franchises. All have their natural and holy advantages, but those are the best which are most clear by their riches and force."

"I pray you, worshipful Heinrich, grant me but a single favor, an' you love me so much as a hair?"

"Name thy will, smith."

"That I may speak of this among the towns men!—such wisdom, and conclusion so evident, should not be cast to the winds!"

"Thou knowest I do not discourse for vain applause."

"By my father's bones! I will touch upon it with discretion, most honorable Burgomaster, and not as one of vain speech—your honor knows the difference between a mere street babbler and one that hath a shop."

"Have it as thou wilt; but I take not the merit of originality, for there are many good and substantial citizens, and some statesmen, who think much in this manner"

"Well, it is happy that God hath not gifted all alike, else might there have been great and unreasonable equality, and some would have arrived to honors they were little able to bear. But having so clearly explained your most excellent motives, worshipful Heinrich, wilt condescend to lighten the march by an application of its truth to the enterprise on which we go forth?"

"That may be done readily, for no tower in the Palatinate is more obvious. Here is Limburg, and yon is Deurckheim; rival communities, as it were, in interests and hopes, and of necessity but little disposed to do each other favor. Nature, which is a great master of all questions of right and wrong sayeth that Deurckheim shall not harm Limburg, nor Limburg, Deurckheim.—Is this clear?"

"Himmel! as the flame of a furnace, honorable Burgomaster."

"Now, it being thus settled, that there shall be no interference in each other's concerns, we yield to necessity, and go forth armed, in order to prevent Limburg doing wrong to a principle that all just men admit to be inviolable. You perceive the nicety we confess that what we do is weak in argument, and the greater need it should be strong in execution. We are no madcaps to unsettle a principle to gain our ends, but then all must have heed to their interests, and what we do is with a reserve of doctrine."

"This relieves my soul from a mountain!" exclaimed the smith, who had listened with a sort of earnestness that denotes honesty of purpose; "naught can be more just, and woe to him that shall gainsay it, while back of mine carries harness!"

In this manner did Heinrich and his lieutenant ighten the way by subtle discourse, and by arguments that we feel some consciousness may subject us to the imputation of plagiarisms, but for which we can vouch as genuine, on the authority of Christian Kinzel, already so often named.

The high and disinterested intellect that is active in regulating the interests of the world has been so often alluded to, in other places and on different occasions, that it is quite useless to expatiate on it here. We have already said, that Heinrich Frey was a stout friend of the conservative principle, which, reduced to practice, means little more than, that

> "They shall get, who have the power,
> And they shall keep, who can."

Justice, like liberality, has great reservations, and perhaps there are few countries in the present advanced condition of the human species, that does not daily employ some philosophy of the same involved character as this of Heinrich, supported by reasoning as lucid, irresistible, and nervous.

The direction in which the band of Deurckheimers proceeded, led them, by a tortuous way, it is true, but surely, to the side of the valley on which the castle of Hartenburg stood. Heinrich, however, brought his followers to a halt long before they had made the circuit which would have been necessary to reach the hold of Count Emich. The place he chose for the collection and review of the band, was about midway between Deurckheim and the castle, pursuing a line that conformed to the sinuosities and variations of the foot of the mountain. It was in an open grove, where the shadows of the trees effectually concealed the presence of the unusual company. Here refreshments were taken by a , for the good people of the town were much addicted to practices of this consolatory nature, and the occasion must have been doubly urgent that could induce them to overlook the calls of the appetite.

"Seest thou aught of our allies, honest smith?" demanded Heinrich of his lieutenant, who had been sent a short distance along the brow of the hill to reconnoitre. "It were unseemly in men so trained as our friends, to be lacking at need."

"Doubt them not, Master Heinrich. I know the knaves well; they merely tarry to lighten their packs by the way, in consumptions like this of our own. Dost see the manner in which the Benedictines affect tranquillity, worshipful Burgomaster?"

"'Tis their usual ghostly hypocrisy, brave Dietrich; but we shall uncloak them! Good will come of our enterprise, for, of a truth, by this spirit on our part, which shall for ever demonstrate the necessity of not meddling in the concerns of a neighbor, we settle all uncertainties between us. By the Kings of Koeln! is it to be tolerated, that a gownsman shall hoodwink a townsman to the day of judgment?—Is there not a light in the Abbey-chapel?"

"The reverend fathers pray against their enemies. Dost think, worshipful Burgomaster, that the tale concerning the manner in which those heavy stones were carried upon Limburg hill, has received small additions by oft telling?"

"It may be thus, Dietrich; for naught, unless it may be damp snow, gaineth more by repeated rolling, than your story."

"And gold," rejoined the smith, chuckling in a manner not to displease his superior, since it palpably intimated the idea he entertained of the Burgomaster's success in accumulating money, an idea that is always pleasant to those who deem prosperity of this nature to be the principal end of life

—"Gold well rolled increases marvellously! I am of your mind, Master Heinrich; for to speak truth, I much question whether the Evil Spirit would have troubled himself with so light an affair as carrying the smaller materials a foot.—As to the heavy columns, and the hewn key-stones, with other loads of weight, it was not so much beneath his character, and may be considered as probable. I have never contradicted that part of the legend, for it hath likelihood to back it, but—ha! here cometh the succor."

The approach of a band of men, who came from the direction of Hartenburg, always keeping along the margin of the hills, and within the shadows, absorbed all attention. This second party was treble the force of the townsmen, like them it was armed, and, like them, it showed every sign of military preparation. When it had halted, which it did at a little distance from the band of Heinrich, as if it were not deemed advisable to blend the two bodies in one, a warrior advanced to the spot where the Burgomaster had taken post. The new comer was well but lightly armed, wearing head-piece and harness, and carrying his sword at rest.

"Who leadeth the Deurckheimers?" he demanded, when near enough to trust his voice.

"Their poor Burgomaster, in person; would there had been a better for the duty!"

"Welcome, worshipful sir," said the other, bowing with more than usual respect. "In my turn, I come at the head of Count Emich's followers."

"How art thou styled, brave captain?"

"'Tis a name but little worthy to be classed with yours, Herr Frey. But such as it is, I disown it not. I am Berchthold Hintermayer."

"Umph!—A young leader for so grave an enterprise!—I had hoped for the honor of thy lord's company."

"I am commanded to explain this matter to your

worship." Berchthold then walked aside with the Burgomaster, while Dietrich proceeded to take a nearer view of the allied force.

It is well known to most of our readers, that every baron of note, at the time of which we write, entertained more or fewer dependants, who, succeeding to the regularly banded vassals of the earlier ages, held a sort of middle station between the servitor and the soldier. There stands a noble ruin, called Pierrefont, within a day's ride of Paris, and on the very verge of a royal forest,—a forest that in some of its features approaches nearer to an American wood than any we have yet met in the other hemisphere,—which castle of Pierrefont is known to have been the hold of one of these warlike nobles, who did many and manifest wrongs to the lieges of the king, even in an age considerably later than this of our tale. In short, European society, just then, was in the state of transition, beginning to reject the trammels of feudalism, and struggling to wear its bonds, at least in a new and less troublesome form. But the importance and political authority of the Counts of Leiningen fully entitled them to preserve a train that barons of lesser note were beginning to abandon, and consequently all of their castles had many of these loose followers, who have since been entirely superseded by the regularly embodied and trained troops of our own time.

The smith found much to approve, and something to censure, in the party that Berchthold had led to their support. So far as recklessness of character and object, audacity in acts, and indifference to moral checks, were concerned, a better troop could not have been desired, for more than half of them were men who lived by the excesses of the community, occupying exactly that position in the social scale that fungi do in the vegetable, or that sores and blotches fill in the physical economy of the species

But in respect to thewes and sinews, a primary consideratiou with the smith in estimating the value of every man he saw, they were much inferior, as a body, to the townsmen, in whom orderly living gainful and regular industry, had permitted the animal to become developed. There was, however, a band of peasants, drawn from among the mountains, or inhabitants of the hamlet beneath the castle walls, who, though less menacing in air, and bold of speech, were youths that Dietrich thought only required the Deurckheim training to become heroes.

When Heinrich and Berchthold rejoined their respective followers, after the private discourse, all discontent was banished from the former's brow, and both immediately occupied themselves in making the dispositions necessary to the success of the common enterprise. The wood, in which they had halted, lay directly opposite to the inner extremity of the Abbey hill, from which it was separated by a broad and perfectly even meadow. The distance, though not great, was sufficient to render it probable, that the approach of the invaders would be seen by some of the sentinels, who, there was little doubt, the men-at-arms, lent by the Elector to the monks, maintained, were it only for their own security. Limburg was not a fortress, its impunity being due altogether to the moral power that the Church, to which it belonged, still wielded, though it were so much weakened in that part of Germany; but its walls were high and solid, its towers numerous, its edifices massive, and all was so disposed that a body within, resolutely bent on resistance, might well have set at defiance a force like that which now came against it.

Of all these truths Heinrich was sensible, for he had shown courage and gained experience in the defence of places, during a life that was now past its meridian, and which had been necessarily spent amid the tumults and contentions of that troubled age. He looked about him, therefore, with greater seriousness, in order to ascertain on whom he might rely, and the fine and collected deportment of Berchthold Hintermayer gave him that sort of satisfaction which brave men feel by communion with kindred spirits in the moment of danger. When every necessary disposition was made, the party advanced, moving deliberately to preserve their order, and conscious that breath would be necessary in mounting the steep acclivity.

Perhaps there is no time in which the ingenuity of man is more active, than in those moments when he has a sensitive consciousness of being wrong, and consequently a feverish desire to vindicate his works or acts to himself, as well as to others. A deep conviction of truth, and the certainty of being right, fortifies the mind with a high moral dignity, that even disinclines it to the humility of vindication. Thus he who rushes from a dispute in which his own convictions cause him to distrust his own arguments, into rash and general asseverations, betrays the goadings of conscience rather than spirit, and weakens the very cause that it may be his wish to establish. An arrogant assumption of knowledge, especially in matters that our previous habits and education rather disqualify than teach us to comprehend; can only lead to contradiction and detection; and although circumstances may lend a momentary and fallacious support to error, the triumph of truth is as certain as its punishments are severe. Happily, this is an age, in which no sophistry can long escape unscathed, nor any injury to natural justice go long unrequited. No matter where the wrong to truth has been committed—on the throne, or in the cabinet, in the senate, or by means of the press—society is certain to avenge itself for the deceptions of which it has been the dupe, and its final judgments are recorded on that opinion which lasts long after the specious triumphs of the plausible are forgotten. It were well that they who abuse their situations, by a reckless disregard of consequences, in order to obtain a momentary object, oftener remembered this fact, for they would spare themselves the mortification, and in some cases the infamy, that is so sure to rest on him who disregards right to attain an end.

Heinrich Frey greatly distrusted the lawfulness of the enterprise in which he was engaged; for, unlike his companions, he had the responsibility of advising, as well as that of execution, on his head. He had, therefore, a restless wish to find reasons of justification for what he did; and as he marched slowly across the meadows, with Berchthold and the smith at his side, his tongue gave utterance to his thoughts.

"There cannot be any manner of doubt of the necessity and justice of what we do to Limburg, Master Hintermayer," he said; for men usually affirm in all dubious cases with a confidence precisely in an inverse ratio to the distrust they feel of the rectitude of their cause:—"else why are we here? Is Limburg for ever to trouble the valley and the plain, with its accursed exactions and avarice, or are we slaves for shaven monks to trample on?"

"There are sufficient reasons, of a truth, for what we do, Herr Burgomaster," answered Berchthold, whose mind had taken a strong bias to the new change in religious opinions, that were then fast gaining ground. "When we have so good motives, let us look no farther."

"Nay, young man, I am certain that the honest smith here will say, no nail that he drives into hoof can be too well clenched."

"That fact is out of all question, Master Berchthold," answered Dietrich, "and therefore must his worship be right in the whole argument."

"Let it be so; I shall never gainsay the necessity of breaking up a nest of drones."

"I call them not drones, young Berchthold, nor do I come to break them up; but simply to show the world, that he who would deal with the affairs of Deurckheim, hath need of a lesson to teach him not to enter his neighbor's grounds."

"This is wholesome, and will bring great credit on our town!" responded the smith. "The more the pity that we do not press the same matter home upon the Elector too, who hath of late raised new pretensions to our earnings."

"With the Elector the affair may not be discussed. for his interference is of too strong a quality to call upon our manhood in maintaining the right of non interference. These subtle questions of law are not to be learned over a furnace, but need nice capacities to render them clear; but clear they are,—to all who have the power to understand them. It is more than probable, that to thee, Dietrich, they are not so manifest; but wert thou one of the town council, thou shouldst look into the question with different eyes."

"That I doubt not, honorable Heinrich, that I doubt not. Could but such an honor light on one of my name and breeding—Himmel! the worshipful council should find a man ready to believe any nicety of this sort, or indeed of any other sort!"

"Ha! There is a light at yonder loop!" exclaimed Berchthold. "This bodes well."

"Hast a friend in the Abbey?"

"Go to, Herr Burgomaster—This touches on excommunication;—but I much like yon light at the loop!"

"Let there be silence," whispered Heinrich to those in his rear, who passed the order to their fellows. "We draw near."

The party was now at the foot of the hill. Not a

sign of their approach being known had yet met them; unless a single taper placed at a dungeon-loop could thus be interpreted. On the contrary, the stillness already described in the approach of Ulrike, reigned over the whole of the vast pile. But, neither Heinrich nor his companion liked this fearful quiet, for it boded a defence the more serious when it did come. They would have greatly preferred an open resistance, and nothing would have more relieved the minds of the two leaders, than to have been able to command a rush, under a hot discharge from the arquebusiers of Duke Friedrich But this relief was refused them, and the whole band reached a point of the hill, under a flanking tower, where it became necessary to abandon all idea of cover, and to make a swift movement, to gain the road. It was the rush of this evolution which first disturbed the monks in the chapel. The second interruption proceeded from the ruder sounds of the assault, that immediately after was made upon the outer gate, itself.

CHAPTER XIX.

"I'll never
Be such a ghostling to obey instinct, but stand
As if a man were author of himself,
And knew no other line."

Coriolanus.

THE assailants, as has been seen, were led by the Burgomaster, and his two lieutenants, Berchthold and the smith. Close at the heels of the latter followed three of his own journeymen, each, like his master, armed with a massive sledge. No sooner did the party reach the gate, than these artisans commenced the duty of pioneers, with great readiness and skill. At the third blow, from Dietrich's brawny arm, the gate flew open, and those in front rushed into the court.

"Who art thou?" cried Berchthold, seizing a man who knelt with a knee on another's breast, immediately across his passage. "Speak, for this is not a moment of trifling!"

"Master Forester, be less hot, and remember thy friends. Dost not see it is Gottlob, that holdeth the convent porter, lest the knave should use the additional bars. There are strangers within, and. to consult his ease, the faithless varlet hath not done his fastenings properly, else mightest thou have pounded till Duke Friedrich's men were upon thee."

"Bravely done, foster brother! Thy signal was seen and counted on; but, since thou knowest the ways so well, lead on, at once, against the men-at-arms."

"Himmel! The rogues have bristly beards, well grizzled with war, and may not like to have their sleep thus suddenly broken; but service must be done—Choose the most godly of thy followers, worshipful Burgomaster, to go against the monks, who are fortified in their choir, and well armed with prayer; while I will lead the more carnal to another sort of work against the Elector's people."

While this short dialogue had place, the whole of the assailants poured through the gate, their officers endeavoring to maintain something like order, among the ill-trained band. All felt the imperious necessity of first disposing of the troops; for as respects the monks themselves, there was certainly no cause of immediate apprehension. A few were left, therefore, to guard the gate, while Heinrich, guided by the cow-herd, led his followers toward the buildings, where the men-at-arms were known to lodge.

If we were to say that the party advanced to this attack without concern, we should overrate their valor, and do the reputation of the Elector's men injustice. There was sacrilege in the invasion of the convent, according to the predominant opinions of the age; for though Protestantism had made great progress, even reformers had grievous doubts in severing the bonds of habit and long-established prejudices. To this lurking sentiment was added the unaccountable silence that still reigned among the men-at-arms, who, as Gottlob had said, were known to be excellent soldiers at need. They lay in the rear of the Abbot's dwelling, and were sufficiently intrenched behind walls, and among the gardens, to make a fierce resistance.

But all these considerations rather flashed upon the minds of the leaders, than they were maturely weighed. In the moment of assault there is little leisure for thought, especially when the affair gets to be as far advanced as this we are now describing. The men rushed towards the point of attack, accordingly, beset by misgivings rather than entertaining any very clear ideas of the dangers they ran.

Gottlob had evidently made the best of the time he had been at liberty in the Abbey, to render himself master of the intricate windings of the different passages. He was soon at the door of the Abbot's abode, which was dashed into splinters by a single blow of Dietrich's sledge, when there poured a stream of reckless, and we may add lawless, soldiery through the empty apartments. In another moment, the whole of the assailants were in the grounds, in the rear of this portion of the dwellings.

As there is nothing that more powerfully rebukes violence than a calm firmness, so is there nothing so appalling to or so likely to repulse an assault, as a coolness that seems to set the onset at defiance. In such moments, the imagination is apt to become more formidable than the missiles of an enemy; conjuring dangers in the place of those, which, in the ordinary course of warfare, might be lightly estimated were they seen. Every one knows, that the moment which precedes the shock of battle, is by far the most trying to the constancy of man, and a reservation of the means of resistance is prolonging that moment, and of course increasing its influence.

Every man among the hostile band, even to the leaders, felt the influence of this mysterious quiet among the troops of the Elector. So imposing in fact did it become, that they halted in a group, a position of all others most likely to expose them to defeat,—and there was a low rumor of mines and ambuscades.

Berchthold perceived that the moment was critical, and that there was imminent danger of defeat.

"Follow!" he cried, waving his sword, and springing towards the silent buildings in which it was known the men-at-arms were quartered. He was valiantly seconded by the Burgomaster and the smith, when the whole party resumed its courage, and advanced tumultuously against the doors and windows. The sounds of the sledges, and the yielding of bars and bolts, came next; after which the rush penetrated to the interior. The cries of the assailants rang among empty vaults. There was the straw, the remnants of food, the odor of past debauches, and all the usual disgusting signs of ill-regulated barracks; for in that day, neatness and method did not descend far below the condition of the affluent; but no cry answered cry, no sword or arquebuse was raised to meet the blow of the invader. Stupor was the first feeling, on gaining the knowledge of this important fact. Then Heinrich and Berchthold both issued orders to bring the captured porter, who was in the centre of the assailants, before them.

"Explain this," said the Burgomaster, authoritatively; "what hath become of Duke Friedrich's followers?"

"They departed at the turn of the night, worshipful Herr, leaving Limburg to the care of its patron saint."

"Gone! whither, and in what manner?—If thou deceivest me, knave, thy saint Benedict himself shall not save thee from a flaying!"

"I pray you be not angered, great magistrate, for I say nothing but truth. There came an order from the Elector, as the sun set, recalling his meanest warrior: for, it is said, he is sore pressed, and hath great need of succor."

The silence which followed this explanation, was succeeded by a shout, and individuals began to steal eagerly away from the main body, bent on their own designs of pillage.

"What road took the Duke's men?"

"Worshipful Heinrich, they went down by the horse-path, in great secrecy and order, and passed up the opposite mountain, in order to escape troubling the townsmen to open the gates at that late hour. It was their intention to cross the cedars of the Heidenmauer, and, descending on the other side of the camp, to gain the plain in the rear of Deurckheim."

There no longer remained a doubt that the conquest was achieved, and the entire party broke off in bands; some to execute their private orders, and others, like those who had already proved delinquent, to look after their own particular interests.

Until this moment not a solitary straggler had gone near the chapel. As it was not the wish of those who had planned the assault, to do personal injury to any of the fraternity, the orders had been so worded, as to leave this portion of the Abbey for a time unvisited, in the expectation that the monks would profit by the omission, to escape by some of the many private posterns that communicated with the cloisters. But, as there no longer was an armed enemy to subdue, it now became necessary to think of the fraternity. The process of sacking their dormitories was already far advanced, and the bursts of exultation, that began to issue from the buildings announced that the rich and commodious dwelling of the Abbot himself was undergoing a similar summary process.

"Himmel!" muttered Gottlob, who from the moment of his liberation had not quitted the side of his foster brother, "our castle rogues are taking deep looks into the books of the most reverend Bonifacius, Master Berchthold! It were good to tell them which are Latin, at least, lest they burthen their shoulders with learning they can never use."

"Let the knaves plunder," replied Heinrich, gruffly; "as much evil as good hath come from that store of letters, and it will be all the better for Deurckheim were the damnable ammunition of the Benedictines a little less plenty. There are those on the plains who doubt that necromancy is bound up in some of the volumes that bear a saint's name on their backs."

Perhaps Berchthold might have remonstrated, had not his instinct told him, that remonstrance on such a subject, in that moment of riot and confusion, would have been worse than useless. The consequence was, that valuable works and numerous manuscripts, which had been collected during centuries of learned ease, were abandoned to the humor of men incapable of estimating their value, or even of understanding their objects.

"Let us to the monks," said Heinrich, sheathing his heavy blade, for the first time since they had quitted the wood. "Friend smith, thou wilt look to the duties here, and see that what is done is done thoroughly. Remember that thy metal is well heated, and on the anvil, waiting thy pleasure; it must be beaten flat, lest at another day it be remoulded into a weapon to do us harm. Go to, Dietrich; thou knowest what we of the town would have, and what we expect of thy skill."

Taking Berchthold by the arm, the Burgomaster led the way towards that far-famed pile, the Abbey-church. They were followed by a body of some twenty chosen artisans, who, throughout the whole of that eventful night, kept close to the two leaders, like men who had been selected for this particular duty."

The same ominous silence reigned around the chapel as had rendered the approach to the quarters of the men-at-arms imposing. But here the invaders went against a different enemy. With most then living, the mysterious power of the Church still possessed a deep and fearful interest. Dissenters had spoken boldly, and the current of public opinion had begun to set strongly against the Romish Church, in all that region, it is true; but it is not easy to eradicate by the mere efforts of reason, the deep roots that are thrown out by habit and sentiment. At this very hour, we see nearly the entire civilized world committing gross and evident wrongs, and justifying its acts, if we look closely into its philosophy, on a plea little better than that of a sickly taste formed by practices which in themselves cannot be plausibly vindicated. The very vicious effects of every system are quoted as arguments in favor of its continuance; for change is thought to be, and sometimes is, a greater evil than the existing wrong; and men, in millions, are doomed to continue degraded, ignorant, and brutal, simply because vicious opinions refuse all sympathy with those whose hopeless lot it has been to have fallen, by the adventitious chances of life, beneath the ban of society. In this manner does error beget error, until even philosophy and justice are satisfied with making abortive attempts to palliate a disease that a bolder and better practice might radically cure. It will not occasion surprise, therefore, when we say, that both Heinrich and Berchthold had heavy misgivings concerning the merit of their enterprise, as they drew near the church. Perhaps no man ever much preceded his age, without at moments distrusting his own principles; and it is certain, that Luther himself was often obliged to wrestle with harassing doubts. Berchthold was less troubled, however, than his companion, for he acted under the orders of a superior, and was both younger and better taught than the Burgomaster. The first of these facts was sufficient of itself, under his habits, to remove a load of responsibility from his shoulders, while the latter not only weakened the influence of previous opinions, but caused those which he had adopted to be well fortified. In short, there existed between Heinrich and Berchthold that sort of difference which all must have remarked in the advancing age in which we live, between him who has inherited his ideas from generations that have passed, and him who obtains them from his contemporaries. The young Forester had grown into manhood since the voice of the Reformer was first heard in Germany, and as it happened to be his lot to dwell among those who listened to the new opinions, he had imbibed most of their motives of dissent, without ever having been much subject to the counteracting influence of an opposite persuasion. It is in this gradual manner, that nearly all salutary moral changes are effected, since they who first entertain them, are rarely able to do more, in their generation, than to check the progress of habit; while the duty of causing the current to flow backward, and to take a new direction, devolves on their successors.

In believing that Wilhelm of Venloo would be foremost in deserting his post, in this moment of outrage and tumult, the authors of the assault did him injustice. Though little likely to incur the haz ards, or to covet the honors of martyrdom, the masculine mind of the Abbot elevated him altogether above the influence of any very abject passion; and if he had not self-command to curtail the appetites, he had a dignity of intellect which rarely deserts the mentally-gifted in situations of difficulty. When Heinrich and Berchthold, therefore, entered the church, they found the entire community in the choir remaining, like Roman senators, to receive the blow in their collective and official character. There might have been artifice, as well as magnanimity, in the resolution which had decided Bonifacius to adopt this course; for, coming as they did from the scene of brutal violence without, those who entered the church were much impressed by the quiet solemnity which met them.

The candles still burned before the altar, the lamps threw their flickering light on the quaint architecture and the gorgeous ornaments of the chapel, while every pale face and shaven head beneath, looked like some consecrated watchman, placed near the shrine to protect it from pollution. Each monk was in his stall, with the exception of the Prior and Father Johan, who had stationed themselves on the steps of the altar; the first as the officiating priest of the late mass, and the latter under an impulse of his governing and natural exaggeration, which moved him to throw his person as a shield before the vessel that contained the host. The Abbot was on his throne, motionless, indisposed to yield, and haughty, though with features that betrayed great and condensed passion.

The Burgomaster and Berchthold advanced into the choir alone, for their followers remained in the body of the church, in obedience to a sign from the former. Both were uncovered, and while they walked slowly up the choir, scarce a head moved.

Eveiy eye seemed riveted, by a common spell, on the crucifix of precious stones and ivory that stood upon the altar. The blood of Heinrich creeped under the influence of this solemn calm, and by the time he had reached the steps, where he stood confronted equally to the Abbot and the Prior, for the former of whom he had quite as much fear as hatred, and for the latter an unfeigned love and reverence, the resolution of the honest Burgomaster was sensibly weakened.

"Who art thou?" demanded Bonifacius, admirably timing his question, by the indecision and the quailing eye of him he addressed.

"By Saint Benedict! my face is no such stranger in Limburg that you put this question, most holy Abbot," answered Heinrich, making an effort to imitate the other's composure, that was very sensible to himself, but better concealed from others; "though not shaven and blessed, like a monk, I am one well known to most that dwell in or near Deurckheim!"

"I had better said, '*What* art thou?' Thy name and office are known to me, Heinrich Frey; but in what character dost thou now presume to enter Limburg church, and to show this want of reverence to our altars?"

"To speak thee fairly, reverend Bonifacius, 'tis in the character of the head-man of Deurckheim, a much-injured and long-abused town, that is tired of monkish exactions and monkish pride, and which hath at length assumed the office of doing itself justice, that I appear. We are here to night, not as peaceful citizens bent on prayers and hymn-singing, but armed, as thou seest, and bold in the intention to do away a nuisance from the neighborhood for ever."

"Thy words are as little friendly as thy guise, and what thou sayest here, but too well answers to hat which thy rude followers perform beyond the walls of this consecrated spot. Hast thou well pondered on this bold step of thy town, Herr Heinrich?"

"If often pondering be well pondering, it hath been before us, Bonifacius, at different meetings, and in various discussions, any time this year past."

"And hast thou no dread of Rome?"

"That is an authority which lessens daily in this region, holy Benedictine. Not to deal doubly by thee, of the two we have most distrusted the anger of Duke Friedrich; but that fear is diminished by the certainty that he hath so much on his hands just now, that his thoughts cannot easily turn to other affairs. We did not know, in sooth, that he had recalled his men-at-arms, but had counted on some angry discussion with those obstinate warriors; and thou wilt easily comprehend that their absence hath, in no manner, lessened our faith in our own cause."

"The Elector may regain his power, when a day of reckoning will come for those who have dared to profit by his present distress."

"We are traders and artisans, good Bonifacius, and have made our estimates with some nicety. If the Abbey must be paid for—an event by no means certain—we shall count the bargain profitable so long as it cannot be rebuilt. Brother Luther, we think, is laying a corner-stone that will prevent the devil from ever attempting to set up that which we now propose to throw down."

"This is thy final answer, Burgomaster?"

"Nay, I say not that, Abbot. Send in thy terms to the town-council to-morrow, and, if we can entertain them, it may happen that a present accommodation shall stop all further claims. But what has here been so happily commenced, must be as happily finished."

"Then before I quit these holy walls, hearken to my malediction," returned Bonifacius, rising with priestly and practised dignity:—"on thee and on thy town—on all that call thee magistrate—parent——"

"Stay the dreadful words!" cried a piercing female voice from among the columns behind the choir. "Reverend and holy Abbot, have mercy!" added Ulrike, pale, trembling, and shaken equally with horror and alarm, though her eye was bright and wild, like that of one sustained by more than human purpose: "Holy Priest, forbear! He knows not what he does. Madness hath seized on him and on the town. They are but tools in the hands of one more powerful than they."

At the appearance of Ulrike, Bonifacius resumed his seat, disposed to await the effect of her appeal.

"Thou here!" said Heinrich, regarding his wife with surprise, but entirely without anger or suspicion.

"Happily here, to avert this fearful crime from thee and thy household."

"I had thought thee at thy prayers with the poor Herr von Ritterstein, in his comfortless hermitage of the Heidenmauer!"

"And canst thou think of the deed which hath driven the Herr Odo to this penitence and suffering, and stand here armed and desperate! Thou seest that years do not suffice to relieve a soul on which the weight of sacrilege rests; oh! hadst thou been with me, to witness the agony that preyed upon poor Odo, as he knelt at yonder step, listening to the mass that hath this night been said in his behalf, thou mightest better know how deep is the wound made on the heart that hath been seared by God's anger!"

"This is most strange!" rejoined the wondering Burgomaster; "that those whom I had hoped well disposed of, and that in a manner neither to suspect nor to trouble our enterprise, should cross us at the moment when all is so near completion! Sapperment! young Berchthold, thou seest in what manner matrimony clogs the stoutest of us, though girded with the sword."

"And thou, Berchthold Hintermayer, son of my dearest friend—child of my fondest hope,—thou comest, too, on this unholy errand, like the midnight robber, stealing upon the unarmed and consecrated!"

"None love, or none reverence thee, more than I, Madame Ulrike," answered the youth, bowing with sincere respect; "but wert thou to address thy speech to the Herr Heinrich, it would go at once to him who directs our movements."

"Then on thee, Burgomaster, will be thrown the heaviest load of Heaven's displeasure, as on the leader of the outrage. What matters it that the Benedictines are grasping, or overweening in their respect for themselves, or that some among them have forgotten their vows? Is not this temple devoted to God? Are not these his altars, before which thou hast dared to come, with a hostile heart and an angry purpose?"

"Go to, good Ulrike," returned Heinrich, saluting the cold but ever handsome cheek of his wife, who leaned her head on his shoulder to recall her faculties, while she firmly held his hand with both her own, as if to stay his acts; "Go to, thou art excellent in thy way, but what can thy sex know of policy? This matter hath been had up before many councils; and—by my beard!—tongue of woman cannot shake the resolutions of Deurckheim. Go, depart with thy nurse, and leave us to do our pleasure."

"Is it thy pleasure, Heinrich, to brave Heaven Dost thou not know, that the crimes of the parent are visited on the child—that the wrong done to-day however we may triumph in present success, is sure to revisit us in the dread shape of punishment? Were there no other power than conscience, so long as that fearful scourge remains on earth, 'tis vain to expect immunity. Dost thou owe all to thy Deurckheim council and its selfish policy? Hast thou forgotten the hour that my pious parents gave thee my hand, and the manner in which thou then plighted thy faith to protect me and mine, to assume the place of these departed friends, to be father, and mother, and husband, to her thou took to thy bosom? Is Meta—that child of our mutual esteem—naught, that thou triflest with her peace and hopes? Lay aside, then, these hasty intentions, and turn thy mind to thine own abode; bethink thee of those whom nature and the law condemn to suffer for thy faults, or to whom both have given the dearer right to rejoice in thy clemency and mercy."

"Was ever woman so bent on crossing the noble duties of man!" said the Burgomaster, who, spite of himself, had been sensibly moved by this hasty and comprehensive picture of his domestic duties, and who was greatly troubled to find the means of extricating himself from the position in which he stood.—"Thou art better in thy chamber, good Ulrike. Meta will hear of this onset, and have her fears.—Go then, and calm the child; thou shalt have such escort as becometh my quality and thy deserts."

"Berchthold, I make the last appeal to thee. This cruel father, this negligent husband, is too madly bent on his council, and on the wild policy of the town, to remember God! But thou hast young hopes, and sentiments that become thy years and virtue. Dost think, rash boy, that one like Meta will dare trust the last chance of happiness to a participator in this crime, when such an inheritance of guilt will be the portion that shall descend from her own father?"

A stir among the monks, who had hitherto listened

with an attention that vacillated between hope and fear, interrupted the answers of the wavering Burgomaster, and his young companion. The movement was caused by the entrance of the group, which, until now, had stood aloof in the obscurity of the great aisle, but which seized the moment of doubt, to advance into the centre of the choir. One closely muffled, walked from out its centre, and throwing aside the cloak that had concealed his form, showed the armed person of Emich of Leiningen. The moment Ulrike recognized the unbending eye of the Baron, she buried her face in her hands, and quitted the place. She went not unattended, however, for both her husband and Berchthold followed anxiously; nor did either return to the work of the night, until he had seen the heart-stricken wife and mother under the protection of a well-chosen company of the townsmen.

CHAPTER XX.

"He, who the sword of heaven will bear,
Should be as holy as severe—"
Measure for Measure.

The first glances between Emich and Bonifacius were filled with those passions which each had so long dissembled, and of which the reader has already had glimpses during the more unguarded moments of the recent debauch. In the eyes of the Count, triumph mingled with hatred; while there still remained a slight covering of artifice and caution about the lineaments of the Abbot, masks that he scarcely thought it yet expedient to throw entirely aside.

"We owe this visit, then, to thee, Herr Emich?" said the latter, struggling to appear calm.

"And to thine own desert, most holy Bonifacius."

"What wouldst thou, audacious Baron?"

"Peace in this oft-violated valley—humility in shaven crowns—religion without hypocrisy—and mine own."

"I will not talk to thee of Heaven, bold man, for the word were blasphemy in such a presence; but thou art not yet so lost to worldly policy as to overlook the punishment of the Empire. Hast thou well counted thy gold, and art thou sure thy coffers are sufficiently stored to rebuild the sainted pile which thy hand would fain destroy—or dost think thy riches can replace all that pious princes have here bestowed, during ages in which the Church hath been duly reverenced?"

"As to thy vessels and precious stones, reverend Abbot, it shall be my heed to preserve them to meet this demand, which haply may never be made; and as to the cost of rebuilding the Abbey, why the same notable workman that helped first to set it up, will owe me a good turn for punishing those that outwitted him, and sent him away without the promised boon of souls. Though, God's truth! were the fact fairly dived into, I am of opinion that Limburg, after all, hath sent more customers to his furnaces, than all the drinking-inns and pot-houses of the Palatinate!"

This sally of their Lord produced a general and deriding laugh among his followers, who now began to flock into the church from other parts of the Abbey, with the expectation that there was rich plunder to be had in the sanctuary. It was about this time, too, that a brand was cast among the straw of the barracks, and the strong light which glared through the stained windows very effectually told the monks of the inefficiency of further remonstrances.

Notwithstanding his known licentiousness, and the

general freedom of his life, the Abbot had imbibed, from the high objects of his calling, by that secret process that renders even the least deserving in some measure subject to the influence of their professions, a cast of dignity, and perhaps we might add even of sincerity (for there is often a strange admixture of inherent faith and practical unbelief about the dissolute) that caused him frequently to rise to the level of his most solemn duties. A character strong and masculine as his, could not be aroused without displaying some of its latent energies, be it for good or be it for evil; and Emich had doubts of the result, when he witnessed the manner in which his enemy succeeded in repressing his fierce resentment, and the expression of clerical dignity and official calmness that reigned in his countenance. The Abbot arose, like a prelate in the undisturbed exercise of his functions, and raising his voice, so as to send his words to the deepest recesses of the chapel, he spoke after the manner of the peculiar rites of the Church he served.

"God, in his hidden wisdom, hath permitted to the wicked a momentary triumph," he said; "we search not now into the reasons of this mysterious dispensation; the truth will be known in his own time:—but, as servitors of the altar—as guardians of this holy sanctuary—as the sworn and professed of Heaven—as one consecrated and blessed—there remaineth a solemn, an imperative duty to perform."

"Bonifacius, beware!" interrupted the Count of Leiningen; "thou dealest not now with burgomasters and weeping wives."

"In the behalf, then, of that God to whom this shrine hath been raised," continued the unmoved Abbot, "in his holy interest, and in his holy name"—

"At thy peril, priest!" and Emich shook, partly in anger, and partly in a terror he could scarce explain.

"As his unworthy but necessary minister—as consecrated and blessed—gifted with the power by the head of the Church, and now required to use it, do I pronounce thee"—

"Where are ye, followers of Hartenburg? Down with the silly maledictions of this mad monk; remember ye are not trembling women, to need a Benedictine's blessing!"

The voice of Emich was drowned, as well as that of the Abbot, by the noises that were now raised in the chapel. The first interruption came from a long dark instrument, that was thrust from out of the aisle behind the throne of Bonifacius, and within a few feet of his head; an interruption that filled the whole edifice with the wild, plaintive strains of the mountains.

This signal, which came from the cherry-wood trumpet of Gottlob, who rarely went abroad without this badge of his profession, was immediately followed by a general shout from the band of the Count, and by a variety of similar sounds, that were raised by different instruments that had hitherto been mute. The effect of these shrill strains, echoing among the vaulted and fretted roofs, which were brightly illuminated by the growing and fierce light that now pervaded the church, and of the seeming calm of the Abbot, who ended his malediction, spite of the uproar, is left to the reader's imagination. When he had finished the unheard curse, Bonifacius looked about him in gloomy observation.

It was evident to his cool and instructed mind, which was far too earthly in its habits, to cling to any hopes of a merely spiritual nature, that the outrage had already gone so far, as to render it more hazardous to his enemy to retreat than to advance. Signing to the community, he descended slowly, and with dignity, from his throne, and led the way from the choir The ready monks obeyed, the fraternity walking from that extraordinary scene, in their customary silent order. Emich followed the dark procession with a troubled eye, for even the conqueror regards the calm retreat of his foes with uneasiness, and there was an instant of painful distrust of his own purpose, as the last flowing robe vanished through a private door that led to a secret postern, by which the routed Benedictines quitted a mountain, where they had so long dwelt, in the calm, and, we might add, in the ease, of an affluent and privileged seclusion.

The invaders of the Abbey took this open abandonment of the place by its ancient possessors, to be an unequivocal admission of their triumph. There is no moment so likely to produce excesses, as that in which the uncertainty of strife is changed to the certainty of victory. The feelings seem willing to avenge themselves for all their previous doubts, and man is ever too ready to ascribe his successes to some inherent qualities, which give him an apparent right to abuse any advantages that may happen to be their consequence. The band of the castle and the people of the town, among whom a large proportion had to the last distrusted the presence of the community, to which vulgar opinion attributed the power of working miracles, no sooner found themselves, as they believed, in undisputed possession of the mountain, than the reaction of feeling, to which there has just been allusion, urged them to increase their violence, and to redouble those efforts which had momentarily been checked.

A shout of triumph was the common signal for renewing the assault. It was followed by the crashing of windows, and the overthrow of every fixture in the body of the church, that was not too solid to resist their first and ill-directed efforts, and a general mutilation of the monuments and labored statuary. Marble cherubs fell on every side, wings and limbs of angels separated from the trunks, and the grave and bearded visages of many an honored saint were doomed to endure contumely and fractures. Even the inferior altars were no longer respected, but they and their decorations were ruthlessly scattered, as if the enmity of the conquerors was tranferred from hose who had administered at them, to the dreaded Being in whose name the rites had been celebrated.

The reader will imagine the confusion and tumult that attended a scene like this. During the uproar, Emich buried his face in his mantle, and paced to and fro in the choir, which his presence, and perhaps some lingering reverence for the sacred spot, still preserved from violence. He was joined only by the Burgomaster and Berchthold, the remainder of the party having mingled with those who were destroying the chapels and decorations of the church. Heinrich seated himself in one of the vacant stalls, for the recent scene and the subsequent parting with his wife had shaken his resolution; while the young Forester advanced respectfully to the side of his lord.

"Is the Herr Count troubled?" demanded the latter, after a moment of deferential silence.

Emich dropped the cloak, and leaning a hand familiarly on the shoulder of his young servitor, he stood regarding the gorgeous riches and the elaborate beauty of the high altar, all of which was rendered doubly imposing by the powerful light that now illuminated the whole interior of the edifice, which was never more beautiful than as then seen, with its strong relief and deep shadows.

"Berchthold, there is a God!" he said with emphasis.

"None but the fool doubts it, Herr Emich."

"And he hath his ministers on earth—those whom he hath commissioned to do him pleasure, and to burn his incense."

"We have high authority for this belief, my good Lord."

"We have—the authority is high, that hath so much antiquity—which so suits our secret desires—which descends to us from our fathers."

"And which is so supported by proofs, sacred and profane."

"Thou hast been well schooled, good Berchthold, said the Count, looking earnestly at his companion.

"Heaven left me a pious and tender mother, when it took my father away."

Emich continued to lean on the shoulder of Berchthold, while his eye, in which sternness of purpose was singularly blended with the waverings of doubt, never turned from its contemplation of the altar. Above the chased and gilded cabinet which contained the host, was a small picture of the Mother of Christ, delineated in those mild and attractive colors with which the pencil is accustomed to portray the Virgin Wife of Joseph. Her eye seemed to meet the gaze of Emich in sorrow. It was easy to fancy the gentle expression was in reproach of the sacrilege.

"These Benedictines are at length unhoused"—he continued, trying fruitlessly to avert his look from that mild but expressive image; "they have too long ridden roughly on their betters."

Berchthold bowed.

"Dost thou see aught strange, youth, in that image of Maria?"

"'Tis a skilful design, Herr Count, and a fair face to regard."

"Methinks it looks upon this violence with an evil eye!"

"'Tis but the work of an ingenious man, my Lord, and cannot look other than it hath always seemed."

"Dost think thus, Berchthold? There are many who pretend that images and paintings have been known to speak, when it was Heaven's pleasure."

"They relate such legends, my good Lord, but these are events that are little wont to touch those who are not much disposed to see them."

"And yet in these facts had my fathers faith, and in this belief was I trained!"

Berchthold was mute, his own education having been more suited to the growing opinions of the times.

"That God *can* surpass the ordinary workings of nature, to effect his pleasure," continued Emich, "we may at least believe."

"It may be believed, Herr Count, but is it necessary? He who made nature may use it at his pleasure."

"Ha! thou hast no faith in miracles, boy!"

"I am myself a miracle, that tells me every moment of the existence of a superior power; and in that much I bend to its control. But it hath never been my fortune to hear an image speak, or see it do aught else that belongs to the will."

"By my father's bones! but thou art fit to deal with the cunningest knave that wears a cowl! How now, brave followers!" turning towards his people; "leave no vestige of the roguery and abominations that have so long been done within these polluted walls!"

"Herr Count!" said Berchthold eagerly, presuming in his haste to touch the cloak of Emich, "here are the Benedictines!"

The word caused the bold, and at that moment the independent Baron to turn suddenly, laying a hand on his sword, as he did so. But the hand released its grasp, and the features of Emich immediately reverted to their former expression of anxiety and doubt, at what he now beheld.

By this time all of the different edifices which composed the Abbey of Limburg were fired, the church and its immediate appendages alone excepted. The consequence was such an increase of light within the latter, as penetrated the most obscure of its Gothic recesses. The choir, above all, received the strongest illumination; and young Berchthold thought its tracery never appeared so beautiful as in that fearful moment of impending destruction. The candles and lamps of the great altar began to look dim, and all around prevailed the glorious and fiery brightness which accompanies a fierce conflagration. During the instant that Emich was turned towards his people, two monks had come from the sacristy, and placed themselves on the steps of the altar. They were the Prior and Father Johan. The former bore a small ivory crucifix, which from time to time he kissed, while the latter placed at his feet a massive and curiously carved chest, of sufficient size and weight to have required the aid of a lay-brother to bring it from its repository.

The countenance of the Prior was mild, persuasive, and filled with holy concern. That of his companion flushed, excited, and bearing the look of feverish fire, which is the effect of an enthusiasm that springs as much from temperament, as from conviction.

Emich looked at the Benedictines uneasily, and he advanced so near, always attended by the Forester, as to be within reach of his arm.

"'Fore God, but ye are tardy, Fathers," he said, determined to assume an indifference he was far from feeling; "the pious Bonifacius hath departed many minutes, and quickened, as he is, by love of his person, I make no question that his footsteps have already gone down the mountain side!"

"Thou hast at length yielded to the whispering of the devil, Count of Leiningen!" returned the

Prior; "thou art resolute that this blot shall rest upon thy soul!"

"We are not at confession, holy Arnolph, but engaged in a knightly redressing of our rights; if thou hast aught here, that is dear to thee, take it, of God's name, and go thy way. Thou shalt have safe conduct, were it to the gates of Rome; for, of all thy fraternity, thou art he for whom alone I feel regret or amity, in this just enterprise."

"I know not this difference in love, when it touches the existence of our shrine, or the duty that ties us to its service. This question is not between thee and me, Lord Emich, but between thee and God!"

"Have it as thou wilt, Herr Prior, so thou dost but depart in peace."

"I am not weak enough to resist when resistance is vain," mildly answered the Monk; "nor am I quick to desert my post, while there is hope. Thou hast not well bethought thee of this act, Emich; thou hast not remembered thy posterity, nor thy kind interest in the noble Ermengarde!"

"Dost fancy me an uxorious citizen, reverend Arnolph, that thou wouldest fain stop a knight in his onset, by speaking of the good wife and her babes?"

As he concluded, Emich laughed.

"Thou hast not well conceived me. This is not a question of death in battle, or of the grief of those who survive; for such thoughts are, unhappily, but too common with those who rule the earth, to raise disquiet; but I would speak to thee of the long future and of its pains. Dost thou know, irreverend Baron, that the God of Israel—who is my God and thine—the God of Israel hath said, that he will visit the sins of the parent upon the descendant, from generation to generation? and yet, blinded by this specious success, thou seemest to court his anger."

"This may be so or not; for ye of the cloisters have many subtle ways of reasoning as you wish;

but to me it appeareth better that each should suffer for his own sins; and such, I take it, is what the community of Limburg doth now undergo."

"That we have done much evil, and neglected much good, is, alas, too true!"

"By the kings of Koeln! thou art getting to be of our side, holy Arnolph!"

"For such is the common course," continued th unmoved Prior,—"but that thou art not our judge is equally certain. That each does and will suffer for his own acts is beyond denial, but the fearful consequences of crime do not stop with him who hath committed it. This much is taught us by reason and what is still more sure, it is consecrated by words from God's own mouth. Ponder, then, whilst thou may, on the load of sorrow thou art heaping on thy descendants: remember that thou standest there, subject to goading passions, the miserable being thou art, simply that in thy person thou payest the price of a parent's sins. What our common father did, is still avenged on us his children."

"How now, Herr Prior, thou pushest my pedigree much beyond its pretensions. Noble and princely, if thou wilt, but I pass not the dark ages in any of my claims. Let them that have greater ambition pay for the purchase in the way thou namest; I am content with more modern honors."

Emich spoke jeeringly, but the attentive Monk saw that he was troubled.

"If thou hast no thought for posterity—none for thyself—none for thy God, Emich," the latter resumed, "bethink thee of those who have gone before. Hast already forgotten thy visit to the tombs of thy family?"

"Thou hast me there, Arnolph!—those sacred vaults have been thy convent's shield these many months!"

"And thou art now disposed to forget them?"

"If thou wilt ask yon honest men, they will tell thee, Prior, they have no order to spare the meanest of thy marble cherubs, even though it hover over a grave of mine own house."

"Then do I indeed despair of touching thy heart!" answered Father Arnolph, sorrowing as much for the crime as for its consequences. "Then indeed art thou madly and ruthlessly bent, not only on our destruction, but on thine own; for pity for the child, and love of the parent, are equally despised Emich of Leiningen, I curse thee not—this is a weapon too fearful for human hands lightly to wield.—I bless thee not; duty to God forbids the holy office."

"Hold! reverend Arnolph, let us not part in anger—I would, in sooth, crave from thy worthy hands some touch of consolation—if—ay—if there be chapel in this church, for which thou hast more than usual reverence, let it be named, and I swear, by knight's faith, unless the work be already done, it shall stand unscathed amid the ruins, in testimony of my love for thee—or if thou hast aught here of price, whether of monkish or worldly value, point it out, that it may be held safe for thy better leisure. In return, I ask but the parting words of peace."

"'Tis forbidden to those who war against God," returned the grieved Prior, releasing his robe from the eager grasp of the Baron.—"I can and will pray for thee, Emich; but to bless thee were treachery to Heaven!"

So saying, the pious Arnolph buried his face in his dress, to shut out the view of the profanation that was working around him, and withdrew slowly from the choir.

CHAPTER XXI.

> Avaunt!
> Incarnate Lucifer! 'tis holy ground.
> A martyr's ashes now lie there, which make it
> A shrine.—
>
> BYRON.

During the foregoing scene, the Benedictine already known to the reader as Father Johan, had awaited its issue with a species of lofty patience on the steps of the altar. But in a character so exaggerated, there remained little that was purely natural; even the forbearance of the Monk partook of the forced and fervid qualities of his mind. Conventual discipline, deep and involuntary respect for the Prior, and that very disdain which he felt for all gentle means of recalling a sinner to the fold, kept him tolerably tranquil, while Emich and his spiritual superior held their parley; but there was a gleam of wild delight in his eye, when he found, of all that powerful and boasted fraternity, that he alone remained to defend the altars. The feeling of the moment in such a breast, notwithstanding the scene of tumult that rather increased than diminished in the church, was that of triumph. He exulted in his own constancy, and he anticipated the effects which were to follow from his firmness, with the self-complacency of a prurient confidence, and with the settled conviction of an enthusiast.

Emich took little heed of his presence, during the first moments that succeeded the departure of the Prior. There is a majesty, and a quiet energy in truth and sound principles, that happily form their constant buttresses. Without this wise provision of Providence, the world would be hopelessly abandoned to the machinations of those who consider all means lawful, provided the ends tend to their own success. All near the Abbey of Limburg had felt the influence of these high qualities in Father Arnolph, and it is more than probable that, as in the case of the city of Canaan, had the community contained four of his spiritual peers the Abbey would not have fallen

The Count, in particular, who, like all that first break from mental servitude, was so often troubled with strong doubts, had long entertained a deep respect for this monk; and it is not improbable, that had the pious Arnolph fully understood his own power, by an earlier and more vigilant use of his means, he might have found a way to avert the blow that had now alighted on Limburg. But the meekness and modesty of the Prior were qualities as strongly marked as his more active virtues, and the policy of Limburg was not of a character to rely on either for its security.

"There is good in that brother," said Emich to Berchthold, when his thoughtful eye again rose to the face of the young Forester.—"Had he been mitred, instead of Bonifacius, our rights might have still suffered."

"Few are more beloved than Father Arnolph, Herr Count, and none so deserve to be."

"Thou art of this mind! How now, Master Heinrich! art in monkish meditation in thy stall, or dost dispose of the lesson of the virtuous Ulrike, more at thy ease, in a seat where so much substantial carnal aliment hath been digested by godly Benedictines! Come to the front, like a stout soldier and give us the savor of thy good wisdom in this strait."

"Methinks, our work is well-nigh done, Lord Emich," answered Heinrich, complying with the request, "my faithful townsmen are not idle in the chapels and among the tombs, and the sledge of yon smith dealeth with an angel an' it were a bar of molten iron Each stroke leaves a mark that no chisel will repair!"

"Let the knaves amuse themselves; every blow is quickened by the recollection of some hard penance. Thou seest that they place the confessionals in a pile ready for the torch! This is attacking the enemy in his citadel. But Heinrich, is the excellent Ulrike wont to come forth with thee in thy frays against the church? God's judgments! Were Ermengarde of this humor, we should have no hope of salvation in our castle!"

"You do my wife injustice, Herr Count; Ulrike was here to pray, and not to encourage."

"Thou mightest have spared the explanation, for truly such encouragement never did soldier need! Wert privy to the visit,—ha!—wert privy, worthy Burgomaster?"

"To speak you honestly, Herr Emich, I thought the woman otherwise bestowed."

"By the Magi!—in her bed?"

"Nay, at her prayers, but in a different place. But we do her too much honor, noble Emich, to let the movements of a mere housewife occupy our high thoughts in this busy moment."

"Nothing that touches thee is of light concern with thy friends, good Burgomaster," answered the Baron, who pondered with instinctive uneasiness, even in that moment of tumult, on this visit of Ulrike to the Benedictines, at an hour so unusual.

"Thou art well wived, Herr Heinrich, and all that know thy consort do her honor!"

The Burgomaster was a man by far too well satisfied with his own superior merits to harbor jealousy. Self-complacency might have been at the bottom of his security, though it were scarce possible for one even much more addicted by nature to that tormenting passion, to have lived so long in perfect familiarity with the pure mind of Ulrike.

without feeling reverence for its principles and virtue. The sentiments of the Baron were very different; for though in his heart equally convinced of the character of her to whom he alluded, he could not altogether exclude the suspicions of a man of loose habits, nor the uneasiness of one who had himself been discarded. The answer of the husband, however, served to turn the discourse, by giving the Burgomaster an opportunity of placing himself in the most prominent relief.

"A thousand thanks, illustrious Herr," he said, raising his cap; "the woman is not amiss, though much troubled with infirmity on the score of altars and penances. When we shall have fairly disposed of Limburg, another reign will commence among our wives and daughters, and we can hope for more quiet Sabbaths. As to this grace of your present speech, Lord Count, I take it, as it was no doubt meant, to be another pledge of our lasting amity and close alliance."

"Thou talkest well," quickly answered Emich, losing the passing feeling of distrust in the recollection of his present purpose; "no words of friendship are lost, on a true and sworn supporter. Well, Heinrich, is our affair finally achieved?"

"Sapperment! Herr Count, if not finished, it is in a fair way to be so quickly."

"Here remaineth a Benedictine!' said Berchthold, drawing their attention to the Monk, who still maintained his post on the steps of the altar.

"The bees do not relish quitting their hive, while any of the hard earnings are left," said the Count, laughing; "what wouldst thou, Father Johan?—if thy careful mind hath had thought of the precious vessels, make thy choice and depart."

The Benedictine returned the laugh of the noble, with a smile of deep but quiet exultation.

"Assemble thy followers, rude Baron," he said:

"call all within thy control to this sanctified spot for there yet remaineth a power to be overcome of which thou hast not taken heed; at the moment when thou fanciest thyself most secure, art thou nearest to disgrace and to destruction."

As the excited Monk suited his words by a corresponding energy of emphasis and tone, Emich recoiled a step, like one who distrusted a secre mine. The desperate character of Father Johan's enthusiasm was well known, and neither of the three listeners was without apprehension, that the fraternity, aware of the invasion, had plotted some deep design of vengeance, which this exaggerated brother had been deputed to execute.

"Ho! without there!" cried the Count—"Let a party descend quickly to the crypt, and look to the villanies of these pretended saints; cousin of Viederbach," revealing in the eagerness of the moment the presence of this sworn soldier of the Cross, "see thou to our safety, for the Rhodian warfare hath made thee familiar with these treacheries."

The call of the Count, which was uttered like a battle cry, stayed the hands of the destroyers Some rushed to obey the order, while most of the others gathered hastily into the choir. It is certain that the presence of fellow-sufferers diminishes the force of fear, even though it may in truth increase the danger; for such is the constitution of our minds, that they willingly admit the influence of sympathy whether it be in pain or pleasure. When Emich found himself backed by so many of his band, he thought less of the apprehended mine, and he turned to question the Monk, with more of the calmness that became his condition.

"Thou wouldst have the followers of Hartenburg, Father," he said, ironically, "and thou seest now readily they come!"

"I would that all who have listened to schismatics

—all who refuse honor to the holy Church—all who deny Rome—and all that believe themselves on earth freed from the agency of Heaven, now stood before me!" answered the Benedictine, examining the group of heads that clustered among the stalls, with the bright but steady eye of one engrossed with the consciousness of his force. "Thou art in hundreds, Count Leiningen—would it were God' pleasure that it had been in millions!"

"We are of sufficient strength for our object, Monk."

"That remaineth to be seen. Now, listen to a voice from above!—I speak to you, unhallowed ministers of the will of this ambitious Baron—to you, misguided and ignorant tools of a scheme that hath been plotted of evil, and hath been brought forth from the prolific brain of the restless Father of Sin. Ye have come at the heels of your lord, vainly rejoicing in a visible but impotent power—impiously craving the profits of your unholy enterprise, and forgetting God!"—

"By the mass, priest!" interrupted Emich; "thou hast once already given us a sermon to day, and time presseth. If thou hast an enemy to present, bring him forth; but we tire of these churchly offices."

"Thou hast had thy moment of wanton will, abandoned Emich, and now cometh the judgment—seest thou this box of precious relics!—dost thou orget that Limburg is rich in these holy remains, nd that their virtues are yet untried?—Woe to him who scoffeth at their character, and despiseth their power!"

"Stay thy hand, Johan!" cried the Count hastily when he saw that the Monk was about to expose some of those well-known vestiges of mortality to which the Church of Rome then, as now, attributed miraculous interventions; "this is no moment for fooleries!"

"Callest thou this sacred office by so profane a name!—abide the issue, foul-mouthed asperser of our holy authority, and triumph if thou canst!"

The Count was much disturbed, for his reason had far less influence now in supporting him than his ambition. The party in the rear, too, began to waver, for opinion was not then sufficiently confirmed to render the mass indifferent to such an exposure of clerical power. Whatever may be the difference that exists between Christian sects concerning the validity of modern miracles, all will allow, that, when trained in the belief of their reality, the mind is less prepared to resist their influence than that of any other engine by which it can be assailed, since it is placing the impotency of man in direct and obvious collision with the power of the Deity. Before such an exhibition of force, nature offers no means of resistance; and the mysterious and unseen agency by which the wonder is produced, enlists in its interest both the imagination and that innate dread of omnipotence which all possess.

"'Twere well this matter went no farther!" said Emich, uneasily whispering his principal agents.

"Nay, my Lord Count," answered Berchthold, calmly, "it may be good to know the right of the matter. If we are not of Heaven's side in this affair, let it be shown in our own behalf; and if the Benedictines are no better than pretenders, our consciences will be all the easier."

"Thou art presuming, boy—none know the end of this!—Herr Heinrich, thou art silent?"

"What would you have, noble Emich, of a poor Burgomaster? I will own, I think it were more for the advantage of Deurckheim that the matter went no farther."

"Thou hearest, Benedictine!" said the Count, aying the point of his sheathed sword on the richly chased and much reverenced box that the Monk had already unlocked,—"this must stop here!"

"Take away the weapon, Emich of Leiningen,' aid father Johan, with dignity.

The Count obeyed, though he scarce knew why

"This is a fearful instant for the unbeliever," continued the Monk; "the moment is near when our altars shall be avenged—nay, recoil not, bold Baron—remain to the end, ye dissolute and forsaken followers of the wicked, for in vain ye hope to flee the judgment."

There was so much of tranquil enthusiasm in the air and faith of Father Johan, that, spite of a general wish to be at a distance from the relics, curiosity, and the inherent principle of religious awe, held each man spell-bound; though every heart beat quicker as the Monk proceeded, calmly, and with a reverential mien, to expose the bones of saints, the remnants of mantles, the reputed nails of the true cross, and morsels of its wood, with divers other similar memorials of holy events, and of sainted martyrs. Not a foot had power to retire. When all were laid, in solemn silence, on the bright and glowing shrine, Father Johan, crossing himself, again turned to the crowd.

"What may be Heaven's purpose in this strait, I know not," he said; "but withered be the hand, and for ever accursed the soul, of him who dareth violence to these holy vestiges of Christian faith!"

Uttering these ominous words, the Benedictine faced the crucifix, and kneeled in silent prayer. The minute that followed was one of fearful portent to he cause of the invaders. Eye sought eye in doubt, and one regarded the fretted vault, another gazed intently at the speaking image of Maria, as if each expected some miraculous manifestation or divine displeasure. The issue would have been doubtful, had not the cherry-wood trumpet of the cow-herd again sounded most opportunely in his master's behalf. The wily knave blew a well-known and popular imitation of the beasts of his herd, among the arches of th chapel, striking at the effect of what had just passea y the interposition of a familiar and vulgar idea The influence of the ludicrous, at moments when the passions vacillate, or the reason totters, is too well known to need elucidation. It is another of those caprices of humanity that baffle theories, proving how very far we are removed from being the exclusively reasoning animal we are fond of thinking the species.

The expedient of the ready-witted Gottlob produced its full effect. The most ignorant of the castle followers, those even whose dull minds had been on the verge of an abject deference to superstition, took courage at the daring of the cow-herd; and, as the least founded in any belief are commonly the most vociferous in its support, this portion of the band echoed the interruption from fifty hoarse throats. Emich felt like a man reprieved; for under the double influence of his own distrust, and the wavering of his followers, the Count for a moment had fancied his long-meditated destruction of the community of Limburg in great danger of being frustrated.

Encouraged by each other's cries, the invaders returned to their work laughing at their own alarm. The chairs and confessionals had been already heaped in the great aisle, and a brand was thrown into the pile. Fire was applied to the church wherever there was food for the element, and some of the artisans of Deurckheim, better instructed than their looser associates, found the means to light the conflagration in such parts of the roofs and the other superior stories, as would insure the destruction of the pile. In the mean time, all the exterior edifices had been burning, and the whole hill, to the eye of him who dwelt in the valley beneath, presented volumes of red flame, or of lurid smoke.

During the progress of this scene, Emich paced the choir, partly exulting in his success, and partly doubting of its personal fruits. Over the temporal consequences he had well pondered; but the motionless attitude of Father Johan, the presence of the long-reverenced relics, and the denunciations of the Church, still had their terrors for one whose mind had few well-grounded resources to sustain it. From this state of uneasiness he was aroused by the noise of the sledge, at work in the crypt. Followed by Heinrich and Berchthold, the Count hastened to descend to this place, which it will be remembered contained the tombs and the chapel of his race. Here, as above, all was in bright light, and all was in confusion. Most of the princely and noble tombs had already undergone mutilation, and no chapel had been respected. Before that of Hartenburg, however, Albrecht of Viederbach stood, with folded arms and a thoughtful eye. The cloak which, during the commencement of the attack, had served to conceal his person, was now neglected, and he seemed to forget the prudence of disguise, in deep contemplation.

"We have at length got to the monuments of our fathers, cousin;" said the Count, joining him.

"To their very bones, noble Emich!"

"The worthy knights have long slept in evil company; there shall be further rest for them in the chapel of Hartenburg."

"I hope it may be found, Herr Graf, that this ad venture is lawful!"

"How!—dost thou doubt, with the work so near accomplished?"

"By the mass! a soldier of Rhodes might better be fighting your turbaned infidel, than awakening the nobles of his own house from so long a sleep, at so short a summons!"

"Thou canst retire into my hold, Herr Albrecht if thy arm is wearied," said Emich, coldly; "not a malediction can reach thee there."

"That would be poor requital for a free hospitality, cousin; the travelling knight is the ally of the last friend, even though there be some wrong to general duties. But we cavaliers of the island well know, that a retreat, to be honorable, must be orderly, and not out of season. I am with thee, Emich, for the hour, and so no more parley. This was the image of the good Bishop of our line?"

"He had some such reverend office, I do believe; but speak of him as thou wilt, none can say he was a Benedictine."

"It had been better, cousin, since this church is to be sacked, that our predecessors had found other consecrated ground for their dust. Well, we sworn soldiers pass uneven lives! It is now some twelve months or so, that like a loyal and professed Rhodian, I stood to my knees in water, making good a trench against your believer in Houris and your unbeliever in Christ; and now, forsooth, I am here as a spectator (none call me more with honesty), while a Christian altar is overturned, and a brotherhood of shaven monks are sent adrift upon earth, like so many disbanded mercenaries!"

"By the Three Kings! my cousin, thou makest a fit comparison; for like disbanded mercenaries have they gone forth to prey upon society in a new shape.—Spare the angel of my grandfather, good smith," cried Emich, interrupting himself; "if there be any virtue in the image, 'tis for the benefit of our house!"

Dietrich stayed his uplifted arm, and directed the intended blow at another object. The marble flew in vast fragments at each collision with his sledge, and the leaders of the party soon found it necessary to retire, to avoid the random efforts of the heated crowd.

There no longer remained a doubt of the fate of these long-known and much-celebrated conventual buildings. Tomb fell after tomb, monuments were defaced, altars were overturned, chapels sacked, and every object that was in the least likely to resist the action of fire, received such indelible injuries as rendered its restoration difficult or impossible.

During the continuance of their efforts, the conflagration had advanced, as the fierce element that had been called in to assist the destroyers is known to do its work. Most of the dormitories, kitchens, and outer buildings were consumed, so far as the materials allowed, beyond redress; and it became apparent that the great church and its dependencies would soon be untenable.

Emich and his companions were still in the crypt, when a cry reached them, admonishing all within hearing to retreat, lest they become victims to the flames. Berchthold and the smith drove before them the crowd from the crypt, and there was a general rush to gain the outer door.

When the interior of the church was clear, the Count and his followers paused in the court, contemplating the scene, with curious eyes, like men satisfied with their work. No sooner was the common attention directed back towards the spot from whence they had just escaped, than a general cry, that partook equally of wonder and horror, broke from the crowd. As the doors were all thrown wide, nd every cranny of the building was illuminated y the fierce light of the flames that were raging in he roofs, the choir was nearly as visible to those without, as if it stood exposed to the rays of a noonday sun. Father Johan was still kneeling before the altar.

In obedience to the commands of Emich, th sacred shrine had been stript of its precious vessels, but none had presumed to touch a relic. On these long-venerated memorials, the Benedictine kept his eyes riveted, in the firm conviction that, sooner or ater, the power of God would be made manifest in defence of his violated temple.

"The monk! the monk!" exclaimed fifty eager voices.

"I would fain save the fanatic!" said Emich, with great and generous concern.

"He may listen to one who beareth this holy emblem," cried the Knight of Rhodes, releasing his cross from the doublet in which it had been concealed. "Will any come with me, to the rescue of this mad Benedictine?"

There was as much of repentant atonement in the offer of Albrecht of Viederbach, as there was of humanity. But the impulse which led young Berchthold forward, was purely generous. Notwithstanding the imminent peril of the attempt, they darted together into the building, and passed swiftly up the choir. The heat was getting to be oppressive, though the great height of the ceilings still rendered it tolerable. They approached the altar, advising the monk of his danger by their cries.

"Do ye come to be witnesses of Heaven's power?" demanded Father Johan, smiling with the calm of an inveterate enthusiast; "or do ye come, sore-stricken penitents that ye have done this deed?"

"Away, good father!" hurriedly answered Berchthold; "Heaven is against the community to-night; in another minute, yon fiery roof will fall."

"Hearest thou the blasphemer, Lord? Is it thy holy will, that"——

"Listen to a sworn soldier of the cross," interrupted Albrecht, showing his Rhodian emblem—

'we are of one faith, and we will now depart together for another trial."

"Away! false servant! and thou, abandoned boy!—See ye these sainted relics?"—

At a signal from the knight, Berchthold seized the monk by one side, while Albrecht did the sam thing on the other, and he was yet speaking as they bore him down the choir. But they struggled with one that a long-encouraged and morbid view of life had rendered mad. Before they reached the great aisle, the fanatic had liberated himself, and, while his captors were recovering breath, he was again at the foot of the altar. Instead of kneeling, however, Father Johan now seized the most venerated of the relics, which he held on high, audibly imploring Heaven to hasten the manifestation of its majesty.

"He is doomed!" said Albrecht of Viederbach, retiring from the church.

As the Knight of Rhodes rushed through the great door, a massive brand fell from the ceiling upon the pavement, scattering its coals like so many twinkling stars.

"Berchthold! Berchthold!" was shouted from a hundred throats.

"Come forth, rash boy!" cried Emich, with a voice in which agony was blended with the roar of the conflagration.

Berchthold seemed spell-bound. He gazed wistfully at the monk, and darted back again towards the altar. An awful crashing above, which resembled the settling of a mountain of snow about to descend in an avalanche, grated on the ear. The very men who, so short a time before, had come upon the hill ready and prepared to slay, now uttered groans of horror at witnessing the jeopardy of their fellow-creatures; for, whatever we may be in moments of excitement, there are latent sympathies in human nature, which too much use may deaden but which nothing but death can finally extinguish.

"Come forth, young Berchthold! come forth, my gallant forester!" shouted the voice of the Count above the clamor of the crowd, as if rallying his followers with a battle-cry. "He will die with the wretched monk!—The youth is mad!"

Berchthold was struggling with the Benedictine. though none knew what passed between them. There was another crash, and the whole pavement began to glow with fallen brands. Then came a breaking of rafters, and a scattering of fire that denoted the end. The interior of the chapel resembled the burning shower which usually closes a Roman girandola, and the earth shook with the fall of the massive structure. There are horrors on which few human eyes can bear to dwell. At this moment nearly every hand veiled a face, and every head was averted. But the movement lasted only an instant. When the interior was again seen, it appeared a fiery furnace. The altar still stood, however, and Johan miraculously kept his post on its steps. Berchthold had disappeared. The gesticulations of the Benedictine were wilder than ever, and his countenance was that of a man whose reason had hopelessly departed. He kept his feet only for a moment, but withering fell. After which his body was seen to curl like a green twig that is seared by the flames.

CHAPTER XXII.

Masters, you ought to consider with yourse.ves."—
Midsummer Night's Dream.

THE constant moral sentinel that God hath set on watch in every man's breast, but which acts so differently in different circumstances, though, perhaps, in no condition of humiliation and ignorance does it ever entirely desert its trust, is sure to bring repentance with the sense of error. It is vain to say that this innate sentiment of truth, which we call conscience, is the mere result of opinion and habit, since it is even more apparent in the guileless and untrained child than in the most practised man, and nature has so plainly set her mark upon all its workings, as to prove its identity with the fearful being that forms the incorporeal part of our existence. Like all else that is good, it may be weakened and perverted, or be otherwise abused; but, like every thing that comes from the same high source, even amid these vicious changes, it will retain traces of its divine author. We look upon this unwearied monitor as a vestige of that high condition from which the race fell; and we hold it to be beyond dispute, that precisely as men feel and admit its influence do they approach, or recede from, their original condition of innocence.

The destruction of the Abbey was succeeded by most of those signs which attend all acts of violence, in degrees that are proportioned to previous habits Even they who had been most active in accomplishing this long-meditated blow, began to tremble for its consequences; and few in the Palatinate heard of the deed, without holding their breaths like men who expected Heaven would summarily avenge the sacrilege. But in order that the thread of the narrative should not be broken, we will return to our incidents in their proper order, advancing the time but a few days after the night of the conflagration.

The reader will have to imagine another view of the Jaegerthal. There was the same smiling sun, and the same beneficent season; the forest was as green and waving, the meadows were as smooth and dark, the hill-sides as bright beneath the play of light and shade, while the murmuring brook was as limpid and swift, as when first presented to his eye in these pages. Not a hut or cottage was disturbed, either in the hamlets or along the travelled paths, and the Hold of Hartenburg still frowned in feudal power and baronial state, on the well-known pass of the mountains, gloomy, massive, and dark. But the hill of Limburg presented one of those sad and melancholy proofs of the effects of violence which are still scattered over the face of the old world, like so many admonitory beacons of the scenes through which its people have reached their present state of comparative security;—beacons that should be as useful in communicating lessons for the future, as they are pregnant with pictures of the past.

The outer wall remained unharmed, with the single exception of the principal gate, which bore the indelible marks of the smith's sledges; but above this barrier the work of devastation appeared in characters not to be mistaken. Every roof, and there had been fifty, was fallen; every wall, some of which were already tottering, was blackened; and not a tower pointed towards the sky, that did not show marks of the manner in which the flames had wreathed around its slender shaft. Here and there, a small thread of white smoke curled upwards, losing itself in the currents of the air, resembling so many of the lessening symptoms of a volcano after an explosion. A small crucifix, which popular rumor said was wood, but which, in fact, was of painted stone, still kept its place on a gable of the ruined church; and many a peasant addressed to it his silent prayers, firm in the belief that God had protected this image of his sacrifice, throughout the terrors of the memorable night.

In and about the castle, there appeared the usual evidences of a distrustful watch;—such ward as is kept by him who feels that he has justly become obnoxious to the hand of the constituted powers. The gates were closed; the sentinels on the walls and bastions were doubled; and, from time to time, signals were made that communicated with look-outs, so stationed on the hills that they could command views of the roads which led towards the Rhine, beyond the gorge of the valley.

The scene in Deurckheim was different, though it also had some points of resemblance with that in the hold. There was the same apprehension of danger from without, the same watchfulness on the walls and in the towers. and the same unusual display of an armed force. But in a town of this description, it was not easy to imitate the gloomy reserve of baronial state. The citizens grouped together in the streets, the women gossipped as in all sudden and strong cases of excitement, and even the children appeared to reflect the uneasiness and indecision of their parents; for as the hand of authority relaxed in their seniors, most wandered idly and vaguely among the men, listening to catch such loose expressions as might enlighten their growing understandings. The shops were opened, as usual, but many stopped to discourse at the doors, while few entered; and most of the artisans wasted their time in speculations on the consequence of the hardy step of their superiors.

In the mean time there was a council held in the town-hall. Here were assembled all who laid claim to civic authority in Deurckheim, with some who appeared under the claim of their services in the late assault upon the monks. A few of the anxious wives of the burghers, also, were seen collected in the more public rooms of the building; for domestic influence was neither covert nor trifling in that uxorious and simple community. We shall resume the narrative within the walls of this municipal edifice.

The Burgomaster and other chief men were much moved, by the vague apprehension which was the consequence of their hazardous experiment. Some were bold in the audacity of success; some doubted merely because the destruction of the brotherhood seemed too great a good, to come unmixed with evil; some held their opinions in suspense, waiting for events to give a value to their predictions, and others shook their heads in a manner that would appear to imply a secret knowledge of consequences that were not apparent to vulgar faculties. The latter class was more remarkable for its pretension to exclusive merit than for numbers, and would have been equally prompt to exaggerate the advantages of the recent measure, had the public pulse just then been beating on the access. But the public pulse was on the decline, and, as we have said, seeing and understanding all the advantages that were to be hoped from the defeat of Bonifacius, uncertainty quickened most imaginations in a manner to conjure disagreeable pictures of the future. Even Heinrich who wanted for neither moral nor physical resolution, was disturbed at his own victory, though if questioned he could scarcely have told the reason why. This uneasiness was heightened by the fact, that most of his compeers regarded him as the man, on whom the weight of the Church's and of the Elector's displeasure was most likely to fall, though it is more than probable that his situation would have been far less prominent, had there been no question of any results but such as were agreeable.

This sort of distinction, so isolated in defeat, and so social in prosperity, is a species of revenge that society is very apt to take of all who pretend to be wiser or better than itself, by presuming to point the way in cases of doubtful expediency, or in presuming to lead the way in those that require decision and nerve. He alone is certain of an unenvied reputation who, in preceding the main body in the great march of events, leaves no very sensible space between him and his fellows; while he alone can hope for impunity. who keeps so near his backers as to be able to confound himself in the general mass, when singularity brings comment and censure.

Heinrich fully felt the awkwardness of his position, and, just then, he would gladly have compounded for less of the fame acquired by the bold manner in which he had led the attack, in order to be rid of some of his anxiety. Still a species of warlike instinct led him to put the best face on the affair, and when he addressed his colleagues, it was with cheerfulness in his tones, however little there might have been of that desirable feeling in his heart.

"Well, brethren," he said, looking around at the knot of well-known faces, which surrounded him in the gravity of civic authority, "this weighty matter is, at length, happily, and, as it has been effected without bloodshed, I may say, peaceably over! The Benedictines are departed, and though the excellent Abbot hath taken post in a neighboring abbey, whence he sends forth brave words to frighten those who are unused to more dangerous missiles, it will be long before we shall again hear Limburg bell tolling in the Jaergerthal."

"For that I can swear," said the smith, who was among the inferiors that crowded a corner of the hall, occupying as little space as possible, in deference to their head-men; — "my own sledge hath helped to put the fine-tuned instrument out of tune!"

"We are now met to hear further propositions from the monks; but as the hour set for the arrival of their agent is not yet come, we can lighten the moments by such discourse as the circumstances may seem to require. Hast any thing to urge that will ease the minds of the timid, brother Wolfgang? —if so, of God's name, give it utterance, that w may know the worst at once."

The affinity between Wolfgang and Heinrich existed altogether in their civic relations. The former, although he coveted the anticipated advantages that were to result from the downfall of Limburg, had a constitutional deference for all superior power, and was unable to enjoy the triumph, without the bitterest misgivings concerning the displeasure of the Elector and Rome. He was aged, too,—a fact that served to heighten the tremor of tones, that, by a very general convention, are termed raven.

"It is wise to call upon the experienced and wise, for counsel, in pressing straits," returned the old burgher, "for years teach the folly of every thing human, inclining us to look at the world with moderation, and with less love for ourselves, and our interests—"

"Brother Wolfgang, thou art not yet yielding so fast as thou wouldest have us believe," interrupted Heinrich, who particularly disliked any discouraging views of the future. "Thou art but a boy—the difference between us cannot be greater than some five-and-twenty years."

"Not that, not that;—I count but three-and-seventy, and thou mayest fairly number fifty-and-five."

"Thou heapest honors on me I little deserve, friend Wolfgang. I shall not number the days thou namest these many months, and time marches fast enough without any fillips from us to help him. If I have yet seen more than fifty-four, may my fathers arise from their graves to claim the little they left behind, when they took leave of earth!"

"Words will make neither young, but I could wish we had found means to lay this unquiet spirit of Limburg, without so much violence and danger to ourselves. I am old, and have little interest in life, except to see those who will come after me happy and peaceful. Thou knowest that I have neither chick nor child, neighbor Heinrich, and the heart of such a man can only beat for all. 'T were, indeed, folly in me to think of much else, than of that great future which lies before us."

"Sapperment!" exclaimed the smith, who was disposed to presume a little on the spirit he had shown in the late attack.—"Worshipful Burgomaster, were Master Wolfgang to deal out some of his stores a little freely to the Benedictines, the whole affair might be quietly settled, and Deurckheim would be a great gainer. I warrant you now, that Bonifacius would be glad to receive a well-told sum in gold, without question or farther account, in lieu of his lodgings and fare in Limburg, of which he was only a life-tenant at best. At least, such had been my humor, an' it had pleased Heaven to have made me a Benedictine, and Bonifacius a smith."

"And where is this gold to be had, bold-speaking artisan?" demanded the aged burgher, severely.

"Where but from your untouched stores, venerable Wolfgang," answered the single-minded smith; "thou art old, father, and, as thou truly sayest, without offspring; the hold of life is getting loose, and to deal with thee in frankness, I see no manner in which the evil may be so readily turned from our town."

"Peace, senseless talker! dost think thy betters have no other employment for their goods than to cast them to the winds, as thy sparks scatter at the stroke of the sledge? The little I have hath been gained with sore toil and much saving, and it may yet be needed to keep want and beggary from my door. Nay, nay, when we are young we think the dirt may be turned to gold; hot blood and lusty limbs cause us to believe man equal to any labor, ay, even to living without food; but when experience and tribulation have taught us truth, we come to know neighbors, the value of pence. I am of a long living stock, Heaven help us! and there is greate likelihood of my yet becoming a charge to the town than of my ever doing a tithe of that, this heedless smith hath hinted."

"By St. Benedict, master! I hinted naught: what I said was in plain words, and it is this, that one so venerable for his years, and so respected for his means, might do great good in this strait! Such an act would sweeten the few days thou yet hast."

"Get thee away, fellow; thou talkest of death an' it were a joke. Do not the young go to their graves as well as the old, and are there not instances of thousands that have outlived their means? No, I much fear that this matter will not be appeased without mulcting the artisans in heavy sums;—but happily, most that belong to the crafts are young and able to pay!"

The reply of the smith, who was getting warm in a dispute in which he believed all the merit was on his own side, was cut short by a movement among the populace, who crowded the outer door of the town-house; the burghers seemed uneasy, as if they saw a crisis was near, and then a beadle announced the arrival of a messenger from the routed community of Limburg. The civic authorities of Deurckheim, although assembled expressly with the expectation of such a visit, were, like all men of but indifferently regulated minds, taken by surprise at the moment. Nothing was digested, no plan of operations had been proposed and, although all had dreamed for several nights o the very subject before them, not one of them all had thought upon it. Still it was now necessary to act, and after a little bustle, which had no other object than an idle attempt to impose upon the senses of the messenger, by a senseless parade, orders were given that the latter should be admitted.

The agent of the monks was himself a Benedictine. He entered the hall, attended only by the city-guard who had received him at the gate, with his cowl so far drawn upon his head as to conceal the features. There was a moment of curiosity, and the name of "Father Siegfried" was whispered from one to another, as each judged of the man by the exterior.

"Uncover, of Heaven's mercy! Father," said Heinrich, "and seat thyself as freely in the town-hall of Deurckheim, as if thou wert at thine ease in the ancient cloisters of Limburg. We are lions in the attack, but harmless as thy marble cherubs, when there is not occasion for your true manly qualities; so take thy seat, of God's name! and be of good cheer;—none will harm thee."

The voice of the Burgomaster lost its confidence as he concluded. The Benedictine was calmly removing the cowl; and when the cloth fell, it exposed the respected features of Father Arnolph.

"He that comes in the service of him I call master, needeth not this assurance," answered the monk; "still I rejoice to find ye in this mood, and not bent on maintaining an original error, by further outrages. It is never too late to see our faults, nor yet to repair them."

"I cry thy mercy, Holy Prior! we had taken thee for a very different member of the fraternity, and thou art not the less welcome for being him thou art."

Heinrich arose respectfully, and his example was followed by all present. The Prior seemed pleased and a glow, like that which a benevolent hope creates, passed athwart his countenance. With perfect simplicity he took the offered stool, as the least obtrusive manner of inducing the burghers to resume their seats. The experiment produced tne effect he intended.

"I should pretend to an indifference I do not feel, were I to say, Heinrich Frey, that I come among you, men to whom I have often administered the rites of the church during long and watchful years, without the wish to find that my ministrations are remembered."

"If there dwelleth knave in Deurckheim whose heart hath not been touched by thy good works, Father, the hound is without bowels, and unfit to live among honest people."

"Most true!" exclaimed the smith, in his audible by-play. "The Burgomaster doth us all justice! I never struck spark from iron, more freely than I will render respect to the most reverend Prior. His prayers are like tried steel, and next to those of him of the hermitage are in most esteem among us. Fill me an abbey with such men, and for one, I shall be ready to trust all our salvation to their godliness, without thought or concern for ourselves. Sapperment! could such a community be found, it would be a great relief to the laymen, and more particularly to your artisan, who might turn all his thoughts to his craft, with the certainty of being watched by men capable of setting the quickest-witted devil at defiance!"

Arnolph listened to this digression with patience, and he acknowledged the courtesy and friendliness of his reception, by a slow inclination of the head. He was too much accustomed to hear these temporal applications of the spiritual interests of which he was a minister, to be surprised at any thing; and he was too meek on the subject of his own deserving. to despise any because they were weaker than himself. The Christian religion seems to be divided into two great classes of worshippers; those who think its consolations are most palpable in their direct and worldly form, and those whose aspirations are so spiritualized, and whose thoughts are so sublimated, as to consider it a metaphysical theory, in which the principal object is to preserve the logical harmony. For ourselves, we believe it to be a dispensation from God, to those of his creatures who are fearfully composed of the material and immaterial, and that so far as it is connected with our probation here, it is never to be considered as entirely distinct from one or the other of the great attributes of our nature. It is evident that such were not the views of the honest smith; and it is probable, had the matter been thoroughly sifted, it would have been found that, as respects Deurckheim, he was altogether of the popular party.

"Thou comest, Father, like the dove to the ark, the bearer of the olive-branch," resumed Heinrich; "though for our northern regions a leaf of the oak would more likely have been the emblem, had Ararat been one of these well-wooded hills of ours."

"I come to offer the conditions of our brotherhood, and to endeavor to persuade the misguided in Deurckheim to accept them. The holy abbots, with the right reverend fathers in God, the Bishops of Spires and Worms, now assembled in the latter city, have permitted me to be the bearer of their terms, an office I have sought, lest another should forget to entreat and influence, in the desire to menace."

"Gott bewahre! thou hast done well, as is thy wont, excellent Arnolph! Threats are about as useful with Deurckheim, as the holy water is in our rhenish, both being well enough in their places; but he that cannot be driven must be led, and liquor that is right good in itself needeth no flavor from the church. As for this old misunderstanding between Limburg of the one side, and the noble Count of Hartenburg with our unworthy town of the other, the matter may be said to be now of easy adjustment, since the late events have cleared it of its greatest difficulty ; and so, from my heart, I wish thee joy of thy mission, and felicitate the town that it hath to treat with one so skilful and so reasonable. Thou wilt find us in a friendly humor, and ready to meet thee half-way; for I know not the man in Deurckheim that desireth to push the controversy a foot further, or who is not at heart content."

"No, that would be out of reason and charity," said the smith, speaking again among the auditors, "We ought to show these Benedictines an example of moderation, neighbors; and therefore for one, though no better than a poor artisan that gaineth his bread by blows on the anvil, do I agree with the worshipful Heinrich, and say, of God's name! let us be reasonable in our demands, and be content with as little as may be, in the settlement of our dispute."

The Prior listened patiently, as usual, but a hectic glowed, for an instant, on his cheek. It disappeared, and the benevolent blue eye was again seen shining amid features that the cloister and the closet had long since robbed of all other bloom. "Ye know, burghers of Deurckheim," he answered, "that in assailing the altars of Limburg ye set a double power at defiance;—that of the Church, as it is constituted and protected on earth, and that of God. My errand, at this moment, is to speak of the first. Our Father of Worms is sorely angered, and he has not failed to address himself directly and promptly to our Father at Rome. In addition to this reverend appeal, messengers have been dispatched to both the Elector and Emperor, as well as to divers of the Ecclesiastical Princes who rule on the banks of the Rhine. This is a fearful array of power to be met by a mountain baron, and a city whose walls can be measured by the leg in so short a time. But chiefly would I lay stress on the evil that may flow from the displeasure of the Head of the Church."

"And should he read the late exploit with severity, reverend Prior, what are we to look to, as its fruits?"

"To be denounced as excluded from the fold, and to be left to the wickedness and folly of your own hearts. In a word, excommunication."

"Umph!—this might prove a short way of recruiting the followers of Brother Luther! thou knowest, holy Arnolph, that men look more and more closely, every day, into these disputed points."

"Would that they looked with more humility and understanding! If ye consider the denunciations and benedictions of him to whom has been confided the authority to bless and to curse, as of little weight, no words of mine can heighten their effect; but all among ye who are not prepared to go the length that your Burgomaster hath just hinted, may deem it prudent to pause, ere they incur the heavy risk of living under such a weight of Heaven's displeasure."

The burghers regarded each other in doubt, few among them being yet prepared to push resistance so far. Some inwardly trembled, for habit and tradition were too strong for the new opinions; some shrewdly weighed the temporal rather than the spiritual consequences, and others ruminated on the possibility of enduring the anathema in so good company. There are thousands that are willing to encounter danger in large bodies, who shrink from its hazards alone; and perhaps the soldier goes to the charge quite as much stimulated by the sympathy of association, as he is sustained by the dread of shame or the desire of renown. The civic counsellors of Deurckheim now found themselves in some such plight, and each man felt assurance or doubt, much as he happened to meet with either of those feelings expressed in the eyes of his neighbor

"Have ye any less godly proposition to make?" asked Heinrich, who perceived that the moral part of his civic support began to waver, "for these are points in which we are better skilled, than on those that touch your doctrinal niceties."

"I am commanded to say, that, as becomes their divine office, the brotherhood of Limburg is disposed to pardon and forget, inasmuch as duty will allow, the late act of Deurckheim, on conditions that may be named."

"Ay, this is christian-like, and will meet with a ready return, in our dispositions. On our side, too, holy Prior, there is every wish to forget the past, and to look only to a quiet and friendly future—do I interpret the intentions of the town well, my neighbors?"

"To the letter!—no clerk could do it better."—"Yes, we are of the community's mind; it is wise to live at peace, and to pardon and overlook;" were ready answers to this appeal.

"Thou hearest, father! a better mood no minister or messenger need wish! 'Fore Heaven! we are all of one mind in this particular; and I know not that the man would find safety in Deurckheim, who should talk of aught but peace!"

"It is to be mourned, that ye have not always been of this humor; I come not, however, to reproach, but to reclaim; not to defy, but to persuade; not to intimidate, but to convince. Here are the written propositions of the holy divines by whom I am charged with this office of mediator, and I leave it for a time to your private consultations. When ye shall have well digested this fit offer, I will come among ye in peace and friendliness."

The written proposals were received, and the

whole assembly rose to do the Prior honor. As the latter left the hall, he asked permission of several of the burghers, among whom was Heinrich Frey, to visit their families, in the spirit of Christian guardianship. The desired consents were obtained without demur or doubt, on the part of any; for whatever may be said or thought of the errors of public opinion, it is usually right where the means are possessed of at all giving it a true direction. The high estimation in which Arnolph was held, by the mere force of popular instinct, was never more plainly seen than on the present occasion, when even those who had so lately warred against the community, threw open their doors without reserve; though it was well known, that the late policy of the town had many a secret enemy, and many a bitter commentator, in that sex which is sometimes as slow to incite to violence and resistance, as at others it is thoughtless and hasty.

CHAPTER XXIII.

"What well-appointed leader fronts us here?"
King Henry IV.

THE missive of the monks was written in Latin. At that period few wrote but the learned, and every noble or town was obliged to maintain a scholar to perform what are now the commonest duties of intercourse. The clerkly agent of Deurckheim had been educated for the Church, and had even received the tonsure; but some irregularities of life, which, as it would appear, were not within the pale of clerical privileges, or which had been so unguarded as to bring scandal on the profession, compelled him to give his destinies a new direction. As happens with most men who have expended much time and labor in qualifying themselves for any particular pursuit, and who are unexpectedly driven from its exercise, this individual, who was named Ludwig, and who was often ironically styled in common parlance Father Ludwig, never completely succeeded in repairing the injury done by the first false step he had made. His acquirement procured for him a certain amount of consideration but as he was known to be somewhat free in his manner of life, and, especially as schism grew strong in Germany, a bold sceptic on most of the distinctive doctrines of the Catholic Church, he ever wore about his character some of that fancied looseness, which insensibly attaches itself to all renegades, whether their motives be more or less corrupt. Still as he was known to be instructed, the multitude ascribed more virtue to his secession than it would have imputed to the withdrawal from the fold of fifty sincere believers; for most believed there were means of judging that belonged to the initiated, which did not fall to the lot of those who worshipped in the outer court. We have daily proofs that this weakness reaches into the temporal interests of life, and that opinions are valued in proportion as there is believed to be some secret means of acquiring information; though men rarely conceal any thing that they know which may be revealed, and few indeed are disposed to "hide their lights under a bushel."

Ludwig forgot no part of the intonation or emphasis, while he uttered the unintelligible phrases of the monkish missive. His auditors listened the more attentively, because they did not understand a syllable of what was said; attention seeming usually to be riveted in an inverse ratio to the facilities of comprehension. Perhaps some of the higher dignitaries flattered themselves, that their inferiors might be duped into the belief of their attainments; a fact that could not fail to increase their influence, since there is no better evidence of the innate aspirations of our intellectual being, than the universal deference that is paid to knowledge. We have hazarded this supposition against the civic authorities of Deurckheim, because we believe it depends upon a general principle of human ambition; and because in our own case, we well remember hearing out a sermon of more than an hour's duration delivered in Low Dutch, and in a damp church in Holland, when not a word, from the text to the benediction, was understood.

"Right learnedly worded, and no doubt of proper courtesy!" exclaimed Heinrich, when the letter was ended, and while the clerk was clearing his spectacles, preparatory to the more vulgar version—"It is a happy strife, neighbors, in which such language passes between the parties; for it proves that charity is stronger than malice, and that reason is not forgotten merely because there have been blows!"

"I have rarely heard braver words," answered a fellow-burgher, "or those that are better penned!"

"Potz-tausend!" muttered the smith; "it were almost a sin to dispossess men that can write thus!"

Murmurs of approbation passed through the crowd, and not an individual was there, with the solitary exception of a gaping idiot that had stolen into the hall, who did not affect to have received more or less pleasure from the communication. Even the idiot had his share of satisfaction, for, by the pure force of sympathy, he caught gleamings of a delight that seemed so strong and so general.

Ludwig now commenced translating the letter into the harsh, energetic, German of the Rhine. The wonderful capabilities of the language enabled him to convert the generalities and comprehensive terms of the Latin, with a minuteness of signification, which put the loss of any shade of idea utterly out of the question.

What the monks had meant, and perhaps even more, was laboriously, and with malignant pleasure, rendered; and so rendered, as to give to each xpression the fullest weight and meaning.

We have no intention of attempting the office of translating this harsh summons ourselves, but must be content with a brief summary of its contents. The instrument opened with a greeting that was not unlike those which were sent, in the first ages of the present dispensation, from the apostles to the churches of the east. It then contained a short but pointed narrative of the recent events, which were qualified in a way that the reader can easily imagine; it proceeded to refer to the spiritual and temporal authorities from which the brotherhood had assurances of support; and it concluded by demanding, under the penalty of incurring every earthly and heavenly risk, an enormous sum in gold, as a pecuniary reparation for the injury done—a complete and absolute submission of the town to the jurisdiction of the community, even more than was ever before pretended to—a public and general acknowledgment of error, with a variety of penances and pilgrimages to be performed by functionaries that were named—and the delivery of Heinrich Frey, with eleven others of the principal inhabitants, into the Abbot's hands as hostages, until all of these exactions and conditions should be completely and satisfactorily fulfilled.

"Wh—e—e—e—w!" whistled Heinrich, when Ludwig ended, after a most provoking prolixity, that had completely exhausted the Burgomaster's patience. "Himmel! here is a victory that is likely to cost us our means, our characters, our liberties, our consciences, and our ease! Are the monks mad, Master Ludwig or art thou sporting with our credulity:—Do they really speak of hostages, and of gold?"

"Of a surety, worshipful Herr, and seemingly with a right good will."

"Wilt read the part touching the hostages again, in the Latin; thou mayest have indiscreetly overlooked a conjunction or a pronoun, as I think thou callest these notable figures of speech."

"Ay, it were well to judge of the letter by the Latin," echoed the smith; "one never knows the quality of his metal, at the first touch of the hammer."

Ludwig read, a second time, extracts in the original, and, through a species of waggery, by which he often took a secret and consolatory revenge for the indignities he frequently received from the ignorant, and which served him as food of merriment and as a vent to his confined humors in occasional interviews with others of his own class, he gave with singular emphasis the terms of greeting, which were, as usual, embellished with phrases of priestly benediction, as the part that especially demanded the prompt delivery of Heinrich Frey and his fellows into the hands of the Benedictines.

"Gott bewahre!" cried the Burgomaster, who had shifted a leg each time the clerk glanced an eye at him over his spectacles—"I have other concerns than to sit in a cell, and Deurckheim would fare but badly were the town left without so large a share of its knowledge and experience. Prithee, Master Ludwig, give us the kinder language of these Benedictines; for methinks there may be found some words of peace in the blessings they bestow.

The crafty clerk now read, in the original, the strongest of the denunciations, and the parts of the letter which so peremptorily demanded the hostages.

"How now, knave!" said the hasty Burgomaster, "thou hast not been faithful in thy former readings!

Thou hearest, neighbors, I am named especially in their benedictions; for you must know, worthy burghers, that Henricus means Heinrich, and Frey well pronounced, is much the same in all languages This I know from long experience in these cunning instruments. I owe the reverend Benedictines grac for their good wishes, expressed with this particu larity; though the manner in which they introduce the hostages is unseemly."

"I thought when it came to the worst," muttered the smith, "that Master Heinrich would be considered with especial favor. This it is, brother artisans, to be honored in one's town, and to have a name!"

"There sounds a parley!" interrupted the Burgomaster. "Can these crafty monks have dared to trifle with us, by sending the choicest of their flock to hold us in discourse, while they steal upon us in armor?"

The idea was evidently unpleasant to most of the council, and to none more so than to the aged Wolfgang, whose years would seem to have given less value to his personal safety than to the rest. Many quitted the hall, while those that remained appeared to be detained more by their apprehensions than by their fortitude. Heinrich, who was constitutionally firm, continued the most undisturbed of them all, though even he went from window to window, like a man that was uneasy.

"If the godly villains have done this treachery, let them look to it—we are not vassals to be hoodwinked with a cowl!"

"Perhaps, worshipful and wise Heinrich," said the crafty Ludwig, "they send the trumpet, in readiness to receive the hostages."

"The holy magi curse them, and their impudent long-winded musician!—How now, fellow!—who maketh this tan—ta—ra—ra at our gate?"

"The noble Count of Hartenburg is at the valley side of the town, honorable Burgomaster, with a stout troop of mounted followers," announced the breathless runner, who came on this errand. "He chafes at the delay, but as the order to keep fast is so rigid, the captain of the watch dares not unbar and unbolt without permission had."

"Bid the valiant and faithful burgher undo his fastenings, o' Heaven's name!—and right speedily. We should have bethought us, excellent neighbors, of the chances of this visit, and had a care that our princely friend were without this cause of complaint. But we should rejoice, too, that our people are so true, as to keep their trust even against one so known and honored. I warrant ye, neighbors, were it the imperial Karl himself, he would fare no better:—"

Heinrich was interrupted while vaunting and extolling the civic discipline, by the trampling of horses' feet on the pavement below the windows, and on looking out he saw Emich and all his cortége coolly alighting.

"Umph!" ejaculated the Burgomaster—"go forth, and do reverence to my Lord the Count."

The council awaited in deep silence the appearance of their visitor. Emich entered the hall with the assured step of a superior, and with a countenance that was clouded. He bowed to the salutations of the council, signed for his armed followers to await at the door, and walked himself to the seat which Heinrich had previously vacated, and which in truth was virtually the throne of Deurckheim. Placing his heavy form in the chair, with the air of one accustomed to fill it, he again bowed, and made a gesture of the hand, which the burghers understood to be an invitation to be seated. With doubting faces the awed authorities submitted, receiving that permission as a boon, which they were ready so lately themselves to urge as a civility. Heinrich looked surprised, but, accustomed to pay great deference to his noble friend, he returned the bow and smile—for he was especially saluted with a smile—and took the second place.

"It was not well, my worthy townsmen, to clos your gates thus churlishly against me," commenced the baron; "there are rights and honors that ought to be respected, at all hours and seasons, and I marvel that this need be taught to the Deurckheimers by a Count of Leiningen. I and my train were held at parlance at your barriers, an' we had been so many wandering gipsies, or some of the free bands that sell their arquebuses and lances to the highest bidder!"

"That there may have been some little delay, my Lord Count—" answered Heinrich—

"Little, Burgomaster! dost thou call that little which keeps a noble of Leiningen chafing at a gate, amid dust and heat, and gaping mouths? thou knowest not the spirit of our steeds, Herr Frey, if thou imaginest they like such sudden checks of the curb. We are of high mettle, horses and riders, and must have our way when fairly spurred!"

"There was every desire, nobly born Emich, to do you honor, and to undo our bolts as speedily as might be done; for this end we were about to depute the necessary orders, when we were suddenly favored with your gracious and high dispensing company. We doubt not that the captain of the watch reasoned with himself, and did that, of good intention and of his own accord, which he would speedily have been called upon to do, by our com mands."

"God's truth! that may not prove so true," answered Emich, laughing. "Our impatience was stronger than your bolts, and lest the same oversight might renew the inconvenience, we found means to enter with little formality."

The burghers in general seemed greatly troubled, and Heinrich was greatly surprised. The baron saw that enough had been said, for the moment; and assuming a more gracious mien, he continued in another strain.

"Well, loving townsmen," he said, "it is now a happy week, since all our desires have been accomplished. The Benedictines are defeated, the Jaegerthal is at peace and under the sway of its rightful Lord, and yet the sun rises and sets as before, the heavens seem as smiling, the rains as refreshing, and all our hopes as reasonable, as of old! There is to be no miracle in their behalf, Herr Heinrich, and we may fain sleep in peace."

"That may depend, Lord Count, on other humors than ours. Here are reports abroad that are any thing but pleasant to the ear, and our honest townsmen are troubled lest, after doing good service in behalf of their betters, they may yet be made to pay all the charges of the victory."

"Set their hearts at peace, worthy Burgomaster, for I have not thrust a hand into the ecclesiastical flame, without thought of keeping it from being scorched. Thou knowest I have friends, and 'twill not be easy to put a Count of Leiningen to the ban."

"Nay, we doubt but little, illustrious noble, of your safety, and of your house's; our fear is for ourselves."

"Thou hast only to lean on me, Master Frey. When the tie between us shall be explained more clearly to the Emperor and the Diet, and when our loving wishes, as respects each other, shall be better understood, all will know that to strike Deurckheim is to aim a blow at me. Whence cometh this sudden fear, for last reports touching your condition said that the town was firm of heart, and bent on joining Luther, rather than confess?"

"Sapperment! the heart must not always be judged by the countenance! Here is the smith, who is seldom of a bright visage, but were it said that his heart is as black as his face, great injustice would be done the man."

A movement and a murmur betrayed the admiration of those who crowded the door, at this figure of the Burgomaster.

"Thou hast some reason for this sudden despondency?" rejoined the Count, glancing a look of indifference at the artisans.

"Why, to speak the truth, Lord Emich, Bonifacius hath sent us a missive, written in very fair Latin, and in a scholarly manner, that threatens us to a man with every Christian wish, from plagues to downright and incurable damnation."

"And art thou troubled, Heinrich, at a scrawl of unintelligible words!"

"I know not what is to be understood, Herr Count, if a demand for Heinrich Frey, with eleven others of our most respected, as hostages, doubtless to be kept from their affairs in some convent cells, on hard fare, and hard penance, for weary months, be not plain! To this they add demands for gold, with pilgrimages, and penances, and other godly recreations."

"By whose hand got ye this?"

"By that of the honest Prior, a man of so much bowels, that I marvel he should be the bearer of a message so unwelcome and so uncharitable. But the best of us have our moments of weakness, for all are not always thoughtful or just."

"Ha! Arnolph is afoot!—Hath he departed?"

"He tarries, my good lord; for look you, we have not yet determined on the fashion of our reply."

"Thou wouldst not have thought of sending answer, without taking counsel of me, Herr Frey!" said Emich, sharply, and much in the manner that a parent reproves his child. "I am luckily arrived, and the matter shall be looked to. Have ye bethought ye of the fitting terms?"

"No doubt all have bethought them much, though as yet, none have uttered their secret opinions. For one, I cry out loudly against all hostages, though none could be readier than I to undergo this risk to serve the town; but it is admitting an error in too plain evidence, and carrieth with it a confession that our faith is not to be depended on."

This sentiment, which had long been struggling in Heinrich's breast, met with an audible echo in that of every one of the eleven who were likely, by situation and years, to be chosen for this honorable distinction; and every man among them uttered some proper phrase concerning the value of character, and the necessity of so demeaning themselves, as not to cheapen that of Deurckheim. Emich listened coolly, for it was of great indifference to him how much the burghers were alarmed, since their fears could only induce them the more to seek support from his interest and power.

"Thou hast then refused the conditions?"

"We have done nothing, Herr Count, but we have thought much and sorely, as hath just been said. I take it, the gold and the hostages will find but little favor among us; but, rather than keep the Palatinate in a disturbed and insecure state, and as we are quiet burghers, who look to peace and the means of getting their bread, our answer may not be so hort, could the matter be brought down to a few chosen penitents and pilgrimages. Though half of Brother Luther's mind in many things, it were well to get quit of even the chances of damnation, for a few sore feet and stripes, that might be so managed as to do little civic harm."

"By the lineage of my house! excellent Heinrich, thou dost but echo my thoughts. The Prior is a man with bowels, and this matter shall be speedily arranged. We must bethink us of the details, for these monks are close calculators, and on a time are said to have outwitted Lucifer. First then, there shall be an offering of gold."

"Nay, my Lord Count will consider the means of our town!"—

"Peace, honest Heinrich," whispered Emich, leaning towards the place where the Burgomaster and two or three of the principal members of the council sat—"We have accounts from the Hebrews at Koeln, which say the Limburg treasures may be well applied, in this manner, to purchase a little peace. We will be liberal as becomes our names," he now spoke to all, "and not send the brotherhood naked into a world, which is getting every day less disposed to clothe them; we must drain our coffers rather than they should starve, and this point may be looked upon as settled. As for our penitents and pilgrims, the castle and the town shall equally furnish a share. I can send the lieutenant of my men-at-arms, who hath a nimble foot—Gottlob the cow-herd, to whom punishment is fairly due, on many general accounts—and others doubtless that may be found. What good, of this nature, can Deurckheim supply?"

"We are a homely people, high-born Graf, and having fewer virtues than our betters, are not so well gifted either in vices. As becometh a middle state, we are content with no great excess in the one or the other of the more striking qualities; and yet I doubt not, neighbors, that at need there might be among us men, who would not fare the worse for wholesome correction and fitting penances?"

Heinrich looked about him, in an inquiring manner, while each burgher passed the investigation on to the next, as men forward a glance that they wish to think has no application to themselves. The crowd at the door recoiled a pace, and heads were turned curiously, and eyes roamed among the inferiors, with quite as much expression as had just been done by their superiors.

"There are delinquents, young and thoughtless varlets, who vex the town with their ribaldry and noise, that it might do to scourge with the church's rod,"—suggested the tremulous and aged Wolfgang.

"St. Benedict will be put off with none of these," bluffly answered the Burgomaster; "he must have men of substance and of some esteem, or the affair will be as far as ever from a happy conclusion. What thinkest thou, honest and patriotic Dietrich?—Thou hast a constitution to endure, and a heart of iron."

"Tausend sex und zwanzig!" returned the smith; 'you little know all my ailings, most worshipful masters, if you think I am near this force! I have difficulties of breath, that are only at peace near the heat of the forge, and my heart gets soft as a feather on a journey. Then there is the wife and the young to wail my absence, and I am not scholar enough to repeat a prayer more than some six or ten times in a day."

This excuse did not appear to satisfy the council, who, acting on that principle of exaction which is found among all people and in all communities, felt disposed to recollect the former services of the artisan, as a sort of apology for further claims on his exertions.

"Nay, for one that hath ever been so free at the wish of Deurckheim, this plea cometh with an ill grace," answered Heinrich,—a sentiment that was audibly repeated in a general exclamation of discontent by all the other burghers.—

"We expected other reply from thee!"

"Well, since the worshipful council expects—but there will be the wife and the young, with none to care for them!"—

"That difficulty may be disposed of—thou hast six, if I remember, in thy household?"

"Ten, honorable Heinrich—not a mouth less than half a score, and all of an age to require much food and strong."

"Here are all but two of our dozen, in a word, noble Emich," promptly added the Burgomaster; "and of a scriptural quality, for we are told, the prayers and sacrifices of the young and innocent are acceptable. Thanks, honest smith, and more than thanks: thou shalt have marks of a quality different from those left by the scourge. No doubt the others may be picked up among the useless and idle."

"Our affairs seem settled, loving burghers," answered the Count. "Leave me to dispose of the question of indemnity, and look ye to the penitents, and to the seemliness of the atonement. Ye may retire, ye that throng the way."—The mandate was hurriedly obeyed, and the door closed.—"As for support at Heidelburg and Madrid," continued the Count, "the matter hath been looked to; and should the complaint be pushed beyond decency at Rome, we have always brother Luther as an ally. Bonifacius wanteth not for understanding, and when he looks deeper into our defences, and into the humor of the times, I know him for one that will be disposed to stay an evil, before it becomes an incurable sore. These shaven crowns, master Heinrich, are not like us fathers of families, much troubled for posterity; for they leave no name or blood behind them; and so long as we can fairly satisfy their present longings, the truce may be considered as more than half concluded. To strip a churchman of his hoardings, needeth but a bold spirit, a present bribe, and a strong hand."

The whole council murmured its approval of this reasoning, and the discussion now took a turn more inclining to the details.

Emich grew gracious, and the burghers bolder. Some even laughed openly at their late apprehensions, and nearly all thought they saw a final settlement of this long-disputed and serious question. The Prior, who had been engaged in visits of religious charity in the town, was soon summoned, and the Count assumed the office of communicating the common answer.

The meeting between Emich and Father Arnolph was characteristic. It took place in the public hall, and in the presence of a few of the principal burghers. The Count was at first disposed to be haughty, imperious, and even repulsive; but the Monk was meek, earnest, and calm. The effect of this forbearance was quickly apparent. Their intercourse soon grew more courteous, for Emich, when not excited, or misled by the cupidity that disgraced the age, possessed most of the breeding of his peers. On the other hand, Arnolph never lost sight of his duties, the chiefest of which he believed to be charity.

"Thou art the bearer of the olive-branch, holy Prior," said the Count, as they took their seats, after some little previous parley; "and pity 'tis, that all who wear the cowl, did not as well comprehend the pleasantest quality of their sacred characters. The world would grow less quarrelsome, and we who worship in the court of the temple, would be less disturbed by doubts touching those who lift its veil."

"I did not look to hold discussion of clerkly duties with thee, Lord Count, when my superior sent me on this errand to the town of Deurckheim," mildly answered the monk, indifferent to the other's wily compliments. "Am I, then, to consider the castle and the council as one?"

"In heart, humor, and interests;—I might add also, in rights and sovereignty; for, now all question of the Abbey is settled, the ancient temporal rule is replaced.—Say I well, loving burghers?"

"Umph!" ejaculated Heinrich. The rest bent their heads, though doubtingly like men taken by surprise. But Emich seemed perfectly satisfied.

"It is of no great moment who governs here, since the wrong done to God and our brotherhood must be repaired by those who have committed it. Hast thou examined the missive of the Abbey, Herr Burgomaster, and art ready with the reply?"

"This duty hath been done, reverend Arnolph, and here is our answer. As for the letter, it is our mature opinion, that it hath been indited in a fair hand, and in very learned Latin, as befitteth a brotherhood of so much repute. We deem this more creditable, since there have been some late heavy losses in books, and he who did this might not have the customary aid of materials to which use had made him familiar. As for what hath been said in the way of greeting and benedictions, holy Prior, we are thankful, and most especially for the part that is of thy share, which we esteem to be of particular unction; in mine own behalf, especially would I thank all of the convent for the manner in which my name hath been introduced into their good wishes; though I must add, it were better that he who wrote had been content to stop there, since these frequent introductions of private personages, in matters of general concernment, are apt to raise envy and other evil passions. As respecting, moreover, any especial pilgrimages and penances in my own person, I feel not the occasion, as would doubtless be the fact at need, since we see most men pricked on to these mortifications by their own consciences."

"The expiation is not sought for particular consolation, neither is it desired as a balm to the Convent's wounds, but as an humble and a necessary atonement to God. In this view have we deemed it important to choose those who are most esteemed among men, since it is before the eyes of mankind that the expiation must be made. I am the bearer of similar proposals to the Castle, and, by high ecclesiastical authority, am I charged to demand that its well-born Lord, himself, make these acknowledgments in his own person. The sacrifice of the honored and innocent hath more flavor than that of the mean and wicked."

"Potz Tausend!" muttered Heinrich.—"I see little use for leading a clean life with such doctrines and discipline!"

But Emich heard the proposal without a frown Bold, haughty, and audacious, he was also deeply artful and superstitious. For years, his rude mind had been tormented by conflicting passions—those of cupidity and religious dread; and now that the former was satisfied, he had begun to reflect seriously of appeasing his latent apprehensions in some effectual manner. Plans of various expiatory offerings had already crossed his mind, and so far from hearing the declaration of the Benedictine with resentment, he entertained the idea with pleasure. It seemed an easy and cheap expedient of satisfying all scruples; for the re-establishment of the community on the hill of Limburg was a condition he knew to be entirely out of the question, in the present state of the public mind in Germany. In this humor, then, did he reply. The conference of course proceeded harmoniously, and it was protracted for several hours. But as its results will be more regularly developed in the course of the narrative, we shall not anticipate events.

CHAPTER XXIV.

"In a strange land
Such things, however trivial, reach the heart,
And through the heart the head, clearing away
The narrow notions that grew up at home,
And in their place grafting good will to all"—
Rogers.

It is necessary to advance a few weeks in the order of time; a change that will bring us to the middle of the warm and generous month of July. The hour was towards the close of day, and the place and scenery such as it is now our duty to describe.

Let the reader imagine a high naked down, whose surface was slightly broken by irregularities. Scarce a tree was visible over the whole of its bald face, though a few stunted shrubs betrayed the efforts of the earth to push forth a meager vegetation. The air was pure, thin, and volatile, and, together with the soft blue of the void, denoted a great elevation above the vapors and impurities which linger nearer to regions that lie on the level of the sea. Notwithstanding these never-failing signs of a mountain country, here and there were to be seen distant peaks, that shot upward into the fierce light, glittering with everlasting frost. Along one side of this naked expanse, the land fell suddenly away, towards a long, narrow, sheet of water, which lay a thousand feet below. The shores of this lake, for such it was, were clothed with innumerable white dwellings, and garnished with hamlets and vineyards while a walled town, with its towers and battlements, occasionally darkened the shores. But these were objects scarcely to be seen, from the precise situation which we desire the mind of the reader to occupy. In the distant view, always in that direction, one favorably placed might have seen a vast range of undulating country, stretching towards the north and east, that had the usual characteristics of a region in which Alpine mountains begin gradually to melt into the plain. This region was beautified with several spots of dark blue, resembling so many deep reflections of the skies, which were sheets of limpid and tranquil water. Towards the south and west, the down was bounded by a natural wall of rude and gray rock, that rose, in nearly all its line, to the elevation of a mountain, and which shot up to a giddy height, near its centre, in two pointed cones, that, by their forms, coupled with other circumstances that shall be soon explained, had obtained the name of the 'Mitres.'

Near the barrier of mountain, and almost directly beneath these natural mitres, was a small village, whose houses, constructed of wood, had the wide roofs, numerous windows, and the peculiar resin-like color of Swiss habitations.

The place was a hamlet rather than a village, and most of the land around it lay at waste, like all that was visible for miles, in every direction. On a rising ground near the hamlet, from which it was separated merely by a large esplanade, or green as we should be apt to term the spot, stood one of those mazes of roofs, chimneys, and towers, which in that age, and indeed even now, mark a conventual pile. The edifices were large, complicated in their forms and order, and had been constructed without much architectural knowledge or taste; the air of the whole being that of rude but abundant wealth. In the centre was a church, or chapel, evidently of ancient existence and simple origin, though its quaint outlines were elaborately decorated.

after the fashion of the times, by a variety of after thoughts, and in a manner to show that means were not wanting to render the whole more magnificent, and that the fault of the construction lay rather in the first idea, than in any subsequent ability or inclination to repair it.

The site of this hamlet and down was in the celebrated Canton of Schwytz, a small district that has since given its name to the heroic confederation, that occupies so much of the country among and near the Western Alps. Its name was Einsiedlen; the monastic buildings belonged to a convent of Benedictines, and the church contained one of the shrines even then most in repute, after that of Loretto. Time and revolutions have since elevated our Lady of Einsiedlen, perhaps, to the very highest rank among the pilgrimages of the Catholic; for we have lately seen thousands crowding her altars, while we found the Santa Casa abandoned chiefly to the care of its guardians, or subject to the casual inspection of curious heretics.

Having thus described the spot to which the scene is shifted, it is proper to refer to the actors.

At a point distant less than a league from the hamlet, and on the side of the open down just mentioned, which lies next to the steep ascent from the lake of Zurich, and in the direction of the Rhine, there came a group of travellers of both sexes, and apparently of all ages, between declining manhood and vigorous youth. They were afoot, wearing the garb and symbols of pilgrims. Weariness had caused them to lengthen their line, and they went in pairs, the strongest in front, the feeble and more fatigued in the rear.

In advance marched two men. One wore the gown and cowl of a Benedictine, while he carried, like the rest, the staff and wallet of a pilgrim. His companion had the usual mantle decorated with scollop shells, and also bore his scrip and stick. The others had the same attire, with the usual exceptions that distinguish the sexes. They consisted of two men of middle age, who followed those in front; two of each sex in pairs, all still young and active; two females, who were in their prime, though wearied and sad; and a maiden, who dragged her limbs after them with a difficulty disproportioned to her years. At the side of the latter was a crone, whose infirmities and age had enabled her to obtain the indulgence of an ass, on which she was seated comparatively at her ease; though, by a license that had been winked at by the monk, her saddle was encumbered with the scrips of most of the female penitents. In the rear of all came two males, who seemed to form a sort of rear guard to the whole party.

This group was composed of the Prior and Emich, who led the van; of Heinrich, and Dietrich, the smith; of Gisela and Gottlob, with a youth and maiden from Deurckheim; of Ulrike and Lottchen, of Meta and Ilse, and of M. Latouche and the Knight of Rhodes. These were the penitents chosen to expiate the late offence to the majesty of God, by prayers and mortifications before the shrine of Einsiedlen. The temporal question had been partially put at rest, by the intrigues and influence of the Count, backed, as he was, by timely applications of gold, and by the increasing heresy that had effectually shaken the authority of the Church throughout all Germany, and which had sufficiently apprized the practised Bonifacius, and his superiors, of the expediency of using great moderation in their demands.

"St. Benedict make us thankful, holy father!" said the Count, as his gratified eye first beheld the long wished-for roofs of the convent.—"We have journeyed a weary distance; and this snail's pace, which, in deference to the weak, we are bound to observe, but little suits the impatience of a warrior, accustomed to steed and spur. Thou hast often visited this sacred shrine, pious Arnolph?"

The Monk had stopped, and with a tearful eye he stood gazing, in religious reverence, at the distant pile. Then kneeling on the grass, he prayed while the others, accustomed to these sudden demonstrations of zeal, gladly rested their limbs, the while.

"Never before hath eye of mine greeted yon holy pile," answered the Prior, as they slowly resumed their journey; "though often, in night dreams, hath my soul yearned for the privilege!"

"Methinks, father, thou hast little occasion for penitence, or pilgrimage:—thou, whose life hath rolled on in deeds of Christian charity and love."

"Each day brings its evil, and each day should have its expiation."

"Truly, not in marches over stony and mountain paths, like these we travel. Einsiedlen must have especial virtue, to draw men so far from their homes to do it honor. Hast the history of the shrine at command, reverend Prior?"

"It should be known to all Christians, and chiefly to the pilgrim. I had thought thee instructed in these great events!"

"By the Magi!—to speak thee honestly, Father Arnolph, the little friendship which hath subsisted between Limburg and my house, had given a disrelish for any Benedictine miracle, let it be of what quality it would; but now that we are likely to be so lovingly united, I could gladly hear the tale, which will at least serve to divert our thoughts from a subject so grovelling as our own feet; for to conceal nothing, mine make most importunate appeals to be at rest!"

"Our journey draweth near its end; but, as thy

request is reasonable, it shall be answered. Listen, then, Emich, and may the lesson profit thy soul! During the reign of the illustrious and warlike Charlemagne, who governed Gaul, with so much of our Germany and the country of the Franks, there lived a youth of the ancient family of Hohenzollern, branches of which still possess principalities and marches in the empire. The name of this learned and pious youth was Meinard. Early fatigued with the vanities of life, he sought a hermitage, nearer than this to the banks of that lake which we so lately crossed at Rapperschwyl. But, overburdened by the number of the curious and pious who visited his cell, the holy Meinard, after seven years of prayer, retired to a clear fountain, which must still run near yonder church, where another cell and a chapel were built for him, expressly by command of Hildegarde, a royal lady, and the Abbess of a monastery in the town of Zurich. Here Meinard lived and here he died, filled with grace, and greatly blessed by godly exercises."

"Father, had he a profitable and happy end, in this wild region?"

"Spiritually, nothing could have been more desirable; temporally, naught more foul. He died by the hands of vile assassins, to whom he had rendered hospitality. The deed was discovered by means of two crows, who followed the murderers to Zurich, where they were taken and executed—at least, so sayeth tradition. In a later age, the holy Meinard was canonized by Benedict VIII. For nearly half a century, the cell of Meinard, though in great request as a place of prayer, remained without a tenant; but at the end of that period, Beurun, a canon of the house of Burgundy, which house then ruled most of the country far and near, caused the chapel and cell to be repaired, replaced the image of the blessed Maria, and devoted his own life to the her mitage. The neighboring Seigneurs and Barons contributed to endow the place, and divers holy men joined themselves to the service of the altar, from which circumstance the shrine obtained the name of our 'Lady of the Hermits,' its true appellation to this hour. It would weary thee to listen to the tale of miracles performed in virtue of their prayers, even in that early and less gifted condition of the place; but its reputation so circulated, that many came from afar to see and to believe. In the process of time, a regular community was established, and the church thou seest was erected, containing in its nave the original cell, chapel, and image of Saint Meinard. Of the brotherhood, Saint Eberhaud was named the Abbot."

"I had thought there was still higher virtue in the place!" observed Emich, when the Prior paused, and seemingly a little disappointed; for your deep sinner as little likes a simple dispensation, as the drunkard relishes small drinks.

"Thou shalt hear. When the buildings were completed, and it became necessary to consecrate the place, agreeably to the forms and usages of the Church, Conrad, Bishop of Constance, was invited to discharge the holy office. Here cometh the wonderful favor of Heaven! As Conrad of Constance, with other pious men, arose to pray, at midnight of the day appointed for the service, they suddenly heard divine music most sweetly chanted by angels. Though sore amazed and impressed, they were still sufficiently masters of their reason to discover that the unseen beings sang the prescribed formula of the consecration, that office which they were preparing themselves to perform a few hours later. Satisfied with this especial and wonderful interference, Conrad would have abstained from repeating a service which had already been thus performed, but for the demands and outcries of the ignorant. But when, after hours of delay, he was about to yield to their impatience, a clear voice three times admonished him of the blasphemy, by saying, 'Cease, brother! thy chapel is divinely consecrated!' From that moment the place is so esteemed, and all our rites are performed as at a shrine of high behest and particular virtue."

Emich crossed himself devoutly, having listened in perfect faith, and with deep interest;—for at that moment early impressions were stronger than the modern doubts.

"It is good to be here, father," he reverently answered; "I would that Ermengarde, and all of my house, were at my side! But are there any especial favors accorded to those who come hither, in a fitting temper, in the way of temporal gifts or political considerations; since, being before a shrine so holy, I could fain profit by the sore pains and privations by which the grace is gained?"

The Prior seemed mortified, for, though he lent the faith required by the opinions of the age, to the tradition he had recounted, he was too well instructed in the true doctrines of his Church, not to perceive the false bias of his companion's mind. The embarrassment caused a silence, during which the reader is to imagine that they passed on, giving place to other personages of the tale.

Before turning to another group, however, we desire to say distinctly, that, in relating the manner of the miraculous consecration of the chapel of 'Our Lady of the Hermits,' we have wished merely to set the tradition before the reader, without inferring aught for, or against, its authenticity. It is well known that the belief of these supernatural interferences of Divine Power forms no necessary part of doctrine, even in that Church which is said to be the most favored by these dispensations; and it ought always to be remembered, that those sects which impugn these visible and physical signs of Omnipotence, entertain opinions, of a more purely spiritual character, that are scarcely less out of the course of ordinary and vulgar nature. In cases in which there exist so nice shades of distinction, and in which truth is so difficult of discovery, it is our duty to limit ourselves to popular facts, and as such have we given the history of Einsiedlen, its Abbey and its Virgin. The opinion of Father Arnolph is the local opinion of our own times, and it is the opinion of thousands who, even now, yearly frequent the shrine.

Heinrich and the smith were the couple next to the Count and the Prior, and of course they were the next to cross the stage:

"It is no doubt much, or I may add altogether as you say, worshipful Burgomaster"——

"Brother Pilgrim;" ruefully interrupted Heinrich.

"I should have said, Brother Worshipful Pilgrim,—though, Heaven it knows, the familiarity goes nigh to choke me!—but it is much as you say, that whether we cling to Rome, or finally settle quietly into the new worship of Brother Luther, this journey ought, in all fairness, to be set down to our account, as of so much virtue; for, look you, brother worshipful, it is made at the cost of Christian flesh and blood, and therefore should it be savory, without much particularity concerning mere outward appearances. I do not think, were truth spoken, that wielding the sledge a twelvemonth would have done this injury to my feet!"

"Have mercy on thyself and me, good smith, and think less of these trifling grievances. What Heaven wills must happen, else would one of thy merit have risen higher in the world."

"Thanks, Worshipful Brother Pilgrim and Burgomaster; I will bethink me of resignation, though these wire-drawn pains are never to the liking of your men of muscle and great courage. A knock o' the head, or the bullet of an arquebuse gives less uneasiness than smaller griefs much endured. Were things properly governed, the penances and pilgrimages, and other expiations of the Church, would be chiefly left to the women."

"We shall see hereafter how Luther hath ordered this: but having ourselves embarked in this journey for the good of Deurckheim, to say nothing of our own souls, it behoveth us to hold out manfully;—a duty the more easily performed, as we can now see the end of it. To speak thee fair, Dietrich, I do not remember ever to have beheld Benedictine abode with so much joy, as this we see at yonder mountain's foot!"

"Be of cheer, most honorable and excellent brother worshipful pilgrim; the trial is near its end, and if we come thus far to do this honor to our own community, why,—Himmel! it is but the price paid for getting rid of another!"

"Be of cheer, truly, brother smith, for it is but some kneeling, and a few stripes that each is to apply to his own back; after which the return will reasonably be more joyous than the advance."

Encouraged by each other, the devotees hobbled on, their heavy massive frames yielding at every step, like those of overgrown oxen which had been but indifferently shod. As they passed by, their places were filled by the four, of whom Gisela and Gottlob formed a part. Among these the discourse was light and trifling, for bodily fatigue had little influence on the joyous buoyancy of such spirits; especially at a moment when they saw before them the immediate termination of their troubles. Not so with those that came next; these were Ulrike and her friend, who moved along the path, like those who were loaded with griefs of the soul.

"God is among these hills, as he is on our plains

Lottchen!" said the former, continuing the discourse. "Yon temple is his shrine, as was that of Limburg; and it is as vain for man to think of forgetting him on earth, as it would be to invade him in that Heaven which is his throne! What he doth is wise, and we will endeavor to submit."

The words of Ulrike were perhaps more touched with resignation than her manner. The latter, though subdued, was filled with sorrow, and her voice was tremulous nearly to tears. Though the exhibition of her melancholy was deep and evident, it was of a character which denotes no extinction of hope. On the other hand, the features, eye, and entire manner of her friend, bore the heavy and fatal impress of incurable woe.

"God is among these hills!" repeated Lottchen, though she scarce seemed to hear the words; "God is among these hills!"

"We approach a much-esteemed shrine, dearest Lottchen: the Being, in whose name it hath been raised, will not permit us to depart from it unblessed."

"We shall be blessed, Ulrike!"

"Thou dwellest hopelessly on thy loss, my Lottchen! Would thou had less thought of the past, and more of the future!"

The smile with which the widow regarded her friend was full of anguish.

"I have no future, Ulrike, but the grave!"

"Dearest Lottchen!—we will speak of this holy shrine!" Emotion smothered her voice.

"Speak of what thou wilt, my friend," answered the childless widow, with a frightful calm. "I see no difference in subjects."

"Lottchen!—not when we discourse of Heaven!"

The widow bowed her vacant eyes to earth, and they passed on. Their footsteps were succeeded by those of the beast ridden by Ilse, and by the falter ing tread of Meta.

"Ay,—yon is the shrine of our Lady of the Hermits!" said the former; "a temple of surpassing virtue! Well, Heaven is not in Churches and chapels, and that of Limburg may yet be spared; the more especially as the brotherhood was far from being of unexceptionable lives. Keep up thy heart, Meta, and think not of weariness, for not a pain dost thou now bear, that will not be returned to thee, another day, in joy, or in some other precious gift. This is Heaven's justice, which is certain to requite all equally, for good or evil. Well-a-day!—it is this certainty that comforteth the godly, and giveth courage to the tottering."

She spoke to an insensible listener. The countenance of Meta, like that of Lottchen, expressed hopelessness, though it were in less palpable and certain signs. The eye was dull but wandering, the cheek pale, the mouth convulsive and at times compressed, the step languid, and the whole being of this young and innocent creature seemed wasting under a premature and unnatural blight! She looked at the convent with indifference, though it brought relief to her bodily pains. The mountains rose dark and rugged near, or glittered in the distance like hills of alabaster, without giving birth to a single exclamation of that delight, which these scenes are known to excite in young breasts; and even the pure void above was gazed at, though it seemed to invite to a more tranquil existence, with vacuity and indifference.

"Ah's me!" continued Ilse, whose observation rarely penetrated beyond her own feelings, and whose tongue was never known to wax weary.—"Ah's me! Meta. O! it must be a wicked world that needs all these pilgrimages and burnings.—But they are only types, child, of the past and of the future; of the 'has been,' and of the 'to come.' First, life is a pilgrimage, and a penance; though few of us think so while journeying on its way, but so it is to all; especially to the little favored—but a penance it is, by means of our ailings and other infirmities, particularly in age; and therefore do I bear with it cheerfully, since penances are to be borne; and the burnings of convents and villages are types of the burnings of the wicked. Thou dost not answer, child?"

"Dost think, nurse, that they who die by fire are blessed!"

"Of what art speaking, Meta!—Poor Berchthold Hintermayer perished, as thou knowest, in the flames of Limburg; so did Father Johan, and so did one, far more evil than either!—Oh! I could reveal secrets, an' I had not a prudent tongue!—But wisdom lieth in prudence, and I say naught: therefore, Meta, be thou silent."

"I will obey thee, nurse."

The tones of the girl trembled, and the smile with which she gladly acquiesced in the demand of Ilse, was such as the sinking invalid gives the kind attendant.

"Thou art dutiful, and it is a merit. I never knew thee more obedient, and less given to merriment or girlish exclamations, than on this very pilgrimage, all of which shows that thy mind is in a happy state for these holy offices. Well-a-day!—the pious A nolph has halted, and now we are about, in sooth, to reap the virtue of all our labors. Oh! an' I had been a monk, thou wouldest have had a leader!"

Ilse beat the sides of the patient animal she rode, and Meta toiled after, as well as her trembling limbs permitted. The Knight and the Abbé came last.

"Thou hast made many of these pious expiations, reverend Abbé?" observed the former, when they had risen the hill, which commanded a view of the convent.

"Never another. Had not chance made me an innocent participator in the destruction of Limburg, this indignity would have been spared."

"How! callest thou a pilgrimage, and prayer at a shrine, an indignity?—thou, a churchman!"

"Gallant Knight, I speak to thee as to a comrade of many days, and of weary passages; as one enlightened. Thou knowest the constitution of earth, and the divers materials that compose society. We have doctrines for all; but practices must be mitigated, like medicaments to the sick. Your pilgrimage is well enough for the peasant, or the citizen, or even for your noble of the Provinces, but their merit is much questioned among us of the capitals—unless, indeed, there should mingle some hope for the future but penance for deeds accomplished we hold to be supererogatory."

"By my rapier! no such doctrine was in vogue at Rhodes, where all ordinances were much respected, and uniformly admitted."

"And had ye then these familiar practices of religion in your daily habits, Sir Knight?"

"I say not in practice; but ever in admission. Thou knowest the distinction, Sir Abbé, between the purity of doctrine, and some constructions of practice."

"That doubtless. Were we to tie the gentle down to all the observances and exactions of a severe theory, there would grow up numberless inconveniences. For myself, had it been possible to preserve the ecclesiastical character, without penance under the odium of this unhappy but accidental visit to our host the Count, I could have dispensed with the last act of the drama."

"'Tis whispered, Herr Latouche, my cousin bethought him, that the presence of an ecclesiastic might prove a cloak to his intentions, and that we owe the pleasure of thy agreeable society to a policy that is deeper than chance!"

Albrecht of Viederbach laughed, as he intimated this ruse of Emich; and his companion, who had long perceived how completely he had been the dupe of his host, for in truth he knew nothing previously of the intended assault, was fain to make the best of his situation. He laughed, in his turn, as the loose of principle make light of any misadventure that may happen to be the consequence of their laxity of morals; and, pressing each other, on their several parts in the late events, the two proceeded leisurely towards the spot where the Prior and Emich, as leaders of the party, had now come to a halt. We shall profit by the occasion to make some necessary explanations.

We are too much accustomed in this Protestant country, to believe, that most of the piety of those who profess the religion of Rome consists in externals. When the great antiquity of this Church shall be remembered, as well as the general tendency, in the early ages, to imitate the forms and habits of their immediate predecessors, it should not occasion surprise if some observances were retained, that cannot very clearly be referred, either to apostolic authority or to reason. The promulgation of abstract truth does not necessarily infer a departure from those practices which have become of value by use, even though they may not materially assist in the attainment of the great end. We have inherited many of the vestments and ceremonies, which are retained in the Protestant churches, from Pagan priests; nor is there any sufficient motive for abandoning them, so long as they aid the decencies of worship, without weakening its real objects. The Pagans themselves probably derived some of these very practices, from those whom we are taught to believe held direct communion with God, and who should have best known in what manner to render human adoration most acceptable to the ruler of the universe.

In this country, Catholicism, in its limited and popular meaning, is no longer catholic, since it is in so small a minority, as to have no perceptible influence on the opinions or customs of the country The outward symbols, the processions, and all the peculiar ceremonies of the Romish Church are confined to the temples, and the eye rarely or never meets any evidence of its existence, beyond their walls. But in Europe the reverse is altogether the case, more particularly in those countries in which the spiritual sway of the head of the Church has not been interrupted by any adventitious changes, proceeding from political revolutions, or other powerful causes. The crucifix, the spear, the cock, the nails, and the sponge, are erected at cross-roads,—chapels dedicated to Mary are seen near many a spring, or at the summit of some weary mountain: while the usual symbols of redemption are found scattered along the highways, marking the site of some death by accident, or the scene of a murder.

In no part of the other hemisphere are these evidences of faith and zeal more common, than in the Catholic cantons of Switzerland. Hermitages are still frequent among the rugged rocks of that region, and it is usual to see near these secluded abodes a sort of minor chapel, that is termed, in ordinary language, a 'station.' These stations are so many tabernacles raised by the way-side, each containing a representation of one of the twelve sufferings of Christ. They are met equally on the side of Vesuvius, overlooking the glorious sea and land, of that unequalled country; among the naked wastes of the Apennines; or buried in gorgeous groves; as accident may have determined their location. In some of the valleys of Switzerland, these little tabernacles dot the mountain side for miles, indicating by zig-zag lines, and white walls, the path that leads from the village beneath to some shrine, that is perhaps perched on the pinnacle of a naked rock, or which stands on a spur of the nearest range.

The shrine of Einsiedlen possessed the usual number of these tabernacles, stretching along the path that communicated with the Lake of Zurich. They were designated in the customary manner; each alluding to some one of those great personal afflictions that preceded the crucifixion, and each having sentences of holy writ, to incite the pious to devotion. Here the pilgrims ordinarily commenced the worship peculiar to the place, and it was here that the Prior now awaited his companions.

CHAPTER XXV.

"Was Godde to serche our hertes and reines,
The best were synners grete;
Christ's vycarr only knowes ne synne,
Ynne alle thys mortall state."

CHATTERTON.

When all were arrived, the pilgrims divided themselves along the path, some kneeling before one tabernacle, and some at another. Ulrike and Lottchen, followed by the pallid Meta, prayed long at each in succession. The other females imitated their example, though evidently with less zeal and earnestness. The Knight of Rhodes and Monsieur Latouche limited their observances to a few genuflexions, and much rapid crossing of themselves with the fingers, appearing to think their general professions of faith possessed a virtue, that superseded the necessity of any extraordinary demonstrations of piety. Heinrich and the smith were more particular in showing respect for the prescribed forms; the latter, who was secretly paid by his townsmen for what he did, feeling himself bound in honor to give them the worth of their money, and the Burgomaster, in addition to his looking for great temporal advantages from the whole affair, being much influenced by paternal regard for Deurckheim. As for Ilse, none was more exact than she; and, we may add, none more ostentatious.

"Hast bethought thee, Dietrich, to say an extra word in behalf of the general interests?" demanded Heinrich, while he patiently awaited the removal of the other, from before the last tabernacle, in order to assume the post himself.

"Nay worshipful Burgomaster—"

"Brother Pilgrim, good smith!"

"Nay, worshipful Brother, and good pilgrim, there was no question of this duty in the understanding."

"Himmel! Art such a hound, Dietrich, as to need a bribe to pray in thine own interest? Do that thou hast promised, for the penance, and in the interest of the monks, and then bethink thee, like an honest artisan, of the town of which thou art a citizen. I never rise from my knees without counting a few beads on the score of Deurckheim, and others for favor on the family of Frey."

"I cry you mercy, honorable Heinrich and excellent brother Pilgrim; the wish is reasonable, and it shall be performed."

The smith then counted off his rosary, making place for the Burgomaster as soon as he could conveniently get through with the duty. In the mean time, Arnolph had prayed devoutly, and with sincere mental abasement, before each station.

The pilgrims then arranged themselves in two lines, a form of approaching the convent of Einsiedlen that is still observed by thousands annually, the men placing themselves on the right of the path in single files, and the females on its left, in a similar order. Arnolph walked ahead, and the whole proceeded. Then began the repetition of the short prayers aloud.

Whoever has wandered much through this remarkable and wild country, must have frequently met with parties of pilgrims, marching in the manner described, and uttering their aspirations in the pure air, as they ascend to, or descend from, the altar of "our Lady of the Snow" on the Rhigi, or wend their way among rocky and giddy paths, seeking or returning from some other shrine. We know of no display of human worship that is more touching or impressive than this. The temple is the most magnificent on earth, the air is as limpid as mountain torrents and a high region can bestow, while sound is conveyed to the ear, in its clearest and most distinct tones, aided perhaps by the echoes of dells that are nearly unfathomable, or of impending masses that appear to prop the skies. Long before the party is seen, the ear announces its approach by the music of the prayers; for music it is in such a place, the notes alternating regularly between the deep bass of the male to the silvery softness of the female voice.

Such was now the effect produced by the advance of our party from the Palatinate. Father Arnolph gave the lead, and the powerful lungs of Heinrich and the smith, though much restrained, uttered the words in tones impressively deep and audible. The response of the women was tremulous, soft, and soothing. In this manner did they proceed for a mile, when they entered the street of the hamlet.

An express had announced to the community of Einsiedlen the approach of the German penitents. By a singular perversion of the humble doctrines of the founder of the religion, far more importance was attached to the expiations and offerings of princes, and of nobles of high degree, than to those which proceeded from sources that were believed to be meaner. All the dwellers of the hamlet, therefore, and most of the others that frequented the shrine, were abroad to witness this expected procession. The name of Emich was whispered from ear to ear, and many curious eyes sought the form of the powerful baron, under the guise common to the whole party. By general consent, after much speculation, the popular opinion settled on the person of the smith, as on the illustrious penitent; a distinction which Dietrich owed to the strength of his lungs, to some advantage in stature, and particularly to the zeal which, as a hireling, he thought it just to throw into his air and manner.

Among the other traditions that serve to give a popular celebrity to the shrine of our Lady of the Hermits, is one which affirms that, on an occasion it is unnecessary to relate, the Son of God, in the form of man, visited this favored shrine. He is said to have assuaged his thirst at the fountain which flows, with Swiss purity and profusion, before the door of the building; and as the clear element has been made to run through different metal tubes, it is a custom of the Pilgrims, as they arrive, to drink a hasty swallow at each, in order to obtain the virtue of a touch so revered. There was also a plate of silver, that had marks which were said to have been left by the fingers of Jesus, and to these it was the practice to apply the hand. The former usage is still universal; though modern cupidity has robbed the temple of the latter evidence of the reputed visit, in consequence of the value of the metal which bore its memorial.

Arnolph halted at the fountain, and, slowly making its circuit, drank at each spout. He was followed by all of his companions. But he passed the silver plate, and entered the building, praying aloud until his foot was on the threshold. Without stopping he advanced and knelt on the cold stones before the shrine, fastening his eye the whle on the carved image of Mary. The others imitated his movements, and, in a few minutes, all were kneeling before the far-famed chapel of the Divine Consecration.

The ancient church of Einsiedlen (for the building has since been replaced by another still larger and more magnificent) had been raised around the spot where the cell of Saint Meinard originally stood. The chapel reputed to have been consecrated by angels, was in this revered cell, and the whole stood in the centre of the more modern edifice. It was small, in comparison with the pile which held it, but of sufficient size to admit of an officiating priest, and to contain many rich offerings of the pious. The whole was encased in marble, blackened by time and the exhalations of lamps; while the front, and part of the sides, permitted a view of the interior, through openings that were protected by gratings curiously and elaborately wrought.

In the farther and dark extremity of this sacred chapel, were the images of the Mother and Child. Their dresses, as is usual at all much-worshipped shrines, were loaded with precious stones and plates of gold. The face of each had a dark and bronzed color, resembling the complexion of the far east, but which probably is a usage connected with the association of an origin and destiny that are superhuman. The whole was illuminated by strong lights, in lamps of silver-gilt, and the effect, to a mind indisposed to doubt, was impressive, and of a singularly mysterious influence. Such was the shrine of our Lady of the Hermits at the time of our tale, and such it continues to be to this day, with some immaterial additions and changes, that are more the results of time than of opinion.

We have visited this resort of Catholic devotion

n that elevated region of hill and frost; have stroll ed, near the close of day, among its numerous and decorated chapels; have seen the bare-kneed peasant of the Black Forest, the swarthy Hungarian, the glittering-eyed Piedmontese, and the fair-haired German, the Tyrolese, and the Swiss, arrive, in groups, wearied and foot-sore; have watched them drinking with holy satisfaction at the several spouts, and, having followed them to the front of the altar, have wondered at the statue-like immovability with which they have remained kneeling, without changing their gaze from that of the unearthly looking image that seemed to engross their souls. Curiosity led us to the spot alone, and at no moment of a pilgrimage in foreign lands, that has now extended to years, do we remember to have felt so completely severed from all to which we were most accustomed, as at that hour. The groups arrived in scores, and, without pausing to exchange a greeting, without thought of lodging or rest, each hurried to the shrine, where he seemed embodied with the stone of the pavement, as, with riveted eye and abased mien, he murmured the first prayers of expiation before the image of Mary.—But to return to the narrative.

For the first hour after the arrival of the expected pilgrims of Deurckheim, not a sign of recognition, or of grace, was manifested in the convent. The officials came and went, as if none but of common character made their expiations; and the fixed eye and swarthy face of the image seemed to return each steady gaze, with supernatural tranquillity. At length Arnolph arose, and, as if his movements were watched, a bell rang in a distant aisle. A lateral door, which communicated with the conventual buildings, opened, and the whole brotherhood issued through it into the body of the church. Arnolph immediately kneeled again, and, by a sign, com manded his companions to maintain their places. Though grievously wearied with their positions, the men complied, but neither of the females had yet stirred.

The Benedictines of Einsiedlen entered the church in the order that has been already described in th processions of Limburg. The junior monks cam first, and the dignitaries last. In that age, thei Abbot was commonly of a noble and ancient, and sometimes of a princely house; for, in maintaining its influence, the Church has rarely been known to overlook the agency of those opinions and prejudices that vulgarly exist among men. In every case, however, the prelate who presided over this favored community, possessed, in virtue of his office, the latter temporal distinction; being created a mitred Abbot and a Prince of the Empire, on the day of his consecration.

During the slow advance of the long line of monks, that now drew near the shrine, there was a chant in the loft, and the deep organ accompanied the words, on a low key. Even Albrecht and the Abbé were much impressed, while Emich fairly trembled, like one that had unwittingly committed himself into the hands of his enemies.

The head of the train swept round the little chapel, and passed with measured steps before the pilgrims. The Prior and the females only prayed the more devoutly, but neither the Count nor the Burgomaster could prevent their truant eyes from watching the movement. Dietrich, little schooled in his duties, fairly arose, and stood repeating reverences to the whole fraternity, as it passed. When the close drew near, Emich endeavored to catch a glance of the Abbot's eyes, hoping to exchange one of those secret signs of courtesy, with which the initiated, in every class of life, know how to express their sympathies. To his confusion, and slightly tc his uneasiness, he saw the well-known countenance of Bonifacius, at the side of the dignitary who presided over the brotherhood of Einsiedlen. The glances of these ancient and seemingly irreconcilable rivals, were such as might have been anticipated. That of Bonifacius was replete with religious pride, and a resentment that was at least momentarily gratified; though it still retained glimmerings of conscious defeat; while that of Emich was fierce, mortified, and alarmed, all in a moment.

But the train swept on, and it was not long ere the music announced the presence of the procession in the choir. Then Arnolph again arose, and, followed by all the pilgrims, he drew near to listen to the vespers. After the prayers, the usual hymn was sung.

"Himmel! master brother Pilgrim," whispered the smith to the Burgomaster, "that should be a voice known to all of Deurckheim!"

"Umph!"—ejaculated Heinrich, who sought the eye of Emich. "These Benedictines sing much in the same strain, Herr Emich, whether it be in Limburg, or here in the church of our Lady of the Hermits."

"By my fathers! master Frey, but thou sayest true! To treat thee as a confidant, I little like this intimate correspondence between the Abbots, and, least of all, to see the reverend Bonifacius enthroned here, in this distant land, much as he was wont to be in our valley. I fear me, Burgomaster, that we have entered lightly on this penance!"

"If you can say this, well-born Emich, what should be the reply of one that hath wife and child, in addition to his own person, in the risk? It would have been better to covet less of Heaven, the least portion of which must naturally be better than the best of that to which we are accustomed on earth, and to be satisfied with the advantages we have

Do you note, noble Count, the friendly manner in which Bonifacius regards us, from time to time?"

"His favors do not escape me, Heinrich;—but peace! we shall learn more, after the vespers are ended."

Then came the soothing power of that remarkable voice. The singer had been presented to the convent of Einsiedlen, by Bonifacius, to whom he was now useless, as a boon that was certain to give him great personal favor: and so it had proved; for in those communities, that passed their lives in the exercise of the offices of the Church, the different shades of excellence in the execution, or the greater external riches and decorations of their several shrines, often usurped the place of a nobler strife in zeal and self-denial. The ceremony now ended, and a brother approaching whispered Father Arnolph. The latter proceeded to the sacristy, attended by the pilgrims, for it was forbidden, even to the trembling Meta, to seek refreshment or rest, until another important duty had been performed.

The sacristy was empty, and they awaited still in silence, while the music of the organ announced the retiring procession of the monks. After some delay, a door opened, and the Abbot of Einsiedlen, accompanied by Bonifacius, appeared. They were alone, with the exception of the treasurer of the Abbey; and as the place was closed, the interview that now took place, was no longer subject to the vulgar gaze.

"Thou art Emich, Count of Hartenburg-Leiningen," said the prelate, distinguishing the noble, spite of his mean attire, by a single glance of an eye accustomed to scan its equals;—"a penitent at our shrine, for wrongs done the Church, and for dishonor to God?"

"I am Emich of Leiningen, holy Abbot!"

"Dost thou disclaim the obligation to be here?"

"And a penitent;—" the words "for being here" being bitterly added, in a mental reservation.

The Abbot regarded him sternly, for he disliked the reluctance of his tongue. Taking Bonifacius apart, they consulted together for a few minutes; then returning to the group of pilgrims, he resumed—

"Thou art now in a land that listeneth to no heresies, Herr von Hartenburg; and it would be wel to remember thy vow, and thy object. Hast thou aught to say?"

Emich slowly undid his scrip, and sought his offerings among its scanty contents.

"This crucifix was obtained by a noble of my house, when a crusader. It is of jasper, as thou seest, reverend Abbot, and it is not otherwise wanting in valuable additions."

The Abbot bowed, in the manner of one indifferent to the richness of the boon, signing to the treasurer to accept the gift. There was then a brief pause.

"This censer was the gift of a noble far less possessed than thee!" said he who kept the treasures of the Abbey, with an emphasis that could not easily be mistaken.

"Thy zeal outstrippeth the limbs of a weary man, brother.—Here is a diamond, that hath been heirloom of my house, a century. 'Twas an emperor's gift!"

"It is well bestowed on our Lady of the Hermits; though she can boast of far richer offerings from names less known than thine."

Emich now hesitated, but only for an instant, and then laid down another gift.

"This vessel is suited to thy offices," he said, "being formed for the altar's services."

"Lay the cup aside;" sternly and severely interrupted Bonifacius: "it cometh of Limburg!"

Emich colored, more in anger than in shame however, for in that age plunder was one of the speediest and most used means of acquiring wealth. He eyed the merciless Abbot, fiercely, but without speaking.

"I have no more," he said; "the wars—the charges of my house—and gold given the routed brotherhood, have left me poor!"

The treasurer turned to Heinrich, with an eloquent expression of countenance.

"Thou wilt remember, master Treasurer, that there is no longer any question of a powerful baron," said the Burgomaster, "but that the little I have to give, cometh of a poor and saddled town. First we offer our wishes and our prayers,—secondly, we present, in all humility, and with the wish they may prove acceptable, these spoons, which may be of use in some of thy many ceremonies,—thirdly, this candlestick, which though small is warranted to be of pure gold, by jewellers of Frankfort:—and lastly, this cord, with which seven of our chief men have grievously and loyally scourged themselves, in reparation of the wrong done thy brethren."

All these offerings were graciously received, and the monk turned to the others. It is unnecessary to repeat the different donations that were made by the inferiors, who came from the castle and the town. That of Gottlob was, or pretended to be, the offending horn, which had so irreverently been sounded near the altar of Limburg, and a piece of gold. The latter was the identical coin he had obtained from Bonifacius, in the interview which led to his arrest; and the other was a cracked instrument, that the roguish cow-herd had often essayed among his native hills, without the least success. In after life, when the spirit of religious party grew bolder, he often boasted of the manner in which he had tricked the Benedictines by bestowing an instrument so useless.

Ulrike made her offering, with sincere and meek penitence. It consisted of a garment for the image of the Virgin, which had been chiefly wrought by her own fair hands, and on which the united tributes of her townswomen had been expended, in the way of ornaments, and in stones of inferior price. The gift was graciously received; for the community had been well instructed in the different characters of the various penitents.

"Hast thou aught in honor of Maria?" demanded the treasurer of Lottchen.

The widowed and childless woman endeavored to speak, but her power failed her. She laid upon the table, however, a neatly bound and illuminated missal; a cap that seemed to have no particular value, except its tassel of gold and green, and a hunting horn; all of which, with many others of the articles named, had made part of the load borne on the furniture of the ass.

"These are unusual gifts at our shrine!" muttered the monk.

"Reverend Benedictine," interrupted Ulrike, nearly breathless in the generous desire to avert pain from her friend, "they are extorted from her who gives, like drops of blood from the heart. This is Lottchen Hintermayer, of whom thou hast doubtless heard?"

The name of Lottchen Hintermayer had never reached the treasurer's ear; but the sweet and persuasive manner of Ulrike prevailed. The monk bowed, and he seemed satisfied. The next that advanced was Meta. The Benedictines all appeared struck by the pallid color of her cheek, and the vacant, hopeless, expression of an eye that had lately been so joyous.

"The journey hath been hard upon our daughter!" said the princely Abbot, with gentleness and concern.

"She is young, reverend Father," answered Ulrike; "but God will temper the wind to the shorn lamb."

The Abbot looked surprised, for the tones of the mother met his ear with an appeal as touching as that of the worn countenance of the girl.

"Is she thy child, good pilgrim?"

"Father, she is—Heaven make me grateful, for its blessed gift!"

Another gaze from the wondering priest, and he gave place to the treasurer, who advanced to receive the offering. The frame of Meta trembled violently, and she placed a hand to her bosom. Drawing forth a paper, she laid it simply before the monk, who gazed at it in wonder.

"What is this?" he asked. "It is the image of a youth, rudely sketched!"

"It meaneth, Father," half whispered Ulrike, "that the heart which loved him, now belongs to God!"

The Abbot bowed, hastily signing to the inferior to accept the offering; and he walked aside to conceal a tear that started to his eye. Meta at that moment fell upon her mother's breast, and was borne silently from the sacristy.

The men followed, and, with a single exception, the two Abbots and the Treasurer were now left alone.

"Hast thou an offering, good woman?" demanded the latter of the female who remained.

"Have I an offering, Father! Dost think I would come thus far with an empty hand? I am Ilse, Frau Frey's nurse, that Deurckheim hath sent on this pilgrimage, as an offering in herself; and such it truly is for frail bones, and threescore and past. We are but poor town's-people of the Palatinate, but then we know what is available at need! There are many reasons why I should come, as thou shalt hear. Firstly, I was in Limburg church, when the deed was"——

"How! did one of thy years go forth on such an expedition?"

"Ay, and on many other expeditions. Firstly, I was with the old Burgomaster, Frau Ulrike's father when there was succor sent to Mannheim; secondly, I beheld, from our hills, the onset between the Elector's men, and the followers of"——

"Dost thou serve the mother of yonder weeping girl?" demanded the Abbot, cutting short the history of Ilse's campaigns.

"And the weeping girl herself, reverend, and holy and princely Abbot, and, if thou wilt, the Burgomaster too, for, at times, in sooth, I serve the whole family."

"Canst thou repeat the history of her sorrow?"

"Naught easier, my lord and Abbot. Firstly, is she youthful, and that is an age when we grieve or are gladdened with little reason; then she is an only child, which is apt to weaken the spirit by indulgence; next, she is fair, which often tempts the heart into various vanities, and, doubtless, into sorrow, among the others; then is she foot-sore, a bitter grief of itself; and, finally, she hath much repentance for this nefarious sin, of which we are not yet purged, and which, unless pardoned, may descend o her, among other bequests from her father."

"It is well. Deposit thy gift, and kneel that I may bless thee."

Ilse did as ordered, after which she withdrew, making many reverences in the act.

As the door closed on the crone, Bonifacius and his brother Abbot quitted the place in company leaving the monk charged with that duty, to care for the wealth that had been so liberally added to the treasury of Einsiedlen.

CHAPTER XXVI.

—"Israel, are these men
The mighty hearts you spoke of?"—
BYRON.

THERE was little resemblance in the characters of the two prelates, beyond that which was the certain consequence of their common employment. If Bonifacius was the most learned, of the strongest intellectual gifts, and, in other particulars relating to the mind, of the higher endowments, the princely Abbot of Einsiedlen had more of those gentle and winning qualities which best adorn the Christian life. Perhaps neither was profoundly and meekly pious, for this was not easy to men surrounded by so many inducements to flatter their innate weaknesses: but both habitually respected the outward observances of their Church; and both, in degrees proportioned to the boldness and sagacity of their respective intellects, yielded faith to the virtue of its offices.

On quitting the sacristy, they proceeded through the cloisters, to the abode of the chief of the community. Here, closeted together, there was a consultation concerning their further proceedings.

"Thou wert of near neighborhood," said he of our Lady of the Hermits, "to this hardy baron, Brother Bonifacius?"

"As thou mayest imagine by the late events. There lay but a few arrow's flights between his castle and our unhappy walls."

"Had ye good understanding of old, or cometh the present difficulty from long-standing grievances?"

"Thou art happy, pious Rudiger, to be locked, as you are, among your frosts and mountains, beyond the reach of noble's arm, and beyond the desires of noble's ambition. Limburg and the craving Counts have scarce known peace since our Abbey's foundation. Your unquiet baron fills some such agency, in respect to our religious communities, as that which the unquiet spirit of the Father of Sin occupies in the moral world."

"And yet, I doubt that the severest blow we are to receive will come from one of ourselves! If all that rumor and missives from the Bishops reveal, be true, this schism of Luther promises us a lasting injury!"

Bonifacius, whose mind penetrated the future much farther than most of his brethren possessed the means of doing, heard this remark gloomily; and he sat brooding over the pictures which a keen imagination presented, while his companion watched the play of his massive features, with intuitive interest.

"Thou art right, princely Abbot," the former at length replied. "To us, both the future and the past are filled with lessons of deep instruction, could we but turn them to present advantage. All that we know of earth shows that each physical thing returns to its elements, when the object of its creation has been accomplished. The tree helps to pile the earth which once nourished its roots; the rock crumbles to the sand of which it was formed; and even man turns to that dust which was animated that he might live. Can we then expect that our Abbeys, or that even the Church itself, in its present temporal organization, will stand for ever?"

"Thou hast done well to qualify thy words by saying temporal, good Bonifacius, for if the body decays, the soul remains; and the essence of our communion is in its spiritual character."

"Hearken, right reverend and noble Rudiger Go ask of Luther the niceties of his creed on this point, and he will tell thee, that he is a believer in the transmigration of souls—that he keepeth this spiritual character, but in a new dress; and that, while he consigns the ancient body to the tomb, he only lightens the imperishable part of a burthen that has grown too heavy to be borne."

"But this is rank rebellion to authority, and flat refusal of doctrine!"

"Of the former, there can be no question; and, as to our German regions, most seem prepared to incur its risks. In respect to doctrine, learned Rudiger, you now broach a thesis which resembles the bells in your convent towers—on which there may be rung endless changes, from the simple chime to a triple-bob-major."

"Nay, reverend Bonifacius, thou treatest a grave subject with irreverent levity. If we are to tolerate these innovations, there is an end of discipline; and I marvel that a dignified priest should so esteem them!"

"Thou dost me injustice, Brother; for what I urge is said in befitting seriousness. The ingenuity of man is so subtle, and his doubts, once engaged, so restless, that when the barrier of discipline is raised, I know no conclusion for which a clever head may not find a reason. Has it never struck thee, reverend Rudiger, that a great error hath been made from the commencement, in founding all our ordinances to regulate society, whether they be of religious or of mere temporal concerns?"

"Thou asketh this of one who hath been accustomed to think of his superiors with respect."

"I touch not on our superiors, nor on their personal qualities. What I would say is, that our theories are too often faulty, inasmuch as they are made to suit former practices; whereas, in a well-ordered world, methinks the theory should come first, and the usage follow as a consequence of suitable conclusions."

"This might have done for him who possessed Eden, but those who came after were compelled to receive things as they were, and to turn them to profit as they might."

"Brother and princely Abbot, thou hast grappled with the dilemma! Could we be placed in the occupancy of this goodly heritage, untrammelled by previously endeared interests, seeing the truth, naught would be easier than to make practice conform to theory; but, being that we are, priest and noble, saint and sinner, philosopher and worldling, why, look you, the theory is driven to conform to the necessities of practice; and hence doctrine, at the best, is but a convertible authority. As a Benedictine, and a lover of Rome, I would that Luther had been satisfied with mere changes in habits, for these may be accommodated to climates and prejudices; but when the flood-gates of discussion are raised, no man can say to what extent, or in what direction, the torrent will flow."

"Thou hast little faith, seemingly, in the quality of reason?"

Bonifacius regarded his companion a moment with an ill-concealed sneer.

"Surely, holy Rudiger," he gravely replied, "thou hast not so long governed thy fellows to put this question to me! Hadst thou said passion, we might right quickly come to an understanding. The corollaries of our animal nature follow reasonably enough from the proposition; but when we quit the visible land-marks of the species, to launch upon the ocean of speculation, we commit ourselves, like the mariner who trusts his magnet, to an unknown cause. He that is a-hungered will eat, and he that is pained will roar; he that hath need of gold will rob, in some shape or other; and he that loveth his ease may prefer quiet to trouble: all this may be calculated, with other inferences that follow; but if thou wilt tell me what course the Lammergeyer will take when he hath soared beyond the Alps, I will tel. thee the direction in which the mind of man wil. steer, when fairly afloat on the sea of speculation and argument."

"The greater the necessity that it should be held n the wholesome limits of discipline and doctrine."

"Were doctrine like our convent walls, all would be well; but being what it is, men become what they are."

"How! Dost thou account faith for naught? I have heard there were brothers of deep piety in Limburg. Father Johan, who perished in defence of thy altars, may go near to be canonized—to say nothing of the excellent Prior, who is here among us on this pilgrimage."

"I count faith for much, excellent brother; and happy is he who can satisfy uneasy scruples by so pleasant an expedient. Brother Johan may be canonized, if our Father of Rome shall see fit, hereafter, and the fallen Limburg will have reason to exult in its member. Still I do not see that the unhappy Johan proveth aught against the nature of doctrine, for, had he been possessed of less pertinacity in certain of his opinions, he would have escaped the fate which befell him."

"Is martyrdom a lot to displease a Christian? Bethink thee of the Fathers, and of their ends!"

"Had Johan bethought him more of their fortunes, his own might have been different. Reverend Abbot, Johan hath long ceased to be a riddle to me;—though I deny not his utility with the peasant and the fervent. But him thou hast last mentioned"—here Bonifacius' leaned a cheek on his hand, and spoke like one that was seriously perplexed—"him thou namedst last—the sincere, and wise, and simple Arnolph, have I never truly comprehended. That man appeareth equally contented in his cel[illegible] n his stall; honored equally in his office, and on this weary pilgrimage; whether in prosperity or in misfortune, he is ever at peace with himself and with others. Here is truly a man that no reasoning of mine hath been able to fathom. He is not ambitious, for thrice hath he refused the mitre! He is sustained by no wild visions or deceitful fantasies, like the unhappy Johan; nor yet is he indifferent to any of the more severe practices of his profession, all of which are observed quietly, and seemingly with satisfaction. He is learned, without the desire of discussion; meek, amid a firmness that would despise the stake; and forgiving to a degree that might lead us to call him easy, but for a consistency that never seemeth to yield to any influence of season, events, or hopes. Truly, this is a man that baffleth all my knowledge!"

Bonifacius, in despite of his acquirements, his masculine intellect, and his acquaintance with men, did not perceive how much he admitted against himself, by expressing his own inability to fathom the motives of the Prior. Nor did the enigma appear to be perfectly intelligible to his companion who listened curiously to the other's description of their brother; much as we hearken to a history of inexplicable or supernatural incidents.

"I have heard much of Arnolph," observed the latter, "though never matter so strange as this;—and yet most seem to love him!"

"Therein is his power!—though often most opposed to me, I cannot say that I myself am indifferent to the man—By our patron saint! I sometimes fain believe I love him! He was among the last t desert our altars, when pressed by this rapaciou noble, and his credulous and silly burghers; and yet was he foremost to forgive the injury when commit ed. But for him, and his high influence with the

Bishops, there might have been blows for blows spite of this schism that hath turned so many in Germany from our support."

"And since thou speakest of the schism, in wha manner dost thou account for an innovation so hardy in a region that is usually esteemed reasonable? There must have been relaxation of authority; foı there is no expedient so certain to prevent heresies, or errors of doctrine, as a Church well established, and which is maintained by fitting authority."

Bonifacius smiled, for even in that early age, his penetrating mind saw the fallacy to which the other was a dupe.

"This is well when there is right; but when there is error, brother, your established authority does but uphold it. The provisions that are made in thy comfortable abode to keep the cold air out, may be the means of keeping foul air within."

"In this manner of reasoning, truth can have no existence!—Thou dreadest doctrine, and thou wilt naught of discipline!"

"Nay, holy Rudiger, in the latter thou greatly misconceiveth me. Of discipline I would have all that is possible; I merely deny that it is any pledge of truth. We are apt to say that a well-ordained and established Church is the buttress of truth, when experience plainly showeth that this discipline doeth more harm to truth, than it can ever serve it. and that simply because there can be but one truth, while there are many modes of discipline; many establishments therefore uphold many errors, or truth hath no identity with itself."

"Thou surprisest me!—Whatever may come of this heresy, as yet, I know of but one assault on ou supremacy; and that cometh of error, as we come of right."

"This is well for Christendom, but what sayeth it

for your Moslem—your fire-worshipper—your Hindoo—your Pagan, and all the rest; any one of whom is just as ready to keep out error by discipline, as we of Rome? Until now, certainly among Christians this evil hath not often happened, though even we are not without our differences: but looking to this advance of the printing art, and of the variety of opinions that are its fruits, I foresee that we are to have many opposing expedients, all of which will be equally well pondered and concocted to keep in truth, and to exclude error. This pretension of high authority, and of close exactions to maintain purity of doctrine, and what we deem truth, is well, as the jurists say, *quoad hoc;* but touching the general question, I do not see its virtue. Now that men enlist with passion in these spiritual discussions, we may look to see various modifications of the Church, all of which will be more or less buttressed by human expedients, as so many preservatives of truth; but when the time shall come that countries and communities are divided among themselves on these subtleties, look you, excellent Rudiger, we may expect to shut in as much error by our laws and establishments, as we shall shut out. I fear heaven is a goal that must be reached by a general mediation, leaving each to give faith to the minor points of doctrine, according to his habits and abilities."

"This savors more of the houseless Abbot than of him who lately had an obedient and flourishing brotherhood!" Rudiger somewhat piquantly rejoined.

Bonifacius was unmoved by the evident allusion, egarding his companion coolly, and like a man who too well knew his own superiority easily to take of ence. His reply, however, would probably have been a retort, notwithstanding this seeming moderation, had not a door opened, and Arnolph quietly entered the room.

The reception of the Prior, by his two mitred brethren, proved the deep respect which had so universally been won by his self-denying qualities. In the great struggle of the conflicting egotism which composes, in a great degree, the principle of most of the actions of this uneasy world, no one s so likely to command universal esteem, as he who appears willing to bear the burthen of life, with as little as possible of its visible benefits, by withdrawing himself from the arena of its contentions. In the great mass, an occasional retreat from the struggle, on the part of those who have few means of success, creates but little feeling of any sort, perhaps; but when he that hath undeniable pretensions exhibits this forbearance, he may be certain of obtaining full credit for all that he possesses, and more, even to the admission of qualifications that would be vehemently denied had he taken a different attitude, in respect to his rivals. Such was, in some measure, the position of Father Arnolph; and Bonifacius himself never struggled to resist his natural impulses towards the pious monk, having a secret persuasion that none of his virtues, however publicly proclaimed, were likely to militate, against his own interests.

"Thou art much wearied, holy Prior," said the Abbot of Einsiedlen, offering a seat to his visitor, with assiduous and flattering attention.

"I count it not, princely Rudiger; having lightened the way with much good discourse, and many prayers: my pilgrims are faint, but, happily arrived, they are now fairly committed to the convent's hospitality."

"Thou hast with thee, reverend Arnolph, a noble of high esteem in thy German country?"

"Of ancient blood, and of great worldly credit," returned the Prior, with reserve.

"What thinkest thou, brother Bonifacius?—It may not be prudent to make any very public manifestations of a difference of treatment, between those who seek our shrine; but do not hospitality and such courtesy as marketh our own breeding, demand some private greetings. Is my opinion suitable, worthy Arnolph?"

"God is no respecter of persons, Abbot of Einsiedlen."

"Can any know this better than ourselves?—But we pretend not to perfection, nor can our judgments be set up as decisive of men's merits, farther than belongs to our office. Ours is an hospitable order, and we are privileged to earn esteem, and therefore doth it appear to me not only becoming but politic to show a noble of this repute, and at a moment when heresy runs mad, that we do not overlook the nature of his sacrifices. Thou art silent, Brother Abbot!"

The Abbot of Limburg listened with secret satisfaction, for he had views of his own that the proposal favored. He was therefore about to give a ready assent, when Arnolph interrupted him.

"I have nobles among my followers, right reverend Abbots," said the latter earnestly; "and I have those that deserve to be more than noble, if deep Christian humility can claim to be so esteemed. I did not come to speak of Emich of Hartenburg, but of spirits sorely bruised, and to beg of thee, in their behalf, a boon of churchly offices."

"Name it, father, and make certain of its fair reception. But it is now late, and no rites of the morrow need defeat our intentions of honest hospitality."

"They, in whose behalf I would speak," said Arnolph, with apparent mortification, "are already without; if admitted, they may best explain their own desires."

The Abbot signified a ready assent to receive these visitors, and the Prior hastened to admit them anticipating a wholesome effect on the minds of his superiors from the interview. When he reappeared, he was followed by Ulrike, Lottchen, and Meta who came after him in the order named. Both the Abbots seemed surprised, for it exceeded their confidence in themselves to admit visitors of that sex, at an hour so equivocal, in the more retired parts of the buildings, and they counted little on the boldness of innocence.

"This exceedeth usage!" exclaimed the superior of Einsiedlen. "It is true, we have our privileges, pious Arnolph, but they are resorted to with great discretion."

"Fear not, holy Abbot," Arnolph calmly answered; "this visit may at least claim to be as harmless as that of those thou hast just named. Speak, virtuous Ulrike, that thy wishes may be known."

Ulrike crossed herself, first casting a tearful eye on the pallid and depressed countenances of her daughter and of her friend.

"We are come to your favored shrine, princely and pious Abbot," she slowly commenced, like one who feared the effects of her own words, "penitents, pilgrims, and acknowledging our sins, in order to expiate a great wrong, and to implore Heaven's pardon. The accomplishment of our wishes hath been promised by the Church, and by one greater than the Church, should we bring with us contrite hearts. In this behalf, then, we have now little to offer, since our pious guide, the beloved and instructed Arnolph, hath taught us to omit no observance nor hath he, in any particular, left us ignorant of the state of mind that best befitteth our present undertaking. But, right reverend Abbot——"

"Proceed, daughter; thou wilt find all here ready

to listen," said Rudiger kindly, observing that her words became choked, and that she continued to cast uneasy looks at Lottchen and Meta. The voice of the speaker sank, but her tones were still more earnest, as she continued.

"Holy Benedictine, aided by Heaven's kindness, I will. In all that toucheth our pilgrimage and its duties, we confide entirely to the pious counsel of the learned and godly Arnolph, and he will tell you that naught material hath by us been neglected. We have prayed, and confessed, and fasted, and done the needed expiations, in a meek mood, and with contrite hearts. We come then to ask a service of this favored community, which, we trust, may not be refused to the Christian."

The Abbot looked surprised, but he awaited her own time to continue.

"It hath pleased Heaven to call away one dear to us, at a short summons," proceeded Ulrike, not without casting another fearful glance at her companions; "and we would ask the powerful prayers of the community of our Lady of the Hermits, in behalf of his soul."

"Of what age was the deceased?"

"God summoned him, reverend Abbot, in early youth."

"By what means did he come to his end?"

"By a sudden display of Heaven's power."

"Died he at peace with God and the Church?"

"Father, his end was sudden and calamitous. None can know the temper of the mind at that awful moment."

"But did he live in the practices of our faith? Thou comest of a region in which there is much heresy, and this is an hour in which the shepherd cannot desert the fold."

Ulrike paused, for the breathing of her friend was thick and audible.

"Princely Abbot, he was a Christian. I held him myself at the font. This humble penitent and pilgrim gave him birth, and to this holy Prior hath he often confessed."

The Abbot greatly disliked the manner of the answers. His brow drew over the eyes, and he turned jealous glances from Arnolph to the females.

"Canst thou vouch for thy penitent?" he demanded abruptly of the Prior.

"His soul hath need of masses."

"Was he tainted with the heresy of the times?"

Arnolph paused. His mind underwent a severe struggle, for, while he distrusted the opinions of Berchthold, he knew nothing that a scrupulous and conscientious judge could fairly construe into unequivocal evidence of his dereliction from the Church.

"Thou dost not answer, Prior!"

"God hath not gifted me with knowledge to judge the secret heart."

"Ha! this grows plainer. Reverend Bonifacius, canst thou say aught of this?"

The dethroned Abbot of Limburg had, at first, listened to the dialogue with indifference. There had even been an ironical smile on his lips while Ulrike was speaking, but when Arnolph was questioned, it disappeared in an active and a curious desire to know in what manner a man so conscientious would extricate himself from the dilemma. Thus directly questioned, however, he found himself obliged to become a party in the discourse.

"I well know, princely and pious Rudiger, that heresy is rife in our misguided Palatinate," he answered; "else would not the Abbot of Limburg be a houseless guest in Einsiedlen."

"Thou hearest, daughter! The youth is suspected of having died an enemy of the Church."

"The greater the errors, if this be true, the greater the need that prayers be offered for his soul."

"This would be truly aiding Lucifer in his designs to overturn our tabernacles, and a weakness not to be indulged. I am grieved to be compelled to show this discipline to one of thy seeming zeal, but our altars cannot be defiled by sacrifices in behalf of those who despise them. Was the youth connected with the fall of Limburg ?"

"Father, he died in the crush of its roofs," said Ulrike, in nearly inaudible syllables; "and we deem the manner of his end another reason why extraordinary masses should be said in his behalf."

"Thou askest an impossibility. Were we to yield to our pity, in these cases of desperate heresies, it would discourage the faithful, and embolden those who are already too independent."

"Father !" said a tremulous and low, but eager voice.

"What wouldest thou, daughter ?" asked the Abbot, turning to Lottchen.

"Listen to a mother's prayer. The boy was born and educated in the bosom of the Church. For reasons at which I do not repine, Heaven early showed its displeasure on his father and on me. We were rich, and we became poor; we were esteemed of men, and we learned how much better is the support of God. We submitted; and when we saw those who had once looked up to us in respect, looking down upon us in scorn, we kissed the child, were grateful, and did not repine. Even this trial was not sufficient—the father was taken from his pains and mortifications, and my son put on the livery of a baron. I will not say—I cannot say—my strength would have been equal to all this of itself. An angel, in the form of this constant and excellent woman, was sent to sustain me. Until the late wrong to Limburg, we had our hopes and our hours of happiness—but that crime defeated all. My boy hath perished by a just anger, and I remain to implore Heaven in his behalf. Wilt thou refuse the Church's succor to a childless mother, who, this favor obtained, will be ready to bless God and die?"

"Thou troublest me, daughter; but I beg thee to remember I am but the guardian of a high and sacred trust."

"Father!" said a second and still more thrilling appeal.

"Thou too, child! What wouldest thou of one but too ready to yield, were it not for duty?"

Meta had kneeled, and throwing back the hood of her pilgrim's mantle, the change left her bloodless face exposed to the Abbot's view. The girl seemed severely struggling with herself; then, finding encouragement in her mother's eye, she was able to continue.

"I know, most holy and very reverend Abbot," she commenced, with an evidently regulated phraseology, like one who had been instructed how to make the appeal, "that the Church hath need of much discipline; without which there would be neither duration nor order in its existence. This hath my mother taught me; and we both admit it, and prize the truth. For this reason have we submitted ourselves to all its ordinances, never failing to confess and worship, or to observe fasts and saints' days. Even the mitred Bonifacius, there, will not deny this, as respects either of us——"

Meta delayed, as if inviting the Abbot to gainsay her words if he could; but Bonifacius was silent.

"As for him that hath died," resumed Meta, whose voice sounded like plaintive music, "this is the truth. He was born a Christian, and he never said aught in my presence against the Church. Thou canst not think, father, that he who sought my esteem, would strive to gain it by means that no Chrisman girl could respect? That he was often at the Abbey confessionals I know; and that he was in favor with this holy Prior, thou hast but to ask, to learn. In going against Limburg, he did but obey his lord, as others have often done before; and surely all that fall in battle are not to be hopelessly condemned. If there is heresy in Germany, is it not enough of itself to endure so great a danger in life, that the dead must be abandoned to their past acts, without succor from the Church, or thought from their friends? Oh! thou wilt think better, holy but cruel Rudiger, of thy hasty decision. Give us then masses for poor Berchthold! I know not what Bonifacius may have said to thee in secret, concerning the youth, but this much would I say in his favor, in presence of the assembled earth—more pious son, more faithful follower, a braver at need, a more gentle in intercourse, a truer or kinder heart than his, does not now beat in the Palatinate! I know not but I exceed the limits of a maiden's speech, in what I say," continued the girl ardently, a bright spot shining on each cheek amid her tears, "but the dead are mute, and if those they loved are cold to their wants, in what manner is Heaven to know their cruel need?"

"Good daughter," interrupted the Abbot, who began to feel distressed, "we will think of this. Go thou to thy rest,—and may God bless thee!"

"Nay, I cannot sleep while the soul of Berchthold endures this jeopardy! Perhaps the Church will demand penance in his behalf. My mother Lottchen is no longer young and strong, as formerly; but thou seest, father, what I am! Name what thou wilt —pilgrimages, fasts, stripes, prayers, or vigils, are alike to me. Nay, think not that I regard them! Thou canst not bestow more happiness than to give this task for poor Berchthold's sake. Oh! hadst thou known him, holy Monk, so kind with the weak, so gentle with us maidens, and so true, thou wouldest not, nay, thou couldest not need another prayer to grant the masses!"

"Bonifacius, is there no means of justifying the concession?"

"I would speak with thee, brother," answered he of Limburg, who, with a thoughtful countenance, awaited his companion a little apart from the others.

The conference of the two prelates was short, but it was decisive.

"Take away the child," said the Abbot Rudiger, to Ulrike; "the weight of Heaven's displeasure must be borne."

The Prior sighed heavily; but he signed for the females to obey, like one who saw the uselessness of further entreaties. Leading the way, he left the Abbot's abode, his companions following; nor did a murmur escape either, while giving this proof of patient submission. It was only when Ulrike and Lottchen had reached the open air, that they found the helpless girl they supported was without sensibility. As fits of fainting had been common of late, her mother felt no great alarm, nor was it long before all the female pilgrims sought the pillows they so much needed.

CHAPTER XXVII.

"Fy, uncle Beaufort! I have heard you preach,
That malice was a great and grievous sin:"—
King Henry VI.

THE social character of a Benedictine community has been mentioned in one of the earlier chapters. That of Einsiedlen, though charged with the worship of altars especially favored, formed no exception to the general rule. If any thing, the number of distinguished pilgrims that frequented its shrine, rendered it liable to more than usual demands on its hospitality; demands that were met by a suitable attention to the rules of the brotherhood. Even Loretto has its palace for the entertainment of such princes as can descend from their thrones to knee, in the 'santa casa;' for policy, not to speak of a more generous motive, requires that the path should be smoothed to those devotees who are unaccustomed to encounter difficulties. In conformity with the rule of their order, then, though dwelling in the secluded and wild region already described, the fraternity of our Lady of the Hermits, had their Abbot's abode, their lodgings for the stranger, and their stores of cheer, as well as their cells and their religious rites.

It was about three hours after the interview related in the last chapter—a time that brings us near he turn of the night—that we shall return to the arrative. The scene is a banqueting-hall, or, to speak in more measured phrase, a private refectory, in which the princely Abbot was wont to entertain those in whose behalf he saw sufficient reasons to exercise more than ordinary attention and favor. There was no great show of luxury in the ordinary decorations of the place, for a useless display of its means formed no part of the system of a community that chiefly existed by the liberality of the pious Still the hall was as well arranged as comported with the rude habits of the age, in that secluded region—habits that consulted the substantial portion of human enjoyments far more than those elaborate and effeminate inventions, which use has since rendered nearly indispensable to later generations. The floor was of tile, not very nicely polished; the wall were wainscoted in dark oak; and the ceiling had a rude attempt to represent the supper given at the marriage of Cana, and the miracle of the wine. Notwithstanding it was midsummer, a cheerful fire blazed in a chimney of huge dimensions; the size of the apartment and the keen air of the mountains rendering such an auxiliary not only agreeable, but necessary. The board was spacious and well covered, offering a generous display of those healthful and warm liquors, which have so long given the Rhine additional estimation with every traveller of taste.

Around the table were placed the Abbot, and his unhoused peer, Bonifacius; a favorite or two of the community of Einsiedlen; with Emich, the Knight of Rhodes, the Abbé, Heinrich Frey, and the smith. The former were in their usual conventual robes; while the latter were confounded, so far as externals were concerned, in their dresses of pilgrims. Dietrich owed his present advantage altogether to the fortuitous circumstance of being found in so good company, divested of the usual distinguishing marks of his rank. If Bonifacius was at all aware of his character, indifference or policy prevented its exposure.

Had one been suddenly introduced to this midnight scene, he would scarce have recognized the weary penitent and the reproving churchman, in the jovial cheer and boon companionship of the hour The appetite was already more than satisfied, and many a glass had been quaffed in honor of both hosts and guests, ere the precise moment to which we transfer the action of the tale.

The princely prelate occupied the seat of honor, as became his high rank, while Bonifacius was seated at one elbow, and the Count of Hartenburg at the other. The great consideration due to the first, as well as his personal character and mild manners, had served to preserve all outward appearances of amity and courteous intercourse between his neighbors, neither of whom had as yet suffered the slightest intimation of their former knowledge of each other to escape him. This polite duplicity, which we have reason to think is of very ancient origin, and in which Albrecht of Viederbach and Monsieur Latouche assisted with rare felicity, aided in curbing the feelings of their inferiors, who, being less trained in the seemliness of deception, might otherwise have given vent to some of their bodily pains, by allusions of an irritating and questionable nature.

"Thou findest our liquors palatable?" courteously observed the Abbot, as we shall, *par excellence*, now distinguish him of Einsiedlen. "This of the silver cup, cometh from the liberality of thy late Elector, who had occasion to send votive offerings, in behalf of the illness of one of his family, to our Lady of the Hermits, and who had the grace to accompany the memorial to the convent treasury by this sign of private regard; and that thou seemest most to relish, is a neighborly boon from our brother of Saint Gall, than whom more generous churchman does not wear a cowl. Thou knowest, son, that the matter of good wine hath long been the subject of especial care with that thriving brotherhood."

"Thou overratest my knowledge of history, princey Abbot," returned Emich, setting down the glass.

however, in a manner to show that his familiarity with good liquors might safely be assumed. "We of the lower countries waste but little time on these studies, trusting chiefly to those who dwell at the universities for the truth of what we hear. If he of Saint Gall dispenseth much of this goodly liquor, certes it were well that our spiritual guardians sent us, on occasions, to make our pilgrimages in that region, which cannot be far from this, unless my geography is greatly in fault."

"Thou couldest not have better divined, hadst thou been a doctor of Wittenberg, or of Rome itself! Considering our mountain paths, and the insufficiency of the bridges and other conveniences, it may require two suns to urge a beast from our convent gate to that of our brother of Saint Gall, though, on emergencies, we have succeeded, by means of faithful footmen, in getting tidings to their ears within the day and night. Saint Gall is a wealthy and well-bestowed Abbey, of very ancient existence, and of much repute as the haven of letters, during the darkest period, learned Bonifacius, of our more modern times; though the late increase of its town, and the growing turbulence of the times, have not permitted it to escape, with impunity, from the dangers that now beset all of Rome."

This was the first allusion which had been made to the events that had so singularly brought the present company together; and, but for the address and self-command of Bonifacius, it might have brought on a discussion that would not have proved agreeable.

"Saint Gall and its merits are unknown to none who wear the frock of Saint Benedict," he said, with admirable composure. "Thou hast well said that its walls were, for many ages, the sole protectors of learning in our Europe; for without the diligence and fidelity of its Abbots and brotherhood, much that is now preserved and prized would have been irretrievably lost to posterity and to ourselves."

"I doubt not, reverend Benedictine," observed Emich, speaking courteously across the Abbot to Bonifacius, much as a well-bred guest at board addresses a convive to whom he is otherwise a stranger, "that this rare taste in liquors, of which there has just been question, is the fruit of the excellent knowledge which you extol?"

"That is a point I shall not hastily decide," returned Bonifacius, smiling. "It may be so, for we have accounts of sore discord, between Saint Gall and others even of the Church, touching the uses and qualities of their wines."

"That have we, and right faithfully recorded!" rejoined the Abbot. "There was the war between the Prince Bishop of Basle and our brethren of Saint Gall, that led to sore contentions and heavy losses."

"How! did the desire to partake, urge our Rhenish prelate to push adventure so far, as to come this distance in quest of liquor?"

"Thou art in error, son pilgrim, concerning the nature of Saint Gall's stores. We have vineyards, it is true, among these mountains, as witness those on the shores of the neighboring lake of Zurich, as well as others that might be named; but our country wines will warm the blood of peasant only. He that hath tasted better, seldom fills his cup with liquor that comes from any region this side the farther border of Swabia—your vines of the Rheingau in specialty; whereas the territories of Saint Gall lie still farther from those favored countries than we ourselves."

"You have need to explain, princely Abbot; for that the Baslois should come in our direction, in quest of good liquor, is clear enough, whereas the war you have named, would have sent him farther from his object."

"Thou hast not come hither, son, without marking the course of the Rhine, on whose banks thou hast so long journeyed. This great stream, though so turbulent and dangerous among the mountains, is of much use in procuring our supplies. By means of the lake of Constance, and the lower river, heavy burthens arrive at the very territory of our sister Abbey; and the dispute to which there has been allusion, came of the fact that the right reverend prelate of Basle would fain have demanded toll on the purchases of the Abbey. Thou mayest remember, brother," looking towards Bonifacius, "that when both were tired of blows, the good Bishop sent to demand 'What the Virgin had done, that the churchmen above should slay her people?' and that he received for a merry answer the question of, 'What has Saint Gall done, that thou shouldest stop his wines?'"

The listeners laughed, in low simpers, like men amused with this characteristic narrative; for such incidents were yet too recent to excite much other reflection, even among churchmen, than what was connected with the vulgar temporal interests of the incident.

"By the Magi! holy and princely Abbot, thy tale giveth additional flavor!" said Emich, who greatly enjoyed the quarrel; "it moreover serveth to shut out thoughts that come from aching bones and weary feet."

"Thy pilgrimage, son, will bring its rewards, as well as its pains. Should it be a means of removing thee, for a time, from the heresies of Germany, and of placing thee and thine in more friendly communion with the Church, the toil will not be lost."

"As such do I esteem the duty," returned Emich, tossing off his glass, after steadily regarding the liquor a moment by the fire-light. "Saint Gall had the right of the matter; and he who would not take up arms for this, did not deserve to wear them. How now, Herr Frey! Thou art silent?"

"Not more so, I trust, nobly-born Emich, than becometh one on a pilgrimage; and one who hath need to bethink him of his duties, lest his town should have cause to reproach him with negligence."

"God's truth, Master Burgomaster! If any here have reason to bethink them of Deurckheim, it is the city's sovereign and lord. So cheer up, and let us lighten the load we carry, always under the favor and good graces of this hospitable and well-endowed brotherhood."

"Thou art a servitor of the cross?" demanded the Abbot of Albrecht of Viederback, beckoning the Knight to come nearer.

"An indifferent one, princely and pious Rudiger, and, I might say, one that hath yielded to the seductions of company and good fellowship, not to speak of the force of blood; else would he have been spared this expiation."

"Nay, I name not thy pursuit with the intent to reproach;" interrupted the courteous prelate. "Such liberty does not become hospitality. We make a difference within these walls between the confessional and the board."

"The distinction is just, and promises perpetuity and lasting respect to our faith, spite of all heresies. The rock on which this Brother Luther and his followers will split, holy Abbot—at least, it so seemeth to an uninstructed capacity—is the desire to refine beyond men's means of endurance. Religion, like chivalry, is good in its way; but neither the priest nor the knight can bear his armor at all times and seasons. Your schismatic hath the desire to convert the layman into a monk, whereas the beauty of creation is its order; and he that is charged with the cure of souls, is sufficient for his object, without laying this constant burthen on the shoulders of him that hath already more of temporal cares than he can bear."

"Were others more of thy mind, son, we should have less trouble, and better discipline. Our altars are not useless, and if they who frequent them, could be content to think that we are sufficient for their safety, the world would be saved much disputation, and haply some shedding of blood. But with these safe and creditable opinions, Sir Knight and Pilgrim," continued the Abbot, dropping his voice to a more confidential key, "it may be permitted me to express surprise, that I see thee one of a penitence commanded for violence done a convent!"

Albrecht of Viederbach shrugged his shoulders, and glanced meaningly towards his cousin.

"What will you, right noble and reverend Prelate!—We are but the creatures of accident. There is respect due to fellowship and hospitality, to say naught of the claims of blood and kindred. The evil turn of the Rhodian warfare, some longings to look again at our German fields, for the father-land keeps its hold of us more particularly in adversity, with the habits of an unsettled existence, served to lead me to the castle of Hartenburg; and fairly entered, it will excite no wonder that the guest was ready to lend his sword, in a short foray, to the host. These sallies, as thou well knowest, princely Rudiger, are not so rare as to be deemed miracles."

"What thou sayest is true," returned the Abbot, always speaking as it were aside to the Knight, and manifesting no great surprise at this avowal of principles, that were common enough in that age, and which have descended in a different form to our own, since we daily see men, in the gravest affairs of a nation, putting their morality at the disposal of party, rather than incur the odium of being wanting in this species of social faith. "What thou sayest is very true, and may well furnish thy plea with the

Grand Master. Thou mayest on many accounts too, find this pilgrimage wholesome."

"Doubt it not, reverend Abbot. We had little time during the siege, to pay due attention to the rites; and the general looseness of our lives, since driven from the island, has left long arrears to settle; a fact that I endeavor to remember now."

"And thy associate—he of gentle mien; hath he not also connexion with the Church?"

Albrecht turned to whisper the reply.

"'Tis but one that circulates under the frock, holy Benedictine—a youth that hath been the dupe of Lord Emich; for to speak thee fair, my cousin wanteth not of the policy necessary to his condition and to the habits of a sage government."

The Abbot smiled in a way to show a good intelligence between him and his companion. After this, they talked apart earnestly for a while, beckoning Monsieur Latouche to make one of their party, after sundry glances in his direction. In the mean time, the general discourse proceeded among the other guests.

"I was sorrowed to hear, reverend Benedictine," proceeded the Count, purposely avoiding the eye of Bonifacius, by addressing himself to one of the brotherhood of Einsiedlen, "that thy community hath refused us masses, for the soul of one that fell in that unhappy dispute which is the cause of our present pleasure, in being in so goodly company. I loved the youth, and would fain deal liberally by those that remember his present necessities."

"Hath the matter been fairly put to those having the right to decide?" demanded the monk, showing by the direction of his eye, that he meant his superior.

"They tell me it hath, and put touchingly; but without success. I trust there has been no hostile interference, in this affair, which concerneth no less than a soul, and ought to be dealt by tenderly."

"I know of but one, and that is the Father of Evil himself, that hath an enmity to souls!" answered the monk, with very honest surprise—"As for us, it is our pleasure to be of use on all such occasions; and that especially when the request is preferred by friends of the deceased, that are worthy of so much higher favor."

"Dost thou call those who overturn altars," sai Bonifacius, sternly, and with great firmness of voice,—"who visit the temple with the armed hand, and who defy the Church, worthy of her favors!"

"Reverend Abbot!"—

"Nay, let him give his humor vent," said Emich, proudly—"The cold air and a roofless head are apt to move the temper. I would fain have met thee, Bonifacius, in amity, as should have been the case, after our solemn treaty, and all the reparations that are made; but the desire to rule, it would seem, does not abandon thee, even in banishment!"

"Thou art deceived in imagining that I shall forget myself, or my office, rude Emich;—the question put was to the Benedictine, and not to thee."

"Then let the Benedictine answer. I ask thee, Father, is it becoming or just, that the soul of a youth of good repute, of moral life, and of reasonable earthly hopes, should be refused aid, on the mere grudge of ancient hostility, or haply that there were some passages at his death, that might have been better avoided?"

"The Church must judge for itself, noble Pilgrim and decide on those rules which regulate its course!"

"By the sainted eleven thousand!—Thou forgettest, that all usages have been respected, and that the masses are not asked as the beggar imploreth alms, but that fairly counted gold is proffered in behalf of the youth. If enough has not been done in this way, I swear to thee, Bonifacius, since it would seem thy influence here is so strong, that on my re turn there shall be further offerings on his account. Berchthold was very dear to me, and I would not have it said that all memory of the boy is lost beneath the ashes of Limburg."

Though both in their several ways were irascible, violent, and unaccustomed to control, neither Emich nor Bonifacius was wanting in that species of self-command, which is so necessary to men intrusted with the care of important interests. They had early learned to bring feeling more or less in subjection to their policy; and though not quite equal to a cold and managed display of indifference on such subjects as too closely crossed their views, it required a certain combination of excitement to induce either, unnecessarily, to betray his true emotions. Their personal intercourse had, in consequence of this affected moderation, been less violent and wrangling, than would otherwise have proved, for it did not often happen that both found themselves wrought up to the point of explosion, precisely at the same instant; and he that happened to remain the coolest, stood as a check on the passions of him who had momentarily forgotten appearances. But for this fact, the ill-timed and ill-worded question of the Count might have produced an immediate rupture, to the injury of the pilgrims' interests, and to the great scandal of the brotherhood of Einsiedlen: as it was, however, Bonifacius listened with outward courtesy, and answered more like one that remembered his priestly office than his particular injuries.

"Had it been my good fortune, Herr Pilgrim," he said calmly, "to have remained in charge of altars so esteemed, as to be sought on such a behalf, thy application in favor of the youth would have received meet attention; but thou now addresseth a prelate, that, like thee, is indebted to the hospitality of these excellent brothers, for a roof to cover his head."

"Nay, I know not," added the Count a little confused by this sudden humility, "but rather than desert so young a soul in this strait, and soul of a servitor whom I so much loved, that I would not even now endow some chapel—of a size and decorations suited to his station while living."

"On Limburg hill, Herr Emich?"

"Nay, excellent Bonifacius, thou forgettest our loving treaty, this pilgrimage, and other conditions honorably fulfilled. Altars can never rise again on Limburg hill, for that were to lose sight of our oaths and promises, which would be a crying sin in both; but altars and chapels may exist elsewhere. Give us then this grace, and look to our gratitude and justice for the reward."

Bonifacius smiled, for he felt his power, and he enjoyed it like a man conscious of having so lately been in the hands of the very baron, who now so earnestly beseeched his favor. It may not be easy for one educated in these later days, to understand the singular contradiction, which led Emich of Hartenburg, the destroyer of Limburg, thus to entreat a monk; but he who would properly understand his character, must remember the durability of impressions made in youth, the dread mystery that is attached to the unknown future, and, most of all, the flagrant inconsistencies, that are always the fruits of a struggle between principles and interests,—between the force of reason and the desires of selfishness.

"Thou accusest me unwarrantably, when thou sayest that our oaths, or our loving treaty is forgotten, pious Pilgrim," returned the Benedictine; "both are respected and well remembered, as thou wilt see, in the end. But there is a feature in this request of thine, that hath apparently escaped unwittingly one of thy known justice and impartiality. Thy forester is well known for having greatly affected the heresy that is ripe in Germany—"

"Nay, Bonifacius, here must be an error,"—interrupted the Count; "thou hast his very mother in our pilgrimage; and dost think a proselyte of Luther would undertake so grievous pain to satisfy Rome?"

"We speak of the child; and not of the parent, Herr Pilgrim. Had all that were trained in better principles observed the opinions of their fathers, our age would have been spared this heresy. Of the boy's irreverence there can be little doubt, since mine own ears have been my witnesses."

"How, hast thou ever shrived the youth, reverend Abbot?" demanded Emich in surprise. "I did not think thee of so great condescension to one of his hopes, nor—by the mass! did I think the youth so weak, as to touch on disputed points at the confessional!"

"There are other acknowledgments made, Herr Pilgrim, than those which are heard in the Church, or under the cloak of her mysteries. There was formerly a question between us, noble Count, amicably settled, and in a merry manner that need not now be named."

"Touching certain vineyards!" rejoined Emich laughing, "The fact is not so distant as to be forgotten, though neither my cousin nor this good Abbé proved as stanch in that matter as had been expected!"

"Thy forester did better service. Thou mayst also remember there were certain discussions then had, and that the bold boy ventured on a comparison of the tree trimmed of its useless branches, and the tree suffered to stand in its deformity."

"Wilt thou abandon a soul to jeopardy for speech light as this, Herr Bonifacius? God's justice! This promiseth but little in mine own behalf, at some future day. Berchthold, heated and warm in the interest of his lord, threw out hints that might other wise have been spared; moreover, the greater the sinner, Father, the greater need of masses and prayers."

"This will not I gainsay—my objection goeth no

farther than to urge that those who are willing to live by the counsels of Luther, should be also willing to seek salvation by his means."

"Friends and pilgrims," said the Abbot of Einsiedlen approaching the table, from which he had retired a little, to converse more freely with the Abbot and the Knight of Rhodes—"the hour is at hand which has been set to celebrate an early mass in behalf of this pilgrimage. The bell is giving the first summons, and it is meet that we retire to prepare ourselves for the duty."

At this interruption Bonifacius, who saw a storm gathering, gladly arose, and instantly withdrew, the rest dropped off, according to their several conditions; Emich and his cousin retiring with the leisure of men more accustomed to make others wait, than of hastening their movements to the injury of their own convenience.

After perusing this scene, we admonish the reader to spare his remarks, until the subject has been well pondered in his mind. In portraying what past in the private refectory of the convent of our Lady of the Hermits, we wish to convey no censure on any particular persuasion, or sect, or order of Christians, but simply to exhibit the habits and opinions of the age in which the individuals of this legend existed. Let those who are disposed to be hypercritical, or censorious in their remarks, coolly look around them, and, first making the necessary allowances for the new aspects of society, put the question, whether contradictions as apparent, inconsistencies nearly as irreconcileable with truth, and selfishness almost as gross and as unjust, is not now manifest equally among the adherents of Rome, and the proselytes of Luther, as any that have been here represented. We may claim to have improved on the opinions and practices of our predecessors, but we are still far from being the consistent and equitable creatures that, it is to be hoped, we are yet destined to become.

CHAPTER XXVIII.

"Forbear to judge, for we are sinners all.'
King Henry VI.

Among the expiations prescribed to the pilgrims of Deurckheim and Hartenburg, there had been included an especial and early morning service, the one to which they were now summoned. Time had been allowed the weaker portion of the party to rest, while the stronger had been employed in the manner described in the preceding chapter. Certain self-inflicted stripes it was taken for granted had been duly bestowed, at different periods, during the long journey from the Palatinate.

It was an hour after the separation of the abbey guests that the procession of Benedictines swept out of the cloisters into the body of the church. Though far from being a community remarkable for the austerity of its practices, it was not unusual for monks of all orders, to quit their pallets on extraordinary occasions, and to break the stillness of night with the music and service of the altar. When the spirit comes thus fresh from repose, and in a disposition suited to the object, into the immediate presence of the Deity, incense and praise so free from the dross of humanity, must come nearer to that high purity which adorns the worship of angels than any other that can ascend from man, since it is at such a moment that all least feel the burthen of their corporeal adjunct.

Even in the daily parochial duty, the good Catholics still observe a uniformity and rigidity of practice that are unknown even in this land of Puritan origin. The church-bell is heard in every village, with the first dawn of light; at indicated hours, all within hearing of its sound are admonished to recall their thoughts from earth, by addressing a prayer to

God; and with the close of day, the flock is once again summoned to the fold, at the service of vespers. These are beautiful and touching memorials of our duties, and when practised in sincerity, cannot fail to keep the mind in better subjection to the great authority that directs all our destinies. In countries where the husbandmen dwell together in villages, the practice is easy, and we hold its loss to be one of the greatest disadvantages of our own diffuse distribution of rural population; a distribution which is also the reason why we must for ever be wanting in several other features of social intercourse, that give to life more or less of its poetical charm. Happily there are, on the other hand, accompanying advantages that perhaps more than serve as offsets to this, as to most other similar anomalies in our usages.

The arrangements of a Benedictine chapel, and the decorations of its altars, together with the manner in which the brotherhood occupy their stalls in the choir, have been too often mentioned in these pages, to require repetition. Long accustomed to these exercises, the monks were early in their places, though they for whom the mass was to be said were not all as punctual.

Ulrike and Lottchen, with the rest of the females, entered the church in a body, while the men, as is usual in matters that touch the finer feelings, were the last. Emich and the Burgomaster, however, finally made their appearance, followed by their companions, the whole betraying by their drowsy air, that they had been endeavoring to sleep off the late repast, and to recover from their fatigue.

During the mass, the companions of Lottchen and Ulrike exhibited exemplary devotion, and a close attention to the service; but the gaping of the Count and his circle, the wandering eyes, and finally the profound repose of several, sufficiently showed that the ethereal part of their natures was altogether unequal to the mastery of that which was material.

There was a procession from the choir to the shrine, and prayers were said, as on the previous day, with the eyes of all riveted on the unearthly countenance of Maria. As each was left to judge for himself of the manner in which he discharged his particular duties, there was a very sensible difference in the time occupied by the several devotees, in the performance of the common vows. The females appeared to be embodied with the stone, and there were entire minutes during which their motionless forms would have seemed to be as inanimate as the image on which they gazed, but for the heaving of a breast, or an occasional tremor,—outward and visible signs of the workings of the spirit within. Meta kneeled between her mother and Lottchen, her whole soul apparently engrossed in devotion. As she studied the bright eye that gleamed upon her from the depths of that mysteriour chapel, illuminated as it was by gorgeous and bright lamps, her fancy transformed the image into a being sainted and blessed by the choice of God; and her own gentle spirit clung to the delusion, as one replete with a hope to cheer her own desolation. She thought of the future, and of the grave; of the rewards of the just, and of Heaven; of that endless eternity and its fruition in which she confided,—and the ties of earth began sensibly to lessen. There was a holy desire to be at rest. But, notwithstanding the spiritual nature of her employment, the form of Berchthold, gay in the green garb of a forester, with laughing eye, light step, and cheerful voice, mingled in all the pictures of her imagination. Now he appeared a saint, robed and bearded, as she had been wont to see those holy men represented in works of art, and yet, by a contradiction wrought by her own heart, always bright and youthful and now she thought him gifted with wings, and united to the beings of that heavenly choir, which had so many representatives around her suspended between the roof and the pavement of the edifice Singular as it may seem to some of our readers, so busy and so alluring was the working of her imagination at this thrilling moment, that the mourning and affectionate girl had rarely spent an hour of more holy enjoyment, than this which she passed before the shrine of our Lady of the Hermits.

Very different were the sensations of Lottchen. Her griefs were those in which the fancy had no share. She wept for the child to which she had given birth; for the stay of her age, and for the pride of her life. No fancy could betray the imagination of a mother, nor could any workings of the mind convert the sad reality into aught but the bitter truth. Still Lottchen found consolation in her prayers. Religious faith was active, though imagination slumbered; for nothing can be more different than the delusions of the one, and the deep sustained convictions of the other; and she was able to find a solace for her sorrow, by looking with calm, Christian hope beyond the interests of life.

The sentiments and feelings of Ulrike differed from those of her friend, only in the degree, and in the peculiarity of those circumstances which directed her maternal solicitude to a still living object. But Ulrike, kind, true, and warm of heart, had tenderly regarded the lost Berchthold. Had there been no other motive than the fact of his being the offspring of Lottchen, she could not have been indifferent to him; but, accustomed, as she had been for years, to look forward to his union with Meta, she felt his loss little less than she would have mourned over that of a child of her own.

Not so with Heinrich. The bold and spirited

support he received from Berchthold during the assault, had sensibly won upon his esteem, for the affinities between the brave are amongst the strongest; but the Burgomaster had not passed a life in the indulgence of a passion so engrossing, and so incurable, as the love of gain, readily to cast aside all his intentions and objects, at the impulse of a purely generous feeling. He would freely have given of his beloved stores to the youth; but to bestow Meta was, in his eyes, to bestow all, and, under his habits, it seemed to be giving gold without an equivalent, to give his daughter's hand to a penniless husband. There are some who accumulate for the advantages that are incidental to wealth; others hoard under the goadings of an abstract and nearly inexplicable passion; while another set heap together their means, as boys roll up snow, with a delight in witnessing how large a mass may be collected by their agency. Heinrich was of the latter class, subject, however, to a relish for the general results of wealth, and like all men who deem money as an end and not as a means, he was in the practice of considering the last measure of his policy, which was intended to double the stock by the marriage of his daughter, as the happiest and the greatest stroke of a fortunate and prosperous life. And yet Heinrich Frey had his moments of strong natural feeling, and the manner in which Meta mourned for the death of Berchthold touched him, to a degree that might have disposed him to say he regretted the fate of his young lieutenant, as much on her account as on his own. It is more than probable, however, could Berchthold have been suddenly restored to life, that the Burgomaster would have returned to his former mode of thinking, and would have thought the resuscitation of the young forester sufficient, of itself, to assuage the grief of a whole family.

Heinrich and the Count were among the first to quit their suppliant attitudes before the shrine. They had each said the required number of prayers, and brushing their knees, the two pilgrims strolled away, deeper into the body of the Church, like men well satisfied with themselves. But, while so ready to give relief to his own bones, the Burgomaster kept a vigilant eye on Dietrich, who, being a hired penitent, was expected to give Deurckheim the full worth of its money, in the way of mortifications and *aves.*

Most of the lights in the choir had been extinguished, and the aisles of the edifice were dimly visible, by means of a few scattered candles, that burned almost without ceasing, before the altars of different subordinate chapels. As they walked down the great aisle, Emich slowly laid a hand on the shoulder of his companion, seeming to invite his close attention, by the grave and meaning manner of the action.

"I could wish that our poor Berchthold, after all, had the virtue of masses from these servitors of our Lady of the Hermits!" said the Count. "If there be especial savor in any of this description of prayers, methinks it must be among men who watch a shrine of which they tell all these miracles!"

"Your wish, nobly-born-brother-pilgrim-and-friend, is but the expression of mine own. To own the truth, I have thought of little else, while going through the *aves*, but to devise the means of persuading the holy Abbot, at a reasonable rate, to change his mind, and honestly to let the youth's soul benefit by his intercessions."

"Thou hast not well bethought thee altogether, friend Heinrich, of thine own errand here!"

"Sapperment! What would you, Herr Emich, from a man of my years and education? One gets to be so ready with the words by oft repeating, that going through the beads is much like tapping with a finger while the eye looks over an account. But to speak of the boy—were we to bid higher for these masses, it might raise the present price, and we be uselessly losers; for, as I understand the question, the amount given in no manner changes the true value of the intercession to the defunct."

"Heinrich," returned the Count, musingly, "they say that Brother Luther denounces these *post mortem* prayers, as vain and of none avail!"

"That would alter the case greatly, Lord Count-and-brother-pilgrim. One could wish to be sure in an affair of this delicacy, for if the monk of Wittenburg hath reason of his side, we lose our gold; and if he hath wrong, the soul of Berchthold may be none the better for our doubts!"

"We laymen are sorely pressed between the two opinions, worthy Burgomaster, and I could fain wish that these reformers would bring the question speedily to a conclusion. By the mass! there are moments when I am ready to throw away the rosary, and to take Duke Friedrich of Saxony's side of the question, as being the most reasonable and manly. But, then again, should he prove wrong, thou know'st, Heinrich, we lose the benefit of chapels built, of *aves* said, of gold often paid, and the high protection of Rome! Thou seest the strait of poor Berchthold, and this only for some little freedom of discourse!"

Heinrich sighed, for he felt the force of the di lemma, and he appeared to ponder well before he answered. Edging nearer to the Count, like a man who felt he was about to utter dangerous sentiments in a delicate situation, he whispered the reply.

"Here Emich," he said, "we are but dust, and that of no very excellent quality. The potter's ware hath its utility, if well baked and otherwise prepared; but of what use is man when the breath hath departed? They say the soul remains, and that it must be cared for, neither of which will I dispute; but is it reasonable to buy out a patent of salvation, for an intangible thing, with current coin? Look to that knave, the smith!—Your pardon, nobly-born Count—but here hath our town engaged the rogue to do penance in its behalf, and my eyes are no sooner off him, than his lips become as stationary as the wings of a mill in a calm. Duty to Deurckheim demands that I should give him a jog, after which, with your gracious leave, we will look further into the philosophy of that in which we were dealing.'

Se saying, the zealous Heinrich hurried down the aisle towards his religious mercenary, with a laudable and sensitive watchfulness over the interests of his constituents. He found the smith perfectly immovable, and it was only by repeated and vigorous shakes, that he succeeded in arousing his auxiliary from a profound slumber.

In the meanwhile, Emich walked on, still occupied by his reflections. On reaching the gate of the choir, he was about to retrace his steps, when he was privately beckoned, by one whose dusky form appeared at a side door of the church, to draw nearer. On approaching, Emich found that his old rival, Bonifacius, awaited his coming.

The salutations of these ancient enemies were courteous, but distant. After a short parley, however, they withdrew in company; and it was past the turn of the day, ere the Count of Hartenburg reappeared among the pilgrims. The details of what passed in this secret conference were never known to the public, though subsequent events gave reason to believe that they had reference to the final settlement of the long-contested existence of Limburg in the Jaergerthal. It was known generally in the Abbey, that the Abbot Rudiger made one of the council, and that its termination was friendly. Those who were disposed to be critical, intimated in after days, that, in this dispute, as in most others in which the weak and humble lend themselves to the views of the great and the strong, they for whom the battle had been fought, and whose apparently implacable enmities had sown discord among their followers, suddenly found means to appease their resentments, and to still the tempest they had raised, in such a manner as to suffer most of its consequences to fall on the heads of their allies. This result, which appears to be universal with those who have the imprudence to connect themselves indissolubly with friends who can irretrievably dispose of their destinies, was perhaps to be looked for, since the man, or the community, that is so weak as to confide too implicitly in the faith of the powerful, whether considered individually or as nations, may at once consider itself a tool to favor views that have little connexion with its own interests. In cases of this nature, men are wont to share the fate of the orange-skin, which is thrown away after being sucked; and communities themselves are apt to undergo some such changes as those which mark the existence of the courser, which is first pampered and caressed, then driven upon the pole, and which commonly ends its career at the plow.

During the time Bonifacius and Emich were arranging their secret treaty, in the best manner that the former could hope for, in the actual state of Germany, and to the entire satisfaction of the latter, the ceremonies of the expiation proceeded. Aroused from his sleep, Dietrich endeavored to compensate for lost time by renewed diligence, and the Burgomaster himself, apprehensive that the negligence of the hireling might bring a calamity on the town, joined himself to the party, with as much zeal as if he had as yet done nothing towards effecting the object of their journey.

The sun had fallen far towards the west, when the pilgrims finally took their departure for the Palatinate. Father Arnolph was again at their head, and, blessed by the Abbot and in favor with the Church, the whole went their way, if not with lightened hearts, at least with bodies much refreshed, with hopes rekindled, and with packs materially diminished in size.

Ulrike and Lottchen paused when they reached the boundary of the plain, where they could command a parting view of the Abbey. Here they, and Meta, and indeed most of the party, prayed long and fervently; or at least so seemed to pray. When they arose from their knees, the Prior, whose whole time while at the convent had been deeply occupied by religious exercises, and whose spirit had been refreshed, in a degree proportioned to his sincerity and faith, came to the side of the principal group of the females, his eye beaming with holy hope, and his face displaying innate peace of mind.

"Ye are now, daughters, about to take leave, for ever, of the shrine of our Lady of the Hermits," he said. "If ye have seen aught to lessen the high expectation with which the pious are apt to draw near this sacred altar, ascribe it to that frailty which is inherent in the nature of man; and if ye have reaped consolation and encouragement, from your offerings and prayers, ye may, with all security, impute it to the goodness of God. And thou, my child," he added with paternal tenderness, addressing Meta—"thou hast been sorely tried in thy young life,—but God is with thee, as he is in yon blue sky—in that sun of molten gold—in yonder icy pile that props the heavens, and in all his works, that are so glorious in our eyes! Turn with me to yonder mountain, that from its form is called the Mitre. Regard it well—Dost see aught in particular?"

"'Tis an abrupt and dreary pile of rock, Father;" answered Meta.

"Seest thou naught else—on its highest summit?"

Meta looked intently, for in sooth there did appea

the uppermost pinnacle of the mass, an object so small, and so like a line, that, at first, she passed a hand across her eye to remove a floating hair from before her sight.

"Father!" exclaimed the girl, clasping her hands fervently, "I behold a cross!"

"That rock is the type of God's durable justice;—That cross is the pledge of his grace and love. Go thy way, daughter, and have hope."

The pilgrims turned and descended the mountain in musing silence. That evening they crossed the lake, and slept within the ancient walls of the romantic town of Rapperschwyl. On the following day, the pilgrimage being now happily accomplished, they proceeded toward their own distant habitations, descending the Rhine in boats.

CHAPTER XXIX.

> "But thou art clay—and canst but comprehend
> That which was clay, and such thou shalt behold."
>
> *Cain.*

The return of the pilgrims was a happy moment to all who dwelt in Deurckheim. Many prayers had been offered in their behalf, during the long absence, and divers vague reports of their progress and success, had been eagerly swallowed by their friends and townsmen. When, however, the Burgomaster and his companions were actually seen entering their gates, the good citizens ran to and fro, in troubled delight, and the greetings, especially among the gentler sex, were mingled with many tears. Emich and his followers did not appear, having taken a private path to the castle of Hartenburg.

The simple and still Catholic (though wavering) burghers had felt many doubts, concerning the fruits of their bold policy, while the expiatory penance was pending. Their town was in the midst of a region that is perhaps more pregnant with wild legends, even at this hour, than any other of equal extent in Europe; and it can be easily conceived that, under such circumstances, the imaginations of a people who had been, as it were, nurtured in superstition, would not be likely to slumber. In effect, numberless startling rumors were rife, in the town, the valley, and on the plain. Some spoke of fiery crosses gleaming at night above the walls of the fallen Abbey; others whispered of midnight chants, and spectre-like processions, that had been heard or seen among the ruined towers; while one peasant, in particular, asseverated that he had held discourse with the spirit of Father Johan. These tales found credulous auditors or not, according to the capacity of the listener; and to these may be added another, that was accompanied by such circumstances of confirmation, as are apt momentarily to affect the minds of those, even, who are little wont to lend attention to any incidents of miraculous nature.

A peasant, in crossing the chase by a retired path, was said to have encountered Berchthold, clad in his dress of green, wearing the hunting-horn and cap, and girded with the usual *couteau-de-chasse*, or, in fine, much as he was first presented to the reader in our early pages. The youth was described to have been hot on the chase of a roebuck, and flushed with exercise. From time to time, he was said to wind his horn. The hounds were near, obedient as usual to his call, and indeed the vision was described as partaking of most of the usual accompaniments of the daily exercise of the forester.

Had the tale ended here, it might have passed off among the thousand other similar wonderful sights, that were then related in that wonder-loving country, and been forgotten. But it was accompanied with positive circumstances, that addressed them selves, in a manner not to be disputed, to the senses. The two favorite hounds of the forester had been missing for some weeks, and, from time to time, cries resembling theirs were unequivocally heard, ringing among the arches of the forest, and filling the echoes of the mountains.

This extraordinary confirmation of the tale of the boor, occurred the week preceding the return of the pilgrims. The latter found their townsmen under a strong excitement from this cause, for that very day, nearly half the population of Deurckheim had been into the pass of the Haart which was described in the opening chapter of this work, and with their own ears had heard the deep baying of the hounds. It was only after the first felicitations of the return were over, and during the night which followed, that the pilgrims learned this unusual circumstance. It reached Emich himself, however, ere his foot crossed the threshold of his castle.

On the following day, Deurckheim presented a picture of pleased but troubled excitement. Its population was happy in the return of their chosen and best, but troubled with the marvellous incident of the dogs, and by the wild rumors that accompanied it; rumors which thickened every hour by corroborating details from different sources. Early that very morning a new occurrence helped to increase the excitement.

From the moment that the Abbey was destroyed, not an individual had dared to enter its tottering walls. Two peasants of the Jaegerthal, incited by cupidity, had indeed secretly made the attempt, but they returned with the report of strange sights, and of fearful groans existing within the consecrated pile The rumor of this failure, together with a lingering respect for altars that had been so long reverenced, effectually secured the spot against all similar expeditions. The alarm spread to the Heidenmauer, for, by a confusion of incidents, that is far from unusual in popular rumors, an account of Ilse, concerning the passage of the armed band through the cedars, on the night of the assault, coupled with the general distrust that was attached to the place, had been so perverted and embellished, as effectually to leave the ancient camp to its solitude. Some said that even the spirits of the Pagans had been aroused by the sacrilege, from the sleep of centuries, and others argued that, as the hermit was known to have perished in the conflagration, it was a spot accursed. The secret of the true name, and of the history of the Anchorite, was now generally known, and men so blended the late events with former offences, as to create a theory to satisfy their own longings for the marvellous; though, as is usual in most of these cases of supernatural agency, it might not have stood the test of a severe logical and philosophical investigation.

During the night which succeeded the return of the pilgrims, there had been a grave consultation among the civic authorities, on the subject of all these extraordinary tales and spectacles. The alarm had reached an inconvenient point, and the best manner of quieting it was now gravely debated. There was not a burgher present at the discussion, who felt himself free from the general uneasiness: but men, and especially men in authority, ordinarily choose to affect a confidence they are frequently far from feeling. In this spirit, then, was the matter discussed and decided. We shall refer to the succeeding events for the explanation.

Just as the sun began to shed his warmth into the valley, the people of Deurckheim, with few exceptions, collected without that gate which the Count of Hartenburg had so unceremoniously forced. Here they were marshalled by citizens appointed to that duty, in the usual order of a religious procession. In front went the pilgrims, to whom an especial virtue was attached, in consequence of their recent journey; then came the parochial clergy, with the ordinary emblems of Catholic worship; the burghers succeeded, and last of all followed the women and children, without much attention to order. When all were duly arranged, the crowd proceeded, accompanied by a chant of the choristers, and taking the direction of Limburg.

"This is a short pilgrimage, brother Dietrich," said the Burgomaster, who in his quality of a Christian of peculiar savor was still associated with the smith, "and little likely to weary the limbs; still had the town been as active and true, as we who have visited the mountains, this little affair of a few barking hounds, and some midnight moans in the Abbey ruins, would have been ready settled to our hands. But a town without its head, is like a man without his reason."

"You count on an easy deliverance then, honorable Heinrich, from this outcry of devils and unbidden guests! For mine own particular exercises, I will declare that, though sufficiently foot-sore with what hath already been done, I could wish the journey were longer, and the enemy more human."

"Go to, smith; thou art not to believe above half of what thou hast heard. The readiness to give faith to idle rumors forms a chief distinction between the vagrant and the householder—the man of weakness, and the man of wisdom. Were it decent, between a magistrate and an artisan, I would hold thee some hazard of coin, now, that this affair turns out very different from what thou expectest; and I do not account thee, Dietrich, an every-day swallower of lies."

"If your worship would but hint what a fair dealing man ought in truth to believe—?"

"Why look you, smith, here is all that I expect from the inquiry, though we hunt and exercise for a month. It will be found that there is no pack of hounds at all, loose or in leash, but at most a dog or two, that may be beset or not, as the case shall prove, next, thou wilt see that this tale of Father Johan chasing young Berchthold, while the boy hunts a roe-buck, is altogether an invention, since the monk was the last man to give loose to such a scampering, noisy device; as for the Forester, my life on it, his appearance too will end in footmarks, or perhaps some other modest sign that he desires the masses refused by the Benedictines; for I know not the youth that would be less likely needlessly to disturb a neighborhood, with his own particular concerns, than Berchthold Hintermayer, living or dead."

A general start, and a common murmur among his companions, caused Heinrich to terminate his explanations. The head of the procession had reached the gorge, and, as it was about to turn into the valley, the trampling of many hoofs became audible. Feelings so highly wrought were easily excited to a painful degree, and the common expectation, for the moment, seemed to be some supernatural exhibition. A whirlwind of dust swept round the point of the hill, and Count Emich, with a train of well-mounted followers, appeared from its cloud. It was so common to meet religious processions of this nature, that the Count would not have manifested surprise, had he been ignorant of the motive which induced the population of Deurckheim to quit its walls; but, already apprized of their intentions, he hastily dismounted and approached the Burgomaster, cap in hand.

"Thou goest to exercise, worshipful Emich," he said

"and love for my town hath quickened our steps, that no honor or attention should be wanting to those I love.—hast a place among thy pilgrims, for a poor baron and his friends?"

The offer was gladly accepted, courage being quickened by every appearance of succor. Emich, though equipped as a cavalier, was therefore willingly received among his fellow-travellers. The delay caused by this interruption ended, the procession, or rather the throng, for eagerness and anxiety and curiosity had nearly broken all order, proceeded towards the ascent of the mountain.

The ruins of Limburg, then recent and still blackened with smoke, were found in the deep silence of utter desertion. To judge from appearances, not a footstep had trodden them, since the moment when the band of the assailants had last poured through the gates, after a tumultuous triumph which had been so chilled by the awful catastrophe of the falling roofs. If that party had drawn near the Abbey in expectation of a sudden and furious assault, this slowly advanced with a troubled apprehension of witnessing some fearful manifestation of superhuman power. Both were disappointed. The unresisted success of the assailants is known, and the procession now proceeded with the same impunity; though many a voice faltered in the chant as they entered the spoiled and desolate church. Nothing however occurred to justify their alarm.

Encouraged by this pacific tranquillity, and desirous of giving proofs of their personal superiority to vulgar terrors, the Count and Heinrich commanded the throng to remain in the great aisle of the church, while they proceeded together into the choir. They found the usual evidences of a fierce conflagration at every step, but nothing to create surprise, until hey arrived at the mouldering altar.

'Himmel!" exclaimed the Burgomaster, hastily

pulling back his noble friend by the cloak,—"Your foot was about to do disreverence to the bones of a Christian, my Lord Count!—For Christian Father Johan was, beyond all question, though one more given to damnation than to charity."

Emich recoiled, for he saw in truth, that with heedless step, he had been near crushing these revolting remnants of mortality.

"Here died a wild enthusiast!" he said, moving the skeleton with the point of his sheathed sword.

"And here he is still, nobly-born Graf!—This settles the question of the monk chasing young Berchthold through the forest, and among the cedars of the Heidenmauer, and it would be well to show these remains to the people."

The hint was improved, and the throng was summoned to bear witness, that the bones of Johan still lay on the precise spot, in which he had died. While the curious and the timid were whispering their opinions of this discovery, the two leaders descended to the crypt.

This portion of the edifice had suffered least by the fire. Protected by the superior pavement, and constructed altogether of stone, it had received no very material injury, but that which had been inflicted by the sledges of the invaders. Fragments of the tombs lay scattered on every side, and here and there a wreath of smoke had left its mark upon a wall; but Emich saw with regret, that he owed the demolition of the altar, and of the other memorials of his race, entirely to his own precipitation.

"I will cause the bones of my fathers to be interred elsewhere," he said, musingly;—"this is no sepulchre for an honored stock!"

"Umph!—They have long and creditably decayed where they lie, Herr Emich, and it would have been well had they been left beneath the cover of their ancient marbles: but our artisans showed unusual agility in this part of their toil, in honor, no doubt, of an illustrious house."

"None of my race shall sleep within walls accursed by Benedictines! Hark!—what movement is that above, good Heinrich?"

"The townsmen have doubtless fallen upon the bones of the hermit, and of young Berchthold. Shall we go up, Lord Count, and see that fitting reverence be paid their remains? The Forester has claims upon us all, and as for Odo Von Ritterstein, his crime would be deemed all the lighter in these days, moreover he was betrothed to Ulrike in their youth."

"Heinrich, thy wife was very fair;—she had many suitors!"

"I cry your mercy, noble Count; I never heard but of poor Odo, and myself. The former was put out of the question by his own madness, and as for the latter, he is such as Heaven was pleased to make him: an indifferent lover and husband if you will, but a man of some credit and substance among his equals."

The Count did not care to dispute the possession of these qualities with his friend, and they left the crypt, with a common desire to pay proper respect to the remains of poor Berchthold. To their mutual surprise the church was found deserted. By the clamor of voices without, however, it was easy to perceive that some extraordinary incident had drawn away the members of the procession, in a body. Curious to have so violent an interruption of the proceedings explained, the two chiefs, for Heinrich was still entitled to be so styled, hastened down the great aisle, picking their way among fallen fragments, towards the great door. Near the latter, they were again shocked by the spectacle of the charred skeleton of Johan, which seemingly had been dropped under the impulse of some sudden and great confusion.

"Himmel!" muttered the Burgomaster, while he

hurried after his leader, "they have deserted the bones of the Benedictine!—can it be, Lord Emich, that some fiery miracle, after all our unbelief, hath wrought this fear?"

Emich made no reply, but issued into the court with the air of an offended master. The first glimpse, however, that he caught of the group, which now thronged the ruined walls of the minor buildings, whence there was a view of the surrounding country, and particularly of parts of the adjacent hill of the Heidenmauer, convinced him that the present was no moment to exhibit displeasure. Climbing up a piece of fallen stone-work, he found himself on a fragment of wall, surrounded by fifty silent, wondering countenances, among whom he recognised several of his own most trusty followers.

"What meaneth this disrespect of the service, and so sudden an abandonment of the remains of the monk?" demanded the baron,—vainly looking about him, in the hope of finding some quicker explanation by means of his own eyes.

"Hath not my Lord the Count seen and heard?" muttered the nearest vassal.

"What—knave? I have seen nought, but pallid and frightened fools, nor heard more than beating hearts! Wilt thou explain this, varlet—for, though something of a rogue, thou, at least, art no coward?" Emich addressed himself to Gottlob.

"It may not be so easy of explanation as is thought, Lord Count," returned the cow-herd gravely: "the people have come hither with this speed, inasmuch as the cries of the supernatural dogs have been heard, and some say the person of poor Berchthold hath been again seen!"

The Count smiled contemptuously, though he knew the speaker sufficiently well to be surprised at the concern which was very unequivocally painted in his face.

"Thou wert attached to my Forester?"

"Lord Emich, we were friends, if one of so humble station may use the word, when speaking of a youth that served so near the person of our master. Like his, my own family once knew better days, and we often met in the chase, which I was wont to cross, coming or going to the pastures. I loved poor Berchthold, nobly-born Count, and still love his memory."

"I believe thou hast better stuff in thee, than some idle and silly deeds would give reason to believe. I have remembered thy good will on various occasions, and especially thy cleverness in making the signals, on the night these walls were overturned, and thou wilt find thyself named to the employment left vacant by my late Forester's unhappy end."

Gottlob endeavored to thank his master, but he was too much troubled by real grief for the loss of his friend, to find consolation in his own preferment.

"My services are my Lord Count's," he answered, "but, though ready to do as commanded, I could well wish that Berchthold were here to do that for me, which—"

"Listen!—Hark!"—cried a hundred voices.

Emich started, and bent forward in fixed attention. The day was clear and cloudless, and the air of the hills pure as a genial breeze and a bright sun could bestow. Favored by such circumstances, and amid a silence that was breathing and eloquent, there were borne across the valley the well known cries of hounds on the scent. In that region and age, none dared hunt, and indeed none possessed the means of hunting, but the feudal Lord. Since the late events, his chases had been unentered with this view, and the death of Berchthold, who had especial privileges in this respect, had left them without another who might dare to imitate his habits.

"This is at least bold!" said Emich, when the cries had passed away: "hath any other near dogs of that noble breed?"

"We never heard of other!"

"None would dare use them;" were the answers.

"I know those throats—they are, of a certainty, the favorite hounds of my poor Forester! Have not the dogs escaped the leash, to play their gambols at will among the deer?"

"In that case, Lord Count, would tried hounds remain abroad for weeks?" answered Gottlob. "It is now a sennight since these cries have been first heard, and yet no one has seen the dogs, from that hour to this, unless as some one of our hinds says they have in sooth been seen running madly on the scent."

"'Tis said, mein Herr Graf," put in another, "that Berchthold, himself, hath been viewed in their company, his garments floating in the wind, while he flew along, keeping even pace with the dogs, an' he had been swift of foot as they!"

"With Father Johan at his heels, cowl undone and robe streaming like a penon, by way of religious amusement!" added the Count, laughing. "Dost not see, dotard, that the crackling bones of thy monk are still in the ruin?"

The hind was daunted by his master's manner, but nothing convinced. There then succeeded a long and expecting silence, for this little by-play near the Count had not in the least affected the solemn attention of the mass. At length the throats of these mysterious dogs again opened, and the cries indeed appeared like those of hounds rushing from beneath the cover of woods into the open air. In a few moments they were repeated, and beyond all dispute, they were now upon the open heath that surrounded the Teufelstein. The crisis grew alarming for the local superstitions of such a place, in the commencement of the sixteenth century. Even Emich wavered. Though he had a vague perception of the inconsistency of living dogs being hunted by a dead Forester, still there were so many means of getting over this immaterial difficulty, when the greater point of the supernatural chase was admitted, that he found little relief in the objection. Descending from the wall, he was in the act of beckoning the priests and Heinrich to his side, when a general shout arose among the male spectators, while the women rushed in a body around Ulrike, who was kneeling, with Lottchen and Meta, before the great crucifix of the ancient court of the convent. In the twinkling of an eye, Emich re-occupied his place on the wall, which shook with the impetus of his heavy rush.

"What meaneth this disrespectful tumult?" angrily demanded the baron.

"The hounds!—mein Herr Graf!—the hounds!" answered fifty breathless peasants.

"Explain this outcry, Gottlob,"

"My Lord Count, we have seen the dogs leaping past yonder margin of the hill,—here,—just in a line with the spot where the Teufelstein lies. I know the dear animals well, Herr Emich, and believe me, they are truly the old favourites of Berchthold."

"And Berchthold!" continued one or twc of the more decided lovers of the marvellous,—"we saw the late Forester, great Emich, bounding after the dogs an' he had wings!"

The matter grew serious, and the Count slowly descended to the court, determined to bring the affair to some speedy explanation.

CHAPTER XXX.

"By the Apostle Paul, shadows to-night
Have struck more terror to the soul of Richard,
Than can the substance of ten thousand soldiers——"
Richard III.

The consultation that now took place was between the principal laymen. The connection which the Church had so long maintained with supernatural agencies, determined Emich, who was jealous of its again obtaining its lost ascendency in that country, to exclude the officiating priests altogether from the decision he was about to take. Were we to say that the Count of Hartenburg gave full faith to the rumors concerning the spirit of his late Forester, having been seen engaged in the chase, as when in the flesh, we should probably not do entire credit to his intelligence and habits of thinking, but were we to say, that he was altogether free from superstition and alarm on this difficult point, we should attribute to him a degree of philosophy and a mental independence, which in that age was the property only of the learned and reflecting, and not always even of them. Astrology, in particular, had taken strong hold of the imaginations of those who even pretended to general science; and when the mind once admits of theories of a character so little in accordance with homely reason, it opens the avenues to a multitude of collateral weaknesses of the same nature, which seem to follow as the necessary corollaries of the main proposition.

The necessity of a prompt solution of the question was admitted by all of those whom the Count consulted. Many had begun to whisper that the extraordinary visitation was a consequence of the sacrilege, and that it was hopeless to expect peace, or exemption from supernatural plagues, until the Benedictines were restored to their Abbey and their former rights Though Emich felt convinced that this idea came originally from the monks, through some of their secret and paid agents, he saw no manner of defeating it so effectually as that of demonstrating the falsity of the rumor. In our time, and in this land, a weapon that was forged by a miracle, would be apt to become useless of itself; but in the other hemisphere, there still exist entire countries, that are yet partially governed by agents of this description. At the period of the tale, the public mind was so uninstructed and dependent, that the very men who were most interested in defeating the popular delirium of the hour, had great difficulty in overcoming their own doubts. It has been seen that Emich, though much disposed to throw off the dominion of the Church, so far clung to his ancient prejudices, as secretly to distrust the very power he was about to defy, and to entertain grave scruples not only of the policy, but of the lawfulness of the step his ambition had urged him to adopt. In this manner does man become the instrument of the various passions and motives that beset him, now yielding, or now struggling to resist, as a stronger inducement is presented to his mind; always professing to be governed by reason and constrained by principles, while in truth he rarely consents to consult the one, or to respect the other, until both are offered through the direct medium of some engrossing interest, that requires an immediate and active attention. Then indeed his faculties become suddenly enlightened, and he eagerly presses into his service every argument that offers, the plausible as well as the sound; and thus it happens that we frequently see whole communities making a moral pirouette in a breath, adopting this year a set of principles that are quite in opposition to all they had ever before professed. Fortunately, all that is thus gained on sound principles is apt to continue, since whatever may be the waywardness of those who profess them, principles themselves are immutable, and when once fairly admitted, are not easily dispossessed by the bastard doctrines of expediency and error. These changes are gradual as respect those avant-couriers of thought, who prepare the way for the advance of nations, but who, in general so far precede their contemporaries, as to be utterly out of view at the effectual moment of the reformation, or revolution, or by whatever name these sudden summersets are styled; but as respects the mass, they often occur by a coup-de-main; an entire people awakening, as it were, by magic, to the virtues of a new set of maxims, much as the eye turns from the view of one scenic representation to that of its successor.

Our object in this tale is, to represent society, under its ordinary faces, in the act of passing from the influence of one set of governing principles to that of another. Had our efforts been confined to the workings of a single and a master mind, the picture, however true as regards the individual, would have been false in reference to a community; since such a study would have been no more than following out the deductions of philosophy and reason —something the worse, perhaps, for its connection with humanity; whereas, he that would represent the world, or any material portion of the world, must draw the passions and the more vulgar interests in the boldest colors, and be content with pourtraying the intellectual part, in a very subdued background. We know not that any will be disposed to make the reflection that our labors are intended to suggest, and without which they will scarcely be useful; but, while we admit the imperfection of what has been here done, we feel satisfied that he who does consider it coolly and in candor, will be disposed to allow, that our picture is sufficiently true for its object.

We have written in vain, should it now be necessary to dwell on the nature of the misgivings that harassed the minds of the Count and Heinrich, as they descended the hill of Limburg, at the head of the new procession. Policy, and the determination to secure advantages that had been so dearly obtained, urged them on; while doubt and all the progeny of ancient prejudices, contributed to their distrust.

The people advanced much in the same order as that in which they had ascended to the ruins of the Abbey. The pilgrims were in front, followed closely by the parochial priests, and their choirs; while the rest succeed in an eager, trembling, curious, and devout crowd. Religious change existed, as yet, rather in doctrine, and among the few, than in the practices of the many; and all the rites, it will be remembered, were those usually observed by the church of Rome on an occasion of exorcism, or of an especial supplication to be released from a mysterious display of Heaven's displeasure. The Count and Heinrich, as became their stations, walked boldly in advance; for, whatever might have been the extent and nature of their distrust, it was wisely and successfully concealed from all but themselves—even the worthy Burgomaster entertained a respectful opinion of the Noble's firmness, and the latter much wondering at a man of Heinrich's education and habits of life, being able to show a resolution that he thought more properly belonged to philosophy. They passed up towards the plain of the Heidenmauer, by the hollow way that has already been twice mentioned in these pages—once in the Introduction, and again, as the path by which Ulrike descended on her way to the Abbey, on the night of its destruction. Until near the summit, nothing occurred to create new uneasiness; and as the choristers increased the depth of their chant, the leaders began to feel a vague hope of escaping from farther interruption. As the moments passed, the Count breathed freer, and he already fancied that he had proved the Heidenmauer to be a spot as harmless as any other in the Palatinate.

"You have often pricked courser over this wild common of the Devil, noble and fearless Count," said Heinrich, when they drew near the margin of the superior plain—"One so accustomed to its view is not easily troubled by the cries and vagaries of a leash of uneasy dogs, though they might be kenneled beneath the shade of the Teufelstein!"

"Thou mayest well say often, good Heinrich When but an urchin, my excellent father was wont to train his chargers on this height, and it was often my pleasure to be of the party. Then our hunts frequently drove the deer from the cover of the chases to this open ground—"

The Count paused, for a swift, pattering rush, like that of the feet of hounds beating the ground, was audible, just above their heads, though the edge of the mountain still kept the face of the level ground from being seen. Spite of their resolution, the two leaders came to a dead halt—a delay which those in the rear were compelled to imitate.

"The common hath its tenants, Herr Frey," said Emich, gravely, but in a tone of a man resolute to struggle for his rights; "it will soon be seen if they are disposed to admit the sovereignty of their feudal lord."

Without waiting for an answer, the Count spite of himself muttered an *ave*, and mounted with sturdy limbs to the summit. The first glance was rapid, uneasy, and distrustful; but nothing rewarded the look. The naked rock of the Teufelstein lay in the ancient bed—where it had probably been left, by some revolution of the earth's crust. three thousand years before—gray, solitary, and weather-worn as at this hour; the grassy common had not a hoof or foot over the whole of its surface; and the cedars of the deserted camp sighed in the breeze, as usual, dark, melancholy, and suited to the traditions which had given them interest.

"Here is nothing!" said the Count, drawing a heavy breath, which he would fain ascribe to the difficulty of the ascent.

"Herr von Hartenburg, God is here, as he is among the hills we have lately quitted—on that fair and wide plain below—and in thy hold!—"

"Prithee, good Ulrike, we will of this another time. We touch now on the destruction of a silly legend, and of some recent alarms."

At a wave of his hand the procession proceeded taking the direction of the ancient gateway of the camp, the choir renewing its chant, and the same leaders always in advance.

It is not necessary to say that the Heidenmauer was approached, on this solemn occasion, with beating hearts. No man of reflection and proper feeling can ever visit a spot like this, without fancying a picture that is fraught with pleasing melancholy. The certainty that he has before his eyes the remains of a work, raised by the hands of beings who existed so many centuries before him in that great chain of events which unites the past with the present, and that his feet tread earth that has been trodden equally by the Roman and the Hun, is sufficient of itself to raise a train of thought allied to the wonderful and grand. But to these certain and natural sensations was now added a dread of omnipotence and the apprehension of instantly witnessing some supernatural effect.

Not a word was uttered, until Emich and the Burgomaster turned to pass the pile of stones which mark the position of the ancient wall, by means of the gateway already named, when the former, encouraged by the tranquillity, again spoke.

"The ear is often a treacherous companion, friend Burgomaster," he said, "and like the tongue, unless duly watched, may lead to misunderstandings. No doubt we both thought, at the moment, that we heard the feet of hounds beating the earth, as on a hunt; thou now seest, by means of one sense, that the other hath served us false. But we approach the end of our little pilgrimage, and we will halt, while I speak the people in explanation of our opinions and intentions."

Heinrich gave the signal, and the choir ceased its chant, while the crowd drew near to listen. The Count both saw and felt that he touched the real crisis, in the furtherance of his own views, as opposed to those of the brotherhood, and he determined, by a severe effort, not only to overcome his enemies, but himself. In this mood, he spoke.

"Ye are here, my honest friends and vassals," he commenced, "both as the faithful who respect the usefulness of the altar when rightly served, and as men who are disposed to see and judge for themselves. This camp, as ye witness by its remains, was once occupied by armed bands of warriors who, in their day, fought and fortified, suffered and were happy, bled and died, conquered or were vanquished, much as we see those who carry arms in our own time, perform these several acts, or submit to these several misfortunes. The report that their spirits frequent the spot, is as little likely to be true, as that the spirits of all who have fallen with arms in their hands remain near the earth that hath swallowed their blood; a belief that would leave no place in our fair Palatinate without its ghostly tenant. As for this late alarm, concerning my Forester, poor Berchthold Hintermayer, it is the less probable from the character of the youth, who well knew when living the disrelish I have felt for all such tales, and my particular desire to banish them altogether from the Jaegerthal.

as well as from his known modesty and dutiful obedience. You see plainly that here are no dogs—"

Emich met with a startling contradiction. Just as his tongue, which was getting fluent with the impunity that had so far attended his declarations uttered the latter word, the long drawn cries of hounds were heard. Fifty strong German exclamations escaped the crowd, which waved like a troubled sea. The sounds came from among the trees in the very centre of the dreaded Heidenmauer, and seemed only the more unearthly from rising beneath that gloomy canopy of cedars.

"Let us go on!" cried the Count, excited nearly to madness, and seizing the handle of his sword with iron grasp. "Tis but a hound! Some miscreant hath loosened the dog from his leash, and he scents the footsteps of his late master, who had the habit of visiting the holy hermit that dwelt here of late——"

"Hush!" interrupted Lottchen, advancing hurriedly, and with a wild eye, from the throng of females. "God is about to reveal his power, for some great end? I know—I know—that footstep—"

She was fearfully interrupted, for while speaking, the hounds rushed out of the grove, in the swift, mad manner common to the animal, and made a rapid circuit around the form of the dazzled, and giddy woman. In the next moment, a tottering wall gave way to the powerful leap of a human foot, and Lottchen lay senseless on the bosom of her son!

We draw a veil before the sudden fear, the general surprise, the tears, the delight, and the more regulated joy of the next hour.

At the end of that period, the scene had altogether changed. The chant was ended, the order of the procession was forgotten, and a burning curiosity had taken place of all sensations of superstitious dread. But the authority of Emich had driven the crowd back upon the common of the Teufelstein.

where it was compelled to content itself, for the moment, with conjectures, and with tales of similar sudden changes from the incarnate to the carnate, that were reputed to have taken place in the eventful history of the borders of the Rhine.

The principal group of actors had retired a little within the cover of the cedars, where, favoured by the walls and the trees, they remained unseen from without. Young Berchthold was seated on a fragment of fallen wall, supporting his still half incredulous mother in his arms, a position which he had received the Count's peremptory, but kind orders to occupy. Meta was kneeling before Lottchen, whose hand she held in her own, though the bright eye and glowing face of the girl followed, with undisguised and ingenuous interest, every glance and movement of the countenance of the youth. The emotions of that hour were too powerful for concealment, and had there been any secret concerning her sentiments, surprise and the sudden burst of feeling that was its consequence, would have wrung it from her heart. Ulrike kneeled too, supporting the head of her friend, but smiling and happy. The Knight of Rhodes, the Abbe, Heinrich and the smith paced back and forth, as sentinels to keep the curious at a distance, though occasionally stopping to catch sentences of the discourse. Emich leaned on his sword, rejoicing that his apprehensions were groundless, and we should do injustice to his rude but not ungenerous feelings, did we not say, glad to find that Berchthold was still in the flesh. When we add, that the dogs played their frisky gambols around the crowd on the common, which could hardly yet believe in their earthly character, our picture is finished.

The deserving of this world may be divided into two great classes; the actively and the passively good. Ulrike belonged to the former, for though she felt as strongly as most others, an instinctive recti tude rarely failed to suggest some affirmative duty for every crisis that arrived. It was she, then, (and we here beg to tell the reader plainly, she is our heroine,) that gave such a direction to the discourse as was most likely to explain what was unknown, without harassing anew feelings that had been so long and so sorely tried.

"And thou art now absolved from thy vow, Berchthold?" she asked, after one of those short interruptions, in which the exquisite happiness of such a meeting was best expressed by silent sympathy. "The Benedictines have no longer any claim to thy silence?"

"They set the return of the pilgrims as their own period, and, as I first learned the agreeable tidings by seeing you all in the procession, I had called in the hounds, who were scouring the chase, and was about to hurry down to present myself, when I met you all at the gateway of the camp. Our meeting would have taken place in the valley, but that duty required me first to visit the Herr Odo Von Ritterstein——"

"The Herr Von Ritterstein!" exclaimed Ulrike, turning pale.

"What of my ancient comrade, the Herr Odo, boy?" demanded Emich. "This is the first we have heard of him since the night the abbey fell."

"I have told my tale badly," returned Berchthold, laughing and blushing, for he was neither too old nor too practised to blush, "since I have forgotten to name the Herr Odo."

"Thou told us of a companion," rejoined his mother, glancing a look at Ulrike, and raising herself from the support of her son, instinctively alive to her friend's embarrassment, "but thou called him merely a religious."

"I should have said the holy Hermit, whom all now know to be the Baron Von Ritterstein. When obliged to fly from the falling roof, I met the Herr Odo kneeling before an altar, and recalling the form of one who had shown me much favour, it was he that I dragged with me to the crypt.—I surely spoke of our wounds and helplessness!"

"True; but without naming thy companion."

"It was the Herr Odo, Heaven be praised! When the monks found us, on the following day unable to resist, and weakened with hunger and loss of blood, we were secretly removed together, as ye have heard, and cared for in a manner to restore us both, in good time, to our strength and to the use of our limbs. Why the Benedictines chose to keep us secret, I know not; but this silly tale of the supernatural huntsman, and of dogs loosened from their leash, would seem to prove that they had hopes of still working on the superstition of the country."

"Wilhelm of Venloo had nought to do with this!" exclaimed Emich, who had been musing deeply. "The underlings have continued the game after it was abandoned by their betters."

"This may be so, my good Lord; for I thought Father Bonifacius more than disposed to let us depart. But we were kept until the matters of the compensation and of the pilgrimage were settled. They found us easy abettors in their plot, if plot to work upon the fears of Deurckheim was in their policy; for when they pledged their faith that my two mothers and dearest Meta had been let into the secret of our safety, I felt no extraordinary haste to quit leeches so skilful, and so likely to make a speedy cure of our hurts."

"And did Bonifacius affirm this lie?"

"I say not the Abbot, my Lord Count, but most certainly the Brothers Cuno and Siegfried said all this and more—the malediction of a wronged son, and of a most foully treated mother"—

His mouth was stopped by the hand of Meta.

"We will forgive past sorrow for the present joy;" murmured the weeping girl.

The angry and flushed brow of Berchthold grew more calm, and the discourse continued in a gentler strain.

Emich now walked away to join the Burgomaster, and together they endeavoured to penetrate the motives which had led the monks to practise their deception. In the possession of so effectual a key, the solution of the problem was not difficult. The meeting of Bonifacius and the Count at Einsiedlen had been maturely planned, and the uncertain state of the public mind in the valley and town was encouraged, as so much make-weight in the final settlement of the Convent's claims; for in that age, the men of the cloisters, knew well how to turn every weakness of humanity to good purpose, so far as their own interests were concerned.

CHAPTER XXXI.

'Tis over, and her lovely cheek is now
On her hard pillow— *Rogers.*

On the following morning the Count of Hartenburg took horse at an early hour. His train, however, showed that the journey was to be short. But Monsieur Latouche, who mounted in company, wore the attire and furniture of a traveller. It was in truth the moment when Emich, having used this quasi churchman for his own ends, was about to dismiss him, with as much courtesy and grace as the circumstances seemed to require. Perhaps no picture of the different faces presented by a church that had so long enjoyed an undisputed monopoly in christendom, and which, as a consequence, betrayed so strong a tendency to abuses, would have been complete without some notice of such characters as the Knight of the Cross and the Abbé; and it was, moreover, our duty, as faithful chroniclers, to speak of things as they existed, although the accessories might not have a very capital connection with the interest of the principal subject. But here our slight relations with the Abbé are to cease altogether, his host having treated him, as many politic rulers treat others of his profession, purely as the instrument of his own views. Albrecht of Viederbach was prepared to accompany his boon associate far as Mannheim, but with the intention to return, the unsettled state of his order, and his consanguinity with the Count, rendering such a course both expedient and agreeable. Young Berchthold, too, was in the saddle, his lord having, by especial favour, commanded the Forester to keep at his crupper.

The cavalcade ambled slowly down the Jaegerthal, the Count courteously endeavoring to show the departing Abbé, by a species of misty logic that appears to be the poetical atmosphere of diplomacy, that he was fully justified by circumstances for affecting all that had been done, and the latter acquiescing as readily in his conclusions, as if he did not feel that he had been an egregious dupe.

"Thou wilt see this matter rightly represented among thy friends, Master Latouche," concluded the Baron—"should there be question of it, at the court of thy Francis:—whom may Heaven quickly restore to his longing people—the right valiant and loyal Prince and gentleman!"

"I will take upon myself, high-born and ingenuous Emich, to see thee fully justified, whenever there shall be discussion of thy great warfare and exquisite policy at the court of France. Nay,—by the mass! should our jurists, or our statesmen take upon themselves to prove to the world that thy house hath been wrong in this immortal enterprise, I pledge thee my faith to answer their reasons, both logically and politically, to their eternal shame and confusion."

As Monsieur Latouche uttered this promise with an unequivocal sneer, he thought himself fully aveng ed, for the silly part he had been made to act in the Count's intrigues. At a later day he often told the tale, always concluding with a recital of this bold and ironical allusion to the petty history of the Jaegerthal, which not only he, but a certain portion of his listeners, seemed to think gave him altogether the best of the affair. Satisfied with his success, the Abbé pricked on, to repeat it to the knight, who laughed in his sleeve at his friend while he most extolled his wit, the two riding ahead in a manner to leave Emich an occasion to speak in confidence with his Forester.

"Hast treated of this affair with Heinrich, as I bid thee, boy?" demanded the Count, in a manner between authority and affection, that he was much accustomed to use with Berchthold.

"I have, my Lord Count, and right pressingly, as my heart urged, but with little hope of benefit."

"How?—Doth the silly burgher still count upon his marks, after what hath passed! Didst tell him of the interest I take in the marriage, and of my intent to name thee to higher duties, in my villages?"

"None of these favors were forgotten, or aught else that a keen desire could suggest, or a willing memory recall."

"What answer had the burgher?"

Berchthold colored, hesitating to reply. It was only when Emich sternly repeated the question, that the truth was extorted from him; for nought but truth would one so loyal consent to use.

"He said, Herr Count, that if it was your pleasure to name a husband for his child, it should also be your pleasure to see that he was not a beggar. I do but give the words of the Herr Frey; for which liberty, I beg my lord to hold me free of all disrespect."

"The niggardly miser! These hounds of Deurckheim shall be made to know their master—But be of cheer, boy; our tears and pilgrimages shall not be wasted, and thou shalt soon wive with a fairer and better, as becometh him I love."

"Nay, Herr Emich, I do beseech and implore"—

"Ha! Yon is the drivelling Heinrich seated on a rock of this ravine, like a vidette watching the marauders! Prick forward, Berchthold, and desire my noble friends to tarry at the Town-Hall making their compliments;—as for thee, thou mayest humour thy folly, and greet the smiling face of the pretty Meta the while."

The Forester dashed ahead like an arrow: while the Count reined his own courser aside, turning into that ravine by which the path led to the Heidenmauer, when the ascent was made from the side of the valley. Emich was soon at the Burgomaster's side, having thrown his bridle to a servitor that followed.

"How is this, brother Heinrich!" he cried, displeasure disappearing in habitual policy and well practised management—"art still bent on exorcism, or hast neglected some offices, in yester's pilgrimage?"

"Praised be St. Benedict, or Brother Luther!—for I know not fairly to which the merit is most due—our Deurckheim is in a thrice happy disposition, as touching all witchcraft, and devilry, or even churchly miracles. This mystery of the hounds being so happily settled, the public mind seemeth to have taken a sudden change, and from sweating in broad daylight at the nestling of a mouse, or the hop of a cricket, our crones are ready to set demonology and Lucifer himself at defiance."

"The lucky clearing up of that difficulty will, in sooth, do much to favour the late Saxon opinions and may go near to set the monk of Wittenburg firmly upon his feet, in our country. Thou seest, Heinrich, that a dilemma so unriddled is worth a library of musty Latin maxims."

"That is it, Herr Emich, and the more especially as we are a reasoning town. Our minds once fairly enlightened, it is no easy matter to throw them into the shade again. It was seen how sorely the best of us were troubled with a couple of vagrant dogs so lately as yesterday, and now I much question if the whole of the gallant pack would so much as raise a doubt! We have had a lucky escape, Lord Count, for another day of uncertainty would have gone nigh to set up Limburg church again, and that without the masonry of the devil. There is nought so potent in an argument, as a little apprehension of losses or of plagues thrown into the scale. Wisdom weighs light against profit or fear."

"It is well as it is, though Limburg roof will never again cover Limburg wall, friend Heinrich, while an Emich rules in Hartenburg and Deurckheim."—The Count saw the cloud on the Burgomaster's brow as he uttered the latter word, and slapping him familiarly on a shoulder, he added so quickly as to prevent reflection:—"But how now, Herr Frey; why art at watch in this solitary ravine?"

Heinrich was flattered by the noble's condescension, and not displeased to have a listener to his tale. First looking about him to see that no one could overhear their discourse, he answered on a lower key, in the manner in which communications that needs confidence are usually made.

"You know, Herr Emich, this weakness of Ulrike, concerning hermitages and monks, altars and saints' days, with all those other practices of which we may now reasonably expect to be quit, since late rumors speak marvels of Luther's success. Well the good woman would have a wish to come upon the Heidenmauer this morning, and as there had been some warm argument between us, and the poor wife had wept much concerning marrying our child with young Berchthold, a measure out of all prudence and reason, as you must see, nobly-born Count, I was fain willing to escort her thus far, that she might give vent to her sorrow in godly discourse with the hermit."

"And Ulrike is above, in the cedars, with the anchorite?"

"As sure as I am here waiting her return, Lord Count."

"Thou art a gallant husband, Master Frey!—Wert wont of old to resort much with the Herr Odo Von Ritterstein—he who playeth this masquerade of penitence and seclusion?"

"Sapperment!—I never could endure the arrogant! But Ulrike fancieth he hath qualities that are not so evil, and a woman's taste, like a child's humors, is easiest altered by giving it scope."

Emich laid both hands on the shoulders of his companion, looking him full and earnestly in the face. The glances that were exchanged in this attitude, were pregnant with meaning. That of the Count expressed the distrust, the contempt, and the wonder of a man of loose life, while that of the Burgomaster, by appearing to reflect the character of the woman who had so long been his wife, expressed volumes in her favor. No language could have said more for Ulrike's principles and purity, than the simple, hearty, and unalterable confidence of the man who necessarily had so many opportunities of knowing her. Neither spoke, until the Count, releasing his grasp, walked slowly up the mountain, saying in a voice which proved how strongly he felt—

'I would thy consort had been noble Heinrich!"

"Nay, my good lord," answered the Burgomaster, "the wish were scarcely kind to a friend! In that case, I could not have wived the Frau."

"Tell me, good Heinrich—for I never heard the history of thy love—wert thou and thy proposal well received, when first offered to the virgin heart of Herr Hailtzinger's daughter?"

The Burgomaster was not displeased with an opportunity of alluding to a success that had made him the envy of his equals.

"The end must speak for the means, Herr Count," he answered chuckling. "Ulrike is none of your free and froward spirits to jump out of a window, or to meet a youth more than half-way, but such encouragement as becometh maiden diffidence was not wanting, or mine own ill opinion of myself might have kept me a bachelor to this hour."

Emich chafed to hear such language coming from one he so little respected, and applied to one he had really loved. The effort to swallow his spleen produced a short silence, of which we shall avail ourselves to transfer the scene to the hut of the hermit, where there was an interview that proved decisive of the future fortunes of several of the characters of our tale.

The day which succeeded the restoration of Berchthold had been one of general joy and felicitation in Deurckheim. There was an end to the doubts of the timid and superstitious, concerning an especial and an angry visitation from Heaven, as a merited punishment for overturning the altars of the Abbey, and few were so destitute of good feeling, not to sympathize in the happiness of those who had so bitterly mourned the fancied death of the Forester. As is usual in cases of violent transitions, the reaction helped to lessen the influence of the monks, and even those most inclined to doubt, were now encouraged to hope that the religious change, which was so fast gaining ground, might not produce all the horrors that had been dreaded.

Heinrich has revealed the nature of the discussion that took place between himself and his wife. The latter had endeavored in vain to seize the favorable moment to work upon the feelings of the Burgomaster, in the interests of the lovers; but, though sincerely glad that a youth who had shown such mettle in danger was not the victim of his courage, Heinrich was not of a temperament to let any admiration of generous deeds affect the settled policy of a whole life. It was at the close of this useless and painful conference, that the mother suddenly demanded permission of her husband to visit the hermit, who had been left, as before the recent events, in undisturbed possession of the dreaded Heidenmauer.

Any other than a man constituted like Heinrich might, at such a moment, have heard this request with distrust. But strong in his opinion of himself, and accustomed to confide in his wife, the obstinate Burgomaster hailed the application as a means of relieving him from a discussion, in which, while he scarce knew how plausibly to defend his opinion, he was resolutely determined not to yield. The manner in which he volunteered to accompany his wife, and in which he remained patiently awaiting her return, and the commencement of his dialogue with Emich are known. With this short explanation, we shall shift the scene to the hut of the Anchorite.

Odo of Ritterstein was pale with loss of blood from the wounds received from a fragment of the falling roof, but paler still by the force of that inward fire which consumed him. The features of his fair and gentle companion were not bright, as usual, though nought could rob Ulrike of that winning beauty, which owed so much of its charm to expression. Both appeared agitated with what had already passed between them, and perhaps still more by those feelings, which each had struggled to conceal.

"Thou hast indeed had many moving passages in thy life, Odo," said the gentle Ulrike, who was seemingly listening to some recital from the other's lips "and this last miraculous escape from death is among the most wonderful."

"That I should have perished beneath the roof of Limburg, on the anniversary of my crime, and with the fall of those altars I violated, would have been so just a manifestation of Heaven's displeasure, Ulrike, that even now I can scarce believe I am permitted to live! Thou then thought in common with others, that I had been released from this life of wo?"

"Thou lookest with an unthankful eye at what thou hast of hope and favor, or thou wouldst not use a term so ungrateful in speaking of thy sorrows. Remember, Odo, that our joys, in this being, are tainted with mortality, and that thy unhappiness does not surpass that of thousands who still struggle with their duties."

"This is the difference between the unquiet ocean and tranquil waters—between the oak and the reed! The current of thy calm existence may be ruffled by the casual interruption of some trifling obstacle, but the gentle surface soon subsides, leaving the element limpid and without stain! Thy course is that of the flowing and pure spring, while mine is the torrent's mad and turbulent leaps. Thou hast indeed well said, Ulrike, God did not form us for each other!"

"Whatever nature may have done towards suiting our dispositions and desires, Odo, Providence and the world's usages have interposed to defeat."

The hermit gazed at the mild speaker with eyes so fixed and dazzling, that she bowed her own look to the earth.

"No," he murmured rapidly, "Heaven and earth have different destinies—the lion and the lamb different instincts!"

"Nay, I will none of this disreputable depreciation of thyself, poor Odo. That thou hast been erring, we shall not deny—for who is without reproach?—but that thou meritest these harsh epithets, none but thyself would venture to affirm."

"I have met with many enigmas, Ulrike, in an eventful and busy life—I have seen those who worked both good and evil—encountered those who have defeated their own ends by their own wayward means—but never have I known one so devoted to the right, that seemed so disposed to extenuate the sinner's faults!"

"Then hast thou never met the true lover of God or known a Christian. It matters not, Odo, whether we admit of this or that form of faith—the fruit of the right tree is charity and self-abasement, and these teach us to think humbly of ourselves and kindly of others."

"Thou began early to practise these golden rules, or surely thou never wouldst have forgotten thine own excellence, or have been ready to sacrifice it to the heedless impulses of one so reckless as him to whom thou wast betrothed!"

The eye of Ulrike grew brighter, but it was merely because a tinge of color diffused itself on her features.

"I know not for what good purpose, Herr Von Ritterstein," she said, "that these allusions are now made. You know that I have come to make a last effort to secure the peace of Meta. Berchthold spoke to me of your intention to reward the service he did your life, and I have now to say, that if in ought you can do the youth favor, the moment when it will be most acceptable, hath come—for Lottchen has been too sorely stricken to bear up long against further grief."

The Hermit was reproved. He turned slowly to one of his receptacles of worldly stores, and drew forth a packet. The rattling told his companion that it was of parchment, and she waited the result with curious interest.

"I will scarce say, Ulrike," he replied, "that this deed is the price of a life that is scarce worth the gift. Early in my acquaintance with young Berchthold and Meta, I wrung their secret from them; and from that moment it hath been my greatest pleasure to devise means to secure the happiness of one so dear to thee. I found in the child, the simple, ingenuous faith which was so admirable in the mother, and shall I say that reverence for the latter quickened the desire to serve her offspring?"

"I certainly owe thee thanks, Herr Von Ritterstein, for the constancy of this good opinion," returned Ulrike, showing sensibility.

"Thank me not, but rather deem the desire to serve thy child a tribute that repentant error gladly pays to virtue. Thou knowest that I am the last of my race, and there remained nought but to endow some religious house, to let my estate and gold pass to the feudal prince, or to do this."

"I could not have thought it easy to effect this change, in opposition to the Elector's interests!"

"Those have been looked to; a present fine has smoothed the way, and these parchments contain all that is necessary to install young Berchthold as my substitute and heir."

"Friend!—dear, generous friend!" exclaimed the mother, moved to tears, for, at that moment, Ulrike saw nothing but the future happiness of her child assured, and Berchthold restored to more than his former hopes—"generous and noble Odo!"

The hermit arose, and placed the parchment in her hand, in the manner of one long prepared to perform the act.

"And now, Ulrike," he said with a forced calm, "this solemn and imperative duty done, there remaineth but the last leave-taking."

"Leave-taking!—Thou wilt live with Meta and Berchthold,—the castle of Ritterstein will be thy resting-place, after so much sorrow and suffering!"

"This may not be—my vow—my duties—Ulrike, I fear, my prudence forbids."

"Thy prudence!—Thou art no longer young, dear Odo,—privations thou hast hitherto despised will overload thy increasing years, and we shall not be happy with the knowledge that thou art suffering for the very conveniences which thine own liberality hath conferred on others."

"Habit hath taken nature's place, and the hermitage and the camp are no longer strangers to me. If thou wouldst secure not only my peace, but my salvation, Ulrike, let me depart. I have already lingered too long near a scene which is filled with recollections that prove dread enemies to the penitent."

Ulrike recoiled, and her cheek blanched to paleness. Every limb trembled, for that quick sympathy, which neither time nor duty had entirely extinguished, silently admonished her of his meaning. There was a fervor in his voice, too, that thrilled on her ear like tones which, spite of all her care, the truant imagination would sometimes recall; for, in no subsequent condition of life, can a woman entirely forget the long cherished sounds with which true love first greets the maiden ear.

"Odo," said a voice so gentle that it caused the heart of the anchorite to beat, "when dost thou think to depart?"

"This day—this hour—this minute."

"I believe—yes,—thou art right to go!"

"Ulrike, God will keep thee in mind. Pray often for me."

"Farewell, dear Odo."

"God bless thee—may he have mercy on me!"

There was then a short pause. The hermit approached and lifted his hands in the attitude of benediction; twice he seemed about to clasp the unresisting Ulrike to his bosom, but her meek, tearful countenance repressed the act, and, muttering a prayer, he rushed from the hut. Left to herself, Ulrike sank on a stool, and remained like an image of wo, tears flowing in streams down her cheeks.

Some minutes elapsed before the wife of Heinrich Frey was aroused from her forgetfulness. Then the approach of footsteps told her that she was no longer alone. For the first time in her life, Ulrike endeavored to conceal her emotion with a sentiment of shame: but ere this could be effected, the Count and Heinrich entered.

"What hast done with poor Odo Von Ritterstein, good Frau; that man of sin and sorrow?" demanded the latter, in his hearty, unsuspecting manner.

"He has left us, Heinrich."

"For his castle!—well, the man hath had his share of sorrow, and ease may not yet come too late. The life of Odo, Lord Count, hath not been, like our own histories, of a nature to make him content. Had that affair of the host, though at the best but an irreverent and unwarrantable act, happened in these days, less might have been thought of it; and then, (tapping his wife's cheek) to lose Ulrike's favor was no slight calamity of itself.—But what have we here?"

"'Tis a deed, by which the Herr Von Ritterstein invests Berchthold with his worldly effects."

The Burgomaster hastily unfolded the ample parchment. At a glance, though unable to comprehend the Latin of the instrument, his accustomed eye saw that all the usual appliances were there. Turning suddenly to Emich, for he was not slow to comprehend the cause of the gift, he exclaimed—

"Here is manna in the wilderness! Our differences are all happily settled, nobly-born Count, and next to according the hand of Meta to the owner of the lands of Ritterstein, I hold it a pleasure to oblige an illustrious friend and patron. Henceforth, Herr Emich, let there be nought but fair words between us."

Since entering the hut, the Count had not spoken His look had studied the tearful eyes, and colorless cheeks of Ulrike, and he put his own constructions on the scene. Still he did the fair wife of the burgher justice, for, though less credulous than Heinrich on the subject of his consort's affections, he too well knew the spotless character of her mind, to change the opinion her virtue had extorted from him, in early youth. He accepted the conditions of his friend, with as much apparent frankness as they were offered, and, after a few short explanations, the whole party left the Heidenmauer together.

Our task is ended. On the following day Berchthold and Meta were united. The Castle and the Town vied with each other doing in honor to the nuptials, and Ulrike and Lottchen endeavored to forget their own permanent causes of sorrow in the happiness of their children.

In due time Berchthold took possession of his lands, removing with his bride and mother to the Castle of Ritterstein, which he always affected to hold merely as the trustee of its absent owner. Gottlob was promoted in his service, and having succeeded in persuading Gisela to forget the gay cavalier who had frequented Hartenburg, these two wayward spirits settled down into a half-loving, half-wrangling couple, for the rest of their lives.

Deurckheim, as is commonly the case with the secondary actors in most great changes, shared the fate of the frogs in the fable; it got rid of the Benedictines for a new master, and though the Burgomaster and Dietrich, in after life, had many wise discourses concerning the nature of the revolution of Limburg, as the first affected to call the destruction of the Abbey, he never could very clearly explain to the understanding of the latter, the great principles of its merits. Still the smith was not the less an admirer of the Count, and to this day his descendants show the figure of a marble cherub, as a trophy brought away by their ancestor on that occasion.

Bonifacius and his monks found shelter in other convents, each endeavoring to lessen the blow, by such expedients as best suited his tastes and character. The pious Arnolph persevered to the end, and, believing charity to be the fairest attribute of the Christian, he never ceased to pray for the enemies of the church, or to toil that they might have the benefit of his intercession.

As for Odo Von Ritterstein, the country was long moved by different tales of his fate. One rumor—and it had much currency—said he was serving in company with Albrecht of Viderbach, who rejoined his brother knights, and that he died on the sands of Africa. But there is another tradition extant in the Jaergethal, touching his end. It it is said, that, thirty years later, after Heinrich, and Emich of Leiningen, and most of the other actors of this legend, had been called to their great accounts, an aged wanderer came to the gate of Ritterstein, demanding shelter for the night. He is reported to have been well received by Meta, her husband and son being then absent in the wars, and to have greatly interested his hostess, by the histories he gave of customs and events in distant regions. Pleased with her guest, the Madame Von Ritterstein (for Berchthold had purchased this appellation by his courage) urged him to rest himself another day within her walls. From communicating, the stranger began to inquire and he so knew how to put his questions, that he soon obtained the history of the family. Ulrike was the last he named; and the younger female inmates of the castle fancied that his manner changed as he listened to the account of the close of her life, and of her peaceful and pious end. The stranger departed that very day, nor would his visit probably have been remembered, had not his body been shortly after found in the hut of the Heidenmauer, stiffened by death. Those who love to throw a coloring of romance over the affections, are fond of believing this was the Hermit, who had found a secret satisfaction, even at the close of so long a life, in breathing his last on the spot where he had finally separated from the woman he had so long and fruitlessly loved.

To this tradition—true or false—we attach no importance. Our object has been to show, by a rapidly-traced picture of life, the reluctant manner in which the mind of man abandons old, to receive new, impressions—the inconsistencies between profession and practice—the error in confounding the good with the bad, in any sect or persuasion—the common and governing principles that control the selfish, under every shade and degree of existence—and the high and immutable qualities of the good, the virtuous, and of the really noble.

THE END